APPALACHIAN MUSHROOMS

APPALACHIAN MUSHROOMS

a field guide

Walter E. Sturgeon

OHIO UNIVERSITY PRESS

ATHENS

Ohio University Press, Athens, Ohio 45701
ohioswallow.com
© 2018 by Ohio University Press
All rights reserved

Printed in the United States of America
Ohio University Press books are printed on acid-free paper ∞ ™

28 27 26 25 24 23 22 21 20 19   5 4 3 2

Library of Congress Cataloging-in-Publication Data

Names: Sturgeon, Walt, author.
Title: Appalachian mushrooms : a field guide / Walter E. Sturgeon.
Description: Athens, Ohio : Ohio University Press, [2018] | Includes
   bibliographical references and index.
Identifiers: LCCN 2018019624| ISBN 9780821423257 (pb : alk. paper) | ISBN
   9780821446393 (pdf)
Subjects: LCSH: Mushrooms--Appalachian Mountains--Identification.
Classification: LCC QK605 .S78 2018 | DDC 579.6--dc23
LC record available at https://lccn.loc.gov/2018019624

CONTENTS

THIS BOOK IS an introduction and identification guide to many of the wild mushrooms found in Appalachian forests and fields. Included in this book is information about edibility. Every effort has been made to provide the most accurate information available relating to the species discussed here. However, many more species occur in these woodlands than can be included in this book. Wild mushrooms may be poisonous, and some poisonous species may resemble edible varieties discussed here. Even if not generally poisonous, other wild mushrooms may cause allergic or other negative reactions in particular individuals. Before eating a wild mushroom, be absolutely certain that it is not poisonous *and that it has been identified correctly*.

Neither the author nor Ohio University Press makes any warranty as to the safety of consuming wild mushrooms, and they do not accept responsibility for any health problems, consequences, or symptoms arising from the reader's ingestion of them. The reader consumes these mushrooms at his or her own risk. This is also true for individual or allergic reactions to generally accepted edible species. *The consumer must exercise caution in consuming wild mushrooms*. The author recommends consulting other reference books, websites, and local mushroom club experts before making a decision to eat a mushroom. Furthermore, many edible wild mushroom species are toxic if eaten raw. Edibility information here refers to thoroughly cooked mushrooms.

WILD MUSHROOMS OCCUR in all Appalachian habitats, including soil, moss, humus, living trees, dead wood, and manure. Some wild mushrooms have specialized habitats that include insects, other fungi, nutshells, and aphid exudates. Wild mushrooms exhibit an amazing diversity, and there are many more species than can be included in a field guide.

Mushrooms described in this book have been found in the Appalachian region that includes parts of northern Georgia, South Carolina, North Carolina, eastern Tennessee, Kentucky, Virginia, West Virginia, western Maryland, eastern Ohio, Pennsylvania, New York, and the New England states. There is considerable overlap in range, but some species common in New England, for example, are rare or absent in Georgia.

Many species are undescribed and lack a scientific or common name. The number of species in the Appalachian region is unknown. Estimates of close to three thousand species of macro fungi have been proposed. This book has included all of the popular edible species as well as many of the most common poisonous varieties. Some less common interesting species are found in this text as well.

The mushrooms in this book can be identified using features visible to the naked eye. DNA studies have revealed that in some cases mushrooms that are morphologically identical are actually not the same species. Many familiar mushrooms have incorrectly carried names belonging to their European look-alikes. This has resulted in some species temporarily being technically nameless and lumped together as complexes or groups. None of these groups contain look-alike species that differ significantly in edibility. In the future, the species within these complexes will be sorted out. There will be many new species of morels and chanterelles, for example, but all will remain as popular edibles regardless of what they are called.

The search for wild mushrooms is a scavenger hunt that enables the hunter to enjoy some of his or her quarry as food. The natural beauty of wild mushrooms soon becomes apparent. Delving a bit deeper, we see that it is important and fascinating to learn their ecological importance as recyclers, symbionts, insect killers, and a food source for many insects and animals. The finding and subsequent identification of a mushroom may lead to the discovery of much more than food in the amazing fungi kingdom.

ACKNOWLEDGMENTS

THROUGH THEIR SUPPORT and by generously sharing their knowledge, many people have contributed to the publication of this book. I would like first to acknowledge my father, Thomas H. Sturgeon, who introduced me at an early age to the joys of discovering morels in the old orchard and field mushrooms in the pasture. I would like to extend a special thank you to my wife, Trish, who has been very patient with my spending many hours doing field work and working on this book.

Mycological knowledge has come from many individuals. William Roody has been a constant source of knowledge, field experience, and support over many years. The list of other individuals who have shared their knowledge and given support is long and includes Alan Bessette, Arleen Bessette, Ernst Both, Todd Elliot, Richard Grimm, Emily Johnson, Jay Justice, Gary Lincoff, Renee LeBeuf, Teresa Marrone, Hank Mashburn, Shannon Nix, John Plischke III, and Rod Tulloss.

Two large organizations and their forays have been an inspiration and have provided great learning opportunities. The North American Mycological Association and the Northeast Mycological Federation hold yearly large mushroom forays that offer enjoyable learning experiences. In addition, many local mycological clubs have been instrumental in sharing their local mushroom foray events. These include the Mycological Society of Toronto, the Ohio Mushroom Society, and the West Virginia Mushroom Club.

I would also like to thank Alan Bessette, Arleen Bessette, Todd Elliot, and William Roody for permission to use their photos in this book.

INTRODUCTION

Mushrooms and Macro Fungi

ALL OF THE fleshy and woody fungi fruit bodies in the woods and fields are there for one purpose, reproduction. Microscopic spores are produced somewhere on the fruit body. The part of the organism that produces these reproductive structures is mostly unseen in the substrate as it goes about its lifestyle of procuring nutrients in a saprobic, parasitic, or symbiotic manner. These hidden filaments or strands are known collectively as mycelium. When in the soil or humus, the mycelium can cover large areas. Without chlorophyll and unable to produce its own food, the fungal mycelium uses chemicals to break down its food and then absorbs the nutrients through its cell walls. The mycelium in some mushroom species forms a coating on plant roots, where there is a symbiotic relationship called mycorrhiza. In other species the mycelium is parasitic, aggressively attacking a living plant, insect, or other fungus, killing the host and using it for food. Many macro fungi are saprobes, obtaining their nutrients from dead plant material. They are nature's primary recyclers. Many macro fungi can be parasitic at times and saprobic at other times. Some mycorrhizal fungi can also be saprobic at times.

The terms mushroom, toadstool, fleshy fungus, and macro fungi all refer to the reproductive organ of a fungus but could also refer to the organism itself. None of these terms have a scientific meaning. Non–macro fungi include molds, rusts, mildews, and yeasts. These fungi do not produce large fruiting bodies. Defining the fungus kingdom is difficult. Simply stated, a fungus is a stationary organism that reproduces by spores, lacks chlorophyll, and can't produce its own food. It is neither a plant nor an animal. The fungi kingdom is huge and diverse. Mushrooms and macro fungi are a great introduction to the vast world of fungi. In the following pages the reader should learn to identify and eat distinctive edible species as well as to identify and avoid poisonous mushrooms. More important, the book should help the reader discover the ecology and beauty of these colorful and fascinating life forms that are all around us but are all too often overlooked.

Mushroom taxonomy continues to evolve, which has resulted in the occurrence of many synonyms. A scientific name is created by the person who described the species and published the description in a scientific journal. The name, often abbreviated, follows the species name. Name changes result from new taxonomic information or discovery that the species had previously been published with a different name. Those synonyms selected for use here are the ones the reader is most likely to encounter in recent field guides. The term "Misapplied Name" refers to a name that was commonly used for a mushroom but was discovered to belong to another, similar-looking species.

MUSHROOM IDENTIFICATION

THE COLLECTION PROCESS is the first step in mushroom identification. Equipment should include a basket, knife or trowel, and wax or paper bags to keep each collection separate. Large mushrooms can be wrapped in wax paper. Plastic bags are not preferred since they can accelerate the decomposition of the fruit bodies. Do not put more than one kind in each bag. A hand lens is a useful tool for observing small features such as scales or hairs. Care should be taken to collect the whole mushroom, using the knife or trowel to dig to get the bottom of the stem. The base of the stem may have a bulb or remnants of the universal veil, which are important identification features. Note the kinds of trees in the area. Was the mushroom growing on wood, soil, humus, moss, or wood mulch? Those species with specialized habitats—such as those growing on other mushrooms, nut shells, or cones—are usually easily identified.

At home or in the lab, the first step in identifying a mushroom with gills or pores is to determine the color of a spore deposit. This deposit—called a spore print—is made by removing the stem and laying the cap with the gill or the pore side down on a sheet of white paper. Covering the cap with an inverted bowl helps protect it from drying out. After several hours, remove the cover and the mushroom cap. If the mushroom is not sterile, there will be a visible deposit of microscopic spores. The specimen chosen should be mature but not overripe. The color of the spore print is the first step in the identification of a mushroom. Colors range from white to black and include greenish, cream, yellow, ochre, lavender, dark purplish, pink, salmon, and various shades of brown. Many of the common mushrooms have white spores. It is sometimes possible to determine the color of the spores by looking at the mature gills, but a spore print is the only way to be sure.

Identifying a single mushroom is difficult. It is best to have a collection, including young, old, and intermediate stages. Note the presence or absence of a partial veil covering the gills in the button stage. Is there a ring on the stem or flaps of tissue on the cap margin? Is the ring skirt-like or a simple ring? Note the colors of all parts including the cut flesh. Is there a color change when the flesh is exposed? If the mushroom has whitish spores, look for the presence of latex on the cut gills and flesh.

Are the surfaces of the cap and stem bald, hairy, wrinkled, dry, or slimy? Note the gill attachment to the stem. It could be free from the stem, notched, or running down the stem. Stature can be important. Is the stem longer than the cap is wide or vice versa? Note the odor by sniffing the gills, pores, or a bit of the crushed flesh.

Making a spore print can also be useful for some polypores and spine fungi. Many of the other non-gilled species can be identified without making a spore print by observing the features and following the keys.

There are many more species in Appalachia than can be included in a field guide. If a mushroom does not quite fit the description, it likely is not included in this book. Do not try to force your mushroom into a description that does not quite fit. Conversely, consider that young mushrooms can look very different from old ones, and wet caps can look different from dry ones. Read the descriptions closely. Identifying a mushroom from just a picture can be very difficult. Photos often represent mushrooms in pristine or at least in good condition. Mushrooms may look very different owing to age and environmental conditions.

Gilled Mushrooms

SPORE COLOR IS the starting point for identifying gilled mushrooms. Make a spore print as described in the section of this book titled "Mushroom Identification."

Many genera will have white- to cream-colored spores. Some of these spore deposits will be a bit yellowish or, rarely, tinged violet. The common groups of mostly medium to large species are here separated into eight distinctive genera.

Amanita species have at first a universal veil, which at maturity leaves remnants at the stem base or warts on the cap. They generally have stems longer than the cap width. Of the white-spored mushrooms, this is the only genus with a universal veil. Because of toxic look-alikes, species in this genus are not recommended as edibles for beginners.

Russula species are generally squat mushrooms. Most have very brittle gills and all have brittle flesh. The gills are attached broadly to the stem. Ranging from white to black, many are colorful, with shades of red and green. Mild-tasting species are often edible, but they are also popular with slugs, rodents, and insect larvae.

Lactarius and *Lactifluus* species are generally squat mushrooms with gills that exude latex when cut or damaged. The gills are attached broadly to the stem. Species with mild latex are mostly edible. They are rather coarse textured.

Hygrocybe and *Hygrophorus* species are called wax caps. Their flesh has a waxy texture that can usually be felt by crushing a bit of the cap between thumb and forefinger. *Gliophorus* and *Humidicutis* species are also wax caps. *Gliophorus* species have glutinous caps and stems. Many of the species in these genera are edible, but the waxy texture, mild flavor, and often slimy caps are not popular features for most people who consume edible mushrooms.

Tricholoma is a genus of mostly gray, brown, yellowish, or white mushrooms with gills that are notched at the stem. They generally fruit in the fall. They lack latex and a universal veil. A few have a partial veil. Their flesh is not waxy textured. Many have a mealy odor. Not many species are recommended as edibles for beginning collectors.

Other white-spored mushrooms are diverse and include many genera. They have been keyed out here using size, habitat, presence or absence of a partial veil, and whether the stem is central or off center. There are many good edible mushrooms in this group.

Colored-spored genera are keyed out using spore color, habitat, size, cap color, and the presence or absence of a partial veil. There are many edible species in this group. The large, rusty-brown-spored genus *Cortinarius* has been treated separately. Species in this large genus have a spider web-like cortina veil when young. Many are beautiful, but it is not a genus with many edible species.

Non-Gilled Mushrooms

MANY FLESHY FUNGI do not have gills. These include species with many shapes, textures, and forms.

Pored fungi include the boletes and polypores. Boletes and some polypores have stems. Many polypores have a shelving growth on wood and lack stems. Many polypores are fibrous or woody in texture. There are some good edibles as well. Boletes generally have a typical umbrella shape and fleshy fruiting bodies that typically occur on the ground. Many boletes are popular edibles. These two groups are keyed out separately using size, habitat, general shape, color, taste, pore shape, and fruiting-body toughness. Spore color can also be useful.

Chanterelles are keyed out using color, size, and undersurface features. They often have a funnel shape. Their underside is usually wrinkled or nearly gill-like. Several of these are good edible species.

Coral-like fungi are keyed out based on habitat, texture, color, and whether they are branched or not. Unbranched club fungi are included here. A few are edible. Many are hard to identify.

Spine fungi are keyed out using color, habitat, texture, and presence or absence of a stem. The spines are sometimes referred to as teeth or whiskers. Those that are terrestrial have stems and a typical mushroom shape. The wood-rotting species lack a stem or have a very rudimentary stem. There are good edibles in the genera *Hydnum* and *Hericium*.

Puffballs and their relatives are keyed out using size, colors, presence or absence of a stem, and other distinctive features. Most of these lack stems, but stinkhorns and species of the stalked puffballs in the genus *Calostoma* do have stems. Many of the larger, roundish puffballs are edible but rather bland, much like tofu. The best puffball dishes incorporate more flavorful species and often garlic and butter or bacon!

Cup fungi as presented here range from fragile cups to firm or gelatinous urn-like fruitings. Most are found on dead wood. Color is used as a primary distinguishing feature, along with the presence or absence of hairs. These features, along with size and fleshiness, will enable the reader to identify the species covered in this book. Three crust-like fungi are included in this section. No truly good edibles are in this group.

Jelly fungi are gelatinous and here include species with rubbery fruiting bodies. They are keyed out using color, habitat, and shape. Used in the kitchen for their texture, this is a bland-tasting group.

Morels and false morels have stems and wrinkled to honeycombed caps. Morels are generally considered among the best edible mushrooms in the world. Because some are poisonous, false morels should probably not be eaten even though there are edible species. These two groups are keyed out using color, shape, size, and cap texture.

APPALACHIAN MUSHROOMS

AMANITA

MUSHROOMS IN THIS mostly mycorrhizal, white-spored genus are characterized by being at first enveloped by a universal veil of tissue called a volva. Sometimes the volva is membranous and breaks cleanly, leaving a sack-like structure at the bottom of the stem and no warts or patches on the cap (rarely with a single patch). In some species the universal veil is friable, leaving warts on the cap, on the stem base, or in the surrounding soil. These warts may wash off the cap in rainy weather. There are a few species where the volva is powdery and may not leave much of a trace. Some have a partial veil that may form a ring on the stem. Others lack a partial veil and do not have a ring. These are generally long-legged mushrooms that usually have stems longer than the width of the caps. As considered in the key, small refers to caps 3 in. wide or less. Medium caps are 3–5 in. in diameter. Large caps are over 5 in. wide. Keep in mind that these are general guidelines and that there will be some variation.

There are many poisonous species in this genus. Three species have caused many serious and sometimes fatal poisonings. The white Destroying Angel complex, or *Amanita bisporigera*, is the common one in Appalachia. Less common is *Amanita sturgeonii*, which is known to have caused one fatal poisoning. The greenish Death Cap, or *Amanita phalloides*, is rare in the region, but its range has been expanding and may someday become common. Poisoning from these species usually follows a six- to twenty-four-hour delay between ingestion and the onset of symptoms. Liver failure or at least liver damage is caused by the toxins in these mushrooms. Other serious poisonings have been caused by several *Amanita* species with different toxins, including *Amanita velatipes* (p. 15) and *Amanita muscaria* (p. 14).

The species illustrated here show examples of both membranous and friable universal veils. The gray species illustrated here (p. 2) with universal veil warts is undescribed and is related to *Amanita velatipes* (p. 15) and *Amanita pantherina* (not illustrated). The orange mushroom with yellow universal veil fragments is *Amanita flavoconia* (p. 2). Examples of species with a membranous, sack-like volva are the orange *Amanita banningiana* (not illustrated) and the whitish *Amanita sturgeonii* (p. 2).

Amanita pantherina complex

Amanita sturgeonii

Amanita banningiana

Amanita flavoconia

Key to *Amanita*

No ring on the stem

1. Cap bright red to orangish red with whitish warts: *Amanita parcivolvata* (p. 7)
2. Cap gray with a powdery dusting: *Amanita farinosa* (p. 6)
3. Cap gray to brownish; bald: *Amanita vaginata* (p. 5)
4. Cap orange, brownish orange to yellowish brown: *Amanita amerifulva* (p. 4)

With a skirt-like ring on the stem and a sack-like volva; lacking cap warts

1. Cap white; common: *Amanita bisporigera* (p. 9)
2. Cap white with brownish or olivaceous tints in age; uncommon: *Amanita sturgeonii* (p. 2)
3. Cap red to orange: *Amanita jacksonii* (p. 8)

With a skirt-like ring on the stem and warts or patches on the cap

1. Cap small to medium, yellowish orange; striate; stem with a collared bulb: *Amanita frostiana* (p. 13)
2. Cap small to medium; yellowish orange; not striate; stem lacking a collar: *Amanita flavoconia* (p. 2)
3. Cap medium to large; yellowish orange; stem base usually with 2–3 rings of tissue: *Amanita muscaria* (p. 14)
4. Cap medium to large; cream to tan or whitish; stem base with a collar: *Amanita velatipes* (p. 15)
5. Cap medium to large; brown or white; stem with a prominent bulb that often has a vertical cleft; crushed flesh smells similar to raw potatoes: *Amanita brunnescens* (p. 16)
6. Cap medium to large; brownish to whitish; stem bulb inconspicuous; crushed flesh smells sweet or fruity: *Amanita submaculata* (p. 17)
7. Cap medium to large; with sordid reddish brown stains; odor not distinctive: *Amanita rubescens* (p. 18)
8. Cap small to medium; white with numerous warts; stem bulb prominent: *Amanita abrupta* (p. 19)

SCIENTIFIC NAME: *Amanita amerifulva* **Tulloss nom. prov.**
MISAPPLIED NAMES: *Amanita fulva* Fr., *Amanitopsis fulva* (Fr.) W. G. Sm.
COMMON NAME: Tawny Grisette
FAMILY: Amanitaceae

CAP: Up to 4 in. wide; deep orangish brown at first, becoming yellowish brown, paler to whitish near the prominently striate margin, remaining brownish over the broadly umbonate disc; convex to broadly convex, becoming nearly flat; surface bald; viscid when wet

FLESH: White, sometimes tinted orange near the cap cuticle, unchanging when bruised; thin; soft; odor and taste not distinctive

GILLS: Whitish; free or barely reaching the stem; close; edges even; no partial veil

STEM: Up to 5 in. long; whitish to pale brownish; equal or enlarged downward; base with a whitish to tawny-brown sack-like volval surface bald to slightly hairy; no ring

SPORE PRINT: White

ECOLOGY: Mycorrhizal on soil, humus, moss, or on very rotten wood in a variety of habitats from bogs to upland forests; associated trees include hemlock, pines, and beech; summer and fall; common

EDIBILITY: Although edible, consuming any *Amanita* is discouraged until one has much experience identifying mushrooms. Its flavor is mild and rather uninteresting

COMMENTS: Technically our Tawny Grisette does not have an official name. It has been provisionally named *Amanita amerifulva* by North American *Amanita* expert, Rodham Tulloss. For years it and other look-alike species have been called *Amanita fulva*, which is a name belonging to a similar European species. As with so many mushrooms, there are closely related yet different species that have been lumped together in the past. Until officially described and published, the current name for the species shown here is temporary until a description and new name is proposed and accepted.

Amanita amerifulva

SCIENTIFIC NAME: *Amanita vaginata* (Bull.) Lam.

SYNONYM: *Amanitopsis vaginata* (Bull.) Roze

COMMON NAME: Grisette

FAMILY: Amanitaceae

Cap: Up to 4 in. wide; gray to grayish brown; convex to flat; umbonate; surface viscid when wet, bald; margin prominently striate

FLESH: White; thin, soft; not discoloring when damaged; odor and taste not distinctive

GILLS: White; free; close, becoming more distant in age; narrow; edges even; no partial veil

STEM: Up to 7 in. long; white; tapering upward from a white sack-like volva; solid; surface dry, smooth, or with flattened hairs; no ring

SPORE PRINT: White

ECOLOGY: Mycorrhizal with oaks and other broadleaf trees and conifers; summer and fall; common in humus, moss, and lawns in parks and wood edges

EDIBILITY: Edible but not recommended owing to possible confusion with poisonous species

COMMENTS: This is actually an apparently large group of many species previously lumped under this name. Much work is needed to sort out this complex. The likelihood is that the species illustrated may someday have a new name with many similar look-alikes. The mushrooms haven't changed, just our knowledge of them.

Amanita vaginata

SCIENTIFIC NAME: *Amanita farinosa* Schwein.

SYNONYM: None

COMMON NAME: Powdery Amanita

FAMILY: Amanitaceae

CAP: Up to 3 in. wide; dark gray to whitish gray, at times brownish over the disc; convex to flat; surface dry; center covered with brownish-gray powder becoming thinner at the usually striate margin, which is whitish at times

FLESH: White; thin; soft; unchanging when exposed; odor not distinctive; taste unknown

GILLS: White; barely reaching the stem or free; close; edges flocculose; no partial veil

STEM: Up to 3 in. long; white to gray; equal down to a small basal bulb that is decorated with gray powder; solid; surface bald, smooth to powdery, or flocculose; no ring present

SPORE PRINT: White

ECOLOGY: Mycorrhizal; found in association with oaks, hickories, and beech, occasionally under conifers; solitary to scattered in soil, humus, and moss in broadleaf forests, parks, and wood edges; summer and early fall; common

EDIBILITY: Unknown

COMMENTS: This is a small, common *Amanita* that could be mistaken for a *Russula*; the gills of *Russula* species are broadly attached to the stem, whereas the Powdery Amanita has gills barely reaching the stem or free from it.

Amanita farinosa

SCIENTIFIC NAME: *Amanita parcivolvata* (Peck)
E.-J. Gilbert

SYNONYM: *Amanitopsis parcivolvata* Peck

COMMON NAMES: False Caesar's Mushroom, False Fly Agaric

FAMILY: Amanitaceae

CAP: Up to 4 in. wide; bright red to orangish red or orange, paler toward the margin; convex to broadly convex, then flat in age with a central depression; surface smooth, striate, and bald under a scattering of white to yellow warts or powdery patches; viscid when fresh

FLESH: White to pale yellow, unchanging when cut; firm; odor not distinctive; taste unknown

GILLS: White to yellow; frequently fringed on the edge and dusted with yellow powder; free or barely reaching the stem; close or crowded; broad; no partial veil

STEM: Up to 4½ in. long; pale yellow, equal or tapering slightly upward from a small basal bulb; surface dry and powdery; no ring is present

SPORE PRINT: White

ECOLOGY: Mycorrhizal, associated with oaks and pines; solitary, scattered to gregarious in broadleaf and mixed woods; summer and early fall; fairly common

EDIBILITY: Poisonous

COMMENTS: The lack of a ring and the yellow powdery stem will distinguish this species from *Amanita muscaria* (p. 14) and *Amanita flavoconia* (p. 12). It is probably more common in the oak woods of Appalachia than anywhere else.

Amanita parcivolvata

SCIENTIFIC NAME: *Amanita jacksonii* **Pomerl.**

SYNONYM: *Amanita umbonata* **Pomerl.**

COMMON NAME: American Caesar's Mushroom

FAMILY: **Amanitaceae**

CAP: Up to 6 in. wide; brilliant red, becoming orange to yellowish at the margin; oval becoming convex and finally nearly flat; broadly umbonate in age; surface bald, viscid, and striate

FLESH: Whitish to pale yellow, unchanging when bruised; odor and taste not distinctive

GILLS: Yellow to orangish yellow; free or barely attached to the stem; edges even; covered at first with a yellowish-orange, membranous partial veil

STEM: Up to 6 in. long; yellow with orange to reddish fibers, often in zones; equal or tapering upward; slender; dry, with an apical, skirt-like, yellowish-orange ring; base with a large, white, sack-like volva

VOLVA: White; encases the entire mushroom at first like a chicken egg, then ruptures, leaving a free-limbed sack-like structure at the bottom of the stem; often almost completely buried in the soil; can be appressed against the stipe; contrasts with the yellowish-orange stem

SPORE PRINT: White

ECOLOGY: Mycorrhizal with oaks, hemlock, and pines; scattered to gregarious; summer and early fall; occasional

EDIBILITY: Edible but not recommended; there are several similar species

COMMENTS: This stunning species is very similar to the European *Amanita caesarea*, which is a choice edible. *Amanita jacksonii* differs in having a broad umbo. Although edible, it is not rated as highly as its European cousin. It could be argued that this is the most beautiful mushroom in the Appalachians. *Amanita banningiana* (not illustrated) is similar but is much less robust and its cap is orange to yellowish.

Amanita jacksonii

SCIENTIFIC NAME: *Amanita bisporigera* G. F. Atk.

MISAPPLIED NAMES: *Amanita virosa, Amanita verna*; while not actually synonyms, these names have been given to the North American *Amanita bisporigera* in older field guides

COMMON NAMES: Destroying Angel, Eastern Destroying Angel, Death Angel

FAMILY: Amanitaceae

CAP: Up to 5 in. wide; white, although in age may show some tan at the cap center; nearly oval, becoming convex then flat at maturity; surface dry or slightly tacky; bald, not striate

FLESH: White, unchanging when cut or bruised; odor not distinctive; taste unknown

GILLS: White; free or nearly reaching the stem; close; edges even; covered at first by a membranous, white partial veil

STEM: Up to 6 in. long; white; usually tapers upward slightly from the volva; solid or stuffed with white pith; surface smooth or somewhat floccose, with a delicate skirt-like ring at the apex that may be missing in aged fruitings

VOLVA: White; encasing the entire mushroom at first like an egg, then when the cap emerges it leaves a free-limbed sack-like structure at the bottom of the stem; usually almost completely buried in the soil; at times it can be appressed against the stem

Amanita bisporigera

SPORE PRINT: White

EDIBILITY: Deadly poisonous

ECOLOGY: This species is mycorrhizal with oaks and other broadleaf trees but can also be found in mixed woods, often associating with hemlock; summer and fall; it is a common mushroom in soil, humus, moss, and lawns

COMMENTS: *Amanita bisporigera* has been confused with *Amanita virosa* and *Amanita verna*, which are European Destroying Angels. The taxonomy of the North American species needs work, and there are likely more than one species included under the *Amanita bisporigera* name. In the author's experience the common summer Destroying Angel is a thinner, less robust "species." It is common under oaks. In the late summer and fall there is a much more substantial "species" that occurs under conifers. All of these are white in all parts and all are deadly poisonous. Care must be taken when collecting puffballs for the table so as not to mistake an *Amanita* in the egg stage for a puffball. When cut in half, the Destroying Angel button will have the immature cap and gills visible. This species has caused more fatal poisonings in Appalachia than any other species. The first symptoms of poisoning usually do not occur until several hours after ingestion. The toxins attack the liver and kidneys. It is a prime example of why one should not test the edibility of a mushroom by eating even just one. Consuming a single cap could be a fatal mistake.

Amanita bisporigera

SCIENTIFIC NAME: *Amanita sturgeonii* Tulloss, Q. Cai, and L.V. Kudzma nom. prov.

SYNONYM: None

COMMON NAME: Cemetery Amanita

FAMILY: Amanitaceae

CAP: Up to 4½ in. wide; white, developing brownish or olivaceous stains in age; convex, becoming flat in age; surface bald or rarely with faint brownish universal veil remnants, viscid when wet; margin with veil remnants at times

FLESH: White, unchanging when cut; fairly thick; odor mild to slightly unpleasant; taste unknown

GILLS: White; free from the stem or barely reaching it; close; edges even; covered at first with a white partial veil that may break to form a skirt-like ring or may form remnants on the cap margin

STEM: Up to 3½ in. long; white; surface smooth or with floccose bands; equal or tapering upward from a basal bulb; emerging from a white to buff or brownish sack-like volva

VOLVA: White to brownish; encasing the entire mushroom at first like a chicken egg, then leaving a sack-like structure with a free limb at the bottom of the stem; mid to bottom portions are thicker than the thin opening; often almost completely buried in the soil and can be appressed against the stipe

SPORE PRINT: White

ECOLOGY: Mycorrhizal; scattered to gregarious or in small clusters under oaks, especially red oak, often in lawns; summer and fall; uncommon but locally abundant

EDIBILITY: Deadly poisonous

COMMENTS: This species caused a fatal poisoning in New Jersey. It resembles robust fruitings of the Destroying Angel, *Amanita bisporigera* (p. 10). Its thick volva, cap with brownish or olivaceous tints, robust stature, and usually gregarious habit will help distinguish it.

Amanita sturgeonii

SCIENTIFIC NAME: *Amanita flavoconia* G. F. Atk.

SYNONYM: **None**

COMMON NAME: **Yellow Patches**

FAMILY: **Amanitaceae**

Cap: Up to 3½ in. wide; orange to yellowish orange; ovoid to convex, becoming flat at maturity; surface sticky when wet; not striate or barely so in age; surface covered at first with bright-yellow patches, remnants of the top of the universal veil, which are easily removed or washed off, leaving a bald cap

FLESH: White, buff near the cap; thin; firm; odor mild; taste unknown

GILLS: White; margins may have a yellow dusting from veil remnants; close; barely free; edges even; covered by a yellow partial veil in the button stage

STEM: Up to 4 in. long; yellow, white, or a combination of the two; usually there is yellow near the apex; solid; equal or tapering slightly upward; surface smooth or scurfy, with a yellow, skirt-like ring near the apex; a small bulb at the base may show yellow patches from the universal veil, or these patches may also be on the soil surrounding the stem

SPORE PRINT: White

ECOLOGY: Mycorrhizal; solitary, scattered to gregarious in humus, moss, or lawns under hemlock, red spruce, and other conifers as well as under oaks, beech, and in mixed woods; summer and fall; very common

EDIBILITY: Unknown, probably toxic

COMMENTS: This is a beautiful species when seen with the bright-yellow patches decorating the orange cap. It is abundant and can be found throughout the region. Several species have a similar aspect. *Amanita frostiana* (p. 13) has a striate cap and a more prominent bulb rimmed with yellow material from the universal veil. It is much less common. *Amanita muscaria* (p. 14) is larger and has whitish warts.

Amanita flavoconia

SCIENTIFIC NAME: *Amanita frostiana* (Peck) Sacc.

SYNONYM: None

COMMON NAME: Frost's Amanita

FAMILY: Amanitaceae

CAP: Up to 3½ in. wide; orange to yellowish orange, usually persistently reddish over the disc; surface moist, tacky, bald, with separable yellowish patches of the universal veil; striate.

FLESH: White; thin; odor mild; taste unknown

GILLS: Cream; close; free; edges flocculose; covered at first with a fragile partial veil

STEM: Up to 3½ in. long; white to pale yellowish, with a pale yellow evanescent ring near the apex or midway down the stem; solid; equal down to a distinct white bulb whose top is decorated with yellow remnants of the universal veil; surface dry; bald to flocculose

SPORE PRINT: White

ECOLOGY: Mycorrhizal; solitary to gregarious in humus and moss; associated with pines and oaks; summer and fall; uncommon

EDIBILITY: Unknown, possibly toxic

COMMENTS: This species is uncommon in Appalachian forests, and some reports of it are probably misidentifications of *Amanita flavoconia* (p. 12), which lacks the prominent striations and the collared bulb with the yellow rings around the top.

Amanita frostiana

SCIENTIFIC NAME: *Amanita muscaria* (L.) Lam.

SYNONYM: None (See Comments for nomenclature issues)

COMMON NAME: Fly Agaric

FAMILY: Amanitaceae

CAP: Up to 8 in. wide; orange, reddish orange to yellow; deepest color in the center, fading from sunlight or in age; roundish, becoming convex to broadly convex and eventually nearly flat; surface viscid when wet, covered with a scattering of white cottony warts that may wash off in rainy weather; margin not usually striate, or only faintly so, and may have patches of the universal veil

FLESH: White, thick, unchanging when exposed; odor and taste not distinctive

GILLS: White to cream; free or barely reaching the stem; crowded; broad; edges are minutely hairy; covered at first with a white partial veil

STEM: Up to 8 in. long; white to pale cream or pale yellowish; tapering upward from a white to buff basal bulb; the base usually with two or three rings of tissue; surface dry, finely hairy to cottony scaly, with an apical to mid-stem, skirt-like, white, flaring ring, at times edged in yellow

SPORE PRINT: White

ECOLOGY: Mycorrhizal; solitary, scattered to gregarious in humus, moss, or grass, usually under conifers such as Norway spruce but also under broadleaf trees such as aspens and birches

EDIBILITY: Poisonous and hallucinogenic.

COMMENTS: This mushroom has a long history of use as an intoxicant. It also has caused nausea, dizziness, and digestive issues. It reportedly has been used to kill flies. There are many species and varieties, some with a bright

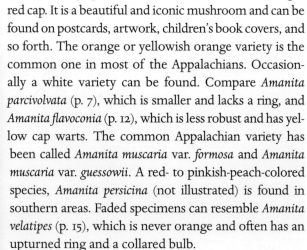

red cap. It is a beautiful and iconic mushroom and can be found on postcards, artwork, children's book covers, and so forth. The orange or yellowish orange variety is the common one in most of the Appalachians. Occasionally a white variety can be found. Compare *Amanita parcivolvata* (p. 7), which is smaller and lacks a ring, and *Amanita flavoconia* (p. 12), which is less robust and has yellow cap warts. The common Appalachian variety has been called *Amanita muscaria* var. *formosa* and *Amanita muscaria* var. *guessowii*. A red- to pinkish-peach-colored species, *Amanita persicina* (not illustrated) is found in southern areas. Faded specimens can resemble *Amanita velatipes* (p. 15), which is never orange and often has an upturned ring and a collared bulb.

Amanita muscaria

SCIENTIFIC NAME: *Amanita velatipes* G. F. Atkinson

SYNONYM: *Amanita pantherina* var. *velatipes* (G. F. Atkinson) D. T. Jenkins

COMMON NAME: Booted Amanita

FAMILY: Amanitaceae

CAP: Up to 8 in. wide; yellow when young, becoming cream to white toward the margin in age, at times cream, buff, or tan all over; may have light brown stains; ovate to bell shaped becoming convex to flat and rarely depressed in the center; surface viscid; obscurely striate, bald, with numerous white, buff, or tan warts that can be washed off in wet weather

FLESH: White; not staining when damaged; odor mild; taste unknown

GILLS: White to pale cream; free; crowded; edges even; covered at first by a membranous partial veil

STEM: Up to 8 in. long; whitish; solid; equal or tapering up slightly from a prominent basal bulb that often has universal veil remnants, sometimes forming bands but terminating at the top with a collar-like rim; with a prominent ring that is unusual in that it is often pulled upward, funnel-like, usually near the middle of the stem; surface bald to silky above the ring, finely hairy to shaggy below

SPORE PRINT: White

ECOLOGY: Mycorrhizal with conifers and broadleaf trees; often in parks and cemeteries; spruce and oak are two frequently observed host trees; scattered to gregarious; at times in arcs or rings; summer and fall; locally common

EDIBILITY: Poisonous

COMMENTS: This large, striking mushroom is set off from the similar *Amanita cothurnata* (not illustrated) by its yellow colors and generally larger size. Pale forms of *Amanita muscaria* (p. 14) are similar but lack the collared bulb and median, upward flaring ring.

Amanita velatipes

SCIENTIFIC NAME: *Amanita brunnescens* G. F. Atk.

SYNONYMS: *Amanita brunnescens* var. *brunnescens* G. F. Atk., *Amanita brunnescens* var. *pallida* L. Krieg

COMMON NAME: Cleft-Foot Amanita

FAMILY: Amanitaceae

CAP: Up to 5 in. wide; dark brown to tan, or whitish with brown stains, often streaked brown; rounded, becoming convex then flat; surface slightly tacky when wet, with white, cottony patches from the universal veil; faintly striate

FLESH: White to brownish, with reddish-brown stains; thin; odor of raw potatoes; taste not recorded

GILLS: White, sometimes with brown stains; close to crowded, free, or just reaching the stem; broad; edges even or flocculose; covered at first with a white partial veil

STEM: Up to 6 in. long; white with brown stains toward the base; equal or narrowing upward; solid, with a white, persistent, skirt-like, apical ring, the edge of which may be brownish; surface smooth to scurfy, flocculose; brown, stained bulb at the base that may have patches of the universal veil along the upper rim; bulb is often prominent and usually has one or more wedge-like vertical clefts

SPORE PRINT: White

ECOLOGY: Mycorrhizal; solitary or gregarious in soil or humus under conifers and broadleaf trees, especially oaks; summer and early fall; common

EDIBILITY: Not recommended; possibly poisonous, and there are similar toxic species

COMMENTS: Whitish forms have been called *Amanita aestivalis* (not illustrated), which may be a distinct species. *Amanita brunnescens* caps can be white and have been described as a variety, namely, as *Amanita brunnescens* var. *pallida*. Collections from the same site can have both brown and whitish caps. Compare with *Amanita submaculata* (p. 17), which has a sweet odor and lacks a prominent basal bulb on the stem.

Amanita brunnescens

SCIENTIFIC NAME: *Amanita submaculata* Peck

SYNONYM: **None**

COMMON NAME: **None**

FAMILY: **Amanitaceae**

CAP: Up to 4 in. wide; gray or dark grayish brown, remaining dark at the center and gray toward the margin; convex becoming almost flat; surface tacky when wet, bald, or with a single tissue patch or a few warts toward the cap center, at times with small, longitudinal, whitish spots, most commonly near the margin

FLESH: White to grayish, thin, unchanging when damaged; odor sweet, fruitlike, at times resembling that of *Pleurotus pulmonarius* (p. 116); taste unknown

GILLS: White, free or barely reaching the stem; close to crowded, edges even; covered at first with a whitish partial veil

STEM: Up to 6 in. long; whitish with brown to dark brown fibrils; solid; tapering slightly upward from a small basal bulb that may have a few universal veil warts; surface fibrillose, may show orangish-brown stains, especially after handling; partial veil forms an apical skirt-like ring

SPORE PRINT: White

ECOLOGY: Mycorrhizal with oaks; solitary to scattered in broadleaf woods and mixed woods of oaks and pines; summer and fall; occasional

EDIBILITY: Unknown

COMMENTS: The sweet odor is unusual in the genus *Amanita*. The cap resembles that of *Amanita brunnescens* (p. 16), a species with a prominent bulb and raw potato odor. Remnants of the universal veil may be visible in the soil around the base of the stem.

Amanita submaculata

SCIENTIFIC NAME: *Amanita rubescens* Pers.

SYNONYM: Provisional name: *Amanita amerirubescens* Tulloss

COMMON NAMES: Blusher, American Blusher

FAMILY: Amanitaceae

CAP: Up to 5½ in. wide; pale tan or yellowish at first, becoming brown with sordid reddish areas; bell shaped at first then convex, becoming flat in age; surface dry or slightly sticky in wet weather; bald, adorned with yellow to gray warts, which are remnants of the universal veil

FLESH: White, staining pinkish red to reddish brown when damaged, this discoloration can often be observed around larvae tunnels; thick; odor and taste mild

GILLS: White or slightly pinkish, staining slowly reddish brown when damaged; free or barely reaching the stem; close; edges even; covered at first by a thin partial veil

STEM: Up to 7 in. long; whitish or with ruddy staining especially near the base; solid; equal or tapering up from a turnip-shaped bulb; smooth or slightly hairy, with a persistent skirt-like ring near the apex

SPORE PRINT: White

ECOLOGY: Mycorrhizal; on soil, litter, and moss in forests and lawns under oaks and pines and in mixed woods; gregarious to scattered; summer and fall; very common

EDIBILITY: Edible but not recommended owing to possible confusion with poisonous look-alikes

COMMENTS: The American cluster of Blusher species differs from the European mushroom originally given this name. As of this writing no new names have been given to several of these variants, including this one, which is a common species in the Appalachians. Historically *Amanita rubescens* was considered a very variable species. Now it is known that several—possibly many—species have been lumped under this name. There is a white form with less prominent, sordid, reddish staining. Similar seriously poisonous species include *Amanita velatipes* (p. 15) and *Amanita pantherina* (not illustrated).

Amanita rubescens

SCIENTIFIC NAME: *Amanita abrupta* Peck
SYNONYM: *Lepidella abrupta* (Peck) E.-J. Gilbert
COMMON NAME: American Abrupt-bulb Lepidella
FAMILY: Amanitaceae

CAP: Up to 3½ in. wide; white, at times tan at the center; surface dry with white or tan pointed or cone-shaped warts that are separable patches of the universal veil; the warts may be washed off in wet weather and on aged caps; convex, becoming flat; surface floccose; margin is not striate and may become cottony

FLESH: White; firm, not staining; odor mild at first becoming unpleasant, resembling spoiled meat in age; taste unknown

GILLS: Whitish or at times with a pale orange cast; close to subdistant; free or barely reaching the stem; edges even or flocculose; covered at first by a white partial veil

STEM: Up to 5 in. long; white; solid with a flimsy skirt-like ring that is smooth on top and often shaggy underneath; nearly equal or slightly tapering upward, with an abrupt white or brown stained bulb at the stem base, which often has a cleft-like depression; surface bald to floccose

SPORE PRINT: White

ECOLOGY: Mycorrhizal; found throughout the Appalachians; it is found on soil and litter in conifer, broadleaf, and mixed forests; summer and fall; fairly common

EDIBILITY: Possibly poisonous

COMMENTS: *Amanita abrupta* is a member of the Lepidella section of *Amanita*. Members of this common section are often large and white with numerous warts or a powdery covering on the caps. Compare with *Amanita cokeri* (not illustrated). The abrupt nonrooting bulb is a key identification feature. *Amanita cokeri* is a more robust species.

Amanita abrupta

RUSSULA

This mycorrhizal genus is characterized by rather squat mushrooms, often with colorful caps. Most species have very brittle gills that crumble when scratched. Many mushrooms in this genus are red or orange. In Appalachia they lack a partial veil, and no volva is present. Stems tend to snap easily when broken. They are an important food source for a variety of animals, including squirrels, box turtles, and slugs. The species in this genus are common in summer and early fall. There are many species, and no current monograph is available. The *Russula* species included in this book can be easily identified without a microscope; however, most *Russula* species require a microscope for identification. Future DNA study will likely reveal many more look-alike species. For those with a microscope and a serious interest in identifying *Russula* species, the following observations are useful.

Make a collection of young and old mushrooms. Getting a heavy spore deposit and carefully noting the color is important. It will range from white, cream, yellow, or ochre. Gill color is useful, as is the presence or absence of gill forking. How far the cap cuticle peels is another relevant observation. Taste is also a useful identification feature. Lastly, observing color changes with the application of chemical reagents such as iron salts ($FeSO_4$) can help clinch the identification.

Species are keyed out here into two groups: those with brittle gills and those with more elastic gills.

Russula species

Russula modesto

Russula species

Key to *Russula*

Gills not brittle (determine by scratching; brittle gills will crumble)

1. Gills quickly staining brown when rubbed: *Russula compacta* (p. 24)
2. Cap with green or purple colors; gills forked toward the margin: *Russula variata* (p. 25)
3. Gills thick, distant, and waxy: *Russula earlei* (p. 23)

Gills brittle (determine by scratching; brittle gills will crumble)

1. Cap purplish, with a whitish bloom at first; often mottled with yellow or green: *Russula mariae* (p. 32)
2. Cap dark red, purplish red to blackish; often fruits early in the season: *Russula vinacea* (p. 33)
3. Cap with patches of green coloration: *Russula parvovirescens* (p. 26)
4. Cap yellowish brown; with granules or patches; odor of rancid cooking oil: *Russula granulata* (p. 28)
5. Cap yellowish brown; lacking granules; odor of almond extract: *Russula grata* (p. 27)
6. Cap yellow to whitish; stem with rows of yellow scales at the base: *Russula ballouii* (p. 29)
7. Cap yellow, at times with orange or pink tints; stem bald to pruinose: *Russula ochroleucoides* (p. 30)
8. Cap white; under conifers; very short stem: *Russula brevipes* (p. 34)
9. Cap grayish buff to brown; gills pale pink to pinkish cinnamon *Russula eccentrica* (p. 31)

SCIENTIFIC NAME: *Russula earlei* Peck

SYNONYM: None

COMMON NAME: Beeswax Russula

FAMILY: Russulaceae

CAP: Up to 4½ in. wide; butterscotch yellow, at times with whitish splotches; convex to broadly convex, becoming nearly flat in age; surface slightly viscid when wet; coarse, irregularly pitted, waxy, and with a granular feel; not striate, or becoming faintly so in age; at times wrinkled

FLESH: Whitish to pale yellow, unchanging when cut; waxy; odor not distinctive; taste mild, slightly bitter to slightly acrid

GILLS: Whitish at first, later colored like the cap or slightly paler, at times with reddish-brown stains; attached to the stem; distant; broad; thick; not brittle; waxy; edges even; no partial veil

STEM: Up to 3 in. long; white to yellowish, at times with reddish-brown stains; equal or tapering in either direction; surface dry, bald

SPORE PRINT: White

ECOLOGY: Mycorrhizal; scattered to gregarious in broadleaf and mixed woods, often in litter under oaks and beech; occasional to locally common

EDIBILITY: Unknown

COMMENTS: This is in a line of primitive *Russula* species. It is a coarse-textured mushroom that looks old even when fresh. The waxy texture resembles that of *Hygrophorus* and *Cuphophyllus* species. Compare with *Cuphophyllus pratensis* (not illustrated), which has decurrent gills and a white, unstaining stem.

Russula earlei

SCIENTIFIC NAME: *Russula compacta* Frost

SYNONYM: None

COMMON NAME: Firm Russula

FAMILY: Russulaceae

CAP: Up to 6 in. wide; whitish to yellowish buff when young, becoming tan to rusty orange and eventually tawny brown; convex to broadly convex and finally nearly flat with a depressed center; slow to decay; surface slightly tacky, bald

FLESH: White, discoloring to yellowish or reddish brown on exposure; thick, firm, brittle; odor fishy; taste unpleasant or slightly acrid

GILLS: White, quickly staining reddish brown when rubbed; attached to the stem; close to crowded; not brittle; edges even; no partial veil

STEM: Up to 4 in. long; whitish at first, soon with reddish-brown areas, staining brown when bruised; sturdy; equal; surface dry, smooth

SPORE PRINT: White

ECOLOGY: Mycorrhizal with oaks and other broadleaf and conifer trees; scattered to gregarious in humus or soil in broadleaf and mixed woods and parks; summer and fall; common

EDIBILITY: Not recommended; reported as edible; the author has tried it and found it unpalatable

COMMENTS: The nonbrittle gills, which rapidly stain brown when rubbed, and the fishy odor are key features. When abundant, the fishy odor can be detected while walking through an overripe patch of this mushroom. *Lactifluus allardii* (p. 50) looks similar but has white latex, which stains greenish.

Russula compacta

SCIENTIFIC NAME: *Russula variata* Banning

SYNONYM: *Russula cyanoxantha* var. *variata* (Banning) Singer

COMMON NAME: Variable Russula

FAMILY: Russulaceae

CAP: Up to 5 in. wide; color extremely variable, usually with some combination of green and purple, also olive green, pinkish, and yellow; convex to broadly convex, becoming flat with a broad central depression; surface smooth or developing small cracks in age; bald; viscid

FLESH: White; thick; brittle; odor not distinctive; taste acrid

GILLS: White to cream, becoming yellowish in age; attached to the stem; crowded; elastic to waxy, not brittle; forking extensively; edges even; no partial veil

STEM: Up to 3 in. long; white; equal or tapering slightly in either direction, or at times enlarged mid-stem; becoming hollow at times; surface bald, smooth, dry

SPORE PRINT: White

ECOLOGY: Solitary, scattered, or gregarious in humus and lawns in broadleaf forests and parks, especially under oaks; summer and fall; common

EDIBILITY: Edible; reportedly the acrid taste dissipates when the mushrooms are thoroughly cooked

COMMENTS: The elastic, repeatedly forking gills are a key feature of this variably colored mushroom. The green version here may eventually be described as a different species. Compare with other green species, such as *Russula parvovirescens* (p. 26) and others, all of which have brittle gills.

Russula variata

SCIENTIFIC NAME: *Russula parvovirescens* Buyck, D. Mitch, and Parrent

MISAPPLIED NAME: *Russula virescens* (Schaeff.) Fr.

COMMON NAME: Green Quilt Brittle-Gill

FAMILY: Russulaceae

CAP: Up to 4 in. wide; grayish green to dull bluish green, in a patchwork pattern, at times with yellowish or tan areas, with the ground color paler than the patches; nearly round at first, becoming convex to broadly convex to flat; center depressed at times; surface dry, dull to velvety; not striate, or only at the margin in age

FLESH: White, not discoloring when damaged; firm; solid; brittle; odor and taste not distinctive

GILLS: White to pale cream; attached to the stem, becoming nearly free in age; close; brittle; edges even; partial veil absent

STEM: Up to 2½ in. long; white, discoloring brownish in age or when handled; equal; at times with a hollow cavity; surface bald, dry

SPORE PRINT: Pale cream

ECOLOGY: Mycorrhizal with conifer and broadleaf trees, especially oaks; solitary, scattered to gregarious in humus in woods and in lawns in parks and cemeteries; summer and fall; common

EDIBILITY: Edible

COMMENTS: Green mushrooms are relatively uncommon, but this one is to be expected every year. It is a favorite of rodents, insects, slugs, and box turtles. Other green *Russula* species include *Russula variata* (p. 25), which has forked gills that are not brittle, and *Russula aeruginea* (not illustrated), which has a smooth cap that does not have a patchwork pattern. Prior to the description of this species, it was referred to as *Russula virescens* (not illustrated), which is a larger species with a non-striate cap and smaller patches that are not usually blue green.

Russula parvovirescens

SCIENTIFIC NAME: *Russula grata* Britzelm
SYNONYM: *Russula laurocerasi* Melzer
COMMON NAME: Almond-Scented Brittlegill
FAMILY: Russulaceae

CAP: Up to 5½ in. wide; dull yellow to brownish yellow, buff in wet conditions; almost round, becoming convex to broadly convex, and finally nearly flat; surface bald, smooth, viscid when wet; markedly striate in age

FLESH: White to yellowish, unchanging when exposed; thick; firm; brittle; odor of almond extract or maraschino cherries, becoming unpleasant in age; taste somewhat acrid

GILLS: Creamy white to yellowish, sometimes with brown stains; brittle; attached to the stem; moderately close; broad; edges even; no partial veil

STEM: Up to 4 in. long; white to yellowish white, often with brown stains; surface smooth, bald, dry

SPORE PRINT: Creamy white to yellowish

ECOLOGY: Mycorrhizal; scattered to gregarious in lawns or humus under broadleaf trees in parks and in mixed woods; common

EDIBILITY: Not edible

COMMENTS: *Russula fragrantissima* (not illustrated) is nearly identical. It tends to be a bit larger and has a foul-smelling odor at maturity and a more acrid or oily taste. Observation of the spore differences are really needed to separate the two. There are reports that there are intermediate collections. It is possible that DNA might reveal that there is only one microscopically variable species. There are other similar species such as *Russula foetentula* (not illustrated), which has reddish-brown stains on the stem base and at times on the cap surface.

Russula grata

SCIENTIFIC NAME: *Russula granulata* Peck

SYNONYM: None

COMMON NAME: Granulated Russula

FAMILY: Russulaceae

CAP: Up to 3 in. wide; yellowish brown to tawny, often darkest at the center; convex, becoming flat at times with an uplifted margin; surface with granules and patches, especially over the center; granules can be lighter, darker, or the same color as the cap cuticle; viscid when wet; striate, sometimes obscurely so; margin incurved at first

FLESH: Whitish or pale yellow; brittle; odor resembling stale cooking oil; rancid to unpleasant; taste slowly acrid

GILLS: Whitish to pale yellow; attached to the stem; close; brittle; often forked near the stem; edges even; no partial veil

STEM: Up to 2½ in. long; white; base at times with brown stains; equal; surface smooth, dry, and bald

SPORE PRINT: Cream

ECOLOGY: Mycorrhizal; solitary, scattered to gregarious in humus and moss in conifer and mixed woodlands; often under hemlock and beech; also in high altitude forests with spruce and fir; summer and fall; common

EDIBILITY: Not edible

COMMENTS: Compare with *Russula grata* (p. 27). Other similar species that are not illustrated here are *Russula fragrantissima* and *Russula foetentula*. These species lack the cap granules. *Russula pulverulenta* (not illustrated) has granules on the stem as well as on the cap.

Russula granulata

SCIENTIFIC NAME: *Russula ballouii* Peck

SYNONYM: None

COMMON NAME: Ballou's Russula

FAMILY: Russulaceae

CAP: Up to 3 in. wide; yellowish ochre, tawny to rusty, paler at times, the cuticle breaking up into small, scale-like patches revealing a creamy, ground color; convex to broadly convex to flat with a central depression; surface bald, dry; not striate, or only faintly so

FLESH: White, moderately thick; odor not distinctive, mealy, or of bread dough; taste usually acrid but mealy or mild at times

GILLS: White to cream colored at times with yellowish stains in insect damaged areas; attached; close to crowded; moderately broad; brittle; edges even; no partial veil

STEM: Up to 1½ in. wide; creamy white above, colored like the cap; equal; solid; surface dry with rows of tawny scales or patches at the base

SPORE PRINT: Cream to very pale yellow

ECOLOGY: Mycorrhizal with oaks and possibly other broadleaf trees; scattered to gregarious in humus and lawns in parks and woodlands; summer; locally abundant

EDIBILITY: Not edible

COMMENTS: A key distinguishing feature is the base of the stem, which has rows of scale-like patches. *Russula compacta* (p. 24) has a similarly colored cap. Its gills are not brittle, and they rapidly stain brown when rubbed. *Russula grata* (p. 27) and several other similar species can easily be separated by their striate caps.

Russula ballouii

SCIENTIFIC NAME: *Russula ochroleucoides* Kauffman

SYNONYM: None

COMMON NAME: Yellow Brittle Gill

FAMILY: Russulaceae

CAP: Up to 4½ in. wide; golden yellow to pale yellow with an orange tint; convex to broadly convex, becoming flat with a depressed center; surface dry, dull velvety at times; not striate, or obscurely so; occasionally with small cracks in age

FLESH: White to buff, unchanging when exposed; firm; brittle; odor not distinctive, or faintly fragrant; taste slowly bitter or acrid

GILLS: White bruising yellowish or brownish eventually; developing brown spots or stains in age; attached to the stem; brittle; close; edges even; no partial veil

STEM: Up to 3 in. long; whitish, at times with yellow or brownish stains; equal; solid becoming spongy; surface bald or minutely pruinose, dry, dull

SPORE PRINT: White to yellowish

ECOLOGY: Mycorrhizal with oaks and beech; scattered to gregarious in broadleaf woods in humus or on lawns in parks; summer and early fall; common

EDIBILITY: Not edible

COMMENTS: *Russula flavida* (not illustrated) is similar but is smaller and has a yellow stem.

Russula ochroleucoides

SCIENTIFIC NAME: *Russula eccentrica* Peck

SYNONYM: None

COMMON NAME: None

FAMILY: Russulaceae

CAP: Up to 5 in. wide; whitish at first, becoming grayish buff to olive buff and finally grayish brown to dark brown; convex to broadly convex and finally flat; surface viscid in wet weather; finely scaly, shiny, or dull

FLESH: Whitish to grayish pink; thick, firm, brittle; odor not distinctive; taste mild or slightly bitter

GILLS: Pale pink to pinkish cinnamon; attached to the stem; very broad; subdistant; with small water droplets at times; numerous short gills; brittle; edges even; no partial veil

STEM: Up to 3 in. long; whitish or at times colored like the cap, with pale brown stains; generally equal or tapering in either direction; surface dry, brittle, bald, or slightly pruinose

SPORE PRINT: White

ECOLOGY: Mycorrhizal; scattered to gregarious in humus in broadleaf woods, especially under oaks; summer; occasional

EDIBILITY: Unknown

COMMENTS: The fairly large, broad, pinkish gills and white spore print are a unique combination.

Russula eccentrica

SCIENTIFIC NAME: *Russula mariae* Peck

SYNONYMS: None

COMMON NAMES: Mary's Russula, Purple Bloom Brittlegill

FAMILY: Russulaceae

CAP: Up to 4 in. wide; purple, at times mottled with yellow or olive colors, or occasionally these colors throughout, center often darkest; convex to broadly convex, becoming flat; surface dry, pruinose, somewhat viscid when wet, velvety with a whitish bloom; only slightly striate in age

FLESH: White, sometimes reddish under the cuticle, unchanging when exposed; thick at the center; odor not distinctive; taste not distinctive, or rarely slightly acrid

GILLS: White to cream or pale yellowish, at times with pinkish edges; attached to the stem; close; brittle; edges even; no partial veil

STEM: Up to 3 in. long; colored like the cap, or white flushed with purple or pink, especially toward the base; equal or swollen at the base or mid-stem; surface bald and dry, or slightly tacky

SPORE PRINT: Creamy to pale yellow

ECOLOGY: Mycorrhizal; solitary, scattered, or gregarious in humus or on lawns under broadleaf trees, especially oaks; common

EDIBILITY: Edible

COMMENTS: This is a common, attractive species in lawns or wood edges under oaks. It was described by Charles Horton Peck, a nineteenth- and early twentieth-century mycologist. He named it after his wife.

Russula mariae

SCIENTIFIC NAME: *Russula vinacea* Burl.

SYNONYM: *Russula krombholtzii* Shaffer

COMMON NAME: Blackish Red Brittlegill

FAMILY: Russulaceae

CAP: Up to 4½ in. wide; variable in color, purplish red, blackish, dark liver red, at times with pink or yellow tones; convex to broadly convex, becoming nearly flat, at times with a depressed center; surface tacky when fresh and moist; bald; faintly striate at times

FLESH: White, unchanging when damaged; brittle; odor not distinctive; taste mild or slightly acrid

GILLS: White becoming creamy or pale yellow, slowly developing rusty-brown stains in age; attached; close; moderately broad; brittle; edges even; no partial veil

STEM: Up to 3 in. long; white, at times becoming grayish and developing rusty-brown spots; equal or tapering upward; surface dry, bald, smooth or slightly wrinkled

SPORE PRINT: White to cream

ECOLOGY: Mycorrhizal; solitary to scattered in humus or moss under broad-leaf trees, especially oaks and hickories; spring through fall; fairly common

EDIBILITY: Reported as edible; the author has not tried it

COMMENTS: This is one of the first *Russula* species to appear in the spring. The often dark-red to blackish cap and early season appearance help distinguish this species from the many other red-capped species in this genus. Identifying red *Russula* species is a challenge. Most are beyond the scope of this book. See the comments in the introduction to the genus.

Russula vinacea

SCIENTIFIC NAME: *Russula brevipes* Peck
SYNONYM: None
COMMON NAME: Short-Stalked Brittlegill
FAMILY: Russulaceae

CAP: Up to 8 in. wide; white to cream, often covered with dirt; convex with a central depression at first becoming nearly flat to funnel shaped in age; surface dry, smooth to fibrillose, becoming cracked at times; margin incurved at first and often remaining so into maturity

FLESH: White, at times staining brownish on exposure; firm, brittle; odor not distinctive, or somewhat unpleasant; taste mild to acrid; taste of variety *acrior* is reportedly very acrid

GILLS: White to creamy or pale yellow, staining reddish brown; subdecurrent; close to crowded; narrow; forking at times; edges even; no partial veil

STEM: Up to 2½ in. long; white to cream, staining brownish; nearly equal; solid, becoming hollow; surface dry, bald

SPORE PRINT: White to cream

ECOLOGY: Mycorrhizal; solitary to gregarious in litter, often partially buried, under pines; summer and fall; common

EDIBILITY: Edible, but generally considered mediocre; the author has not tried it

COMMENTS: This species frequently appears mostly submerged in pine duff. It often occurs with *Lactifluus deceptivus* (p. 41), which looks very similar, but its gills exude latex when damaged. *Russula brevipes* var. *acrior* has a blue band at the stem apex and at times shows blue tints on the gills and cap. Compare with other, similar-sized white mushrooms, such as *Hygrophorus sordidus* (p. 69) and *Tricholoma subresplendens* (p. 91). These usually occur with oaks and are not associated with pines. There are also similar, less common, whitish species (not included here) in the genera *Leucopaxillus* and *Clitocybe*.

Russula brevipes

MILK MUSHROOMS

Lactarius and *Lactifluus*

THESE TWO GENERA of medium to large mushrooms exude latex when the gills or flesh are cut or damaged. Sometimes the latex is scant or watery, and close observation is needed to see it. They are treated in older field guides as all being in the genus *Lactarius*. Macroscopically they are very much alike. General characteristics include white, cream, buff, or yellowish spore deposits; fleshy but rather brittle caps and stems; no partial veil or volva; and a mycorrhizal association with trees. They are rather squat mushrooms, with the cap often being wider than the stem's length. Their sister genus is *Russula*, whose species do not exude latex when cut or damaged, and most species are very brittle. Keys are organized here into three groups: species with acrid white latex; species with mild white latex; and species with colored latex. Several of the species in the genus *Lactifluus* with mild-tasting latex are considered to be good edibles.

Lactarius peckii

Lactifluus lignyotus

Lactarius aspideoides

Lactifluus volemus v. flavus

Key to the Milk Mushrooms, *Lactarius* and *Lactifluus*

Latex acrid or peppery, whitish

Latex rapidly becoming yellow on exposure

1. Under oaks, without prominent reddish-brown stains: *Lactarius chrysorrheus* (p. 38)
2. Under conifers, with reddish-brown stains: *Lactarius vinaceorufescens* (p. 39)

Latex not rapidly changing color on exposure

1. Cap whitish; gills very crowded: *Lactarius piperatus* (p. 40)
2. Cap whitish; gills close to subdistant; covered at first with a pseudo partial veil that does not attach to the stem; mature cap margin slightly stretchy from the remains of the pseudo veil: *Lactarius deceptivus* (p. 41)
3. Cap whitish; gills subdistant or occasionally close; no pseudo veil; cap margin not stretchy: *Lactarius subvellereus* var. *subdistans* (p. 42)
4. Cap bay red to brownish red; dry; not usually zoned; under conifers: *Lactarius rufus* (p. 44)
5. Cap: orangish brown to brick red; dry; zoned under oaks: *Lactarius peckii* (p. 43)
6. Cap orange to yellowish; viscid to tacky; latex may slowly turn yellowish: *Lactarius croceus* (p. 45)
7. Cap gray to pinkish gray; dry; odor of coconut; under conifers: *Lactarius hibbardiae* (p. 46)

8. Cap gray to olive gray or olive buff; dry; under broadleaf trees, especially beech; odor not of coconut: *Lactarius cinereus* (p. 47)

9. Cap dark olive brown to yellowish brown: *Lactarius sordidus* (p. 51)

10. Cap buff, white, or yellowish; distinctly zoned: *Lactarius psammicola* (p. 49)

11. Cap pinkish brown; latex slowly staining tissues greenish: *Lactarius allardii* (p. 50)

12. Cap white to cream, yellow to ochraceous at the center; latex slowly staining tissues yellow: *Lactarius maculatipes* (p. 48)

Latex mild, copious, white to cream

1. Cap orange to yellowish; gills distant to subdistant: *Lactifluus hygrophoroides* (p. 58)

2. Cap orange to yellowish; gills close; fishy odor: *Lactifluus volemus* (p. 59)

3. Cap brownish to brownish orange; often wrinkled: *Lactifluus corrugis* (p. 60)

4. Cap whitish; fishy odor: *Lactifluus luteolus* (p. 62)

5. Cap blackish brown: *Lactarius lignyotus* (p. 61)

Latex mild to slightly peppery, variously colored

1. Latex red; staining tissues greenish; cap pinkish silver: *Lactarius subpurpureus* (p. 56)

2. Latex watery or white; cap reddish brown; under broadleaf trees: *Lactarius quietus* var. *incanus* (p. 57)

3. Scant blue latex, becoming greenish; blue to silver cap: *Lactarius indigo* (p. 52)

4. Latex orange to red; not staining tissues green: *Lactarius thyinos* (p. 53)

5. Latex orange to red; staining gills and flesh green: *Lactarius deterrimus* (p. 54)

6. Latex orange to red, staining gills greenish; flesh bluish: *Lactarius chelidonium* (p. 55)

SCIENTIFIC NAME: *Lactarius chrysorrheus* Fr.

SYNONYM: *Lactifluus chrysorrheus* (Fr.) Kuntze

COMMON NAME: Yellow Drop Milk Cap

FAMILY: Russulaceae

CAP: Up to 3½ in. wide; whitish with brownish spots, pinkish buff; yellowish buff, convex to nearly flat, developing a depressed center; surface faintly zonate at times, moist, sub viscid in wet weather

FLESH: Whitish becoming yellow rather quickly when exposed; thin; odor not distinctive; taste acrid

GILLS: Whitish or very pale yellowish; attached or subdecurrent; close; edges even; no partial veil

LATEX: White, quickly changing to yellow on exposure; not staining the tissues; acrid, often starting mildly acrid and then increasing in intensity; rather copious

STEM: Up to 3 in. long; whitish; generally equal; hollow in age; base hairy at times; surface bald, apex moist to tacky

SPORE PRINT: Buff to yellowish

ECOLOGY: Mycorrhizal with oaks; scattered to gregarious in humus in broadleaf woods; summer and early fall; common

EDIBILITY: Not edible; acrid; gastrointestinal poisonings have occurred with this mushroom

COMMENTS: This mushroom will likely be transferred to the genus *Lactifluus* in the near future. It is a common component of the summer, oak woods mushroom flora. Compare with *Lactarius vinaceorufescens* (p. 39), a common species associated with conifers. It has white latex, quickly changing to yellow on exposure, and it develops sordid reddish-brown stains on the cap, gills, and stem.

Lactarius chrysorrheus

SCIENTIFIC NAME: *Lactarius vinaceorufescens* A. H. Sm.

SYNONYM: None

COMMON NAME: Yellow-Staining Milk Cap

FAMILY: Russulaceae

CAP: Up to 4 in. wide; convex to broadly convex, becoming nearly flat; margin incurved at first; buff, cinnamon pink, cinnamon, vinaceous brown in age; surface viscid, bald, faintly zoned, or with water spots

FLESH: White to pinkish, staining yellow when exposed; fairly thick; odor not distinctive; taste acrid

GILLS: Whitish to pinkish buff, with pinkish to brownish stains, becoming reddish to reddish brown in age; attached to the stem or subdecurrent; close; edges even; no partial veil

LATEX: White on exposure, quickly becoming bright yellow; taste very acrid

STEM: Up to 3 in. long; whitish to pinkish buff with reddish-brown stains; generally equal or slightly enlarged downward; becoming hollow; base with whitish to brown hairs; surface dry, rather smooth, bald

SPORE PRINT: White to pale yellow

ECOLOGY: Mycorrhizal with pines; scattered to gregarious in humus and moss in conifer or mixed woods, often under white pine; summer and fall; common

EDIBILITY: Not edible; acrid

COMMENTS: This species can often be found in large numbers in pine plantations. It often fruits late in the season. Compare with *Lactarius chrysorrheus* (p. 38), which also has latex that quickly turns yellow. It lacks the overall reddish-brown staining and is usually associated with oaks.

Lactarius vinaceorufescens

SCIENTIFIC NAME: *Lactifluus piperatus* (L.) Roussel

SYNONYM: *Lactarius piperatus* (L.) Pers.

COMMON NAME: **Peppery Milk Cap**

FAMILY: **Russulaceae**

CAP: Up to 5½ in. wide; white to creamy white, at times with tan stains in age; convex to flat, becoming depressed in the center to vase shaped; surface dry, bald, not zoned, at times finely wrinkled

FLESH: White, sometimes with yellowish tinges; very firm; odor not distinctive; taste very acrid

GILLS: White to cream, at times with yellowish areas; attached to subdecurrent; very crowded; forking; edges even; no partial veil

LATEX: White, slowly yellowish on exposure; not staining tissues or at times staining the gills yellowish; copious; very acrid

STEM: Up to 3 in. long; white; firm, solid; equal or tapering slightly downward; surface bald, dry

SPORE PRINT: White

ECOLOGY: Mycorrhizal with oaks and other broadleaf trees; scattered to gregarious in humus, grass, and moss; summer and fall; common

EDIBILITY: Not edible; acrid

COMMENTS: Compare with *Lactifluus deceptivus* (p. 41), which has a pseudo veil, and *Lactifluus subvellereus* var. *subdistans* (p. 42), which has subdistant gills. *Lactifluus glaucescens* (not illustrated) is nearly identical. It differs in having latex that dries greenish.

Lactifluus piperatus

SCIENTIFIC NAME: *Lactifluus deceptivus* (Peck) Kuntze

SYNONYM: *Lactarius deceptivus* Peck

COMMON NAME: Deceptive Milk Cap

FAMILY: Russulaceae

CAP: Up to 9 in. wide; white; convex with a broadly depressed center; surface bald, velvety, in age with brown scales, sometimes forming from the center outward; margin enrolled, covering the gills at first and remaining as a stretchy tissue layer at the extreme margin

FLESH: White; thick; firm; coarse; staining brown; odor not distinctive, becoming pungent in age; taste very acrid

GILLS: White or cream, becoming tan in age; attached to subdecurrent; close to subdistant; edges even; forking at times; no true partial veil, but covered when young by a membranous pseudo veil that is not attached to the stem

LATEX: White, unchanging, staining the flesh and gills brown; copious; acrid taste

STEM: Up to 4 in. long; white with brown stains in age; equal or tapering downward; surface dry, velvety, or bald, at times becoming scaly in age

SPORE PRINT: White to pale yellowish buff

ECOLOGY: Mycorrhizal with oak and hemlock; single, scattered, or gregarious in humus or moss in broadleaf and conifer forests; summer and fall; common

EDIBILITY: Not recommended; acrid

COMMENTS: At times this large, white mushroom is one of the most prominent mushrooms in the woods. Two common, white, milk mushrooms with acrid latex, *Lactifluus piperatus* (p. 40) and *Lactifluus subvellereus* (p. 42) lack the marginal pseudo veil. *Russula brevipes* (p. 34) has a very similar appearance but lacks latex.

Lactifluus deceptivus

SCIENTIFIC NAME: *Lactifluus subvellereus* (Peck) Nuytinck
SYNONYM: *Lactarius subvellereus* var. *subdistans* Hesler and A. H. Sm.
COMMON NAME: Fleecy Milk Cap
FAMILY: Russulaceae

CAP: Up to 6 in. wide; white with yellowish or grayish areas; convex with a depressed center, at times becoming funnel shaped; surface dry, velvety to slightly wooly, at times with minute cracks; margin enrolled at first, not cottony but may be floccose in age

FLESH: White, changing to yellowish when cut; compact; hard; odor not distinctive; taste strongly acrid

GILLS: Whitish, becoming yellowish; attached to subdecurrent; subdistant to distant; often with hyaline droplets; narrow; some forking; edges even; no partial veil

LATEX: White, slowly changing to yellow on exposure; staining gills brownish to pinkish brown; copious; strongly acrid

STEM: Up to 2 in. long; white with yellowish or brownish areas; equal or tapered downward; solid; surface dry, velvety

SPORE PRINT: White

ECOLOGY: Mycorrhizal with oaks and possibly other broadleaf trees; single, scattered, or gregarious in lawns, moss, and humus under broad leaf trees in parks and woodlands; summer and early fall; common

EDIBILITY: Not edible; acrid

COMMENTS: The subdistant to distant gills will separate this species from *Lactifluus piperatus* (p. 40), which has crowded gills, and from *Lactifluus deceptivus* (p. 41), which has closer gills and a pseudo veil that leaves a cottony margin.

Lactarius subvellereus
var. *subdistans*

SCIENTIFIC NAME: *Lactarius peckii* Burl.

SYNONYM: None

COMMON NAME: Peck's Milk Mushroom

FAMILY: Russulaceae

CAP: Up to 4 in. wide; orangish brown to brick red, usually with darker concentric zones; broadly convex with a depressed center; surface dry, bald or slightly roughened, occasionally scaly; margin enrolled at first

FLESH: Pale vinaceous brown, not staining when cut; firm; odor not distinctive; taste strongly acrid

GILLS: Pale cinnamon to reddish brown, darker in age or with dark-brown stains; attached to subdecurrent; close; rather narrow; edges even; no partial veil

LATEX: White on exposure; not staining tissues; copious; strongly acrid

STEM: Up to 2½ in. long; tan or colored like the cap, only paler; equal; becoming hollow in age; surface dry, with a whitish bloom when young

SPORE PRINT: White

ECOLOGY: Mycorrhizal with oaks; scattered to gregarious in soil and litter in broadleaf and mixed woods; summer and early fall; common

EDIBILITY: Not edible; acrid

COMMENTS: Tasting the acrid latex of this species will clearly set it apart from *Lactifluus volemus* (p. 59) and similar species.

Lactarius peckii

SCIENTIFIC NAME: *Lactarius rufus* (Scop.) Fr.

SYNONYM: None

COMMON NAME: Red Hot Milk Mushroom

FAMILY: Russulaceae

CAP: Up to 3½ in. broad; bay red to dark brownish red, at times with a whitish bloom when young; rarely zoned; convex becoming flat with a depressed center, umbonate at times; surface moist to dry, not viscid, bald; margin incurved at first, becoming uplifted

FLESH: White with a pinkish or purplish tinge; odor not distinctive; taste intensely acrid

GILLS: Whitish to pinkish tan or darker in age; attached to subdecurrent; narrow; close to crowded, not changing color when damaged; edges even; no partial veil

LATEX: White, unchanging when exposed; not staining tissues; abundant; very acrid, sometimes slowly

STEM: Up to 3½ in. long; colored like the cap; equal or tapering downward; surface bald, dry with a whitish bloom when young

SPORE PRINT: Cream to white or yellowish

ECOLOGY: Mycorrhizal with conifers, especially pines and spruce; often in bogs and wet woods but also in poor soil in dry situations; single, scattered, to gregarious in soil, humus, and moss; late summer and fall; common

EDIBILITY: Not edible; acrid

COMMENTS: There are many similar colored milk mushrooms. This one is set apart by its intensely acrid taste, lack of a distinctive odor, and by its conifer habitat.

Lactarius rufus

SCIENTIFIC NAME: *Lactarius croceus* Burl.

SYNONYM: None

COMMON NAME: None

FAMILY: Russulaceae

CAP: Up to 4 in. wide; bright orange to yellowish orange, fading in age to pale yellow or yellowish tan, at times with zones of darker orange; convex to broadly convex to nearly flat with a depressed center in age; surface viscid when wet, shiny when dry

FLESH: White, staining yellow to orangish yellow when bruised; thick; odor fruity; taste bitter to acrid

GILLS: Whitish, pale yellow to yellowish tan; staining yellow where cut or damaged; attached to subdecurrent; close to subdistant; broad; edges even; no partial veil

LATEX: White slowly turning to yellow; staining gills and flesh yellow; scant; odor not distinctive; taste bitter or acrid, sometimes slowly

STEM: Up to 2½ in. long; whitish, pale orangish yellow or colored like the cap; equal; stuffed becoming hollow; at times with brownish spots; surface bald, at times velvety at the base, dry

SPORE PRINT: Pale yellow

ECOLOGY: Mycorrhizal with oaks; single to scattered in humus and moss in broadleaf and mixed woods; summer and fall; common

EDIBILITY: Not edible; acrid

COMMENTS: Compare with *Lactifluus volemus* (p. 59), which has a dry cap and mild-tasting latex. *Lactarius psammicola* (p. 49) is similar but has a paler and more distinctly zonate cap and often larger size.

Lactarius croceus

SCIENTIFIC NAME: *Lactarius hibbardiae* Peck

SYNONYM: *Lactarius mammosus* Fr.

COMMON NAME: Coconut Milk Cap

FAMILY: Russulaceae

CAP: Up to 3 in. wide; ruddy gray; pinkish brown to dark pinkish gray, paler with age; convex to broadly convex, becoming flat with a depressed center, umbonate at times; surface fibrillose, dry, not striate

FLESH: Whitish, pinkish gray or pinkish brown; odor similar to coconut; taste acrid

GILLS: Cream to pinkish buff, slowly staining brownish where injured; attached to the stem; close to subdistant; edges even; no partial veil

LATEX: White or watery; rather abundant; acrid

STEM: Up to 3½ in. long; whitish or colored like the cap, at times with brownish areas; equal or tapering downward; becoming hollow; surface dry, pruinose

SPORE PRINT: Pale cream

ECOLOGY: Mycorrhizal with conifers; scattered to gregarious in moss or humus, often with hemlock and white pine; late summer and fall; fairly common

EDIBILITY: Unknown

COMMENTS: This is the only mushroom with a coconut odor that one is likely to encounter in the Appalachians. A much paler mushroom with a similar odor is *Lactarius glyciosmus* (not illustrated), which to the author's knowledge has not been found here.

Lactarius hibbardiae

SCIENTIFIC NAME: *Lactarius cinereus* Peck

SYNONYM: *Lactarius cinereus* var. *fagetorum* Hesler and A. H. Sm.

COMMON NAME: None

FAMILY: Russulaceae

CAP: Up to 2¾ in. wide; olive gray to olive buff, with faint violet tinges at times; convex, becoming flat with a depressed center; surface bald or slightly hoary, not zoned, viscid when wet

FLESH: White, unchanging when cut; odor not distinctive; taste acrid

GILLS: White to cream colored, not staining when damaged; attached to sub-decurrent; close; edges even; no partial veil

LATEX: White, unchanging on exposure; acrid; usually fairly abundant

STEM: Up to 3 in. long; colored like the cap or paler; equal becoming enlarged downward; becoming hollow; surface slightly viscid, becoming dry and shiny

SPORE PRINT: Pale yellow

ECOLOGY: Mycorrhizal; scattered to gregarious in humus and moss in broad-leaf and mixed woods, usually under beech; summer and early fall; common

EDIBILITY: Unknown

COMMENTS: This is a common mushroom wherever beech is found. The species described here is probably *Lactarius cinereus* var. *fagetorum*. It is macroscopically very similar to *Lactarius cinereus* var. *cinereus* (not illustrated). Spore measurements are needed to separate the two.

Lactarius cinerus

SCIENTIFIC NAME: *Lactarius maculatipes* Burl.

SYNONYM: None

COMMON NAME: None

FAMILY: Russulaceae

CAP: Up to 4 in. wide; whitish to cream, yellowish or ochraceous at the center, convex to flat with a depressed center and uplifted margin at maturity; surface viscid, bald, at times with pockmarks, obscurely zoned, most often near the margin

FLESH: White, slowly staining yellow; firm; odor not distinctive; taste slowly acrid

GILLS: Whitish, pinkish buff, becoming yellowish; bruising tan; attached to subdecurrent; close to crowded; narrow; sometimes forked; no partial veil

LATEX: White, slowly becoming yellow on exposure; staining tissues yellow; taste slowly acrid

STEM: Up to 3 in. long; whitish; staining yellow; equal or tapering downward; surface with shallow pits, viscid when fresh

SPORE PRINT: Buff to yellowish

ECOLOGY: Mycorrhizal with oaks; scattered to gregarious in humus or grass in broadleaf woodlands and parks; summer and fall; fairly common

EDIBILITY: Unknown

COMMENTS: The pale viscid cap, acrid latex, and pitted stem are key identification features.

Lactarius maculatipes

SCIENTIFIC NAME: *Lactarius psammicola* A. H. Sm.

SYNONYM: None

COMMON NAME: None

FAMILY: Russulaceae

CAP: Up to 6 in. wide; distinctly zoned with yellowish and buff or whitish and buff zones; convex with a central depression; surface bald, viscid; margin arched and enrolled, hairy in *Lactarius psammicola* var. *psammicola*

FLESH: Whitish or with pinkish-cinnamon stains; thick; odor not distinctive; taste acrid

GILLS: Whitish, pinkish buff to cinnamon buff, bruising darker; attached to subdecurrent; close; infrequently forking; edges even; no partial veil

LATEX: White; drying buff; slowly staining tissues pinkish cinnamon; very acrid

STEM: Up to 2 in. long; whitish, discoloring brownish where handled; equal or tapering downward; central or off-center; hard; becoming hollow in age; surface dry, pitted at times

SPORE PRINT: Pinkish buff

ECOLOGY: Mycorrhizal with oaks and possibly other broadleaf trees; scattered to gregarious in grass and humus; summer and early fall; fairly common

EDIBILITY: Not edible; acrid

COMMENTS: This rather large mushroom with a zoned cap is most commonly seen under oaks in parks and cemeteries. Two forms are recognized. *Lactarius psammicola* f. *psammicola* (not illustrated) has a hairy margin, and *Lactarius psammicola* f. *glaber* lacks the hairy margin. The latter form is the most common.

Lactarius psammicola

SCIENTIFIC NAME: *Lactifluus allardii* (Coker) De Crop
SYNONYM: *Lactarius allardii* Coker
COMMON NAME: None
FAMILY: Russulaceae

CAP: Up to 6 in. wide; pinkish brown to reddish brown, whitish where covered by leaves; convex with an enrolled margin, becoming flat with a central depression; surface dry, not zoned, bald or, at times, velvety, not striate

FLESH: White, slowly staining pinkish and then greenish when cut; thick; firm; odor not distinctive, becoming pungent in age; taste acrid

GILLS: Whitish, staining green where damaged; attached to subdecurrent; close to subdistant; forked; edges even; no partial veil

LATEX: White at first, becoming greenish and eventually brown on exposure; copious; taste acrid

STEM: Up to 2 in. long; whitish or tinged the color of the cap; equal or tapering down; surface bald, dry

SPORE PRINT: White to creamy white

ECOLOGY: Mycorrhizal; scattered to gregarious under oak in broadleaf and mixed woodlands; summer and fall; occasional

EDIBILITY: Unknown; not recommended owing to the acrid taste

COMMENTS: Until recently this mushroom was placed in the genus *Lactarius*. The cap surface resembles that of the very common *Russula compacta* (p. 24), which lacks latex and has brown-staining gills.

Lactifluus allardii

SCIENTIFIC NAME: *Lactarius sordidus* Peck

SYNONYM: *Lactarius turpis* (Weinm.) Fr.

COMMON NAME: Sordid Milk Cap

FAMILY: Russulaceae

CAP: Up to 5 in. wide; dark yellowish brown, dark olive brown at the center, at times obscurely zoned; convex to broadly convex, becoming flat, depressed in the center; surface moist or dry, viscid when wet, at first with a felt-like surface

FLESH: White with a pinkish hue, or yellowish; firm; odor not distinctive; taste mild at first, becoming very acrid

GILLS: White to yellowish, staining dull brown to olive brown where damaged; attached to subdecurrent; close; narrow to medium broad; some forking; edges even; no partial veil

LATEX: White to whitish on exposure, not changing, or becoming slightly greenish; staining the gills brown; usually copious; acrid

STEM: Up to 3 in. long; olive or brownish olive, streaked or spotted; surface viscid when wet, with occasional pockmarks; solid becoming hollow

SPORE PRINT: Whitish to cream or pale buff

ECOLOGY: Mycorrhizal; solitary to scattered in moss or humus in conifer and mixed woodlands; late summer and fall; occasional

EDIBILITY: Not edible; acrid

COMMENTS: Considered a synonym of *Lactarius turpis* by some investigators, *Lactarius sordidus* has drab colors that make it easily overlooked. A similar species with a darker greenish-black cap is *Lactarius atroviridis* (not illustrated). It is found under oaks and in mixed woods. Most would not find any of this milk cap group very attractive.

Lactarius sordidus

SCIENTIFIC NAME: *Lactarius indigo* (Schwein.) Fr.

SYNONYM: None

COMMON NAME: Indigo Milk Cap

FAMILY: Russulaceae

CAP: Up to 5 in. wide; blue and silver zones, fading in age to grayish silver with traces of blue, the zones disappearing, at times bruising green; convex to convex depressed, becoming broadly funnel shaped; surface viscid, bald, at times appearing varnished; margin turned under at first

FLESH: Whitish, quickly staining dark blue when exposed; firm; thick; odor not distinctive; taste mild or slightly bitter

GILLS: Indigo blue, dark greenish where damaged, fading to bluish gray and at times with yellowish tints; broadly attached to the stem; crowded; edges even; no partial veil

LATEX: Dark blue, slowly becoming dark green on exposure; staining tissues green; rather scant; taste mild or slightly bitter

STEM: Up to 3 in. long; silver gray with bluish tints, often colored like the cap; usually equal or tapering in either direction; solid at first, becoming hollow; surface viscid at first, soon dry, usually with dark-blue spots

SPORE PRINT: Cream

ECOLOGY: Mycorrhizal with oaks and pines; scattered to gregarious in humus and moss; summer and fall; occasional to locally common

EDIBILITY: Edible

COMMENTS: This is perhaps the most distinctive mushroom in the parks and woodlands of Appalachia. Indigo-blue gills and silvery-blue caps combine with sparse, blue latex to make a unique combination.

Lactarius indigo

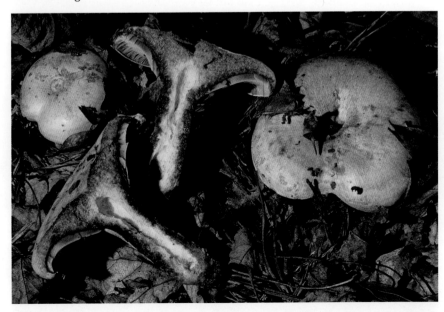

SCIENTIFIC NAME: *Lactarius thyinos* A. H. Sm.

SYNONYM: *Lactarius salmonicolor* R. Heim and Leclair

COMMON NAME: None

FAMILY: Russulaceae

CAP: Up to 4½ in. wide; orange and whitish, often in concentric zones espe-cially toward the margin; convex to broadly convex, becoming flat with a depressed center; surface viscid, bald

FLESH: White to cream or with orange tints, not staining green; rather thin; odor not distinctive; taste not distinctive, or astringent and slightly disagreeable

GILLS: Yellowish orange to orange, staining orange then wine red; attached to subdecurrent; close to subdistant; medium broad; sometimes forked; edges even; no partial veil

LATEX: Orange on exposure, very slowly turning to wine red; scant; taste mild, becoming astringent

STEM: Up to 3 in. long; various shades of orange; equal or tapering toward the base; hollow in age; surface viscid when wet, bald, at times with shal-low pits

SPORE PRINT: Pale yellowish

ECOLOGY: Mycorrhizal with conifers; single to scattered in moss or litter in high altitude, wet conifer, and mixed woods; summer and fall; occasional, and at times common in its preferred habitat

EDIBILITY: Edible

COMMENTS: This is an attractive species common to the boggy woods of Eastern Ontario and New England. It is likely a glacial relict species, which continues to survive on the higher mountains of the Appalachians. *Lac-tarius deterrimus* (p. 54) is similar, but its latex stains the tissues green.

Lactarius thyinos

SCIENTIFIC NAME: *Lactarius deterrimus* Gröger

SYNONYM: *Lactarius deliciosus* var. *deterrimus* (Gröger) Hesler and A. H. Sm.

COMMON NAME: False Saffron Cap

FAMILY: **Russulaceae**

CAP: Up to 4 in. wide; orange at first, then greenish, infused with orange buff, at times yellowish or whitish, zonate at times; convex to broadly convex to nearly flat in age; becoming depressed in the center; surface viscid when wet, bald; margin turned under at first

FLESH: Stem: Up to 2½ in. long; pale orange to whitish, staining reddish and then green; odor and taste not distinctive

GILLS: Orange with reddish-brown or green stains; attached to subdecurrent; subdistant; moderately broad; not forking; edges even; no partial veil

LATEX: Orangish red, unchanging on exposure; staining tissues reddish or green; scanty; mild tasting

STEM: Up to 2 in. long; orange, staining greenish where handled; stuffed becoming hollow; equal; surface smooth, bald

SPORE PRINT: Pale buff

ECOLOGY: Mycorrhizal with conifers, reported with spruce, hemlock, and white pine; scattered to gregarious in wet woods in moss and humus; late summer and fall; locally common

EDIBILITY: Edible; reported as mediocre by some and good by others

COMMENTS: This is a member of the *Lactarius delicosus* group. The mushroom described here is likely different than the species with the same name in Europe. DNA study is needed to sort out this complex. The similar *Lactarius thyinos* (p. 53) can be found at high elevations. It lacks green staining. See the comments under *Lactarius chelidonium* (p. 55) regarding the problems with field identification of this species and *Lactarius deterrimus*.

Lactarius deterrimus

SCIENTIFIC NAME: *Lactarius chelidonium* Peck

SYNONYM: *Lactarius chelidonioides* A. H. Sm.

COMMON NAME: None

FAMILY: Russulaceae

CAP: Up to 3 in. wide; color extremely variable, pale greenish buff, orangish brown, grayish yellow, pinkish brown, or various combinations of these colors, sometimes green in wet weather; sometimes slightly zonate; convex, becoming broadly convex, and then flat with a depressed center, finally funnel shaped; surface bald, slightly viscid when wet; margin turned under at first

FLESH: Blue with orange tones, especially near the gills; odor not distinctive, or slightly fragrant; taste mild, or slightly peppery

GILLS: Dingy yellow, yellowish brown, greenish, or olive buff; attached to subdecurrent; narrow; close to crowded; developing orange or green stains that in wet weather can occasionally turn reddish purple; edges even; no partial veil

LATEX: Dingy yellowish to yellowish brown, staining gills greenish; very scant; taste mild

STEM: Up to 2 in. long; colors similar to the cap or bluish; equal or enlarged downward; rather tough; surface fairly smooth, bald

Spore Print: Pale buff to yellowish

ECOLOGY: Mycorrhizal with pine; often in plantations, where it fruits scattered to gregarious in the needle duff; late summer and fall; occasional to locally common

EDIBILITY: Edible of fair quality

COMMENTS: Recent DNA studies indicate that North American collections of this mushroom are a match for North American collections of what has been called *Lactarius deterrimus* (p. 54). This is a problem for field identification since the two varieties have different-colored latex and different-colored flesh. It is likely that a new name will be created, combining both species into one.

Lactarius chelidonium

SCIENTIFIC NAME: *Lactarius subpurpureus* Peck

SYNONYMS: **None**

COMMON NAME: Wine Red Milk Mushroom

FAMILY: **Russulaceae**

CAP: Up to 4 in. wide; silvery pink or red blended with pinkish gray, at times spotted greenish; convex with a central depression; margin incurved at first; surface moist or tacky, bald, at times faintly striate in age

FLESH: Whitish to pinkish, staining reddish and finally greenish; odor not distinctive; taste mild or slightly bitter

GILLS: Pinkish to wine red, with red and green stains where damaged; attached to subdecurrent; moderately broad; subdistant; edges even; sometimes forked near the stem; no partial veil

LATEX: Wine red; scant; staining tissues reddish and then green; taste mild to faintly acrid

STEM: Up to 3 in. long; colored like the cap, with green stains at times; equal; becoming hollow; surface viscid when wet, bald down to the white mycelium coated base, with reddish spots at times

SPORE PRINT: Cream

ECOLOGY: Mycorrhizal with hemlock and possibly other conifers; single or scattered in humus or moss in conifer or mixed woods; late summer and fall; fairly common

EDIBILITY: Edible

COMMENTS: This is an easily identified milk mushroom. The latex is very scanty and seldom produces droplets.

Lactarius subpurpureus

SCIENTIFIC NAME: *Lactarius quietus* var. *incanus* Hesler and A. H. Sm.

SYNONYM: None

COMMON NAME: Oak Milk Cap

FAMILY: Russulaceae

CAP: Up to 4 in. wide; various shades of reddish brown, usually darker in the center, at times with tan, or purplish hues, sometimes zoned, often with a whitish dusting at first; convex to flat with a depressed center; surface bald or roughened, dry, usually not striate or obscurely so in age; margin incurved at first, becoming expanded to uplifted

FLESH: Whitish or pale pinkish buff; unchanging when cut, or turning slightly pinkish; odor not distinctive, or faintly of maple flavoring; taste mild, or slowly becoming slightly acrid

GILLS: Whitish, pale pinkish or yellowish, becoming brownish spotted, cinnamon in age; attached to subdecurrent; close; edges even; no partial veil

LATEX: White and thick at first, soon becoming watery; not staining tissues; usually scant in age; mild or slowly weakly acrid

STEM: Up to 5 in. long; whitish; often becoming colored like the cap, usually with brown stains; equal or enlarged below; solid becoming hollow; surface dry; silky at first

SPORE PRINT: Pinkish buff

ECOLOGY: Mycorrhizal with oaks; scattered in litter and humus in broadleaf woodlands; summer and fall; common

EDIBILITY: Unknown

COMMENTS: Compare with *Lactarius mutabilis* (not illustrated), which occurs with conifers and has a white to cream spore deposit and mild-tasting, white latex.

Lactarius quietus var. *incanus*

57

SCIENTIFIC NAME: *Lactifluus hygrophoroides* (Berk. and M. A. Curtis) Kuntze

SYNONYM: *Lactarius hygrophoroides* Berk. and M. A. Curtis

COMMON NAME: None

FAMILY: Russulaceae

CAP: Up to 3¼ in. wide; dull orange, pinkish orange, or brownish orange; convex to flat with a central depression; surface dry, bald, velvety at times, not zonate; margin turned under at first, becoming uplifted in age

FLESH: White; firm but brittle; unchanging when exposed; odor and taste not distinctive

GILLS: White, cream, or yellowish buff; unchanging when cut; attached to subdecurrent; subdistant to distant; broad; cross-veined; edges even; no partial veil

LATEX: White, unchanging on exposure, not staining the gills or flesh; copious; mild tasting

STEM: Up to 2½ in. long; orangish brown to orangish yellow; equal; solid; surface dry and bald

SPORE PRINT: White

ECOLOGY: Mycorrhizal; scattered to gregarious in moss or humus in broadleaf and mixed woodlands; it is often found in sandy soil along streams; summer and early fall; common

EDIBILITY: Edible

COMMENTS: Its closest look-alike is *Lactifluus volemus* (p. 59), which has closer gills and prefers a more upland forest. The subdistant to distant gills and mild latex are key features.

Lactifluus hygrophoroides

SCIENTIFIC NAME: *Lactifluus volemus* (Fr.) Kuntze

SYNONYM: *Lactarius volemus* (Fr.) Fr.

COMMON NAMES: Bradley, Leatherback, Apricot Milk Cap,
Tawny Milk Cap

FAMILY: Russulaceae

CAP: Up to 4 in. wide; orange to orangish brown, paler in age; convex to broadly convex, becoming nearly flat with a central depression; surface dry, bald, velvety at times; margin incurved at first and at times wrinkled

FLESH: White; staining brownish; thick; firm; brittle; odor fishy; taste mild

GILLS: White to cream; attached to subdecurrent; close; often forked; with brown stains where damaged; moderately broad; edges even; no partial veil

LATEX: White at first, becoming creamy white and eventually brownish; staining tissues tawny brown; copious; sticky; mild tasting

STEM: Up to 4½ in. long; colored like the cap but paler; equal or tapering slightly downward; surface dry, bald

SPORE PRINT: White

ECOLOGY: Mycorrhizal with oaks and possibly other broadleaf trees; single or scattered in lawns or humus and moss in broadleaf woods and parks; summer and early fall; common

EDIBILITY: Edible and considered by many as very good. The fishy odor disappears when cooked

COMMENTS: Compare with *Lactifluus hygrophoroides* (p. 58), which has distant gills, and *Lactifluus corrugis* (p. 60), which has a darker, wrinkled cap. All three have copious, mild-tasting latex and are edible. *Lactifluus volemus* has a fishy odor that disappears on cooking. Its sticky latex leaves brown stains on fingers, countertops, and baskets. Reports indicate that slow cooking is the best way to bring out the flavor of this mushroom. A yellow variety has been called *Lactifluus volemus* var. *flavus*.

Lactifluus volemus

SCIENTIFIC NAME: *Lactifluus corrugis* (Peck) Kuntze

SYNONYM: *Lactarius corrugis* Peck

COMMON NAME: CORRUGATED MILK CAP

FAMILY: Russulaceae

CAP: Up to 7½ in. wide; variable in color, dark grayish brown, reddish brown, to vinaceous brown, at times deep orange, paler in age; convex, becoming broadly convex and finally flat; surface velvety, dry; not zoned, wrinkled to corrugated, especially near the margin, not striate

FLESH: Whitish, staining brown; thick; firm; odor mild, becoming slightly fishy in age; mild tasting

GILLS: Pale cinnamon pink, pale golden brown; sometimes yellowish to whitish, staining brown where damaged; attached to subdecurrent; close; edges even; no partial veil

LATEX: White, unchanging; staining gills and flesh brown; copious; mild tasting

STEM: Up to 4 in. long; colored like the cap, only paler, at times orangish; equal; solid; surface dry, smooth, bald, or velvety

SPORE PRINT: White

ECOLOGY: Mycorrhizal; solitary, gregarious, or scattered in humus, moss, or soil under broadleaf trees, especially oaks; summer and early fall; common

EDIBILITY: Edible

COMMENTS: *Lactifluus volemus* (p. 59) is very similar. It usually has a brighter orange cap, paler gills, and a strong fishy odor. *Lactarius peckii* (p. 43) has similar colors. It has acrid latex and a zonate cap. *Lactarius rufus* (p. 44) has acrid latex and occurs with conifers.

Lactifluus corrigis

SCIENTIFIC NAME: *Lactarius lignyotus* Fr.
SYNONYM: *Lactifluus lignyotus* (Fr.) Kuntz
COMMON NAME: Chocolate Milky
FAMILY: Russulaceae

CAP: Up to 4 in. wide; striking blackish brown, fading to dingy yellowish brown in age; convex to flat, with the margin uplifted in age; umbonate; surface dry, velvety, not zoned, at times wrinkled, not striate

FLESH: White, staining rosy pink to dull reddish when cut; brittle; odor not distinctive; taste mild or slightly bitter

GILLS: White, becoming ochraceous tan in old age, bruising red; attached to subdecurrent; subdistant; edges even; no partial veil

LATEX: White, abundant; unchanging; staining the gills reddish; mild or slightly bitter tasting

STEM: Up to 4½ in. long; colored like the cap but usually paler; equal or enlarged downward; solid; at times with longitudinal ridges at the apex; surface dry, velvety

SPORE PRINT: Buff to ochre

ECOLOGY: Mycorrhizal with conifers and broadleaf trees, including spruce and oak, often found in moss in bogs; gregarious to scattered; summer and fall; common

EDIBILITY: Not recommended; reports vary, probably not poisonous

COMMENTS: This is a common spruce associate in the higher Appalachians. There are several varieties, including *Lactarius lignyotus* var. *canadensis*, which has dark gill edges, and *Lactarius lignyotus* var. *nigroviolascens*, which has flesh that stains dark violet. *Lactarius lignyotellus* (not illustrated) is a smaller species that has dark gill edges. *Lactarius gerardii* (not illustrated) has more distant gills and is usually paler.

Lactifluus lignyotus

SCIENTIFIC NAME: *Lactifluus luteolus* (Peck) Verbeken

SYNONYM: *Lactarius luteolus* Peck

COMMON NAME: None

FAMILY: Russulaceae

CAP: Up to 2½ in. wide; white to buff, or pale yellowish with tan or yellow stains; convex to flat with a shallow, central depression; surface dry, velvety, somewhat uneven or wrinkled, not zoned or striate

FLESH: White, staining slowly brown where cut; odor fishy; taste not distinctive

GILLS: White to cream, staining brown; attached to subdecurrent; rather thick; close to subdistant; edges even; no partial veil

LATEX: White; unchanging; staining all parts of the mushroom brown; copious; sticky; mild tasting

STEM: Up to 2½ in. long; colored like the cap; equal or tapering downward; solid or stuffed; surface dry, with a velvety bloom, often with brown stains

SPORE PRINT: White to cream

ECOLOGY: Mycorrhizal; usually gregarious or scattered in humus or moss in broadleaf woods, especially with oak; summer and fall; occasional to locally abundant

EDIBILITY: Edible; fishy odor disappears on cooking

COMMENTS: This species is often found along trails in sandy soil.

Lactifluus luteolus

MEDIUM TO LARGE
WHITE-SPORED MUSHROOMS
WITH A WAXY TEXTURE

Hygrophorus

Members of this waxy-textured genus of gilled mushrooms are most common in late summer and fall. Waxiness is a difficult feature to describe and sometimes hard to determine. Crushing a bit of the cap and gills between thumb and finger will usually produce a paraffin-like feel. The gills are attached to the stem. These species form mycorrhiza, often with conifers. Most are medium to large in size. Similar species in *Tricholoma* lack the waxy texture and usually have a notched gill attachment. If a mushroom does not key out, try the *Tricholoma* or *Hygrocybe* keys.

Hygrophorus pudorinus

Hygrophorus eburneus

Key to *Hygrophorus*

1. Cap pinkish with reddish or purple streaks; under conifers: *Hygrophorus purpurascens* (p. 68)
2. Cap tan with a pale margin; under conifers, especially hemlock: *Hygrophorus tennesseensis* (p. 70)
3. Cap yellow and white; glutinous; under pine in the fall: *Hygrophorus flavodiscus* (p. 66)
4. Cap blackish brown to dark olivaceous brown; glutinous; under pine in the fall: *Hygrophorus fuligineus* (p. 67)
5. Cap white; in broadleaf woods, often under oaks: *Hygrophorus sordidus* (p. 69)
6. Cap white; in conifer woods; with yellowish granules on the cap or stem: *Hygrophorus chrysodon* (p. 65)

SCIENTIFIC NAME: *Hygrophorus chrysodon* (Batsch) Fr.

SYNONYM: None

COMMON NAME: Golden Speckled Wax Cap

FAMILY: Hygrophoraceae

CAP: Up to 3½ in. wide; white, at times with a dusting of yellow or yellowish-orange granules on part or all; convex becoming broadly convex to flat, often with a low umbo; surface viscid when wet, shiny when dry, bald where no granules are present; margin finely hairy and turned under at first

FLESH: White; thick; soft; waxy; odor and taste not distinctive

GILLS: White to cream, sometimes yellowish, or edged with yellow; subdecurrent; subdistant; waxy; broad; edges even and thin; no partial veil

STEM: Up to 3½ in. long; white; generally equal; stuffed; surface pruinose, usually with some yellow granules at the apex, lower portion glutinous

SPORE PRINT: White

ECOLOGY: Mycorrhizal; gregarious or scattered in mixed woods under conifers, often hemlock and white pine; can be found in disturbed areas such as roadsides, picnic areas in duff or grass; late summer and fall; fairly common

EDIBILITY: Edible; bland and generally considered mediocre

COMMENTS: The yellow granules can be missing but are usually present somewhere on the cap or stem. There are several white wax cap species, but the yellow granules set this one apart.

Hygrophorus chrysodon

SCIENTIFIC NAME: *Hygrophorus flavodiscus* Frost

SYNONYM: None

COMMON NAME: Yellow Centered Wax Cap

FAMILY: Hygrophoraceae

CAP: Up to 3½ in. wide; white with a yellow center, yellowish all over when young; convex to broadly convex and finally flat; surface bald, glutinous

FLESH: White; thick; firm; odor and taste not distinctive

GILLS: White or slightly pinkish when young; attached to the stem; subdistant; rather thick but tapering to a narrow edge; edges even; covered at first by a hyaline, glutinous partial veil

STEM: Up to 3 in. long; white or with yellowish areas; equal or occasionally tapering downward; solid; surface sheathed with a layer of gluten from the base to near the top of the stem, where it forms a ring-like zone; surface fibrillose under the gluten

SPORE PRINT: White

ECOLOGY: Mycorrhizal; single, scattered, or gregarious in humus or moss in conifer woods, usually associated with white pine; fall; common

EDIBILITY: Edible

COMMENTS: This late-season mushroom can be found under white pine in October and November. It often occurs near *Hygrophorus fuligineus* (p. 67), but it often fruits a bit later. Peeling or removing the slime with a dry cloth before cooking is recommended.

Hygrophorus flavodiscus

SCIENTIFIC NAME: *Hygrophorus fuligineus* Frost

SYNONYM: None

COMMON NAME: Sooty Wax Cap

FAMILY: Hygrophoraceae

CAP: Up to 3½ in. wide; blackish brown at first, becoming dark olivaceous brown or grayish, especially near the margin; orbicular, becoming convex and then flat; surface bald, covered with a layer of hyaline gluten

FLESH: White, tinted gray near the cap cuticle; thick; odor and taste not distinctive

GILLS: White or tinged pinkish; attached to subdecurrent; subdistant; edges even; covered at first with a cortina-like slime veil

STEM: Up to 3½ in. long; white to pale brownish; equal or tapering slightly downward; solid; covered with a slime veil except at the apex, the veil terminates in a ring-like zone; above this zone the surface is silky to floccose

SPORE PRINT: White

ECOLOGY: Mycorrhizal; scattered to gregarious in duff or moss in conifer and mixed woods, usually associated with white pine; fall; common

EDIBILITY: Edible

COMMENTS: This is a late-season wax cap that can often be found near *Hygrophorus flavodiscus* (p. 66). Before cooking, peeling or removing most of the slime with a dry cloth is recommended.

Hygrophorus fuligineus

SCIENTIFIC NAME: *Hygrophorus purpurascens* (Alb. and Schwein.) Fr.

SYNONYM: None

COMMON NAME: Veiled Purple Wax Cap

FAMILY: Hygrophoraceae

CAP: Up to 4½ in wide; pinkish red to purplish red, streaked with darker red areas; convex to broadly convex, finally flat; surface viscid when wet; bald, appressed fibrillose, at times finely scaly in age; margin turned under at first, at times upturned in age

FLESH: White; firm; not staining when cut or bruised; odor not distinctive; taste slightly bitter or not distinctive

GILLS: Pink, reddish or white; attached to subdecurrent; subdistant; narrow; sometimes forked; edges even; covered at first with a semi-membranous or cortinate partial veil

STEM: Up to 3½ in. long; white, streaked with reddish purple; generally equal, or tapering in either direction; solid, surface dry, fibrous, remnants of the partial veil are often present as a ring zone on the upper stem

SPORE PRINT: White

ECOLOGY: Mycorrhizal with conifers; mostly at higher elevations; scattered to gregarious in moss or litter in conifer and mixed woods, often with spruce; late summer and fall; uncommon

EDIBILITY: Edible but rather bitter

COMMENTS: This is a northern species that has remnant populations in the higher altitudes of the Appalachians. Compare with *Hygrophorus russula* (not illustrated), which has similar colors, lacks a partial veil, and occurs in broadleaf woodlands, often with oak.

Hygrophorus purpurascens

SCIENTIFIC NAME: *Hygrophorus sordidus* Peck

SYNONYM: Nonc

COMMON NAMES: Snow White Wax Cap, Sordid Wax Cap

FAMILY: Hygrophoraceae

CAP: Up to 7 in. wide; white or with a yellowish center in age; convex to nearly flat; surface viscid, mostly bald with small hairs in age; margin incurved at first

FLESH: White, unchanging when exposed; thick; waxy; odor not distinctive; taste mild or slightly bitter

GILLS: White, becoming yellowish in age; waxy; adnate to subdecurrent; subdistant; broad; close to subdistant; edges even; intervenose; no partial veil

STEM: Up to 4 in. long; white, slightly brownish from handling; equal or tapering downward, at times with a chiseled base; solid; surface dry, glabrous, or faintly hairy near the apex

SPORE PRINT: White

ECOLOGY: Mycorrhizal with oaks and possibly other broadleaf trees; solitary to usually gregarious in humus or soil; late summer and fall; occasional

EDIBILITY: Edible

COMMENTS: The waxy texture and attached gills will help distinguish this species from other all-white mushrooms. Compare with *Russula brevipes* (p. 34) and *Tricholoma subresplendens* (p. 91).

Hygrophorus sordidus
Photo by Alan Bessette

SCIENTIFIC NAME: *Hygrophorus tennesseensis* A. H. Sm. and Hesler

SYNONYM: None

COMMON NAME: Tennessee Wax Cap

FAMILY: Hygrophoraceae

CAP: Up to 4 in. wide; reddish tan all over at first, then whitish at the margin and remaining tawny to brown at the center; convex with an incurved margin at first, becoming flat, at times with a broad central depression; surface bald, viscid to glutinous when wet; cuticle tastes sour

FLESH: White; thick; firm; odor of raw potatoes; taste bitter

GILLS: White; attached to subdecurrent; subdistant; edges even; no partial veil

STEM: Up to 4 in. long; white; equal or tapering downward; solid; surface dry, usually scurfy at the top, appressed fibrillose below

SPORE PRINT: White

ECOLOGY: Mycorrhizal; gregarious to clustered in coniferous litter; especially under hemlock; late summer and fall; occasional

EDIBILITY: Not edible

COMMENTS: The sour-tasting cuticle (observed by licking), bitter-tasting flesh, and potato odor will distinguish this species from other similar-looking species of *Hygrophorus* and *Tricholoma*.

Hygrophorus tennesseensis

SMALL WHITE-SPORED MUSHROOMS WITH A WAXY TEXTURE

Hygrocybe, Gliophorus, and *Humidicutis*

*H*YGROCYBE IS A GENUS of small, usually terrestrial, waxy, often brightly colored mushrooms. The waxy texture can be determined by the paraffin-like feel of the flesh when crushed. Most have a dry or viscid cap that is not glutinous. *Gliophorus* species are small and have a glutinous cap.

Other waxy-textured genera have been split from *Hygrocybe.* These include *Humidicutis* (p. 84), *Cuphophyllus* (not illustrated), and *Gloioxanthomyces* (p. 72).

If a mushroom does not key out here, try the keys to small, white-spored mushrooms with specialized or various habitats.

Hygrocybe chlorophana

Gloioxanthomyces nitidus

Key to *Hygrocybe, Gliophorus,* and *Humidicutis*

1. Cap glutinous; brownish black to grayish brown: *Gliophorus irrigatus* (p. 83)

2. Cap glutinous; orange, yellow, pinkish, whitish, or violaceous; odor of crushed flesh unpleasant: *Gliophorus laetus* (p. 82)

3. Cap glutinous; reddish orange; yellow, reddish brown, tinged greenish at times; odor mild: *Gliophorus perplexus* (p. 81)

4. Cap glutinous; bright red; very small: *Hygrocybe minutula* (p. 77)

5. Cap dry; grayish brown to buff; odor nitrous: *Hygrocybe nitrata* (p. 79)

6. Cap dry; grayish brown to black; odor sweet: *Neohygrocybe subovina* (p. 80)

7. Cap moist; not viscid; dark orangish red to yellowish orange; gills purplish: *Hygrocybe purpureofolia* (p. 75)

8. Cap moist, not viscid; red to purplish red; gills red with yellow edges; stem red: *Hygrocybe appalachianensis* (p. 76)

9. Cap dry or moist; not viscid; scarlet to orange; gills yellowish; decurrent: *Hygrocybe cantharellus* (p. 73)

10. Cap dry or moist; not viscid; scarlet to orange; gills yellowish; not decurrent: *Hygrocybe miniata* (p. 74)

11. Cap moist; viscid when wet; orange to yellowish orange; gills white or pale yellow: *Hygrocybe flavescens* (p. 78)

12. Cap moist; orange to bright orangish yellow; gills colored like the cap: *Humidicutis marginata* var. *concolor* (p. 84)

SCIENTIFIC NAME: *Hygrocybe cantharellus* (Schwein.) Murrill

SYNONYM: *Hygrophorus cantharellus* (Schwein.) Fr.

COMMON NAME: Chanterelle Wax Cap

FAMILY: Hygrophoraceae

CAP: Up to 1¼ in. wide; convex becoming flattened, often with a central depression; scarlet to reddish orange or yellowish orange, fading in age, margin often yellowish; surface dry, tomentose to finely scaly; margin often scalloped or undulating at maturity

FLESH: Yellowish or colored like the cap; thin; odor not distinctive, or at times of raw potatoes; taste not distinctive

GILLS: Creamy yellow to orange yellow, edges sometimes paler than the faces; subdistant to distant; subdecurrent to decurrent; waxy; thick but with a sharp edge; no partial veil

STEM: Up to 3¼ in. long, typically much longer than the cap width; scarlet to reddish orange or yellowish orange, base yellow or white; equal or tapering downward; cylindrical or compressed; fragile; stuffed or hollow; surface dry or slightly tacky, smooth, bald, dull to satiny

SPORE PRINT: White

ECOLOGY: Probably symbiotic with mosses and possibly other plants; scattered to gregarious in moss, soil, well-decayed wood, and humus in broadleaf and mixed woods, bogs, and lawns; summer and early fall; common

EDIBILITY: Edible but of little value owing to its small size and thin flesh

COMMENTS: Compare with *Hygrocybe miniata* (p. 74), which is a common species that has a shorter stem and whose gills do not run down the stem. *Hygrocybe turunda* (not illustrated) is a similar bog species that has dark, erect hairs on the center of the cap. It is possible that *Hygrocybe cantharellus* represents a complex of very similar species.

Hygrocybe cantharellus

SCIENTIFIC NAME: *Hygrocybe miniata* (P. Kumm.) Fr.

SYNONYM: *Hygrophorus miniatus* (Fr.) Fr.

COMMON NAME: Vermillion Wax Cap

FAMILY: **Hygrophoraceae**

CAP: Up to 1¼ in. wide; scarlet to reddish orange, fading to orange; convex to broadly convex, becoming flat, often with a central depression; surface dry or moist, not viscid, at times becoming fibrillose or slightly scurfy

FLESH: Pale yellow, orange, reddish; thin; odor and taste not distinctive

GILLS: Variable in color, usually yellow but may be reddish or whitish; broadly attached to the stem; subdistant to distant; thick; waxy; edges even; no partial veil

STEM: Up to 3 in. long; red, orange, or yellow; equal or tapering toward the yellowish base; may be compressed; surface moist, not viscid

SPORE PRINT: White

ECOLOGY: Considered to be saprobic but recent studies indicate a possible association with mosses and other plants; gregarious to scattered on the ground, well-decayed wood, and in moss; summer and fall; common

EDIBILITY: Reported as edible; the author has not tried it

COMMENTS: This is one of the most common reddish wax caps. There are many others. None are considered choice edibles. Compare with *Hygrocybe cantharellus* (p. 73), whose gills extend down the stem.

Hygrocybe miniata

SCIENTIFIC NAME: *Hygrocybe purpureofolia* (H. E. Bigelow) **Courtec.**

SYNONYM: *Hygrophorus purpureofolius* H. E. Bigelow

COMMON NAME: Lavender Gilled Wax Cap

FAMILY: Hygrophoraceae

CAP: Up to 2 in. wide; dark orangish red, fading to bright yellowish orange, paler at the margin; conic, becoming convex to nearly flat, with a low, broad umbo; surface bald or with small scales, moist but not tacky or slimy

FLESH: White; thin; waxy; odor and taste not distinctive

GILLS: Lavender to purplish or yellowish orange in age; attached to subdecurrent; subdistant; waxy; edges even; no partial veil

STEM: Up to 3 in. long; yellow to orangish red, base with whitish or violet tints; equal or enlarged downward; hollow; often compressed; surface bald, moist, but not viscid

SPORE PRINT: White

ECOLOGY: Considered to be saprobic, but recent studies indicate a possible association with mosses and other plants; gregarious to scattered on the ground, on well-decayed wood, and in moss in broadleaf and mixed woods; summer and fall; uncommon

EDIBILITY: Unknown

COMMENTS: The combination of a reddish-orange cap and purplish gills make this a distinctive and striking species.

Hygrocybe purpureofolia
Photo by William Roody

SCIENTIFIC NAME: *Hygrocybe appalachianensis* (Hesler and A. H. Sm.) Kronaw

SYNONYM: *Hygrophorus appalachianensis* Hesler and A. H. Sm.

COMMON NAME: Appalachian Wax Cap

FAMILY: Hygrophoraceae

CAP: Up to 2½ in. wide; bright red to deep purplish red, fading to orangish yellow, often with a pale margin; convex to flat, with a depressed center; margin turned under at first, with a yellow edging; surface moist, not viscid, not striate, fibrillose to minutely scaly

FLESH: Yellow tinged orange; odor and taste not distinctive

GILLS: Colored like the cap with yellowish edges; attached to subdecurrent; subdistant to distant; fairly broad; edges even or slightly saw toothed; no partial veil

STEM: Up to 3 in. long; mostly colored like the cap, base yellowish; equal; hollow; compressed at times; surface bald, not viscid

SPORE PRINT: White

ECOLOGY: Considered to be saprobic, but recent studies indicate a possible association with mosses and other plants; gregarious to scattered on the ground, in litter, and in moss; summer and fall; locally common

EDIBILITY: Unknown

COMMENTS: This striking species is aptly named because it is more common in the Appalachian mountain region than any other area. The red stem, at times purplish-red cap, and the yellow gill edges set it apart.

Hygrocybe appalachianensis

SCIENTIFIC NAME: *Hygrocybe minutula* (Peck) Murrill

SYNONYM: *Gliophorus minutulus* (Peck) Kovalenko

COMMON NAME: None

FAMILY: Hygrophoraceae

CAP: Up to ¾ in. wide; scarlet to reddish orange, fading to yellow or orangish yellow in age, not staining black; convex to broadly convex, becoming nearly flat in age; surface glutinous to viscid, bald, obscurely translucent striate at times

FLESH: Colored like the cap or paler; not staining when exposed; thin, fragile; odor and taste not distinctive

GILLS: Yellowish orange or pale orange; attached to the stem or pulling away, with a decurrent tooth; close to subdistant; edges even; no partial veil

STEM: Up to 2 in. long; reddish or yellowish, often paler near the base; equal or tapered downward; fragile; at times constricted and hollow in age; surface bald, viscid, or glutinous

SPORE PRINT: White

ECOLOGY: Probably symbiotic with mosses and possibly other plants; scattered to gregarious in moss, humus, or soil, often in grassy areas under broadleaf trees; late spring, summer, and early fall; uncommon

EDIBILITY: Not edible

COMMENTS: Collecting this fragile mushroom intact requires care. It is very slippery! *Hygrocybe miniata* (p. 74) is larger and has a dry to moist cap.

Hygrocybe minutula

SCIENTIFIC NAME: *Hygrocybe flavescens* (Kauffman) **Singer**

SYNONYM: *Hygrophorus flavescens* (Kauffman) A. H. Sm. and Hesler

COMMON NAME: Golden Wax Cap

FAMILY: Hygrophoraceae

CAP: Up to 2½ in wide; orange, yellowish orange, or orange with a yellow margin; convex to broadly convex, becoming flat; viscid when wet; shiny when dry; bald; obscurely translucent striate; margin turned under at first

FLESH: Yellowish; thin; waxy; odor and taste not distinctive

GILLS: Yellow, white, or pale yellow; notched or occasionally broadly attached to the stem; broad; close to subdistant; waxy; edges even; no partial veil

STEM: Up to 2½ in. long; pale yellow, yellow, orange, usually paler at the base; equal or slightly tapered at the base; often compressed; fragile, splitting easily; surface moist but not viscid

SPORE PRINT: White

ECOLOGY: Considered to be saprobic, but recent studies indicate a possible association with mosses and other plants; gregarious to scattered on the ground, well-decayed wood, and in moss in broadleaf and mixed woods; summer and fall; common

EDIBILITY: Not recommended; reported as edible by some authors, but there are also reports of digestive upsets; even if edible, its thin, waxy flesh does not make it appealing as an esculent

COMMENTS: This is one of the first *Hygrocybe* species to appear in late spring or early summer. *Hygrocybe chlorophana* (p. 71) has a brighter yellow cap and a viscid stem. The author has observed mixed collections fruiting together in gregarious groups.

Hygrocybe flavescens

SCIENTIFIC NAME: *Hygrocybe nitrata* (Pers.) Wünsche

SYNONYM: *Hygrophorus nitratus* (Pers.) Fr.

COMMON NAME: None

FAMILY: Hygrophoraceae

CAP: Up to 2¾ in. wide; grayish brown to buff; bell-shaped at first, becoming convex and finally flat; surface dry, bald at first and then breaking up into fine fibers and squamules

FLESH: Brownish gray; thin; not staining when cut or bruised; odor nitrous, medicinal; taste acidic

GILLS: White with grayish tints; notched; subdistant; broad; waxy; edges even; no partial veil

STEM: Up to 4 in. long; white or grayish; equal or enlarged at the base; surface bald; hollow

SPORE PRINT: White

ECOLOGY: Considered to be saprobic, but recent studies indicate a possible association with mosses and other plants; gregarious to scattered in broad-leaf and conifer woods on the ground, in litter, and in moss; summer and fall; occasional

EDIBILITY: Unknown

COMMENTS: The nitrous odor of this rather drab-colored species will set it apart from other similar mushrooms.

Hygrocybe nitrata

SCIENTIFIC NAME: *Neohygrocybe subovina* (Hesler and A. H. Sm.) Lodge and Padamsee

SYNONYM: *Hygrocybe subovina* (Hesler and A. H. Sm.) Lodge and S. A. Cantrell

COMMON NAME: None

FAMILY: Hygrophoraceae

CAP: Up to 2 in. wide; dark grayish brown when dry, nearly black when moist; convex to broadly convex, becoming flat; surface dry, fibrillose, slightly scaly at times, or smooth

FLESH: Colored about like the cap, at times paler, unchanging when damaged; thick over the center, thin at the margin; odor sweet, like brown sugar; taste not distinctive or slightly soapy

GILLS: Whitish to grayish brown, bruising reddish; just reaching the stem or notched; broad; distant to subdistant; edges usually even but at times distinctly saw-toothed; waxy; no partial veil

STEM: Up to 2½ long; colored about like the cap, at times paler or darker; tapering up or sometimes equal; cylindrical, sometimes compressed; hollow; surface bald, longitudinally striate

SPORE PRINT: White

ECOLOGY: Mycorrhizal; scattered to gregarious in broadleaf and mixed woods, often under oaks; summer and fall

EDIBILITY: Unknown

COMMENTS: The photo shown here was of a collection that lacked the characteristic sweet odor and had saw-tooth gills, which is somewhat unusual. Otherwise it is typical. A very similar species is *Neohygrocybe ovina* (not illustrated), which has an ammonia-like odor.

Neohygrocybe subovina

SCIENTIFIC NAME: *Gliophorus perplexus* (A. H. Sm. and Hesler) Kovalenko

SYNONYM: *Hygrocybe psittacina* var. *perplexa* (A. H. Sm. and Hesler) Arnolds

COMMON NAME: None

FAMILY: Hygrophoraceae

CAP: Up to 1¼ in. wide; variable colors; egg-yolk yellow, reddish orange, reddish brown, at times with green or olivaceous areas; conic to convex, becoming flat in age, at times with a broad umbo; surface glutinous, bald, translucent striate

FLESH: Colored like the cap or paler; thin; odor and taste not distinctive

GILLS: Pale pinkish at first, becoming yellow to yellow orange in age; barely reaching the stem; subdistant; edges even; no partial veil

STEM: Up to 2½ in. long; yellow or yellowish buff or a paler version of the cap color; equal or tapering slightly upward; hollow; surface bald, slimy

SPORE PRINT: White

ECOLOGY: Thought to be saprobic, but its relationships with certain mosses and other plants has yet to be determined; scattered to gregarious in moss, on soil, and on lawns and in broadleaf forests and parks

EDIBILITY: Not poisonous, but too small and slimy to be considered as an edible species

COMMENTS: Once considered a variety of the Parrot Wax Cap, *Gliophorus psittacinus* (not illustrated), which is bright green at first but soon fades to colors similar to those of *Gliophorus perplexus*. All species in the genus *Gliophorus* are slimy and slippery to handle when wet.

Gliophorus perplexus

SCIENTIFIC NAME: *Gliophorus laetus* (Pers.) Herink

SYNONYM: *Hygrocybe laeta* (Pers.) P. Kumm

COMMON NAME: Chameleon Wax Cap

FAMILY: Hygrophoraceae

CAP: Up to 1½ in. wide; very variable in color, with mixtures of orange, yellow, and white, and at times shrimp pink or violaceous; convex to flat, with a central depression; surface bald, slimy when wet, tacky and shiny when dry, translucent striate

FLESH: Whitish, pale orange or pink; thin; odor variable, fishy, skunky, sweet, or not distinctive; taste not distinctive

GILLS: Pink, yellow, whitish, or violet gray; attached to subdecurrent; fairly broad; subdistant; waxy; no partial veil

STEM: Up to 2½ in. long; colored like the cap only paler; equal; surface viscid, bald

SPORE PRINT: White

ECOLOGY: Thought to be saprobic, but its relationships with certain mosses and other plants has yet to be determined; scattered to gregarious in moss, on soil, in broadleaf forests, lawns, and occasionally under conifers; summer and fall; common

EDIBILITY: Not poisonous, but its small size and slime coating will probably discourage its use

COMMENTS: The usually fishy or unpleasant odor of its flesh when crushed, combined with the slippery cap and stem, will distinguish this mushroom. The closest look-alike is *Gliophorus perplexus* (p. 81), which lacks a distinctive odor.

Hygrocybe laeta

SCIENTIFIC NAME: *Gliophorus irrigatus* (Pers.) A. M. Ainsw. and P. M. Kirk

SYNONYMS: *Hygrocybe irrigata* M. M. Moser, *Hygrocybe unguinosa* (Fr.) P. Karst

COMMON NAME: None

FAMILY: Hygrophoraceae

CAP: Up to 1½ in. wide; dark brownish black becoming dark grayish brown in age; convex becoming flat, with an umbo at times; surface glutinous, bald, translucent striate

FLESH: Grayish to white, watery; thin; odor not distinctive, or slightly unpleasant; taste not distinctive

GILLS: Whitish to gray; attached to the stem; thick; waxy; subdistant to distant; edges even; no partial veil

STEM: Up to 2½ in. long; gray to grayish brown; equal; becoming hollow; surface slimy, bald

SPORE PRINT: White

ECOLOGY: Thought to be saprobic, but its relationships with certain mosses and other plants has yet to be determined; scattered to gregarious in broadleaf forests, lawns, and occasionally under conifers; summer and fall; occasional

EDIBILITY: Nonpoisonous, but its small size and slime coating will probably discourage its use

COMMENTS: This dark-colored, slippery mushroom is difficult to collect because it readily slips through the fingers. It is easily overlooked owing to its dark coloration.

Gliophorus irrigatus

SCIENTIFIC NAME: *Humidicutis marginata* var. *concolor* (A. H. Sm.) Malloch

SYNONYMS: *Humidicutis marginata* (Peck) Singer, *Hygrocybe marginata* var. *concolor* (A. H. Sm.) Bessette, A. R. Bessette, Roody, and W. E. Sturgeon

COMMON NAME: None

FAMILY: Hygrophoraceae

CAP: Up to 1½ in. wide; orange yellow to bright golden yellow, at times streaked pale yellow; conic becoming bell-shaped to nearly flat, at times with a broad umbo; surface bald, moist, not striate

FLESH: Yellow; thin; waxy; odor and taste not distinctive

GILLS: Orange yellow to bright golden yellow; attached to the stem or notched; subdistant; broad; waxy; edges even; no partial veil

STEM: Up to 2½ in. long; yellow to pale yellow, sometimes white at the base; equal; hollow; surface bald, moist

SPORE PRINT: White

ECOLOGY: Saprobic; scattered to gregarious in wet woods under conifers and broadleaf trees; summer and fall; common

EDIBILITY: Edible but without much flavor or substance

COMMENTS: Two other varieties are recognized. *Humidicutis marginata* var. *olivacea* has a brownish-olive cap center and is often sharply umbonate. *Humidicutis marginata* var. *marginata* has brilliant-orange gills that remain orange after the cap has faded.

Humidicutis marginata var. *concolor*

SCIENTIFIC NAME: *Chromosera cyanophylla* (Fr.) Redhead, Ammirati, and Norvell

SYNONYM: *Mycena lilacifolia* (Peck) A. H. Sm.

COMMON NAME: None

FAMILY: Hygrophoraceae

CAP: Up to 1 in. wide; color variable, violaceous, or bright yellow when young, fading to pale yellow or whitish; convex to nearly flat, with a central umbilicus; surface viscid, translucent striate

FLESH: Pale, unchanging when exposed; thin; odor mild; taste unknown

GILLS: Lavender fading to pinkish lavender, at times yellow; subdistant; broad; edges even; subdecurrent; no partial veil

STEM: Up to 1 in. long; lavender at first but soon yellowish, fading to pale yellow; equal or with a small basal bulb; hollow; fragile; surface viscid, shiny; base with lavender mycelium

SPORE PRINT: White

ECOLOGY: Saprobic on decorticated conifer logs, often in moss; scattered to gregarious; fruits in cool weather, spring, and fall; occasional

EDIBILITY: Unknown

COMMENTS: When in prime condition, this is an eye-catching little mushroom. The gills keep their lavender color, contrasting nicely with the yellowish caps. It is found throughout Appalachia but is not common and is often overlooked owing to its small size.

Chromosera cyanophylla

Chromosera cyanophylla

85

MEDIUM TO LARGE WHITE-SPORED TERRESTRIAL MUSHROOMS

Tricholoma and Melanoleuca

*T*RICHOLOMA IS A white-spored genus of generally medium to large mushrooms. Many species have a mealy odor. The gill attachment to the stem is typically notched. Many *Tricholoma* species fruit late in the season, often under conifers and after the first frosts. Identification of some of the gray and brown species is very difficult. The species included here can be identified relatively easily. One species of *Melanoleuca* is included here. *Melanoleuca* is a difficult genus to identify in the field. Many species are relatively uncommon. They typically have flat, umbonate caps with uplifted margins in age, and relatively long stems. Only one species is included here.

Melanoleuca alboflavida

Tricholoma intermedium

Tricholoma portentosum

Tricholoma virgatum

Key to *Tricholoma* and *Melanoleuca*

1. With a ring on the stem; cap white with brown fibers: *Tricholoma caligatum* (p. 89)

2. Ring absent; odor mealy; cap with yellowish-brown or reddish-brown scales or fibers: *Tricholoma vaccinum* (p. 94)

3. Ring absent; odor mealy; cap umbonate; cap yellowish to greenish yellow: *Tricholoma davisiae* (p. 95)

4. Ring absent; odor mealy or not distinctive; cap white, may have blue or yellowish stains: *Tricholoma subresplendens* (p. 91)

5. Ring absent; odor fragrant; cap not umbonate, with olive tints: *Tricholoma saponaceum* (p. 93)

6. Ring absent; odor unpleasant, like coal tar; gills white to cream; under conifers: *Tricholoma inamoenum* (p. 90)

7. Ring absent; odor unpleasant, like coal tar; gills yellow to yellowish buff; under broadleaf trees: *Tricholoma odorum* (p. 92)

8. Ring absent; odor fragrant; stem with black scabers: *Melanoleuca verrucipes* (p. 98)

SCIENTIFIC NAME: *Tricholoma caligatum* (Viv.) Ricken

SYNONYM: *Armillaria caligata* (Viv.) Gillet

COMMON NAME: None

FAMILY: Tricholomataceae

CAP: Up to 6 in. wide; white ground color, covered all over or at the center with brown, appressed fibers or scales; nearly round at first, becoming broadly convex to nearly flat; surface dry or tacky when wet; margin turned under and cottony at first, becoming expanded to uplifted, with veil remnants at times

FLESH: White to cream, unchanging when exposed; thick; odor mild; taste very bitter

GILLS: White, with brown stains in age, at times with bluish hues; attached, becoming notched; close to crowded; broad; edges even; at first covered by a thick membranous partial veil

STEM: Up to 4 in. long; white above the ring, brown scaled below, much like the cap; equal or tapering down; surface dry, covered from the base upward with a brown, scaled sheath that ends in a flaring ring, which is white above and brownish below

SPORE PRINT: White

ECOLOGY: Mycorrhizal with oaks and hemlock; scattered to gregarious in humus in broadleaf and mixed woods; late summer, fall, and early winter; locally common

EDIBILITY: Not edible owing to very bitter taste

COMMENTS: This is the common variety in the Appalachians. There are other varieties that have a fragrant odor and mild taste. These are generally considered edible. Future study may reveal new species in this group.

Tricholoma caligatum

89

SCIENTIFIC NAME: *Tricholoma inamoenum* (Fr.) Gillet

SYNONYM: None

COMMON NAME: None

FAMILY: Tricholomataceae

CAP: Up to 2 in. wide; whitish to pale buff; convex to broadly convex, becoming flat, at times with a low, broad umbo; surface smooth and bald

FLESH: White; thick; odor of burning rubber or coal tar; taste unpleasant

GILLS: White to cream; narrowly attached to the stem; subdistant; broad; with numerous short gills; often veined; edges even; no partial veil

STEM: Up to 2½ in. long; white to cream, at times brownish near the base; equal or enlarged downward; solid; surface smooth, pruinose at the apex, dry

SPORE PRINT: White

ECOLOGY: Mycorrhizal; gregarious or scattered in humus or moss under conifers; late summer and fall; occasional

EDIBILITY: Poisonous

COMMENTS: The unpleasant odor is similar to that of swamp gas or dandruff shampoos that contain coal tar.

Tricholoma inamoenum

SCIENTIFIC NAME: *Tricholoma subresplendens* (Murrill) Murrill

SYNONYM: *Melanoleuca subresplendens* Murrill

COMMON NAME: None

FAMILY: Tricholomataceae

CAP: Up to 4¼ in. wide; silky white to cream, at times with yellowish-tan to brownish discolorations, or with bluish tints; convex becoming nearly flat, often with a broad, central umbo; surface viscid when wet, typically with leaves or dirt adhering when dry

FLESH: White, unchanging when exposed; thick at the cap center; odor and taste mealy or not distinctive

GILLS: White to whitish; notched to nearly free in age; close to subdistant; broad; edges uneven, at times becoming scalloped in age; no partial veil

STEM: Up to 4 in. long; whitish, often with yellow or brownish-yellow stains, at times bruising blue or with bluish stains; equal or tapering in either direction; surface dry with silky appressed fibers

SPORE PRINT: White

ECOLOGY: Mycorrhizal; solitary, scattered to gregarious in broadleaf and mixed woods, often with oak and hemlock; late summer and fall; common

EDIBILITY: Unknown

COMMENTS: Compare with *Hygrophorus sordidus* (p. 69), which has a waxy texture, and *Russula brevipes* (p. 34), which is a squat, brittle-capped species found in conifer woods. The absence of a volva and partial veil will separate this species from the deadly *Amanita bisporigera* (p. 9).

Tricholoma subresplendens
Photo by William Roody

SCIENTIFIC NAME: *Tricholoma odorum* Peck

SYNONYM: *Melanoleuca odora* (Peck) Murrill

COMMON NAME: None

FAMILY: Tricholomataceae

CAP: Up to 3½ in. wide; buff to yellowish, center often darker; convex becoming flat; surface dry, smooth, or slightly velvety, occasionally cracking at maturity

FLESH: Pale yellowish to white, unchanging when damaged; fairly thick; odor unpleasant, like coal tar; taste mealy or unpleasant

GILLS: Pale yellow to yellowish buff; narrowly attached to the stem or notched; close; broad; edges even; no partial veil

STEM: Up to 4 in. long; yellowish, whitish or greenish yellow; tapering upward; surface dry, smooth, at times twisted

SPORE PRINT: White

ECOLOGY: Mycorrhizal; scattered to gregarious in humus in oak hickory and beech maple forests; summer and fall; fairly common

EDIBILITY: Not edible

COMMENTS: Compare with *Tricholoma inamoenum* (p. 90), which has a similar odor. It is less common and has paler colors and a conifer habitat. Some mycologists place this species in the genus *Melanoleuca*.

Tricholoma odorum

SCIENTIFIC NAME: *Tricholoma saponaceum* (Fr.) P. Kumm.

SYNONYM: None

COMMON NAME: Soapy Trich

FAMILY: Tricholomataceae

CAP: Up to 4 in. wide; grayish olive, yellowish olive, and olive gray, at times tinged reddish buff; convex to broadly convex, becoming flat in age; surface bald or with appressed fibers, tacky to viscid, at times cracking into scales

FLESH: White, staining pinkish at times, especially in the stem base; thick; odor soapy, pungent, or of corn silk; taste variously reported as not distinctive, sweet, unpleasant, or slightly soapy

GILLS: White to yellowish, sometimes tinted green, at times discoloring orange or pinkish brown; attached or notched; close to subdistant; edges even or slightly eroded; no partial veil

STEM: Up to 3½ in. long; white to pale greenish, at times with pinkish or orange at the base; equal or tapering upward; solid; surface dry, bald, smooth

SPORE PRINT: White

ECOLOGY: Mycorrhizal with conifers and broadleaf trees; solitary, gregarious, or clustered in humus or moss; late summer and fall; common

EDIBILITY: Not edible

COMMENTS: This is a very variable mushroom. It is likely a complex that someday will turn out to be multiple species.

Tricholoma saponaceum

SCIENTIFIC NAME: *Tricholoma vaccinum* (Schaeff.) P. Kumm.

SYNONYM: None

COMMON NAME: Russet Scaly Trich

FAMILY: Tricholomataceae

CAP: Up to 2½ in. wide; background whitish with reddish-brown or yellowish-brown and flattened scales or fibers; conic to convex, becoming broadly convex to nearly flat; surface dry, fibrillose; margin turned under at first and in age, with shaggy veil remnants

FLESH: White to pinkish buff, slowly staining brownish; odor mealy; taste mealy, mild, or bitter

GILLS: Whitish buff when young, staining reddish brown where damaged; attached or notched; close; edges even; covered at first by a whitish cortina

STEM: Up to 3 in. long; whitish, especially at the apex, with orange-brown scales below; equal or slightly enlarged downward; hollow in age; surface fibrillose and dry

SPORE PRINT: White

ECOLOGY: Mycorrhizal; gregarious to scattered in humus and moss in conifer and mixed woods; summer and fall; occasional

EDIBILITY: Not recommended; reported as edible but of poor quality

COMMENTS: Compare with *Tricholoma imbricatum* (not illustrated), which lacks a cortina and has a browner, less scaly cap.

Tricholoma vaccinum

SCIENTIFIC NAME: *Tricholoma davisiae* Peck

SYNONYM: *Melanoleuca davisiae* (Peck) Murrill

COMMON NAME: None

FAMILY: Tricholomataceae

CAP: Up to 6 in. wide; variable in color, usually with a darkish-green to blackish center, yellow, yellowish green, mustard yellow, grayish, nearly iridescent with pinkish or salmon tints; conic to bell-shaped, becoming broadly convex to flat with a prominent umbo; surface dry, with dark, appressed fibrils, with tiny scales near the edge; margin incurved at first, becoming uneven, often uplifted, may be split in age

FLESH: White to buff, at times greenish at first; odor mealy; taste mealy at first, then disagreeable

GILLS: Yellowish to greenish buff, becoming whitish to buff at maturity, at times with orange stains; close to subdistant; notched or barely attached; edges even; no partial veil

STEM: Up to 7 in. long; whitish with greenish yellow on the upper stem; equal or enlarged downward; solid; surface dry and fibrillose

SPORE PRINT: White

ECOLOGY: Mycorrhizal with conifers; scattered to gregarious in humus, often under pines; late summer and fall; occasional

EDIBILITY: Unknown

COMMENTS: This species is more common in New England and Eastern Canada but has been found at various locations in Appalachia. The prominent umbo and colors are important features. Some mycologists place this mushroom in the genus *Melanoleuca*.

Tricholoma davisiae

SCIENTIFIC NAME: *Tricholomopsis rutilans* (Schaeff.) Singer

SYNONYM: None

COMMON NAMES: Red Head, Plums and Custard

FAMILY: Tricholomataceae

CAP: Up to 4 in. wide; yellow ground color covered by red to purplish-red scales and fibers; convex becoming flat; dry

FLESH: Pale yellow; moderately thick; odor not distinctive or slightly fragrant; taste slightly radish-like, bitter, or not distinctive

GILLS: Yellow to whitish; attached, becoming notched; rather narrow; crowded; edges roughened; no partial veil

STEM: Up to 4½ in. long; yellowish, covered with reddish-purple fibers and scales, the apex often without scales; stuffed, rooting at times; often hollow in age

SPORE PRINT: White

ECOLOGY: Saprobic on dead conifer wood; solitary or in small groups; summer and fall; common

EDIBILITY: Not edible

COMMENTS: Among gilled mushrooms of this size, the purplish-red colors over a yellow ground color, and habitat on conifer wood make this a rather easy mushroom to identify.

Tricholomopsis rutilans

SCIENTIFIC NAME: *Tricholomopsis decora* (Fr.) Singer

SYNONYM: None

COMMON NAME: Decorated Mop

FAMILY: Tricholomataceae

CAP: Up to 2¼ in. wide; ground color yellow, buff, whitish or brownish or-ange, with reddish-brown, grayish-brown, or blackish fibers or scales; con-vex becoming flat, at times with a central depression; surface moist when young, then dry in age.

FLESH: Buff to yellow; firm; odor and taste not distinctive

GILLS: Yellow; attached to the stem; close to crowded; narrow; edges even; no partial veil

STEM: Up to 2¼ in. long; yellow with brown, gray, or blackish fibrils; equal or enlarged downward; hollow in age; dry

SPORE PRINT: White

ECOLOGY: Saprobic; solitary to scattered on conifer logs and stumps, espe-cially hemlock; summer and fall; fairly common

EDIBILITY: Poisonous

COMMENTS: The variability of cap and scale colors is an indication that this might be a species complex. More study is needed.

Tricholomopsis decora

SCIENTIFIC NAME: *Melanoleuca verrucipes* (Fr.) Singer

SYNONYM: None

COMMON NAME: None

FAMILY: Tricholomataceae

CAP: Up to 4 in. wide; white to cream; convex to flat, becoming depressed in the center, often umbonate; surface dry, bald, or breaking up into small scales

FLESH: Whitish or buff; unchanging when exposed; rather thick; odor fragrant, similar to anise, reported at times to have an unpleasant component; taste not distinctive, or slightly acrid

GILLS: White; at times pinkish, drying brownish; attached to the stem or pulling away; close to crowded; broad; edges even; no partial veil

STEM: Up to 5 in. long; whitish or tinged pale reddish; equal down to a slightly enlarged base; stuffed; surface dry, covered with black fibers or scabers

SPORE PRINT: White to cream

ECOLOGY: Saprobic; solitary or gregarious in poor soil on lawns or gardens, its favored habitat is wood mulch; spring through fall; uncommon

EDIBILITY: Unknown

COMMENTS: This may be the only *Melanoleuca* species that can be identified with certainty in the field. The blackish fibers on the stem set it apart. The author has seen it from five locations. Its preference for wood chips may mean that it will become more common in the future since it may be an imported species.

Melanoleuca verrucipes

SCIENTIFIC NAME: *Megacollybia rodmanii* R. H. Petersen, K. W. Hughes & Lickey

MISAPPLIED NAME: *Megacollybia platyphylla* (Pers.) Kotl. & Pouzar

COMMON NAMES: Broad Gill, Platterfull Mushroom

FAMILY: Tricholomataceae

CAP: Up to 6 in. wide; gray, brownish gray, paler at times, streaked with dark radial fibers; convex to broadly convex, becoming flat; dry to moist

FLESH: Watery whitish, unchanging when cut; thin; moderately thick at the center; pliant; odor not distinctive; taste mild to slightly bitter

GILLS: White to grayish; barely attached or notched; very broad; subdistant; edges even, becoming uneven to ragged in age; no partial veil

STEM: Up to 6 in. long; white; equal or enlarging downward; tough; surface dry, bald, or with flattened hairs, dry; base usually with white rhizomorphs

SPORE PRINT: White

ECOLOGY: Saprobic on the dead wood of broadleaf trees, solitary to gregarious; spring through fall, most common in late spring

EDIBILITY: Edible with caution; the taste has been compared to that of oyster mushrooms; some have experienced digestive problems especially when it was consumed with alcohol

COMMENTS: This is very common species in late spring in broadleaf forests. The white spores and broad gills will distinguish it from members of the *Pluteus cervinus* complex, which are common in the same habitats. The Broad Gill has been called *Megacollybia platyphylla* but it is now known that this name belongs to a European species.

Megacollybia rodmanii

OTHER WHITE-SPORED MUSHROOMS

T HERE ARE MANY unrelated genera with whitish spores here, and they range in size from small to large. Small mushrooms are those with caps measuring less than 2½ inches, medium mushrooms are those with caps measuring between 2½ and 5 inches, and large mushrooms have caps larger than 5 inches. The medium and large mushrooms are keyed out here in four artificial groups based primarily on habitat and secondarily on stem disposition (central, off-center, lateral, or absent) and the presence or absence of a ring. Two additional keys are provided for small mushrooms, but please note that you will nevertheless find some small mushrooms included with the key to larger species without rings. The most common genera of these small-capped mushrooms are *Mycena*, *Gymnopus*, and *Marasmius*, but there are many others. *Mycena* species are generally fragile, unlike *Marasmius*, *Marasmiellus*, and *Mycetinus* species, which are usually more pliant, with several species that shrivel in dry weather and revive under wet conditions. And although some species of *Gymnopus* and *Marasmius* can be medium sized, most are small.

CLOCKWISE, FROM UPPER LEFT:

Chlorophyllum rachodes

Ossicaulis lignatilis

Echinoderma asperum

Keys to Other White-Spored Mushrooms

White-spored mushrooms on wood, with off-center, lateral, or absent stem and no ring

1. Medium; cap white; thin fleshed; on conifer wood; stem usually off-center: *Pleurocybella porrigens* (p. 117)

2. Medium; cap gray; rubbery with conical spines; stem usually off-center: *Hohenbuehelia mastrucata* (p. 122)

3. Medium to large; cap gray, tan, buff to cream colored; thick flesh; stem usually off-center: *Pleurotus ostreatus* (p. 115)

4. Medium to large; cap white, thin fleshed, usually on broadleaf tree wood; stem usually off-center: *Pleurotus pulmonarius* (p. 116)

5. Medium; cap tan; shoehorn-shaped; often on buried wood; stem off-center: *Hohenbuehelia petaloides* (p. 121)

6. Small to medium; cap violet to brownish or tan; hairy; stem off-center: *Panus neostrigosus* (p. 169)

7. Small to medium; cap greenish, yellowish, or purplish; occurs in the late fall; stem off-center: *Sarcomyxa serotina* (p. 120)

8. Small; gills split along their edges; stem off-center or absent: *Schizophyllum commune* (p. 171)

9. Small; gills not split; gills bioluminescent; stem off-center: *Panellus stipticus* (p. 170)

White-spored mushrooms on wood, with a central stem and no ring

1. Medium; cap with red to purple fibers or scales: *Tricholomopsis rutilans* (p. 96)

2. Medium; cap with brown or blackish fibers or scales: *Tricholomopsis decora* (p. 97)

3. Medium to large; cap whitish with hyaline water spots: *Hypsizygus marmoreus* (p. 125)

4. Medium; cap white; prominently umbilicate; clustered: *Clitocybula abundans* (p. 145)

5. Medium; cap color yellowish white; covered with grayish to brownish fibrils: *Gerronema strombodes* (p. 128)

6. Medium; cap white to cream; stem with gray or black scaber-like fibers; often on wood chips, at times on soil: *Melanoleuca verrucipes* (p. 98)

7. Medium to large; cap gray to brownish gray; gills whitish; very broad: *Megacollybia rodmanii* (p. 99)

8. Medium; cap tawny to yellowish brown; usually densely clustered on broadleaf tree wood; appearing terrestrial at times: *Desarmillaria tabescens* (p. 114)

9. Medium; cap pinkish brown to pale buff; gills saw-toothed: *Lentinellus micheneri* (p. 119)

10. Cap orange; usually densely clustered; dry; on broadleaf tree wood: *Omphalotus illudens* (p. 126)

11. Cap orange, yellowish orange to brownish orange; viscid: *Flammulina velutipes* (p. 165)

12. Cap reddish brown to tan; clustered to gregarious; usually on wood mulch: *Gymnopus luxurians* (p. 151)

13. Cap dark brown to reddish brown; scattered on dead or living wood: *Gymnopus dichrous* (p. 149)

14. Cap brown to tan; occurs on small twigs and leaf litter: *Gymnopus subnudus* (p. 148)

15. Cap brown to grayish brown; furfuraceous stem rooting: *Hymenopellis furfuracea* (p. 160)

White-spored mushrooms on wood, with a central stem and with a ring

1. Cap whitish with a hoary coating at first; ring soon disappearing: *Pleurotus dryinus* (p. 123)

2. Cap whitish with orangish-brown to reddish-brown scales; often on buried wood: *Echinoderma asperum* (p. 124)

3. Cap white with reddish-brown scales; flesh quickly staining yellow to orange when exposed; often on wood chips: *Leucoagaricus americanus* (p. 106)

4. Cap and stem with yellowish-brown fibers; white above the ring: *Leucopholiota decorosa* (p. 110)

5. Cap honey yellow to brownish yellow; often in large clusters: *Armillaria mellea* (p. 112)

6. Cap brown; veil cobwebby, leaving a ring zone; often on buried wood: *Armillaria gallica* (p. 113)

7. Cap tan to brown, with a covering of dark-brown to black hairs: *Armillaria solidipes* (p. 111)

Medium to large white-spored mushrooms on humus or soil, with a ring*

1. Cap with brown scales on a hairy cap surface; flesh staining reddish brown; at times can occur on wood chips: *Chlorophyllum rachodes* (p. 109)

2. Cap with brown scales; flesh not staining when exposed: *Echinoderma asperum* (p. 124)

3. Cap tan to whitish; flesh not staining when exposed; stem longer than the cap width: *Macrolepiota procera* (p. 105)

4. Cap and stem white: *Leucoagaricus leucothites* (p. 107)

   *See also the *Amanita* key for species with a universal veil.

Small white-spored mushrooms on soil, humus, or moss

1. Cap white to yellowish; very fragile; stem with an upturned ring: *Leucocoprinus fragilissimus* (p. 168)
2. Cap white to yellowish; crushed flesh with an unpleasant odor: *Marasmius delectans* (p. 134)
3. Cap white, buff, or tan; crushed flesh with a garlic odor: *Mycetinus scorodnius* (p. 129)
4. Cap rusty brown with radial grooves: *Marasmius fulvoferrugineus* (p. 135)
5. Olive green to yellowish green; at times occurring on wood: *Mycena epipterygia* (p. 142)
6. Violaceous colors on all parts: *Laccaria amethystina* (p. 158)

Small white-spored mushrooms on wood

1. Cap white to gray; gill edges split; stem short and off-center; fan- to shell-shaped: *Schizophyllum commune* (p. 171)
2. Cap tan to buff; gill edges not split; stem short and off-center; semicircular to kidney-shaped: *Panellus stipticus* (p. 170)
3. Cap bright orange fading to yellowish: *Mycena leaiana* (p. 144)
4. Cap rusty-brownish orange; stem with reddish-brown to rusty hairs: *Xeromphalina tenuipes* (p. 164)
5. Cap center dark reddish brown, pinkish outward; margin scalloped: *Mycena haematopus* (p. 140)
6. Cap olive green to yellowish; on conifer wood and debris: *Mycena epipterygia* (p. 142)
7. Cap yellow or violaceous; gills lavender; on conifer wood: *Chromosera cyanophylla* (p. 85)
8. Cap buff, tan, or brownish; usually clustered; on broadleaf tree wood: *Mycena inclinata* (p. 139)
9. Cap brownish orange to reddish brown; clustered or gregarious; on broadleaf tree wood *Marasmius cohaerans* (p. 136)
10. Cap white to pale yellowish tan; surface pleated; on broadleaf tree wood: *Marasmius rotula* (p. 133)
11. Cap whitish; stem base chiseled; crushed flesh has a garlic odor; on broadleaf twigs (also occurs on acorn caps and sweetgum nuts): *Marasmiellus praecutus* (p. 131)
12. Cap whitish to buff; on conifer and rhododendron twigs; substrate with hair-like rhizomorphs: *Mycetinus opacus* (p. 130)
13. Cap, gills, and stem lavender when young: *Baeospora myriadophylla* (p. 157)
14. Cap blue, soon becoming grayish brown with a pale margin: *Mycena subcaerulea* (p. 141)

SCIENTIFIC NAME: *Macrolepiota procera* (Scop.) Singer

SYNONYM: *Lepiota procera* (Scop.) Gray

COMMON NAME: American Parasol Mushroom

FAMILY: Agaricaceae

CAP: Up to 7 in. wide; whitish or pale-tan cuticle, covered with reddish-brown scales that are flat to raised; ovoid, convex, becoming flat, with a low, brown umbo; surface dry; margin often ragged

FLESH: White; not staining when exposed; soft; odor and taste not distinctive

GILLS: White, at times with brown stains; free from the stem; close; broad; edges minutely hairy; covered at first, with a brownish partial veil

STEM: Up to 10 in. long; colored like the cap scales or paler; equal down to a basal bulb; stuffed or hollow; tough; surface dry, fibrous, at times with a snakeskin-like pattern; with a moveable ring near the top

SPORE PRINT: White

ECOLOGY: Saprobic; scattered in lawns, wood edges, and in broadleaf and conifer forests; summer and fall; fairly common

EDIBILITY: The cap is a choice edible, but do discard the stem; best when collected in dry conditions

COMMENTS: This is another example of a mushroom species complex. The true *Macrolepiota procera* is a species known from Europe. Our species differs, but in most guides it can be found under this name. Our Parasol Mushroom will someday have a new name.

Macrolepiota procera

SCIENTIFIC NAME: *Leucoagaricus americanus* (Peck) Vellinga
SYNONYM: *Lepiota americana* (Peck) Sacc.
COMMON NAME: American Lepiota
FAMILY: Agaricaceae

CAP: Up to 4¾ in. wide; at first dark reddish brown to slate gray, when the cap expands it is white with reddish-brown scales, finally becoming reddish brown; oval at first, becoming convex and finally flat with a slight central umbo; surface dry, buttons are bald, soon becoming scaly

FLESH: White, quickly staining yellow to orange and finally reddish, at times especially in age going straight to reddish; rather thin; odor and taste not distinctive

GILLS: White, staining yellowish orange, finally reddish; free from the stem; close; broad in front, narrowed behind; edges even; covered at first by a membranous partial veil that extends down the top of the stem

STEM: Up to 4¾ in. long; ruddy in the early stages, becoming whitish; tapering up from a swollen base or enlarged in the middle; stuffed becoming hollow; surface fibrillose at first, becoming nearly bald; with a collar-like ring

SPORE PRINT: White

ECOLOGY: Saprobic; clustered to gregarious on stumps and woody debris; most common in wood mulched landscaping or sawdust piles, infrequent to rare in woodlands; summer and fall

EDIBILITY: Edible and strongly flavored, it will turn reddish brown in the skillet; some people have experienced gastrointestinal problems, so as with any wild mushroom, try a small portion the first time

COMMENTS: This beautiful and edible urban mushroom will turn dark-reddish brown when cooked. When collected in landscaped areas, care should be taken to make sure the area has not been treated with insecticides or herbicides. *Chlorophyllum rachodes* (p. 109) has a similar aspect, but it has shaggy scales on the cap. The white spore print is an important feature. The greenish-spored lawn species *Chlorophyllum molybdites* (p. 108) is poisonous. Also compare with various species of Amanita, which have scales or warts that are easily separable from the cap.

Leucoagaricus americanus

SCIENTIFIC NAME: *Leucoagaricus leucothites* (Vittad.) Wasser

SYNONYMS: *Leucoagaricus naucinus* (Fr.) Singer, *Lepiota naucina* (Fr.) P. Kumm.

COMMON NAME: Smooth Lepiota

FAMILY: Agaricaceae

CAP: Up to 4½ in. wide; white or grayish white, the center sometimes shows pale-yellowish or tan coloration; oval, becoming convex to nearly flat; surface dry, bald, to fibrillose, or finely scaly

FLESH: White, not staining; soft; thick; odor and taste not distinctive

GILLS: White, becoming pinkish in age, color unchanging when damaged; free from the stem; close; broad; edges even; covered at first by a white, membranous partial veil

STEM: Up to 4¾ in. wide; white, staining pale yellow at times; club-shaped or nearly equal; bald to silky; stuffed, becoming hollow in age; with a white, apical, double-edged ring

SPORE PRINT: White

ECOLOGY: Saprobic; scattered to gregarious in lawns, roadsides, and other disturbed areas, often near spruce trees; abundant some years; summer and most common in the fall

EDIBILITY: Not recommended because some individuals have experienced digestive upsets; beginning collectors should compare with the deadly destroying angel, *Amanita bisporigera* (p. 9), which has a sack-like volva and a skirt-like ring

COMMENTS: On the author's property, Smooth Lepiota appeared one fall on the dirt floor of a shed, along with a population of chipmunk and probably other rodents. In the spring it was shriveled and dry, but it was still there. It is seldom observed having rodent teeth marks. The author does not have an explanation for this species apparently not appealing to rodents.

Leucoagaricus leucothites

SCIENTIFIC NAME: *Chlorophyllum molybdites* (G. Mey.) Massee

SYNONYM: *Lepiota molybdites* (G. Mey.) Sacc.

COMMON NAME: Green-Spored Parasol

FAMILY: Agaricaceae

CAP: Up to 11 in. wide; whitish to very pale tan with a buff-brown to pale-brown center that breaks up into scales as the cap flattens out; nearly round at first, becoming convex, and then nearly flat in age; surface under the scales dry, bald, or finely fibrillose

FLESH: White, unchanging when exposed or staining slightly reddish; thick; odor and taste not distinctive

GILLS: White becoming grayish green or olive green in age; free from the stem; close; broad; edges even; covered at first by a membranous partial veil

STEM: Up to 9 in. long; whitish at first, becoming brownish in age or from handling; equal or with a swollen base; surface dry, bald to finely fibrillose; with a moveable, collar-like, ragged ring on the upper stem, the ring is whitish usually with a reddish-brown underside

SPORE PRINT: Grayish green

ECOLOGY: Saprobic; usually gregarious or in arcs or circles in lawns, fields, and other grassy areas; summer and fall; locally common, especially in southern areas

EDIBILITY: Poisonous; this attractive mushroom has probably caused more mushroom poisonings in Appalachia and eastern North America than any other; severe vomiting, diarrhea, and resultant dehydration are life threatening

COMMENTS: This is a prominent mushroom and can be observed from some distance in a lawn. The caps resemble a scoop of vanilla ice cream with a dollop of caramel sauce. Once considered a southern species, it is now becoming common in some northern areas. Compare with edible species *Leucoagaricus americana* (p. 106), the *Macrolepiota procera* complex (p. 105), and *Chlorophyllum rachodes* (p. 109). The greenish spore print and grassland habitat are important identification features. It is closely related to white-spored species and is the only green-spored species included here.

Chlorophyllum molybdites
Photo by Arleen Bessette

SCIENTIFIC NAME: *Chlorophyllum rachodes* (Vittad.) Vellinga

SYNONYMS: *Macrolepiota rachodes* (Vittad.) Singer, *Lepiota rachodes* (Vittad.) Quél.

COMMON NAME: Shaggy Parasol

FAMILY: Agaricaceae

CAP: Up to 8 in. wide; with a brown cuticle that separates, forming rings of concentric, raised scales and revealing a white or buff hairy coating underneath; rounded to convex, becoming flat in age; surface dry; margin often decorated with partial-veil remnants

FLESH: White to tan, staining pinkish to reddish and then brownish, especially in the lower stem; thick; soft; odor pleasant and taste mild

GILLS: White to buff, staining brown when damaged, becoming brownish in age, especially the edges; close; free; broad; covered at first by a buff to brownish membranous partial veil

STEM: Up to 8 in. long; white above, brownish below, becoming brownish overall in age and when bruised; smooth, enlarged downward, often hollow near the top; may be bulbous, with a double-edged, moveable, white ring near the apex; ring may have a brownish underside

SPORE PRINT: White

ECOLOGY: Saprobic; scattered to gregarious in compost piles, wood mulched flower beds, and lawns; often in the vicinity of spruce trees; the reason for the frequent association with spruce trees is not known; late summer through fall; fairly common

EDIBILITY: Edible and strongly flavored; considered choice by many; compare with the poisonous, grassland species *Chlorophyllum molybdites* (p. 108), which has a greenish spore print and has caused many poisonings in Appalachia

COMMENTS: Resembles *Leucoagaricus americanus* (p. 106), an edible wood mulch species that has flatter scales and stains orange, then red, and finally brown. Another look-alike, *Chlorophyllum brunneum* (not illustrated), is an edible species of western North America and not known from Appalachia.

Chlorophyllus rachodes

SCIENTIFIC NAME: *Leucopholiota decorosa* (Peck) O. K. Mill., T. J. Volk, and Bessette

SYNONYM: *Armillaria decorosa* (Peck) A. H. Sm.

COMMON NAME: None

FAMILY: Tricholomataceae

CAP: Up to 3 in. wide; whitish cap, ground color with brownish scales; orb-shaped, becoming convex, and finally broadly convex to flat; surface dry, covered with rusty-brown to yellowish-brown tufts of fibers or scales; margin incurved at first and fuzzy through maturity

FLESH: White, unchanging when damaged; odor not distinctive; taste mild or slightly bitter

GILLS: White; notched at the stem; close; moderately broad; edges finely scalloped; covered at first by a fibrous-scaly partial veil

STEM: Up to 3 in. long; colored like the cap from the bottom up to the folded-over ring; tapering upward; surface silky white above the ring zone, lower stem surface dry, with scaly, rusty-brown fiber tufts up to and including the ring zone

SPORE PRINT: White

ECOLOGY: Saprobic on the logs and stumps of broadleaf trees, especially sugar maple; late summer and fall; not uncommon in northern broadleaf forests

EDIBILITY: Unknown; reported as edible; the author has not tried it

COMMENTS: The white spores will separate this attractive species from look-alikes in the genus *Pholiota*. Once considered rare to uncommon, the author is now seeing it in several locations most years.

Leucopholiota decorosa

SCIENTIFIC NAME: *Armillaria solidipes* Peck

SYNONYM: *Armillaria ostoyae* (Romagn.) Herink

COMMON NAMES: Podpinki, Stumpy

FAMILY: Physalacriaceae

CAP: Up to 5 in. wide; tan, yellowish brown, or reddish brown; convex to flat with a broad umbo at maturity; surface dry or slightly moist, with a covering of dark reddish-brown to black hairs

FLESH: Whitish, sometimes becoming pinkish brown in age; thick at the center; odor and taste not distinctive

GILLS: White to pinkish with brownish spots; close; adnate to subdecurrent; covered at first with a membranous partial veil that is white with brown patches near the cap margin

STEM: Up to 6 in. long; white with downy hairs above the ring, white to buff below the ring, with white or yellow fibrils, developing brownish stains in age; solid; equal or enlarged above or below; may have black rhizomorphs at the base; surface dry, apex with a whitish ring that often has a brownish edge

SPORE PRINT: Cream

ECOLOGY: Parasitic and saprobic on hemlock and occasionally on broadleaf trees, especially birch; usually clustered; late summer and fall; common

EDIBILITY: Young caps are edible and choice when cooked thoroughly

COMMENTS: Compare with the deadly brown-spored *Galerina marginata* (p. 208). The two species can often be found on the same log at the same time. *Armillaria solidipes* has been called *Armillaria ostoyae*, which is currently thought to be a European species. An edible, uncommon look-alike is *Armillaria gemina* (not illustrated), which occurs on broadleaf logs and stumps. This complex of *Armillaria* and related species can be a challenge to identify. With one exception (*Desarmillaria tabescens,* p. 114), all have a ring, whitish spores, attached gills, and occur on wood. All are edible when well-cooked. While most mushrooms are genetically diverse, this species forms clones. The underground mycelium, which can extend for great distances, has been determined to be the largest living organism on earth.

Armillaria solidipes

SCIENTIFIC NAME: *Armillaria mellea* (Vahl) P. Kumm.

SYNONYM: *Armillariella mellea* (Vahl) P. Karst.

COMMON NAMES: Honey Mushroom, Bootlace Fungus

FAMILY: Physalacriaceae

CAP: Up to 4 in. wide; variable in color, brownish yellow to honey-colored, at times with olivaceous tints; convex becoming nearly flat; surface viscid in wet weather, bald or with yellowish-brown scales or hairs

FLESH: White or watery tan, thick at the disc; not staining when damaged; odor and taste not distinctive

GILLS: Whitish, becoming tan with brown spots in age; subdistant; adnate to subdecurrent; edges even; covered at first with a membranous partial veil

STEM: Up to 6 in. long; variable in color, white, tan, or brown with white fibers, often darker near the base; equal or tapered at the base; tough; surface fibrous, scurfy, with a membranous ring on the upper stem

SPORE PRINT: White

ECOLOGY: Parasitic and saprobic on the wood of broadleaf trees; often in large clusters, at times on soil fruiting from buried roots, rarely on conifer wood; summer and early fall, rarely in late spring; common

EDIBILITY: Edible when cooked thoroughly, toxic when raw; compare with the deadly brown-spored *Galerina marginata* (p. 208)

COMMENTS: What was once considered one variable species is now known to include several Appalachian species, including *Armillaria gallica* (p. 113), *Armillaria solidipes* (p. 111), and *Desarmillaria tabescens* (p. 114). The combination of a membranous ring, honey coloration, and nearly bald cap will distinguish the Honey Mushroom from these closely related species. This species is a virulent parasite that can be very destructive in a woodlot or orchard. Wood that is infected with actively growing Honey Mushroom mycelium will appear to glow in the dark. This phenomenon, sometimes referred to as foxfire, is a result of the mycelium that is infecting the wood being bioluminescent.

Armillaria mellea

SCIENTIFIC NAME: *Armillaria gallica* Marxm. and Romagn.

SYNONYMS: *Armillaria bulbosa* sensu auct. brit. [in the sense of British authors], *Armillaria lutea* Gillet

COMMON NAME: Brown Honey Mushroom

FAMILY: Physalacriaceae

CAP: Up to 3 in. wide; convex, becoming flat in age; rich brown, or pinkish brown to honey brown; surface often bald, moist, or tacky, with or without yellowish hairs; margin usually with yellowish remnants of the partial veil

FLESH: Whitish; thick; unchanging when bruised

GILLS: White, at times with pinkish-brown discoloration; adnate to subdecurrent; close to subdistant; edges even; covered at first by a yellowish to whitish, cobwebby partial veil

STEM: Up to 4 in. long; whitish; swollen base may show yellow or reddish stains; solid; surface dry, rather shaggy with whitish hairs, partial veil may leave a yellowish ring zone

SPORE PRINT: White

ECOLOGY: Saprobic and parasitic, causing a butt rot on the wood of broadleaf trees, occasionally on conifer wood; often appears terrestrial when it inhabits buried roots; usually fruits scattered or in small clusters

EDIBILITY: Edible when cooked thoroughly

COMMENTS: At one time most species of *Armillaria* were called *Armillaria mellea* (p. 112) or *Armillariella mellea*, the Honey Mushroom. What was thought to be one variable species is now known to be many similar species. All are edible but have caused digestive problems when undercooked. Other common species in Appalachia are *Armillaria mellea* (p. 112), *Armillaria solidipes* (p. 111), and *Desarmillaria tabescens* (p. 114). *Armillaria gallica* is darker brown and more likely than any of the other species to have a bulbous stipe base. Its cobwebby veil is also distinctive.

Armillaria gallica

SCIENTIFIC NAME: *Desarmillaria tabescens* (Scop.) R. A. Koch and Aime

SYNONYMS: *Armillariella tabescens* (Scop.) Singer, *Armillaria tabescens* (Scop.) Emel

COMMON NAME: Ringless Honey Mushroom

FAMILY: Physalacriaceae

CAP: Up to 4 in. wide; dark orangish brown to tawny to yellowish brown, becoming drab brown in age; convex becoming flat, in age slightly depressed in the center; surface with dense tufts of hair at the center and flattened hairs near the margin, dry, not striate or only faintly so

FLESH: White, brownish, or becoming brown stained; odor variously described as pleasant, strong, or sweet; taste may be mild, astringent, or slightly bitter

GILLS: White to light pinkish, becoming brown stained in age; subdistant, subdecurrent; edges even; no partial veil

STEM: Up to 8 in. long, white above, gradually darkening to brown downward, typically equal then tapering down to the base; surface fibrous, without a ring

SPORE PRINT: White to cream

ECOLOGY: Parasitic and saprobic on the wood of broadleaf trees, especially oaks and maples; often appears terrestrial because it commonly fruits from buried wood; summer and fall; common

EDIBILITY: Edible and quite good, but like all edible honey mushrooms, thorough cooking is recommended since digestive upsets have occurred when undercooked mushrooms were consumed

COMMENTS: The Ringless Honey Mushroom is a common sight in suburban lawns, where it sometimes fruits from buried roots in large, dense clusters. It is the easiest mushroom in the *Armillaria* complex to identify, because it lacks a ring. This species often appears in hot, humid, and rather dry conditions when other gilled mushrooms are scarce. Compare with the poisonous *Omphalotus illudens* (p. 126), which is orange.

Desarmillaria tabescens

SCIENTIFIC NAME: *Pleurotus ostreatus* (Jacq.) P. Kumm.

SYNONYM: None

COMMON NAME: Oyster Mushroom

FAMILY: Pleurotaceae

CAP: Up to 7 in. wide; dark brown, grayish brown, tan, buff to creamy white; convex becoming somewhat flat; kidney-shaped to fan-shaped; surface bald, moist, not striate; margin incurved at first

FLESH: White; thick; odor fragrant, at times anise-like or fruity; taste not distinctive

GILLS: White to grayish or tan; decurrent; close to subdistant; edges even; no partial veil; often inhabited by fungus beetles, which are black with red heads (*Triplax* species)

STEM: Absent or up to 1½ in. long; white to dingy yellowish; when present, stem is eccentric, lateral, or central when fruiting on top of a stump; thick; dry; solid; with whitish hairs near the base

SPORE PRINT: White to grayish lilac

ECOLOGY: Saprobic, but can be parasitic and infect wounds on living trees; scattered or growing shelf-like in overlapping clusters on logs and stumps of broadleaf trees and rarely conifers; throughout the year in cool weather, most common in the fall

EDIBILITY: Edible and choice

COMMENTS: *Pleurotus pulmonarius* (p. 116) is white and has thinner flesh and is often striate. It is common in hot weather, often on beech logs. *Pleurotus populinus* (not illustrated) fruits in the spring on aspen and other *Populus* species. Its odor resembles anise. Both of these are good edibles as well. Various related species are grown commercially and grow-your-own kits are readily available. *Pleurotus ostreatus* has shown the ability to digest toxic inorganic waste. It has also shown promise as a substitute for Styrofoam. All this and it tastes good and is good for you. Avoid the poisonous and stemless *Pleurocybella porrigens* (p. 117), which has thin flesh and occurs on conifer wood in the fall.

Pleurotus ostreatus

SCIENTIFIC NAME: *Pleurotus pulmonarius* (Fr.) Quél.

SYNONYM: None

COMMON NAME: Summer Oyster

FAMILY: Pleurotaceae

CAP: Up to 5 in. wide, whitish to beige; convex to flat; semicircular to fan-shaped or circular when growing on top of a stump; surface moist to dry, not viscid, bald, often striate; margin enrolled at first, becoming wavy in age

FLESH: White; thick at the center, thin at the margin; odor fragrant; taste mild

GILLS: White; decurrent; subdistant; edges even; no partial veil; often inhabited by fungus beetles, which are black with red heads (*Triplax* species)

STEM: Absent or up to 3 in. long; white; eccentric, usually lateral but central when fruiting on top of a stump; surface dry or moist

SPORE PRINT: White to pale grayish lilac

ECOLOGY: Saprobic on the wood of broadleaf trees, especially beech; late spring, summer, and fall; common

EDIBILITY: Edible and good

COMMENTS: The mushroom described here is what is found in Eastern North America. The mushroom with this name in Western North America is probably different. This is another taxonomic issue that needs more work. Compare with *Pleurotus ostreatus* (p. 115), which has darker colors, thicker flesh, and is never striate. *Pleurotus populinus* (not illustrated) fruits in the spring on aspen and other *Populus* species. Its odor resembles anise. All three of these species are edible. Avoid the poisonous and stemless *Pleurocybella porrigens* (p. 117), which has thin flesh and occurs on conifer wood in the fall.

Pleurotus pulmonarius

SCIENTIFIC NAME: *Pleurocybella porrigens* (Pers.) Singer

SYNONYM: None

COMMON NAME: Angel Wings

FAMILY: Marasmiaceae

CAP: Up to 4 in. wide; white; fan- to shell-shaped; shelving; surface dry, bald, or hairy at the point of attachment; margin often slightly incurved, wavy and uplifted

FLESH: White; very thin; odor and taste not distinctive

GILLS: White becoming cream colored; decurrent; crowded; narrow; edges even; no partial veil

STEM: Absent or rudimentary

SPORE PRINT: White

ECOLOGY: Saprobic on the wood of conifers, especially hemlock; solitary to clustered; late summer and fall; common

EDIBILITY: Toxic, possibly deadly poisonous

COMMENTS: Fatal poisonings of people with kidney and liver disease have been reported in Japan. Before these incidents occurred, it was considered an edible species. It has thin flesh and a rather bland taste. It should be admired but not eaten. Edible oyster mushrooms in the genus *Pleurotus* are similar but have thicker flesh and a stem or thick stem-like base, and usually occur on the wood of broadleaf trees.

Pleurocybella porrigens

SCIENTIFIC NAME: *Lentinellus ursinus* (Fr.) Kühner

SYNONYMS: None

COMMON NAME: Bear Lentinus

FAMILY: Auriscalpiaceae

CAP: Up to 4 in. wide; white or buff, dark brown and with brown hairs from the point of attachment

FLESH: Whitish to pale brownish; firm; fairly thick; odor not distinctive or fruity; taste sharply acrid

GILLS: Whitish to pinkish; close to subdistant; broad; no partial veil; sawtoothed

STEM: Absent

SPORE PRINT: Creamy white

ECOLOGY: Saprobic; clustered to gregarious on the dead wood of broadleaf trees; late summer and fall; common

EDIBILITY: Not edible, very acrid

Comments: The author once made the mistake of rubbing his eye after handling a cluster of this species in wet weather. Definitely acrid! The hairy cap and taste will quickly distinguish this mushroom from the various oyster mushrooms in the genus *Pleurotus*.

Lentinellus ursinus

SCIENTIFIC NAME: *Lentinellus micheneri* (Berk. & M. A. Curtis) Pegler

SYNONYMS: *Lentinus omphalodes* (Fr.) Sacc.

COMMON NAME: None

FAMILY: Auriscalpiaceae

CAP: Up to 2 in. wide; pinkish brown becoming pale buff to whitish when dry; convex to flat with a prominent central umbilicus; surface moist, hygrophanous, bald, not striate

FLESH: Whitish to dingy pale yellowish brown; soft; thin; odor not distinctive; taste mild at first, becoming very acrid

GILLS: Whitish to pinkish brown; not bruising; attached to subdecurrent; edges sawtoothed; no partial veil.

STEM: Up to 2 in. long; brown or colored like the cap, the apex may be yellowish or the color of the gills; equal; often grooved lengthwise; dry; tough; central or off-center

SPORE PRINT: Creamy white

ECOLOGY: Saprobic; gregarious or in small clusters on fallen limbs of broadleaf and conifer trees; summer and fall; occasional

EDIBILITY: Not edible, acrid

COMMENTS: The sawtooth gills, acrid taste, and cap with an umbilicus are keys to identifying this mushroom.

Lentinellus micheneri

SCIENTIFIC NAME: *Sarcomyxa serotina* (Pers.) P. Karst.

SYNONYM: *Panellus serotinus* (Pers.) Kühner

COMMON NAME: Late Fall Oyster

FAMILY: Mycenaceae

CAP: Up to 4 in. wide; colors extremely variable, greenish, purplish, dark brown, silvery gray, yellow, or some combination of these, not white and not black; semicircular; surface bald, smooth, slippery, or tacky when wet, in age becoming velvety or fuzzy

FLESH: White, unchanging when damaged; firm, thick; odor not distinctive; taste mild or slightly bitter.

GILLS: Yellowish buff to orangish yellow, becoming brownish; close; attached to subdecurrent; no partial veil

STEM: Yellowish to brownish; short or absent; thick; lateral; surface hairy or with small scales

SPORE PRINT: White or yellowish

ECOLOGY: Saprobic; in groups or overlapping clusters on the dead wood of conifer and broadleaf trees, especially beech; fall and early winter; common

EDIBILITY: Edible, but most find it rather bland; long, slow cooking and squeezing out the moisture before adding oil is recommended

COMMENTS: This is a cold-weather mushroom. It is most common after the first frost. The color range is remarkable. In many field guides it is called *Panellus serotinus.*

Sarcomyxa serotina

SCIENTIFIC NAME: *Hohenbuehelia petaloides* (Bull.)
Schulzer

SYNONYM: *Hohenbuehelia geogenia* (DC.) Singer

COMMON NAME: Shoehorn Oyster

FAMILY: Pleurotaceae

CAP: Up to 4 in. wide; buff, tan, brown, or whitish at times; shoehorn- to deeply funnel-shaped; surface bald, rubbery, moist, and gelatinous

FLESH: Whitish; soft; rubbery; odor and taste mealy

GILLS: White to gray or yellowish; prominently decurrent; close or crowded; edges even or minutely fringed; no partial veil

STEM: Short, nearly absent; whitish to grayish brown; lateral; thick; continuous with the cap; surface dry

SPORE PRINT: White

ECOLOGY: Saprobic; gregarious or in small clusters around stumps or in areas with woody debris; more common in parks and open areas than in the woods; summer and fall; occasional

EDIBILITY: Edible but reportedly of mediocre quality

COMMENTS: Some authors consider *Hohenbuehelia geogenia* to be distinct. Most mycologists now consider that they are the same species.

Hohenbuehelia petaloides

SCIENTIFIC NAME: *Hohenbuehelia mastrucata* (Fr.) **Singer**

SYNONYM: None

COMMON NAME: None

FAMILY: Pleurotaceae

CAP: Up to 2¾ in. wide; dark to light gray, pinkish gray, bluish gray; convex to nearly flat; semicircular to kidney-shaped; laterally attached to the substrate; surface moist, rubbery, covered with thick conical spines, appearing hair-like, not striate

FLESH: Grayish or whitish; thick; somewhat gelatinous or rubbery; odor and taste mealy

GILLS: White to pale gray; close to subdistant; edges even; no partial veil

STEM: Absent or nearly so

SPORE PRINT: White

ECOLOGY: Saprobic; single or in small groups on the dead wood of broadleaf trees, especially maple; summer and fall; rare

EDIBILITY: Unknown

COMMENTS: This species supplements its diet by catching and eating nematodes, which it encounters in the rotten wood. *Hohenbuehelia atrocaerulea* (not illustrated) is similar but paler in color, and it lacks the prominent, gelatinous spines on the cap.

Hohenbuehelia mastrucata

SCIENTIFIC NAME: *Pleurotus dryinus* (Pers.) P. Kumm.

SYNONYM: None

COMMON NAME: Veiled Oyster

FAMILY: Pleurotaceae

CAP: Up to 4 in. wide; white to cream or yellowish, or yellowish tan; convex, becoming broadly convex; surface dry, often with a fine, frosted, or hoary coating, at times with grayish fibrils

FLESH: White; thick; firm; odor somewhat fragrant, often like citrus, becoming sour in age; taste not distinctive

GILLS: White, discoloring to yellow in age or on drying; subdecurrent to decurrent; close to subdistant; edges even; covered at first with a thin, membranous partial veil

STEM: Up to 4 in. long; white; equal or tapered downward; solid; tough; surface dry, floccose to fibrillose, or hairy, especially toward the base; with an evanescent membranous ring

SPORE PRINT: White

ECOLOGY: Saprobic on dead broadleaf tree wood; gregarious or in small clusters; summer and fall; occasional

EDIBILITY: Edible when young

COMMENTS: *Lentinus levis* (not illustrated) is very similar. Its veil is microscopic, and its stem is hairy from the base to the apex. It is possible that both species will end up in the same genus. They will not mate but otherwise are very similar.

Pleurotus dryinus

SCIENTIFIC NAME: *Echinoderma asperum* (Pers.) Bon

SYNONYMS: *Lepiota acutesquamosa* (Weinm.) P. Kumm., *Lepiota aspera* (Pers.) Quél.

COMMON NAME: Sharp-Scaled Lepiota

FAMILY: Agaricaceae

CAP: Up to 4¼ in. wide; nearly orb-shaped, becoming convex and eventually flat; ground color is whitish, surface covered with orangish-brown, reddish-brown, or brownish-gray and easily removable scales; at the cap center the scales are pointed and are part of the cap cuticle

FLESH: White, unchanging when cut or damaged; soft; odor not distinctive or slightly unpleasant; taste not distinctive

GILLS: White to pale cream; free from the stem; crowded; edges even or slightly roughened; covered at first with a white to pinkish, membranous partial veil, which has brownish scales similar to those on the cap

STEM: Up to 4½ in long; whitish with reddish-brown fibers or scales, especially toward the base; equal; becoming hollow in age; surface dry, floccose, base with white mycelial strands; with an apical, white, skirt-like ring that is persistent but rather fragile, the ring sometimes has reddish-brown scales on the edge

SPORE PRINT: White

ECOLOGY: Saprobic; gregarious in humus, wood mulch, and woody debris in broadleaf woods and parks; summer and fall; uncommon to occasional

EDIBILITY: Reported as edible but not recommended owing to its resemblance to species of *Amanita*; the author has not tried it

COMMENTS: The crowded gills and lack of a universal veil will separate this mushroom from species of *Amanita*.

Echinoderma asperum

SCIENTIFIC NAME: *Hypsizygus marmoreus* (Peck) H.E. Bigelow

MISAPPLIED NAME: *Hypsizygus tessulatus* (Bull.) Singer

COMMON NAME: Water Spotted Agaric

FAMILY: Lyophyllaceae

CAP: Up to 6 in. wide; whitish, usually with distinct hyaline spots; convex to nearly flat at maturity; surface bald, dry, becoming cracked in age in dry conditions

FLESH: Whitish; thick; firm; odor not distinctive; taste bitter or not distinctive

GILLS: Whitish to pale buff; barely reaching the stem; at times pulling away and leaving a faint tooth on the stem; close to subdistant; broad; edges even; no partial veil

STEM: Up to 4 in. long; whitish; thick; very tough; off-center; surface dry, bald, to finely hairy, especially at the base; often curved; usually equal, or may taper in either direction

SPORE PRINT: White to pale buff

ECOLOGY: Saprobic; usually gregarious or clustered on the dead wood of broadleaf trees; late summer and fall; fairly common

EDIBILITY: Edible but some find it bitter; boiling is reported to remove the bitter taste

COMMENTs: *Hypsizygus tessulatus* is the name applied to this fairly common mushroom in most field guides. That name, however, should apply to an Asian and commercially grown species marketed as Shimeji, the Brown Beech Mushroom. Some consider the two as synonymous. I am not aware of DNA studies of our wild mushroom comparing it to the Asian species. It seems likely they will turn out to be different species. The whitish, water-spotted entity of the Appalachian broadleaf and mixed forest often has a bitter taste. *Hypsizygus ulmarius* (not illustrated) is a similar species, although it is uncommon and its white cap lacks the water spots.

Hypsizygus marmoreus

SCIENTIFIC NAME: *Omphalotus illudens* (Schwein.) Sacc.

SYNONYM: *Clitocybe illudens* (Schwein.) Sacc.

COMMON NAME: Jack O'Lantern

FAMILY: Marasmiaceae

Cap: Up to 7 in. wide, bright orange to yellowish orange, becoming brownish in age; dry; convex becoming flat to vase shaped in age, often with a central nipple; the margin is turned under at first, becoming flat and wavy at maturity

Gills: Orange, yellowish or tinted the color of the cap; close to subdistant, adnate to subdecurrent; luminescent; no partial veil

FLESH: White to tinted orange or yellowish; odor unpleasantly sweet, or indistinct; taste mild

STEM: Up to 8 in. long, white or yellow becoming streaked with orange; solid; tapered at the base; smooth

SPORE PRINT: Cream to pale yellowish

ECOLOGY: Saprobic on the wood of broadleaf trees, especially oaks; It typically fruits in large clusters on the roots of stumps but can occur scattered and may appear terrestrial when growing from buried wood; summer and fall; common in broadleaf forests, parks, and suburban lots

EDIBILITY: Poisonous, causing gastrointestinal problems and at times visual impairment; This species has been mistaken for an edible *Cantharellus* species. The latter are terrestrial, have broad gill-like folds, and do not grow in large clusters.

COMMENTS: This striking mushroom was given the common name Jack O'Lantern due to the fact that when the fresh gills are observed in very dark conditions, they emit a greenish light. It may take several minutes to observe this phenomenon, the time giving the eyes a chance to adjust. The function of this bioluminescence has not been established. *Omphalotus olearius* is a similar European species.

Omphalotus illudens

SCIENTIFIC NAME: *Pseudoclitocybe cyathiformis* (Bull.) Singer

SYNONYMS: *Cantharellula cyathiformis* (Bull.) Singer, *Clitocybe cyathiformis* (Bull.) P. Kumm.

COMMON NAME: Goblet Mushroom

FAMILY: Tricholomataceae

CAP: Up to 4 in. wide; dark brown to dark grayish brown, hygrophanous, fading to buff or whitish, center remains darker; convex with a depressed center, becoming deeply funnel-shaped; surface bald, moist; margin rivulose at times, not usually striate

FLESH: Grayish, watery; thin; odor of almond extract; taste slightly sweetish or not distinctive

GILLS: White to gray; attached or subdecurrent; close to subdistant; occasionally forked or with veining; edges even; no partial veil

STEM: Up to 4 in. long; whitish to pale buff; equal or tapering upward; stuffed; fibrillose; gray; white mycelium or rhizomorphs at the base; margin rivulose at times

SPORE PRINT: White

ECOLOGY: Saprobic on the dead wood of broadleaf trees; gregarious or in small clusters; late summer and fall; occasional

EDIBILITY: Not recommended; reports are mixed, it has reportedly caused digestive problems for some people; the author has not tried it

COMMENTS: The deep funnel-shaped cap, the habitat on wood, and the color change from wet to dry are diagnostic.

Pseudoclitocybe cyathiformis

SCIENTIFIC NAME: *Gerronema strombodes* (Berk. & Mont.) Singer

SYNONYM: *Chrysomphalina strombodes* (Berk. & Mont.) Clémençon

COMMON NAME: None

FAMILY: Marasmiaceae

CAP: Up to 2 in. wide; ground color yellowish white, covered with grayish to brownish fibrils; convex with an umbilicate center, at times deeply funnel-shaped; surface slightly tacky to dry and somewhat silky; margin uplifted and often split in age

FLESH: Whitish to cream; thin; unchanging when damaged; odor not distinctive or somewhat sweet; taste not distinctive or slightly bitter

GILLS: White, cream, to yellow; decurrent; distant; edges even; no partial veil

STEM: Up to 2½ in long; equal; hollow; surface dry, usually bald, or finely fibrillose

SPORE PRINT: White.

ECOLOGY: Saprobic on dead wood, usually of broadleaf trees; scattered to gregarious or clustered; summer and early fall; fairly common, very abundant some years

EDIBILITY: Unknown

COMMENTS: This species is most common on broadleaf logs but has been observed in spectacular masses on wood chips.

Gerronema strombodes

SCIENTIFIC NAME: *Mycetinis scorodonius* (Fr.) A. W. Wilson and Desjardin

SYNONYM: *Marasmius scorodonius* (Fr.) Fr.

COMMON NAME: Garlic Mushroom

FAMILY: Marasmiaceae

CAP: Up to 1¼ in. wide; brown, fading to buff or pale tan, whitish toward the margin, or in age all over; convex to flat with a central depression, margin becoming uplifted; surface dry, bald, not striate, or obscurely so

FLESH: Whitish, thin; odor and taste strongly of garlic or onions

GILLS: Whitish; attached to free; close to subdistant; fairly broad; edges even; no partial veil

STEM: Up to 2½ in. long; apex whitish to pale tan, dark reddish from the base upward; equal or tapering downward; tough; surface dry, mostly bald, may be hairy at the base

SPORE PRINT: White

ECOLOGY: Scattered to gregarious in litter or grass under conifers or in mixed woods, occasionally on living tree bark; summer and fall; occasional to common

EDIBILITY: Edible; can be used as a garlic seasoning

COMMENTS: The author has experienced the strong odor of this species by simply walking through a patch of them.

Mycetinis scorodonius

SCIENTIFIC NAME: *Mycetinis opacus* (Berk. and M. A. Curtis) A. W. Wilson and Desjardin

SYNONYM: *Marasmiellus opacus* (Berk. and M. A. Curtis) Singer

COMMON NAME: None

FAMILY: Marasmiaceae

CAP: Up to ¾ in. wide; dirty white, grayish, or buff; convex becoming broadly convex to flat with a broad central depression, at times becoming vase-shaped; surface dry, granular, becoming bald, slightly wrinkled at times; not striate

FLESH: Whitish, very thin; odor not distinctive or slightly unpleasant; taste not distinctive

GILLS: Whitish; attached to the stem; distant; prominently veined, forming a lattice; edges even; no partial veil

STEM: Up to 2¼ in. long; colored like the cap or darker; equal; surface dry, bald, or velvety

SPORE PRINT: White

ECOLOGY: Saprobic; scattered to gregarious in mixed woods on the twigs and litter of hemlock and rhododendron and possibly other trees; late spring through fall; very common

EDIBILITY: Unknown

COMMENTS: Although seldom described in field guides, this small species can be the most common agaric in mixed woodlands where hemlock is present. A key feature is the presence of rhizomorphs looking like hairs emanating from the substrate. This species shrivels in dry conditions and then revives during rainy periods.

Mycetinis opacus

SCIENTIFIC NAME: *Marasmiellus praeacutus* (Ellis) Halling

SYNONYM: *Collybia praeacuta* (Ellis) Gilliam

COMMON NAME: None

FAMILY: Marasmiaceae

CAP: Up to 1 in. wide; white or hyaline when young, white at maturity with a pale, ruddy center at times; convex to flat, often with a depressed center; surface bald, dry

FLESH: White; thin; odor and taste similar to garlic or onion

GILLS: White; attached to the stem; distant; thick; broad; often cross-veined or forking; edges even; no partial veil

STEM: Up to 1½ in. long; reddish brown, decorated with whitish fibers and a white bottom; equal or tapering in either direction down to the abruptly pointed base

SPORE PRINT: White to pale cream

ECOLOGY: Saprobic on dead wood and a wide variety of organic debris, including acorn caps, cone scales, conifer needles, and sweetgum nuts; summer and fall; common

EDIBILITY: Unknown

COMMENTS: The combination of garlic odor and reddish, chiseled stem are diagnostic. It is interesting that the stem develops first, looking disproportionately large in relation to the tiny cap.

Marasmiellus praeacutus

SCIENTIFIC NAME: *Collybia cookei* (Bres.) J. D. Arnold

SYNONYM: *Collybia cirrhata* var. *cookei* Bres.

COMMON NAME: None

FAMILY: Tricholomataceae

CAP: Up to ½ in. wide; whitish to pinkish buff with a darker center; convex becoming flat; surface minutely fibrillose or smooth, dry or moist, no partial veil

FLESH: Whitish; thin; odor and taste not distinctive

GILLS: White to pinkish buff; close to subdistant; attached to subdecurrent; edges even; no partial veil

STEM: Up to 2 in. long; white; flexible; surface dry; pruinose above, hairy at the base; attached directly to the host mushroom or via the basal hairs are yellowish tubers called sclerotia

SPORE PRINT: White

ECOLOGY: Saprobic; gregarious on the well-decayed remains of various mushrooms; summer and fall; common; the sclerotia (singular sclerotium) are dense masses of fungal tissue that help the fungus survive unfavorable conditions such as drought, freezing, or lack of a host

EDIBILITY: Unknown

COMMENTS: Twin species are *Collybia tuberosa*, which has a reddish-brown sclerotium, and *Collybia cirrhata* (not illustrated), which lacks a sclerotium. These species also occur on well-decayed, fleshy fungi. The author has seen prolific fruitings of *Collybia cookei* on the remains of the black-staining polypore *Meripilus sumstinei* (p. 312).

Collybia cookei

Collybia tuberosa

SCIENTIFIC NAME: *Marasmius rotula* (Scop.) Fr.

SYNONYM: None

COMMON NAME: Pinwheel Mushroom

FAMILY: Marasmiaceae

CAP: Up to ¾ in. wide; white or pale yellowish, tan in the center; convex with a central, navel-like depression; surface dry, pleated, and bald

FLESH: White; very thin; odor not distinctive; taste slightly bitter or not distinctive

GILLS: White to pale yellow; appearing free but attached to a collar that is free from the stem or at times collapsing on it; distant; rather broad; no partial veil

STEM: Up to 3 in. long; whitish at the apex, reddish brown or black below, becoming nearly all black; equal; shiny; wiry; black rhizomorphs sometimes present at the base

SPORE PRINT: White

ECOLOGY: Saprobic on the dead wood of broadleaf trees, especially beech, often on bark; densely gregarious, scattered or in small clusters; common and most noticeable after rains

EDIBILITY: Unknown, too small to be of interest

COMMENTS: *Marasmius capillaris* (not illustrated) is similar, but it grows on leaves and twigs and has a pale-tan to whitish-gray cap. Like most species in the genus *Marasmius*, in dry weather, this species shrivels and becomes inconspicuous until wet weather revives them and spore dispersal continues. Both species can produce great numbers of fruit bodies.

Marasmius rotula

SCIENTIFIC NAME: *Marasmius delectans* Morgan

SYNONYM: None

COMMON NAME: None

FAMILY: Marasmiaceae

CAP: Up to 1½ in. wide; white to yellowish; convex becoming flat; surface bald; may be somewhat wrinkled, obscurely striate at times; after drying, reviving in wet weather

FLESH: Whitish, very thin; odor mildly fragrant or sometimes strong and unpleasant; taste not distinctive

GILLS: Colored like the cap; notched; subdistant; moderately broad; veined; edges even; no partial veil

STEM: Up to 3 in. long; dark reddish brown to black from the base upward, white at the apex; equal; hollow; base with white mycelium; surface bald, shiny

SPORE PRINT: White

ECOLOGY: Saprobic; scattered on leaf litter in broadleaf and mixed woods; summer and fall; common

EDIBILITY: Unknown

COMMENTS: This species frequently occurs with white mycelium forming mats of leaves. The shiny stem, which darkens from the base up, is a key feature.

Marasmius delectans

SCIENTIFIC NAME: *Marasmius fulvoferrugineus* Gilliam

SYNONYM: None

COMMON NAME: None

FAMILY: Marasmiaceae

CAP: Up to 1¾ in wide; tawny brown to rusty brown; conical or bell-shaped, becoming convex with a small umbo at times; surface radially grooved, dry, bald, or slightly velvety

FLESH: Very thin; tough; odor and taste not distinctive, or slightly mealy

GILLS: White, or yellowish; notched or free from the stem; distant; very broad; intervenose; edges even; no partial veil

STEM: Up to 2½ in. long; black to reddish brown below, pinkish near the apex; generally equal or tapering downward; slender; round or flattened; cartilaginous; surface bald, base with white mycelium

SPORE PRINT: White

ECOLOGY: Saprobic; scattered to gregarious on decaying leaves and humus in broadleaf and mixed woods; common in the southern Appalachians

EDIBILITY: Unknown

COMMENTS: *Marasmius siccus* (not illustrated) is a very similar, common species, but it is smaller and rusty orange. It is more common in northern areas of the region. Both species shrivel in dry conditions and revive in wet weather.

Marasmius fulvoferrugineus

SCIENTIFIC NAME: *Marasmius cohaerens* (Pers.) Cooke and Quél.

SYNONYM: None

COMMON NAME: Fused Marasmius

FAMILY: Marasmiaceae

CAP: Up to 1½ in. wide; brownish orange, reddish brown, darker in the center, fading to whitish with a brownish-orange center; roundish, then convex, becoming flat; surface dry, velvety or bald, wrinkled at times, striate when mature and wet

FLESH: White; thin; odor not distinctive, or pungent and unpleasant; taste mild, slightly bitter, or with an acidic aftertaste

GILLS: White to yellowish white; attached, becoming free in age; subdistant; fairly broad; edges even; no partial veil

STEM: Up to 3 in. long; whitish to yellowish brown at first, darkening from the base upward from nearly black to dark reddish brown; equal; tough; hollow; surface bald but with a rough surface at times

SPORE PRINT: White

ECOLOGY: Saprobic; clustered or gregarious on the dead wood and humus of broadleaf trees; summer and fall; occasional in the northern areas to fairly common in the southern regions of the Appalachians

EDIBILITY: Unknown, generally considered not edible

COMMENTS: Compare with *Marasmius sullivantii* (not illustrated), which grows singly or scattered on broadleaf litter and not on wood.

Marasmius cohaerens

Scientific Name: *Marasmius oreades* (Bolton) Fr.

SYNONYM: None

COMMON NAMES: Fairy Ring Mushroom, Scotch Bonnets

FAMILY: Marasmiaceae

CAP: Up to 2 in. wide; tan, pale cinnamon to buff, hygrophanous, fading to pale buff or whitish; convex, bell-shaped in age; umbonate; surface bald, dry, occasionally striate in age; margin uplifted at maturity, scalloped at times

FLESH: White or watery; thick over the center, thin outward; odor fragrant, similar to bitter almonds; taste not distinctive

GILLS: White, buff, or yellowish tan; notched or free from the stem; subdistant; fairly broad; veined; edges even; no partial veil

STEM: Up to 3 in. long; lower area colored like the cap, paler above; equal; flexible and rather tough; surface dry, bald, minutely hairy at the base

SPORE PRINT: Creamy white

ECOLOGY: Saprobic on the dead roots of new grass, often growing in arcs or circles; it can be found in groups or scattered, as well as in rings in lawns and fields; summer and fall; common

EDIBILITY: The caps are edible and good, but discard the tough stems. This is an excellent species to dehydrate, store, and reconstitute later. The caps revive back to their fresh state. They are meatier than they look.

COMMENTS: Other mushrooms also grow in arcs and circles in lawns. This is the only one in lawns that has a tough stem, that has gills that do not descend to the stem, and that revives when wet. In nature this mushroom may go through several periods of drying and reviving. The fairy rings, also called devil's circles, are steeped in superstition and folklore. Various stories—including ones involving lightning, mating deer, fairies, and the devil—have all been told to explain the rings formed by various mushrooms. In reality the mushroom starts at a given point, consumes its host, and then moves outward in search of more food. The rings get larger every year. It is possible to see where this phenomenon is occurring even when no mushrooms are present. The mycelium releases nutrients, acting like fertilizer, and causing the grass to grow taller and greener.

Marasmius oreades

SCIENTIFIC NAME: *Mycena crocea* Maas Geest.

SYNONYM: *Mycena luteopallens* (Peck) Peck

COMMON NAME: Walnut Mycena

FAMILY: Mycenaceae

CAP: Up to ¾ in. wide; rich yellow to bright orangish yellow, fading to very pale yellow or whitish; oval becoming broadly convex to nearly flat; margin becoming white; surface bald, moist, translucent striate at maturity

FLESH: Pallid to yellowish; very thin; odor and taste not distinctive

GILLS: Yellowish to whitish, at times with pinkish edges; narrowly attached to the stem; subdistant; fairly broad; edges even; no partial veil

STEM: Up to 4 in. long; orange or yellow near the apex, whitish below; equal; surface bald down to a hairy base

SPORE PRINT: White

ECOLOGY: Saprobic on the shells and debris of walnut and hickory nuts; scattered to gregarious; late summer and fall; common

EDIBILITY: Not edible

COMMENTS: The specialized habitat is the best feature in identifying this small, attractive mushroom. It is named in older books as *Mycena luteopallens*. When the original collection was reexamined, it turned out to be a species of *Hygrocybe*.

Mycena crocea

SCIENTIFIC NAME: *Mycena inclinata* (Fr.) Quél.

SYNONYM: None

COMMON NAME: Clustered Bonnet

FAMILY: Mycenaceae

CAP: Up to 2 in. wide; variable colors, buff to reddish-brown center; whitish outward, at times tan or yellowish brown all over; conical to convex to somewhat bell-shaped, often with a broad umbo; translucent striate when moist; bald; tacky; margin scalloped

FLESH: Whitish or tinted yellowish; very thin; odor mealy or rancid; taste mealy

GILLS: White, tinted light gray, at times becoming pinkish or yellowish in age; barely attached to the stem; close to subdistant; edges even; no partial veil

STEM: Up to 4 in. long; usually whitish above, yellowish in the middle, brownish below, in age brownish or yellowish all over; hollow; fragile; base with whitish hairs; upper surface bald or with small fibers

SPORE PRINT: White

ECOLOGY: Saprobic on the dead wood of broadleaf trees, usually densely clustered but occasionally scattered; summer and fall; common

EDIBILITY: Not edible

COMMENTS: This is a good example of North American mushroom using a name given to a European species. It has yet to be determined whether they really are the same. There are many similarly colored *Mycena* species and no doubt more yet to be described. *Mycena galericulata* (not illustrated) is very similar. It reportedly lacks the basal hairs on the stem. It too was described in Europe. The best a field mycologist can do for now is to call them *Mycena inclinata* complex. Much more work needs done to clarify the status of our North American species. No *Mycena* species are considered to be good edibles.

Mycena inclinata

139

SCIENTIFIC NAME: *Mycena haematopus* (Pers.) P. Kumm.

SYNONYM: None

COMMON NAME: Bleeding Mycena

FAMILY: Mycenaceae

CAP: Up to 2 in. wide; dark reddish brown to brownish red at the center, pinkish or paler outward; oval, becoming bell-shaped or conic, finally convex, and then nearly flat; surface pruinose, becoming moist and smooth, translucent striate; margin scalloped

FLESH: Colored like the cap or paler; very thin; exuding a purplish-red liquid when cut; odor not distinctive; taste mild or slightly bitter

GILLS: Whitish, becoming grayish to reddish brown; narrowly attached to the stem; close to subdistant; edges even and colored like the sides; no partial veil

STEM: Up to 4 in. long; reddish brown, brownish red to purple; equal; hollow, when cut exuding a purplish-red liquid; surface pruinose, becoming bald

SPORE PRINT: White

ECOLOGY: Saprobic; usually clustered but scattered or solitary at times on the wood of broadleaf trees, and reported rarely on conifer wood; spring, summer, and fall; common

EDIBILITY: Reported as edible; the author has not tried it

COMMENTS: This is a common species, found often on decorticated logs. *Mycena sanguinolenta* (not illustrated) is similar but has dark-edged gills and typically grows in litter and humus.

Mycena haematopus

SCIENTIFIC NAME: *Mycena subcaerulea* (Peck) Sacc.

SYNONYM: None

COMMON NAME: Blue Mycena

FAMILY: Mycenaceae

CAP: Up to ¾ in. wide; deep blue at first, with an aqua margin, soon becoming brownish or grayish brown; oval, becoming bell-shaped to broadly convex; surface bald, slightly viscid, translucent striate

FLESH: Pallid or grayish; thin; odor and taste not distinctive

GILLS: Whitish or pale grayish, attached to the stem; close; edges slightly fringed at maturity; no partial veil

STEM: Up to 3 in. long; grayish or brownish, bluish near the apex at first but soon fading to the color of the lower area, at first with bluish mycelium at the base, fading to white in age; equal; hollow; surface pruinose

SPORE PRINT: White

ECOLOGY: Saprobic on the dead wood of broadleaf trees, especially oaks; single, gregarious or in small clusters; spring and fall; common

EDIBILITY: Unknown

COMMENTS: Finding a blue mushroom is a visual treat. This one is easily overlooked, and the blue colors fade very quickly.

Mycena subcaerulea

SCIENTIFIC NAME: *Mycena epipterygia* (Scop.) Gray

SYNONYM: *Mycena epipterygia* var. *lignicola* A. H. Smith

COMMON NAME: Yellow Bonnet

FAMILY: Mycenaceae

CAP: Up to ¾ in. wide; olive green, yellowish green, fading to yellowish, margin paler; conic, broadly conic in age; surface bald, sticky

FLESH: Yellowish, very thin; odor mealy or rancid; taste mild or slightly bitter

GILLS: Whitish; attached; subdistant; narrow; edges even; no partial veil

STEM: Up to 3 in. long; yellowish to whitish, at times brown from the base upward; thin; equal, pliant; surface bald or pubescent

SPORE PRINT: White

ECOLOGY: Saprobic on wood and humus in conifer forests; solitary, scattered, or in small groups; late summer and fall; common

EDIBILITY: Unknown

COMMENTS: Several varieties of this species have been described, some of which are now considered separate species by some mycologists. More study is needed to sort out this complex of dainty little mushrooms.

Mycena epipterygia

SCIENTIFIC NAME: *Mycena pura* (Pers.) P. Kumm.

SYNONYM: *Prunulus purus* (Pers.) Murrill

COMMON NAME: Lilac Bonnet

FAMILY: Mycenaceae

CAP: Up to 2 in. wide; variable in coloration, purplish, reddish, lilac gray; conic to convex or bell-shaped; surface smooth, bald, dry or moist; margin striate

FLESH: Grayish to whitish; insubstantial; odor and taste radish-like

GILLS: Whitish or tinged pinkish or lilac; attached to the stem or notched; close to subdistant; broad; veined; edges even; no partial veil

STEM: Up to 4 in. long; whitish or colored like the pileus; equal or enlarged downward; hollow; surface dry, bald, striate, smooth, or with tiny hairs

SPORE PRINT: White

ECOLOGY: Saprobic on soil and humus under broadleaf and conifer trees; solitary, scattered to gregarious; summer and fall; occasional to common

EDIBILITY: Poisonous

COMMENTS: The cap and gills are reportedly faintly bioluminescent. The radish odor is a good feature, but it is a variable mushroom that may be a complex of several closely related species.

Mycena pura

SCIENTIFIC NAME: *Mycena leaiana* (Berk.) Sacc.

SYNONYM: None

COMMON NAME: Orange Mycena

FAMILY: Mycenaceae

CAP: Up to 1¾ in. wide; bright orange to reddish orange, fading to dull orange or yellowish, almost whitish, especially in wet weather; broadly bell-shaped to convex, becoming broadly convex; surface bald, viscid, shining, striate in age

FLESH: Watery white to orangish; soft; thin; odor mealy or not distinctive; taste mealy or not distinctive

GILLS: Orange on the sides; darker orange on the edges; attached; close; rather broad; edges even; no partial veil

STEM: Up to 2½ in. long; orange or yellowish orange; equal; surface bald, viscid to tacky; base with orange hairs

SPORE PRINT: White

ECOLOGY: Saprobic on the dead wood of broadleaf trees, especially beech; usually clustered; late spring through fall; common

EDIBILITY: Not edible

COMMENTS: The radiant orange colors, habitat on wood, and small size set this mushroom apart from any other. The orange coloration will stain fingers and eventually becomes washed out in rainy weather.

Mycena leaiana

SCIENTIFIC NAME: *Clitocybula abundans* (Peck) Singer

SYNONYM: *Fayodia abundans* (Peck) Singer

COMMON NAME: None

FAMILY: Marasmiaceae

CAP: Up to 1½ in. wide; gray or whitish, with a brownish center; convex to flat, with a prominent central depression; surface bald, not striate, but with innate whitish or brown fibrils or streaks, moist when fresh; the margin is curved under at first and often splits in age

FLESH: Watery, whitish, thin, fragile; odor and taste not distinctive

GILLS: White; close; adnate to subdecurrent; narrow, thin; edges even; no partial veil

STEM: Up to 4 in. long; whitish, paler than the cap; often curved; equal; becoming hollow and readily splitting; surface bald, not viscid, smooth, with a silky apex

SPORE PRINT: White

ECOLOGY: Saprobic; densely clustered or gregarious on logs in broadleaf and mixed forests; black birch is a common host; summer and fall; occasional

EDIBILITY: Unknown

COMMENTS: *Clitocybula oculus* is very similar but has a darker cap and small, dark scales on the stem. It is a Northern species and seldom reported in Appalachia.

Clitocybula abundans

SCIENTIFIC NAME: *Lepista tarda* (Peck) Murrill

SYNONYM: *Clitocybe tarda* Peck

COMMON NAME: None

FAMILY: Tricholomataceae

CAP: Up to 2½ in. wide; pale violet with brownish areas, fading to pale buff or whitish; convex to broadly convex and finally flat with a depressed center; surface bald and moist, hygrophanous; margin translucent striate when moist

FLESH: Watery whitish to pinkish brown; thick in the cap center, thin outward; odor not distinctive, or slightly sweet; taste mild, or slightly metallic

GILLS: Pinkish to pale tan with violet tints or pinkish buff; attached to subdecurrent; close to subdistant; edges even; no partial veil

STEM: Up to 2½ in. long; colored like the cap, only paler, with vertical, reddish-brown streaks; equal or tapering in either direction; solid; flexible

SPORE PRINT: Pinkish buff

ECOLOGY: Saprobic in lawns, fields, and compost piles; often forming arcs or circles; summer and fall; common

EDIBILITY: Reported to be edible; the author has not tried it

COMMENTS: In many guides this species is called *Clitocybe tarda*. *Lepista nuda* (p. 147) is larger and more robust.

Lepista tarda

SCIENTIFIC NAME: *Lepista nuda* (Bull.) Cooke

SYNONYM: *Clitocybe nuda* (Bull.) H.bE. Bigelow & A.bH. Sm.

COMMON NAMES: Blewit, Wood Blewit

FAMILY: Tricholomataceae

CAP: Up to 6 in. wide; dark violet at first, fading to various tinges of violet to pinkish tan or buff; convex with an enrolled margin at first, becoming flat; surface bald, moist, hygrophanous; margin not striate or faintly so when wet; no partial veil

FLESH: Violaceous to whitish; firm; thick; odor mildly fragrant or indistinct; taste mild, nutty, or mealy, rarely slightly bitter

GILLS: Pale lavender to violet, becoming pinkish buff to brownish in age; notched; close to crowded; no partial veil

STEM: Up to 3 in. long; pale lavender or whitish; solid; equal or with an enlarged base; surface dry, fibrillose to scurfy; base with whitish or violaceous mycelium; no ring

SPORE PRINT: Pinkish buff

ECOLOGY: Saprobic on a variety of organic materials, can be found in compost piles, lawns, woody debris, pine plantations, and woodlands; scattered to gregarious in cool weather, late summer and fall, or in early winter; at times this species occurs in arcs or rings

EDIBILITY: Edible when well cooked; the quality can range from excellent to poor; habitat and age of the fruitings may influence the taste

COMMENTS: Spore color is important in identifying this species. Avoid any violaceous mushroom with a brown spore deposit. Many species in the brown-spored genus *Cortinarius* have purplish colors. When young, they also have a spider web-like partial veil called a cortina.

Lepista nuda

SCIENTIFIC NAME: *Gymnopus subnudus* (Ellis ex Peck) Halling

SYNONYM: *Collybia subnuda* (Ellis ex Peck) Gilliam

COMMON NAME: None

FAMILY: Marasmiaceae

CAP: Up to 1½ in. wide; cinnamon brown, at times fading to tan of brownish buff, the center usually has a spot that is darker or paler than the rest of the cap; convex to broadly convex and finally flat with a depressed center; surface dry, bald, becoming wrinkled; shriveling when dry, reviving when wet

FLESH: Whitish to brownish; thin; tough; odor not distinctive; taste bitter or peppery, at times mild

GILLS: Whitish to pinkish buff; attached, notched, or, in age, nearly free; subdistant; edges even or slightly scalloped; no partial veil

STEM: Up to 2¾ in. long; buff to pinkish near the top, becoming dark reddish brown from the blackish base upward; equal or flaring upward, compressed at times; lower half of surface dry with grayish or whitish hairs, upper half of the surface dry, smooth, velvety, or with short, whitish hairs

SPORE PRINT: Creamy white

ECOLOGY: Saprobic; scattered to gregarious in leaf litter, humus, and on small twigs in broadleaf woodlands; summer and fall; common

EDIBILITY: Unknown

COMMENTS: Compare with *Gymnopus dichrous* (p. 149), which grows on wood and has a small, black bulb at the base of the stem.

Gymnopus subnudus

SCIENTIFIC NAME: *Gymnopus dichrous* (Berk. and M. A. Curtis) Halling

SYNONYM: *Collybia dichrous* (Berk. and M. A. Curtis) Gilliam

COMMON NAME: None

FAMILY: Marasmiaceae

CAP: Up to 1½ in. wide: dark brown to reddish brown, pale buff to whitish near the margin, becoming light brown to buff when old; convex with a turned-under margin at first, becoming nearly flat; surface dry, bald, slightly wrinkled at times, translucent striate in age

FLESH: White to brownish; thin; tough; odor and taste not distinctive

GILLS: White to pinkish buff, with brown stains in older fruitings; narrowly attached or free from the stem; subdistant; cross veined; no partial veil

STEM: Up to 2 in. long; whitish at first, soon becoming brownish; equal or enlarged at either end; hollow; flexible; with a swollen knob at the base; surface dry, finely hairy, or velvety

SPORE PRINT: White to cream

ECOLOGY: Saprobic on the wood of broadleaf trees; summer and fall; common

EDIBILITY: Unknown

COMMENTS: This is one of the species that shrivels in dry conditions and then revives in rainy weather. This cycle can be repeated several times. Compare with *Gymnopus subnudus* (p. 148), which grows on humus and litter and lacks the swollen base of the stem.

Gymnopus dichrous

SCIENTIFIC NAME: *Gymnopus dryophilus* (Bull.) Murrill

SYNONYM: *Collybia dryophila* (Bull.) P. Kumm.

COMMON NAME: Oak-Loving Collybia

FAMILY: Marasmiaceae

CAP: Up to 2½ in. wide; brown to yellowish tan; convex to flat; margin turned under at first and uplifted in age; surface moist, bald

FLESH: White or yellowish; thin; odor and taste not distinctive

GILLS: White, pale pinkish buff, or yellowish; free or barely reaching the stem; crowded; edges even

STEM: Up to 3½ in. long; whitish or colored like the cap but paler, especially at the apex; equal or enlarged at the base; surface moist, not viscid; flexible; hollow; usually with thin, whitish mycelial strands at the base

SPORE PRINT: Cream or whitish

ECOLOGY: Saprobic; scattered, gregarious or in clusters, at times in arcs or rings; in litter in broadleaf and conifer woodlands; summer and fall; very common

EDIBILITY: Not recommended since reports vary about the edibility of this mushroom, ranging from choice to poisonous; it is reported to accumulate heavy metals, which might be a factor in the mixed reviews; the author has not tried it

COMMENTS: *Rhodocollybia butyracea* (p. 227) is similar but has saw-toothed gill edges. *Gymnopus earleae* (not illustrated) is a similar spring species with a pale-tan cap.

Gymnopus dryophilus

SCIENTIFIC NAME: *Gymnopus luxurians* (Peck) Murrill

SYNONYM: *Collybia luxurians* Peck

COMMON NAME: None

FAMILY: Marasmiaceae

CAP: Up to 3 in. wide; dark reddish brown, fading to tan, margin often whitish; irregular, especially when growing in tight clusters, but generally convex to flat with an upturned margin in age; surface bald, dry or slightly tacky, not striate

FLESH: Whitish to pinkish buff; thick; odor not distinctive; taste unpleasant, bitter

GILLS: White to pinkish buff, brown spotted in age; attached and then pulling away from the stem; close to crowded; fairly broad; edges saw toothed or even, whitish; no partial veil

STEM: Up to 4¾ in. long; whitish above, buff to tan below, with brown stains; equal or enlarged at either end; dry; often twisted; tough; with fine hairs that are easily removable; usually with white mycelial strands at the base

SPORE PRINT: Creamy white

ECOLOGY: Saprobic; usually clustered, at times in groups, in wood chips or growing from buried roots; summer and fall; fairly common

EDIBILITY: Unknown

COMMENTS: This is a common mushroom in wood-mulched flower beds, where it may occur in dense clusters.

Gymnopus luxurians

SCIENTIFIC NAME: *Clitocybe gibba* (Pers.) P. Kumm.

SYNONYMS: *Infundibulicybe gibba* (Pers.) Harmaja, *Clitocybe infundibuliformis* Quél.

COMMON NAMES: Forest Funnel Cap, Funnel Clitocybe

FAMILY: Tricholomataceae

CAP: Up to 3½ in. wide; tan, pinkish tan, yellowish to whitish, especially toward the margin in old fruitings; flat with a central depression, becoming funnel-shaped; bald; dry or slightly moist; not striate or only faintly

FLESH: White or watery; thin; fragile; odor mild or resembling almonds; taste mealy or not distinctive

STEM: Up to 3 in. wide; whitish with white mycelium at the base; equal; dry; smooth; hollow in age; no ring

GILLS: Whitish; close to crowded; usually forked; decurrent; no partial veil

SPORE PRINT: White

ECOLOGY: Saprobic on humus in broadleaf forests, rarely under conifers; summer and fall; common

EDIBILITY: Edible

COMMENTS: This common species is reported by many authors as edible. The author has not tried it. A similar species that occurs under conifers is *Clitocybe squamulosa* (p. 153). It has a brown stem.

Clitocybe gibba

SCIENTIFIC NAME: *Clitocybe squamulosa* (Pers.) P. Kumm.

SYNONYM: *Infundibulicybe squamulosa* (Pers.) Harmaja

COMMON NAME: None

FAMILY: Tricholomotaceae

CAP: Up to 3½ in. wide; tan, brownish orange, paler at the margin in age; flat with a central depression, becoming funnel shaped; bald or fibrillose, may have small scales over the center; dry or slightly moist; not striate or only indistinctly so; no partial veil

FLESH: Whitish to pale buff or watery; thin; fragile; odor mild or mealy; taste not distinctive or slightly unpleasant

GILLS: Whitish to cream; close to crowded; usually forked; decurrent; edges even; no partial veil

STEM: Up to 3 in. long; colored like the cap; close to subdistant; decurrent; with white mycelium at the base; solid; equal or slightly enlarged at the base; surface dry, smooth, or fibrillose

Spore Print: White

ECOLOGY: Saprobic; single, scattered, or gregarious under conifers; summer and fall; occasional

EDIBILITY: Unknown

Comments: Compare with *Clitocybe gibba* (p. 152), which has a whitish stem and is usually under broadleaf trees.

Clitocybe squamulosa

SCIENTIFIC NAME: *Clitocybe robusta* Peck

SYNONYMS: *Lepista robusta* (Peck) Harmaja, *Clitocybe alba* (Bataille) Singer

COMMON NAME: None

FAMILY: Tricholomataceae

CAP: Up to 7 in. wide; white, becoming buff or tan in age; convex at first, becoming nearly flat in age; bald; smooth; dry or slightly viscid in wet weather; margin curved under at first

FLESH: White; thick; odor pungent and unpleasant; taste rancid, unpleasant

GILLS: White, becoming pale buff in age; close to crowded; sometimes forked; even; broadly attached to the stem

STEM: Up to 4 in. long; white to buff; solid, becoming hollow in age; equal down to a club-shaped or bulbous base; surface dry, fibrillose

SPORE PRINT: Pale yellowish

ECOLOGY: Saprobic, usually scattered to gregarious or clustered under broadleaf trees but also in mixed woods; late summer and fall; common

EDIBILITY: Reportedly edible but not palatable

COMMENTS: The unpleasant odor will separate this species from *Lepista irina* (not illustrated) which has a pleasant fragrance and pale pinkish-buff spores. Species of *Leucopaxillus* may appear similar but they also lack the unpleasant odor. This is a robust species commonly found partially covered by fallen leaves.

Clitocybe robusta

SCIENTIFIC NAME: *Ampulloclitocybe clavipes* (Pers.) Redhead, Lutzoni, Moncalvo & Vilgalys

SYNONYM: *Clitocybe clavipes* (Pers.) P. Kumm.

COMMON NAME: Club Foot

FAMILY: Hygrophoraceae

CAP: Up to 3 in. wide; brown to grayish brown or olive brown, at times pale gray especially near the margin; broadly convex to flat, at times becoming funnel-shaped, may have a broad umbo; surface bald, moist

FLESH: Whitish, watery; thick; odor slightly fragrant or fruity; taste mild

STEM: Up to 2½ in. long; colored like the cap or at times buff or whitish; solid becoming hollow; equal down to a basal bulb which usually has a white mycelium coating

GILLS: Whitish or cream colored; close to subdistant; decurrent; sometimes forking

SPORE PRINT: White

ECOLOGY: Saprobic; scattered to gregarious; most common under conifers in late summer but may be found earlier or later in the season; occasional under broadleaf trees and mixed woods; summer and fall; common

EDIBILITY: Not recommended; headaches and rashes have been reported when this species has been consumed with alcohol

COMMENTS: This can be a very common mushroom in pine plantations. It sometimes forms arcs or circles. The common name Club Foot refers to the fact that most fruitings have an enlarged bulb at the bottom of the stem.

Ampulloclitocybe clavipes

SCIENTIFIC NAME: *Baeospora myosura* (Fr.) Singer

SYNONYM: None

COMMON NAME: Conifer Cone Baeospora

FAMILY: Marasmiaceae

CAP: Up to ¾ in. wide; buff with a tan center; convex, becoming broadly convex to nearly flat; surface moist, smooth, bald to slightly velvety

FLESH: Whitish; very thin; odor and taste not distinctive

GILLS: Whitish; free from the stem or barely attached; crowded; narrow; no partial veil

STEM: Up to 2 in. long; white to brownish; equal; hollow; surface hairy to powdery, base with long, white hairs

SPORE PRINT: White

ECOLOGY: Saprobic; usually gregarious on pine and spruce cones; summer and fall; fairly common

EDIBILITY: Unknown; too small to be of culinary value

COMMENTS: The growth on cones and the very crowded gills distinguish this species.

Baeospora myosura

SCIENTIFIC NAME: *Baeospora myriadophylla* (Peck) Singer

SYNONYM: *Mycena myriadophylla* (Peck) Kühner

COMMON NAME: None

FAMILY: Marasmiaceae

CAP: Up to 1½ in. wide; lavender, buff to brownish ochre in age; convex to nearly flat, center becoming depressed; surface bald, smooth, hygrophanous

FLESH: Grayish; very thin; odor and taste not distinctive

GILLS: Lavender, becoming paler in age, becoming tinged ochre brown; attached, becoming nearly free in age; crowded; edges even; no partial veil

STEM: Up to 2 in. long; lavender becoming brownish; equal, cylindrical, or compressed; becoming hollow; surface dry, smooth, base with long, lavender hairs

SPORE PRINT: White

ECOLOGY: Saprobic on decaying wood, often on hemlock; scattered to gregarious; spring, summer, and fall; occasional but fruits regularly in the same site

EDIBILITY: Unknown

COMMENTS: The crowded gills, lavender color when young, and habitat on wood set this mushroom apart from other small mushrooms.

Baeospora myriadophylla

SCIENTIFIC NAME: *Laccaria amethystina* Cooke

SYNONYM: None

COMMON NAME: Amethyst Deceiver

FAMILY: Hydnangiaceae

CAP: Up to 1¾ in. wide; purple, grayish purple, fading to pale reddish violet in age, often darker on the disc; convex to flat, at times with a central depression; surface dry, bald, at times faintly translucent striate

FLESH: Colored like the cap, only paler; thin; odor and taste not distinctive

GILLS: Dark purple or colored like the cap; broadly attached to the stem or subdecurrent; subdistant to distant; thick; no partial veil

STEM: Up to 3 in. long; reddish buff or colored like the cap, only paler; equal or slightly enlarged at the base; finely to coarsely hairy; base with lilac or whitish mycelium

SPORE PRINT: White

ECOLOGY: Mycorrhizal with oak and beech; solitary, scattered, or gregarious in lawns and woodlands; occasional, locally abundant

EDIBILITY: Edible and reportedly quite good; the author has not tried it; its small size makes finding enough for a side dish a challenge

COMMENTS: The small size, purple colors, terrestrial habitat, and white spores make for a distinctive set of characters.

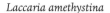

Laccaria amethystina

SCIENTIFIC NAME: *Laccaria ochropurpurea* (Berk.) Peck

SYNONYM: None

COMMON NAME: Purple Gilled Laccaria

FAMILY: Hydnangiaceae

CAP: Up to 5 in. wide; pale lilac buff; grayish buff to whitish; convex becoming flat with a depressed center and uplifted margin; bald, at times fibrous or with fine scales; not striate; margin turned under at first

FLESH: Colored like the cap but paler; thick; firm; tough; odor and taste not distinctive

GILLS: Light to dark purple; attached to subdecurrent; subdistant; rather thick; edges even

STEM: Up to 6 in. long; colored like the cap; equal or swollen at the base, sometimes markedly; solid; surface coarsely fibrous; base with violet or whitish mycelium

SPORE PRINT: Whitish to pale lilac

ECOLOGY: Mycorrhizal; scattered to gregarious in lawns and woodland litter under oak and other broadleaf trees, and also under white pine; summer and fall; common

EDIBILITY: Edible but rather bland

COMMENTS: The white spore print and lack of a cortina will help distinguish this species. It often fruits toward the end of a period when numerous mushroom species have been abundant. *Laccaria trullisata* is similar but occurs in sand, which usually adheres to the fruiting body.

Laccaria ochropurpurea

SCIENTIFIC NAME: *Hymenopellis furfuracea* (Peck) R. H. Petersen

SYNONYMS: *Xerula furfuracea* (Peck) Redhead, Ginns, and Shoemaker, *Oudemansiella radicata* var. *furfuracea* (Peck) Pegler and T. W. K. Young, *Collybia radicata* var. *furfuracea* Peck

COMMON NAME: Rooting Agaric

FAMILY: Physalacriaceae

CAP: Up to 5½ in. wide; brown to grayish brown, darkest on the umbo; convex to flat, with a central umbo; wrinkled around the umbo; velvety at first; surface bald, moist to tacky, or viscid in wet weather, not striate

FLESH: White; thin; odor and taste not distinctive

GILLS: White; attached to the stem but often pulling away, leaving a gill remnant on the stem; subdistant; fairly broad; edges even

STEM: Up to 10 in. long; underground "root" may double the length in extreme cases; apex pale whitish, most of the area below is whitish; equal down to an enlarged base, then becoming much thinner underground; fibrous, rather tough; surface dry, covered with brownish-gray fibers that sometime separate into a snakeskin pattern

SPORE PRINT: White

ECOLOGY: Saprobic; solitary to scattered, often appearing terrestrial but growing from buried wood of broadleaf trees, occasionally above ground from very rotten stumps; summer and fall; common

EDIBILITY: The caps are edible but of mediocre quality

COMMENTS: This genus of white-spored mushrooms is typified by an underground extension of the stem, also known as a false root. *Hymenopellis megalospora* (not illustrated) is a very common parkland species. Its cap is mostly white or grayish, and its stem is not furfuraceous. Over the author's collecting years, these species have been placed in four different genera owing to advancements in taxonomy. Recent studies indicate these species may be returned to the genus *Oudemansiella*. They are the same rather distinctive mushrooms regardless of what name mycologists choose to call them.

Hymenopellis furfuracea

SCIENTIFIC NAME: *Marasmius nigrodiscus* (Peck) Halling

SYNONYM: *Gymnopus nigrodiscus* (Peck) Murrill

COMMON NAME: None

FAMILY: Marasmiaceae

CAP: Up to 4 in. wide; center tan to yellowish brown fading to whitish toward the margin; convex to flat, with a slight flattened umbo; surface dry, bald, hygrophanous, smooth, or wrinkled, with translucent striations when wet

FLESH: Whitish; thin; odor not distinctive, or of bitter almonds or camphor when crushed; taste mild, slightly mealy to slightly bitter

GILLS: White to creamy or pinkish; attached to notched, with a decurrent tooth on the stem, or almost free from the stem; close at first becoming subdistant; edges even; no partial veil

STEM: Up to 4 in. long; whitish or tinted the color of the cap; equal or tapering upward; twisted at times; surface dry, fibrous, with longitudinal grooves

SPORE PRINT: White to pale buff or slightly olivaceous

ECOLOGY: Solitary, scattered, but usually gregarious or in small clusters on humus, soil, and well-decayed wood in broadleaf, conifer, and mixed woods; summer to early fall; occasional

EDIBILITY: Reported to be edible; the author has not tried it

COMMENTS: This is the largest species of *Marasmius*. It resembles *Marasmius cystidiosus* (not illustrated), which differs in having pinkish colors near the margin and not being striate, and is also slightly smaller.

Marasmius nigrodiscus

SCIENTIFIC NAME: *Cantharellula umbonata* (J. F. Gmel.) Singer

SYNONYM: *Hygrophoropsis umbonata* (J. F. Gmel.) Kühner and Romagn.

COMMON NAME: The Grayling

FAMILY: Tricholomataceae

CAP: Up to 2 in. wide; gray to grayish brown, margin slightly paler, at times with white patches; convex to flat and at times funnel-shaped, often with an umbo; surface dry to moist, bald or minutely fibrillose, at times becoming wrinkled; margin turned under at first, upturned in age

FLESH: White; thin; odor and taste not distinctive

GILLS: Whitish to gray, at times with reddish spots; subdecurrent; close to crowded; narrow; repeatedly forking; edges even; no partial veil

STEM: Up to 5 in. long; white to pinkish buff or pale gray; equal; moist, somewhat flexible; surface bald to silky; the base often with a pad of white mycelium that is often water soaked; often bent or twisted

SPORE PRINT: White

ECOLOGY: Saprobic; associated with *Polytrichum* and other mosses; usually scattered to gregarious, occasionally in arcs or circles; summer and fall; fairly common

EDIBILITY: Edible and reportedly quite good

COMMENTS: The occurrence in moss is a key identification feature, along with the equal stem and subdecurrent white gills.

Cantharellula umbonata

SCIENTIFIC NAME: *Xeromphalina kauffmanii* A. H. Smith

SYNONYM: None

COMMON NAME: None

FAMILY: Mycenaceae

CAP: Up to 1 in wide; orange yellow, brownish orange at the center; convex to broadly convex, with a depressed center; surface bald, shiny, becoming striate at times

FLESH: Yellowish; thin; odor and taste not distinctive

GILLS: Pale yellow to pale orange; decurrent; subdistant to distant; cross-veined; edges even; no partial veil

STEM: Up to 2 in. long; yellow above, dark reddish brown below; equal or tapering downward; rather tough; smooth or scurfy downward; base with a tuft of tawny mycelium

SPORE PRINT: White

ECOLOGY: Saprobic or mildly parasitic; densely gregarious in large groups or in clusters, at times in smaller groups on dead and living wood of broadleaf trees; summer and fall; common

EDIBILITY: Not edible

COMMENTS: Its twin-like sister species, *Xeromphalina campanella* (not illustrated), is common on conifer wood, especially hemlock. The photo here was taken on a living wild cherry tree.

Xeromphalina kauffmanii

SCIENTIFIC NAME: *Xeromphalina tenuipes* (Schwein.) A. H. Smith

SYNONYM: None

COMMON NAME: Cross-Veined Mushroom

FAMILY: Mycenaceae

CAP: Up to 2½ in. wide; rusty brownish orange, yellowish toward the margin; convex to broadly convex, becoming flat, often with a broad umbo; surface dry, velvety, or smooth, obscurely striate or lacking striations

FLESH: Watery, brown; thin; odor not distinctive; taste bitter

GILLS: White to yellow; attached, pulling away and often leaving a subdecurrent line on the upper stem; usually cross-veined; close to subdistant; edges even; no partial veil

STEM: Up to 3 in. long; similar in color to the cap or dark brownish orange or brown, usually darkening from the base upward; equal or with a swollen base; compressed at times; surface dry, with a coating of fine, dense, reddish-brown to rusty-orange hairs

SPORE PRINT: White to cream

ECOLOGY: Saprobic; scattered to gregarious on logs, stumps, woody debris of broadleaf trees, especially beech, also on wood chips; late spring and summer; locally abundant

EDIBILITY: Not edible

COMMENTS: This attractive mushroom appears shortly after morel season. The fuzzy stem and general aspect are reminiscent of *Flammulina velutipes* (p. 165), which has a viscid cap and black fuzz on its lower stem.

Xeromphalina tenuipes

SCIENTIFIC NAME: *Flammulina velutipes* (Curtis) Singer

SYNONYM: *Collybia velutipes* (Curtis) P. Kumm.

COMMON NAMES: Winter Mushroom, Velvet Stem

FAMILY: Physalacriaceae

CAP: Up to 2¾ in. wide; orange, yellowish orange, orangish brown, darkest at the center; convex, becoming flat in age; surface bald, slimy when wet, tacky when dry

FLESH: Yellowish; watery; thin; odor pleasant or not distinctive; taste mild

GILLS: Cream to pale yellow; barely attached to the stem or notched, at times subdecurrent; subdistant; broad; edges minutely hairy; no partial veil

STEM: Up to 3 in. long; pale yellowish brown to brownish orange when young, in age brown or blackish brown from a covering of hairs; velvety; generally equal; tough; at times hollow in age

SPORE PRINT: White

ECOLOGY: Saprobic; gregarious to clustered on the wood of broadleaf trees, especially elm, often fruiting from debarked areas; fall, spring, and during thaws in the winter; fairly common

EDIBILITY: Edible and good; the stems are tough and should be discarded; cleaning is a problem as debris sticks to the sticky caps; partial drying before frying is recommended

COMMENTS: When cultivated in dark conditions with high levels of carbon dioxide, the winter mushroom takes on a completely different appearance. The stems are long, the caps are tiny, and the entire fruit body is whitish. It is available in many grocery stores under the name Enoki or Enokitake. It has a mild taste similar to radishes. The wild variety has a sweet flavor when cooked.

Flammulina velutipes

SCIENTIFIC NAME: *Rickenella fibula* (Bull.) Raithelh.

SYNONYM: *Mycena fibula* (Bull.) Kühner

COMMON NAME: Orange Moss Cap

FAMILY: Rickenellaceae

CAP: Up to ½ in. wide; yellowish orange to brownish orange, darkest at the center, which is often depressed, fading in age; convex to broadly convex; surface pruinose, becoming bald, translucent striate, tacky when fresh, soon becoming dry

FLESH: Pale; extremely thin; odor and taste not distinctive

GILLS: Creamy to very pale orange; decurrent; subdistant to distant; edges even; no partial veil

STEM: Up to 2 in. long; yellowish orange to pale yellow, lighter in areas, especially at the base; fragile; hollow; surface dry to moist, finely hairy at first, becoming bald

SPORE PRINT: White

ECOLOGY: Saprobic or possibly in a symbiotic relationship with moss; scattered to gregarious in moss; spring, summer, and fall; common

EDIBILITY: Not edible

COMMENTS: This is one of many small mushrooms found in moss. The cap colors, white spore print, and decurrent gills are distinctive.

Rickenella fibula

SCIENTIFIC NAME: *Cystoderma amianthinum* (Scop.) Fayod

SYNONYMS: *Cystoderma amianthinum* var. *rugosoreticulatum*
(F. Lorinser) Bon

COMMON NAME: Corn Silk Cystoderma

FAMILY: Cystodermataceae

CAP: Up to 1¾ in. wide; pale tan, yellowish tan, pale orangish yellow or brownish; convex to broadly convex and finally flat; nearly smooth or densely granular over the center; often wrinkled; margin often with flaps of veil tissue

FLESH: White; thin; firm; odor strong, reminiscent of sweet corn or corn silk; taste not distinctive, or unpleasant

GILLS: White, at times pale orangish yellow at maturity; attached to the stem or notched; close; edges even or slightly irregular; no partial veil

STEM: Up to 2½ in. long; apex sheathed up to the ring with pale-buff to tan granules, scales, and fibers; pale yellowish to tan above the ring; more or less equal; apex smooth or appressed fibrillose; apical or mid-stem ring is fibrillose, indistinct or at times well-formed

SPORE PRINT: White

ECOLOGY: Saprobic; solitary or in small groups, in moss or needle litter under conifers; summer and fall; more common in northern areas and at higher altitudes

EDIBILITY: Unknown, too small to be of much interest

COMMENTS: Some find the odor of this attractive little mushroom unpleasant. While strong, the author finds it quite pleasant. The frequent association with mosses has not been explained and may indicate a possible symbiotic or parasitic relationship.

Cystoderma amianthinum

SCIENTIFIC NAME: *Leucocoprinus fragilissimus* (Ravenel ex Berk. and M. A. Curtis) Pat.

SYNONYM: *Lepiota fragilissima* (Ravenel ex Berk. and M. A. Curtis) Morgan

COMMON NAME: None

FAMILY: **Agaricaceae**

CAP: Up to 1¾ in. wide; white with a yellowish center; ovate to bell-shaped, becoming flat with a central dark-yellow to tan umbo; at times powdery yellow around the umbo; grooved from the center to the margin; very fragile

FLESH: Whitish or yellowish; very thin and fragile, disintegrating quickly in hot weather; odor and taste not distinctive

GILLS: White or yellowish; free; narrow; distant; often dissolving in hot weather; edges even; covered at first by a whitish partial veil

STEM: Up to 5 in. long; pale yellow, grayish yellow, or whitish; with whitish to yellowish fibers; equal or enlarged downward, at times with a basal bulb; very fragile, often collapsing by mid-afternoon; with a membranous, upturned, whitish, or yellowish ring

SPORE PRINT: White

ECOLOGY: Solitary or scattered on humus in mixed woods; occasional, more common southward

EDIBILITY: Unknown

COMMENTS: This mushroom is best observed in the morning, because by afternoon it will be wilted and collapsed. When at its freshest, it is a striking little mushroom.

Leucocoprinus fragilissimus

SCIENTIFIC NAME: *Panus neostrigosus* Drechsler-Santos and Wartchow

SYNONYMS: *Lentinus strigosus* (Pers.) Fr., *Panus rudis* Fr., *Panus lecomtei* (Fr.) Corner

COMMON NAMES: Hairy Panus, Ruddy Panus

FAMILY: Polyporaceae

CAP: Up to 3 in. wide; purplish at first, becoming reddish brown and finally pinkish tan; kidney- to fan-shaped, broadly funnel-shaped at times; surface dry, densely hairy, may be finely cracked in the center

FLESH: White; tough; thin; odor not distinctive; taste slightly bitter

GILLS: Violet or whitish, becoming yellowish tan in age; decurrent; close; edges even; no partial veil

STEM: Up to 1 in. long; colored like the cap, only paler; short; eccentric, laterally attached, or central when fruiting on top of a stump, absent at times; tough, surface dry, densely hairy

SPORE PRINT: White to cream

ECOLOGY: Saprobic on the wood of broadleaf trees; spring through fall; fairly common

EDIBILITY: Not recommended; while not poisonous, it is tough and hairy

COMMENTS: This species can often be found on the stumps of recently cut broadleaf trees. It is most common in dry, exposed areas rather than in deep woods.

Panus neostrigosus

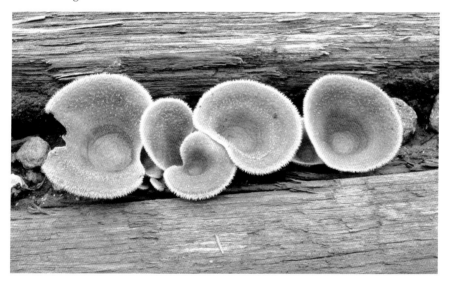

SCIENTIFIC NAME: *Panellus stipticus* (Bull.) P. Karst
SYNONYMS: *Panus stipticus* (Bull.) Fr.
COMMON NAME: **Luminescent Panellus**
FAMILY: **Tricholomataceae**

CAP: Up to 1¼ in. wide; tan; buff or dingy white after frosts, becoming brownish with white scales or patches; semicircular to kidney-shaped or irregular; surface dry, velvety at times, or finely scaly or scurfy

FLESH: Whitish to pale yellowish brown; tough; odor not distinctive; taste variously described as bitter, acrid, and astringent

GILLS: Colored like the cap or paler, becoming rusty brown in winter; attached; close to crowded; cross-veined; edges even or irregular at times; no partial veil

STEM: Up to ¾ in. long; whitish to brownish; very short; eccentric or lateral; surface dry, with white or tan fuzzy hairs

SPORE PRINT: White

ECOLOGY: Saprobic; gregarious or in shelving clusters on the dead wood of broadleaf trees; summer, fall, and early winter; common

EDIBILITY: Not edible

COMMENTS: *Crepidotus* species are similar but are very fragile and have brown spores. *Schizophyllum commune* (p. 171) looks similar, but it has split-edged gills and a fuzzy cap. This little tan mushroom's claim to fame is that when observed in a dark situation, the gills emit a greenish light. It is a reviving species, so it can be collected in dry weather and reconstituted later, and the gills will still glow. It usually takes a few minutes for the eyes to adjust to see the phenomenon. The function of its bioluminescent gills is unknown. Its name refers to it reportedly being used as a styptic to stop bleeding.

Panellus stipticus

SCIENTIFIC NAME: *Schizophyllum commune* Fr.

SYNONYM: None

COMMON NAME: Split Gill

FAMILY: Schizophyllaceae

CAP: Up to 2 in. wide; white to grayish or tan; fan- to shell-shaped or irregular; surface dry to slightly moist, densely hairy; margin incurved, becoming nearly flat when wet

FLESH: Whitish or grayish, brownish at times in age; tough, leathery; odor and taste not distinctive

GILLS: White, gray, or pinkish gray; at times saw-toothed, torn, or irregular; subdistant, narrow; split lengthwise on the edges; no partial veil

STEM: Absent, or a very short extension of the cap

SPORE PRINT: White

ECOLOGY: Saprobic; scattered or in overlapping clusters on the dead wood of broadleaf trees; all seasons; common

EDIBILITY: Not recommended; considered not edible but consumed in some cultures

COMMENTS: The split-edged gills distinguish this species. It is a remarkable, fleshy fungus. It has been found infecting humans with weakened immune systems. Non-fruiting growths of this fungus have been found in the respiratory tract of a newborn baby and on aboriginal toenails. It shrivels in dry conditions and revives in wet weather. *Panellus stipticus* (p. 179) has a similar aspect. Its luminescent gills are not split, and its cap is not hairy.

Schizophyllum commune

COLORED-SPORED MUSHROOMS

WITH SPORE COLORS ranging from salmon pink to black, and including green and many shades of brown, most of the genera here are
saprobes or parasites.

The mostly saprobic, brown-spored genera include *Pholiota*, *Gymnopilus*,
Agrocybe, *Tapinella*, *Crepidotus*, *Galerina*, *Conocybe*, *Simocybe*, and *Bolbitius*. The
saprobic genera with purplish-brown to black spores include *Coprinellus*, *Coprinopsis*, *Coprinus*, *Hypholoma*, *Psathyrella*, *Lacrymaria*, *Gomphidius*, *Stropharia*,
and *Agaricus*.

Inocybe and *Hebeloma* have dull-brown spores and are mycorrhizal species
associated with various tree species. Keys use habitat, spore color, size, and the
presence or absence of a partial veil. The pink-spored group includes species
with ruddy or salmon spores. These are saprobes and parasites and include
Pluteus, *Entoloma*, *Clitopilus*, *Volvariella*, and *Rhodocollybia*.

Pluteus cervinus complex

Lacrymaria lacrymabunda

Agrocybe aceracola

Coprinopsis acuminata

Galerina marginata

Cortinarius is the largest genus of terrestrial, gilled mushrooms, and they can be found on soil, moss, or humus. They are mycorrhizal with a variety of trees. There are likely over one thousand species. They have rusty-brown spores and range in size from small to large. The colors range from white to nearly black. Many are brown or violet. When young, there is a web-like cortina of fibers extending from the cap margin to the stem. When the cap expands, remnants of the cortina can usually be seen as fibers on the stem where they may be spore stained. A few have membranous rings on the stem. Spore prints are typically rusty brown. Only a relatively few species can be identified in the field. Fourteen species are included here. Average cap size here is 3 inches in diameter or smaller for small mushrooms, and 3 inches and larger for medium to large capped species.

Top row (left and right), *Cortinarius* species
Bottom row (left), *Cortinarius* species; (right), *Cortinarius traganus*
Note the web-like cortina from the stem to the cap margin in young caps. The older specimens show spore-stained cortina remnants on the stem.

Keys to Colored-Spored Mushrooms

Cortinarius mushrooms

Cap with a membranous ring on the stem

1. Cap dry; gills distant; medium to large size: *Cortinarius torvus* (p. 193)
2. Cap dry; gills close; medium to large size: *Cortinarius squamulosus* (p. 192)
3. Cap moist to dry; cap yellow to ochre; rather fragile: *Cortinarius caperatus* (p. 190)

Red- or orange-colored gills

1. Cap and gills red: *Cortinarius harrisonii* (p. 182)
2. Cap brownish, gills orange: *Cortinarius cinnamomeus* (p. 181)
3. Cap tawny to yellowish, gills blood red: *Cortinarius semisanguineus* (p. 180)

Viscid cap, smooth or wrinkled, and without a ring

1. Cap smooth; rich reddish orange: *Cortinarius mucosus* (p. 187)
2. Cap wrinkled; yellowish orange to tawny brown: *Cortinarius corrugatus* (p. 185)
3. Cap smooth; orange to yellowish buff; lower stem with shaggy, brownish scales: *Cortinarius trivialis* (p. 188)
4. Cap smooth; purple; convex to flat; small to medium size: *Cortinarius iodes* (p. 189)

Scaly or fibrillose cap at least over the center

1. Medium to large; cap reddish orange to brownish yellow; stem lacking orange bands: *Cortinarius limonius* (p. 183)
2. Medium to large cap; reddish orange to brownish yellow; stem with orange bands: *Cortinarius armillatus* (p. 184)
3. Small to medium cap; light brown to buff: *Cortinarius pholideus* (p. 186)
4. Medium to large; cap dry; silver to pale lilac; convex to flat; odor fruity: *Cortinarius traganus* (p. 191)

Other colored-spored mushrooms

Medium to large mushrooms on wood, with salmon to ruddy-brown spores

1. Gills free; cap hairy; stem with a large, sack-like volva: *Volvariella bombycina* (p. 194)
2. Gills free; cap white; cap tomentose: *Pluteus tomentosulus* (p. 195)

3. Gills free; cap pale to dark brown; not scaly: *Pluteus cervinus* (p. 196)

4. Gills free; cap whitish to pale brown; scales present on the cap center: *Pluteus petasatus* (p. 197)

5. Gills attached; cap buff to orange; with brown spots; gills yellowish: *Rhodocollybia maculata.* var. *scorzonerea* (p. 198)

6. Gills attached; cap silvery to tan or brownish; stem tall and twisted: *Entoloma strictius* var. *isabellinum* (p. 199)

7. Gills decurrent; cap gray to grayish brown; accompanied by cauliflower-like growths: *Entoloma abortivum* (p. 200)

8. Stem absent, or nearly so; cap orange to yellowish orange; fuzzy; shelving; odor often unpleasant: *Phyllotopsis nidulans* (p. 201)

Small and medium mushrooms on wood, with spores various shades of brown

1. On charred wood or burnt wood debris: *Pholiota highlandensis* (p. 202)

2. On dead conifer wood; stem blackish brown and hairy: *Tapinella atrotomentosa* (p. 206)

3. On dead conifer wood; stem lacking; fan-shaped; gills crimped or wrinkled: *Tapinella panuoides* (p. 207)

4. On dead wood; stem absent, or nearly so; cap orange to yellowish orange; fuzzy; shelving; spores pinkish brown; odor often unpleasant: *Phyllotopsis nidulans* (p. 201)

5. Clustered on dead broadleaf wood; cap with raised, tawny scales: *Pholiota squarrosoides* (p. 203)

6. On dead wood; cap with reddish-brown, irregular to triangular, flattened scales: *Pholiota aurivella* (p. 204)

7. On dead wood, often on buried roots; clustered; cap with flattened, brown scales: *Pholiota angustipes* (p. 205)

8. On dead wood; cap brown to yellowish brown; bald: *Galerina marginata* (p. 208)

9. On dead broadleaf wood; cap blackish brown, fading in age; no partial veil: *Agrocybe firma* (p. 211)

10. On dead wood; cap orange to yellowish orange; fragrant odor; bitter taste: *Gymnopilus luteus* (p. 209)

11. On wood; cap with brown scales; gills orange; stem lacking: *Crepidotus crocophyllus* (p. 210)

On wood or buried wood, with purplish-brown to black spores and a partial veil

1. Cap honey colored, becoming white; not scaly; often on buried wood: *Psathyrella candolleana* (p. 212)

2. Cap mostly white, with white to reddish-brown scales; cap tall and longer than its width; usually on buried wood: *Coprinus comatus* (p. 221)

3. Cap hyaline to whitish, with prominent tan scales overall, squat; on wood: *Coprinopsis varieagata* (p. 220)

4. Cap gray to grayish brown; cap center scaly at times; squat; usually on buried wood: *Coprinopsis atramentaria* (p. 219)

5. Cap brown and wrinkled; on dead, broadleaf tree wood: *Psathyrella delineata* (p. 213)

6. Cap wine red, fading to buff in age; stem ring grooved above, with claw-like hooks on the underside; usually on wood mulch: *Stropharia rugosoannulata* (p. 217)

7. Cap yellow to brownish yellow; on broadleaf tree wood; often from buried roots; stem with white rhizomorphs: *Stropharia hardii* (p. 218)

8. Cap tawny, with prominent black hairs; on broadleaf tree wood: *Psathyrella echiniceps* (p. 214)

9. Cap brick red with a yellow or buff margin; on broadleaf tree wood: *Hypholoma lateritium* (p. 215)

10. Cap reddish orange to pale yellowish orange; on conifer wood: *Hypholoma capnoides* (p. 216)

On soil or humus, medium to large, with colored spores and lacking a cortina

1. Spores black to gray; cap glutinous; no stem ring: *Gomphidius glutinosus* (p. 222)

2. Spores purplish brown; cap yellowish; with a stem ring; at times on wood: *Stropharia hardii* (p. 218)

3. Spores dark brown; cap whitish; large size; with a stem ring; odor of anise: *Agaricus arvensis* (p. 223)

4. Spores chocolate brown; cap whitish, medium size; with a ring; no anise odor: *Agaricus campestris* (p. 224)

5. Spores rusty brown; cap with brown scales; partial veil seldom forms a ring; clustered; at times on wood: *Pholiota angustipes* (p. 205)

6. Spores salmon to reddish brown; cap whitish; no stem ring; odor of yeast or bread dough: *Clitopilus prunulus* (p. 225)

7. Spores salmon to reddish brown; cap whitish with cracks; no stem ring: *Clitocella mundula* (p. 226)

8. Spores salmon to reddish brown; cap silver tan or brownish; no stem ring; stem tall and twisted: *Entoloma strictius* var. *isabellinum* (p. 199)

9. Spores pinkish buff; cap bay to reddish brown; gills barely reaching the stem; no stem ring: *Rhodocollybia butyracea* (p. 227)

10. Spores salmon to reddish brown; accompanied by cauliflower-like growths; no stem ring; at times on wood: *Entoloma abortivum* (p. 200)

11. Spores greenish; cap white with brownish patches or scales; with a stem ring: *Chlorophyllum molybdites* (p. 108)

Small and fragile colored-spored mushrooms in various habitats

1. On wood; surrounded by a mat of orange mycelium: *Coprinellus domesticus* (p. 228)

2. On wood; stem absent; cap with brown scales; gills orangish: *Crepidotus crocophyllus* (p. 210)

3. On wood, often wood that is buried; cap usually with shiny granules: *Coprinellus micaceus* (p. 229)

4. On wood; cap brown; margin pale buff; odor of fish or cucumbers: *Macrocystidia cucumis* (p. 235)

5. On wood; cap reddish orange to reddish brown; viscid; fragile: *Bolbitius callistus* (p. 231)

6. On woody debris or manured straw or humus; cap yellowish; viscid; fragile: *Bolbitius titubans* (p. 230)

7. On lawns or wood-rich humus; cap white to buff: *Conocybe apala* (p. 233)

8. On humus or moss; cap orange; spores salmon: *Entoloma quadratum* (p. 236)

9. On humus or moss; cap yellow; spores salmon: *Entoloma murrayi* (p. 237)

10. On humus or moss; cap blackish brown to purplish brown or reddish brown; fibrous: *Inocybe tahquamenonensis* (p. 239)

11. On humus or moss; cap buff to tawny; surface fibrous wooly: *Inocybe unicolor* (p. 242)

12. On humus or moss; cap pinkish to grayish cinnamon; conical; stem purplish brown with white mycelium: *Entoloma conicum* (p. 238)

13. On humus or moss; cap yellowish to reddish tan; surface splitting in a spoke-like pattern: *Inocybe rimosa* (p. 241)

14. On humus or moss; cap purplish; cap dry; conical; odor of crushed flesh unpleasant: *Inocybe lilacina* (p. 240)

15. On aborted *Coprinus comatus*: *Psathyrella epimyces* (p. 243)

16. On aborted *Clitocybe* species: *Volvariella surrecta* (p. 244)

SCIENTIFIC NAME: *Cortinarius semisanguineus* (Fr.) Gillet

SYNONYM: *Dermocybe semisanguinea* (Fr.) M. M. Moser

COMMON NAME: Red-Gilled Cort

FAMILY: Cortinariaceae

CAP: Up to 2½ in. wide; bright golden yellow, tawny, becoming tan to brownish buff in age or after frosts; convex or bell-shaped, becoming broadly convex and then flat, at time with a broad, central umbo; surface dry, not striate, fibrillose; margin turned under at first

FLESH: Whitish to pale yellowish; odor not distinctive, or radish-like; taste mild or slightly bitter

GILLS: Blood red to rusty red; close to subdistant; attached to the stem but pulling away from it in age; at first covered by an ample, yellowish cortina

STEM: Up to 2½ in. long; usually yellow but at times whitish or orange, the base is often yellowish orange; equal; solid; fibrillose; spore-stained fibrous remnants of the cortina sometimes form a ringed zone on the upper stem

SPORE PRINT: Rusty brown

ECOLOGY: Mycorrhizal; scattered in mixed woods in humus or moss, most often under conifers, especially two-needle pines; often found in poor soil; summer and fall; common

EDIBILITY: Not edible

COMMENTS: The contrast of the blood-red gills and golden-yellow cap sets this species apart as one of the most beautiful mushrooms. It is common under planted pines, often in reclaimed mining areas. It is a favorite with those using mushrooms for dyeing.

Cortinarius semisanguineus

SCIENTIFIC NAME: *Cortinarius cinnamomeus* (L.) Fr.

SYNONYM: *Dermocybe cinnamomea* (L.) Wünsche

COMMON NAME: Cinnamon Cort

FAMILY: Cortinariaceae

CAP: Up to 2 in. broad; cinnamon buff, yellowish brown, or reddish brown, paler near the margin; convex, becoming broadly convex, sometimes with a low umbo; surface dry, bald, fibrillose at times

FLESH: Yellowish, sometimes with olive or cinnamon tones; firm; odor and taste not distinctive

GILLS: Orange becoming brownish orange; adnate or notched; subdistant; edges even; when young, with a yellow cortina that becomes brown stained from the spores and soon disappears

STEM: Up to 3 in. long; yellow, yellowish brown to orangish, becoming reddish brown in age; equal or slightly enlarged toward the base; with remnants of the cortina, which are brown from the spores falling on them; base with yellowish mycelium

SPORE PRINT: Rusty Brown

ECOLOGY: Mycorrhizal with conifers, especially pines; in Europe it is reported to form mycorrhiza with sedges; scattered to gregarious in humus and moss; late summer and fall; fairly common

EDIBILITY: Poisonous

COMMENTS: There are many questions surrounding this species. It was described from Europe. North American collections may include one or more species that have yet to be described. The mushroom described and illustrated here is typical of our pine-associated species.

Cortinarius cinnamomeus

SCIENTIFIC NAME: *Cortinarius harrisonii* Ammirati, Niskanen, and Liimat

SYNONYM: None

COMMON NAME: None

FAMILY: **Cortinariaceae**

CAP: Up to 2½ in. wide; bright brick red to brownish red, fading in age; in very wet conditions yellow may bleed through the red; convex or bell-shaped, becoming broadly convex to flat, at times with a broad central umbo; surface dry, silky to fibrillose, at times finely scaly

FLESH: Whitish becoming reddish brown in age; odor and taste not distinctive

GILLS: Bright brick red, becoming brownish red in age; close to subdistant; attached to the stem; broad; covered when young with a yellow to buff cortina

STEM: Up to 2¾ in. long; yellowish overlaid with red fibrils; equal or enlarged slightly downward; hollow; surface dry; base with yellow mycelium

SPORE PRINT: Rusty brown

ECOLOGY: Mycorrhizal; scattered to gregarious in mixed woods, often in association with beech and hemlock; summer and early fall; occasional

EDIBILITY: Not edible

COMMENTS: This species is placed in the Dermocybe group, which includes several species that are used to create colorful dyes. Compare with the nearly identical *Cortinarius marylandensis* (not illustrated), which has pinkish-buff basal mycelium.

Cortinarius harrisonii

SCIENTIFIC NAME: *Cortinarius limonius* (Fr.) Fr.

SYNONYM: None

COMMON NAME: None

FAMILY: **Cortinariaceae**

CAP: Up to 3 in. wide; bright reddish orange becoming brownish yellow when dry; convex to broadly convex, becoming flat in age, sometimes with a broad umbo; surface bald or scaly, hygrophanous

FLESH: Yellowish; thick; odor and taste not distinctive

GILLS: Yellow at first, becoming brownish yellow; reaching the stem, or narrowly attached; close; broad; with a pale-yellow, cortinate partial veil

STEM: Up to 3½ in. long; pale yellow to yellow with orange fibrils, brownish where handled; fibrillose to shaggy; equal or enlarged below, sometimes tapering at the frequently curved bottom; staining brown inside when cut; cortina leaving indistinct fragments on the upper stem

SPORE PRINT: Rusty brown

ECOLOGY: Mycorrhizal; scattered to gregarious in humus under conifers in mixed woods, often found in woodlands with birch, hemlock, and white pine; late summer and fall; occasional

EDIBILITY: Not edible

COMMENTS: The similar *Cortinarius callisteus* (not illustrated) is not known from the Appalachians. It has an unpleasant odor. There are other similar *Cortinarius* species. It is the largest known mushroom genus, with several hundred species in Appalachia.

Cortinarius limonius

SCIENTIFIC NAME: *Cortinarius armillatus* (Fr.) Fr.

SYNONYMS: None

COMMON NAME: Bracelet Cort

FAMILY: Cortinariaceae

CAP: Up to 4 in. wide; brownish orange to reddish brown, yellowish tan at times; hemispherical, becoming bell-shaped or convex, eventually nearly flat with a low, broad umbo; fibrous; surface dry to moist, nearly smooth, becoming radially fibrillose, with small scales over the disc; at maturity the margin may have partial veil remnants

FLESH: Pale buff, tawny or brownish; odor mild, or similar to radish; taste mild or slightly bitter

GILLS: Tawny, becoming rusty brown; attached to the stem, broad; subdistant; covered at first by a whitish, web-like partial veil

STEM: Up to 6 in. long; whitish to tan; tapering up from a swollen base; with one or more orange to reddish-brown bands; apex with a thin, rusty-brown ring zone; dense, white basal mycelium

SPORE PRINT: Rusty brown

ECOLOGY: Mycorrhizal with birch trees; scattered to gregarious in humus in low mixed woods with birch, hemlock, and pine; late summer and early fall; common

EDIBILITY: Poisonous, contains small amounts of orellanine, a slow-acting, potentially very deadly poison

COMMENTS: The orange bands on the stem are a distinct feature of this mushroom. It is a common species in its favored habitat.

Cortinarius armillatus

SCIENTIFIC NAME: *Cortinarius corrugatus* Peck

SYNONYM: None

COMMON NAMES: Wrinkled Cortinarius, Corrugated Cort

FAMILY: Cortinariaceae

CAP: Up to 4 in. wide; yellowish orange, tawny brown, or reddish brown; bell-shaped to convex, becoming broadly convex, with a central umbo; surface distinctly corrugated and wrinkled, except at the center; bald, viscid in wet conditions, tacky or dry in warm and dry conditions

FLESH: White to buff, becoming yellowish to brownish where damaged; thin; firm; odor and taste not distinctive

GILLS: Violet, gray, or whitish, becoming cinnamon brown; attached to the stem; close; broad; edges often eroded in age; when young with a cortinate partial veil

STEM: Up to 5 in. long; yellowish or streaked the color of the cap, especially at the base; equal with a small basal bulb; surface dry or slightly viscid near the base; partial veil remnants usually absent or barely visible

SPORE PRINT: Rusty brown

ECOLOGY: Mycorrhizal; found in humus and moss in mixed woods, often under beech, oak, hemlock, and rhododendron; summer and early fall; common

EDIBILITY: Not edible

COMMENTS: The wrinkled cap and rather tall stature are key features. Compare with *Cortinarius caperatus* (p. 190), which has a rather frosted-appearing cap that is not wrinkled.

Cortinarius corrugatus

SCIENTIFIC NAME: *Cortinarius pholideus* (Lilj.) Fr.

SYNONYM: None

COMMON NAME: Scaly Cort

FAMILY: Cortinariaceae

CAP: Up to 3½ in. wide; light brown to buff, at times yellowish buff or darker brown, the center is dark brown; orb-shaped, becoming convex to broadly convex and eventually flat; surface dry, covered with dark-brown fibrils or scales

FLESH: Dull white, pale violet to buff, at times with brownish-red tints; odor and taste not distinctive

GILLS: Pale violet, becoming grayish brown and finally rusty brown; barely reaching the stem; close to subdistant; narrow; edges even; with a whitish to gray cortinate partial veil

STEM: Up to 4 in. long; pale violet near the apex at first, soon buff with gray or brown scales, patches, or rings from the base up to the ring zone; above the ring dry, white, and smooth; stuffed

SPORE PRINT: Rusty brown

ECOLOGY: Mycorrhizal; scattered to gregarious on soil, moss, or litter and at times on well-decayed wood in moist, mixed forests, often under birches; summer and fall; occasional

EDIBILITY: Not edible

COMMENTS: Its habit of fruiting on wood at times is unusual for a *Cortinarius* and, along with the scaly cap, could lead to confusion with a species of *Pholiota*.

Cortinarius pholideus

SCIENTIFIC NAME: *Cortinarius mucosus* (Bull.) J. Kickx f.

SYNONYM: None

COMMON NAME: None

FAMILY: Cortinariaceae

CAP: Up to 4 in. wide; rich reddish orange, paler around the margin, often fading in age; convex, becoming broadly convex and finally flat; surface bald, viscid; margin not striate, turned under at first

FLESH: Whitish, cream to buff; odor and taste mild

GILLS: Cream or whitish at first, becoming rusty brown; attached to the stem; close; edges even; totally covered at first, by a white slime veil having a cortina encased within

STEM: Up to 6 in. wide; white or tinged very slightly lavender, becoming brownish stained from handling; generally equal; surface covered at first with a viscid coating that dries somewhat in age, with an apical, spore-stained cortina ring zone

SPORE PRINT: Rusty brown

ECOLOGY: Mycorrhizal; single to scattered in humus or moss; associated with conifers, especially two- and three-needle pines, often in poor soil; fall; occasional to common

EDIBILITY: Not edible

COMMENTS: This attractive mushroom can be found late in the season, often after several frosts. The presence of a fibrous cortina is obscured until the remnants form the spore-stained ring on the stem. There are other, similar slimy *Cortinarius* species, including *Cortinarius collinitus* (not illustrated), which has a violet stem, and *Cortinarius trivialis* (p. 188), which has scaly bands on the stem.

Cortinarius mucosus

SCIENTIFIC NAME: *Cortinarius trivialis* J. E. Lange

SYNONYM: None

COMMON NAME: Girdled Webcap

FAMILY: Cortinariaceae

CAP: Up to 4½ in. broad; orange to yellowish buff, usually with brownish areas; convex to flat, at times with a broad umbo; surface bald, viscid to glutinous; margin indistinctly striate

FLESH: Dull white, at times brownish in the stem base; soft; odor and taste not distinctive

GILLS: White, clay, or faintly lilac, becoming rusty; close to subdistant; attached to the stem; edges even; covered when young with a slimy partial veil with an imbedded cortina

STEM: Up to 4¾ in. long; whitish above, the lower areas are banded with zones of shaggy, brownish scales; equal or tapering toward the base; at times with an apical, fibrillose ring zone

SPORE PRINT: Rusty brown

ECOLOGY: Mycorrhizal; scattered to gregarious in humus or moss under aspen and other broadleaf trees; summer and fall; common

EDIBILITY: Not edible

COMMENTS: This is probably a species complex. It is to be expected under quaking and big-tooth aspen. *Cortinarius collinitus* (not illustrated) is similar but lacks the shaggy, brownish zones on the lower stem.

Cortinarius trivialis

188

SCIENTIFIC NAME: *Cortinarius iodes* Berk and M. A. Curtis

SYNONYM: None

COMMON NAME: Viscid Violet Cort

FAMILY: Cortinariaceae

CAP: Up to 2 in. wide; dark purplish or dark lilac, fading in age and developing yellowish spots most commonly at the center; convex to broadly convex, becoming flat; surface slimy when moist, sticky when dry, bald under the slime coating; taste of the slime is mild

FLESH: Pale violet to whitish; soft; odor and taste not distinctive

GILLS: Off-white to violet, becoming grayish brown; close; attached to the stem; edges even; covered at first with a whitish cortina

Stem: Up to 3 in. long; violet or whitish with violet smears; tapering up from an enlarged base or equal; surface viscid, bald, with an evanescent, rusty-brown ring zone near the apex

SPORE PRINT: Rusty brown

ECOLOGY: Mycorrhizal; scattered to gregarious on soil and litter in broadleaf woodlands, especially with oaks and beech; summer and fall; common

EDIBILITY: Not edible

COMMENTS: The nearly identical *Cortinarius iodeoides* (not illustrated) has bitter-tasting slime. *Cortinarius heliotropicus* (not illustrated) is possibly a synonym of one of these two species. *Cortinarius iodes* is the more common of these two look-alikes in the Appalachians. As most collectors do not choose to lick the slimy cap, *Cortinarius iodeoides* may be more common than records indicate. All collections the author has tasted were mild.

Cortinarius iodes

SCIENTIFIC NAME: *Cortinarius caperatus* (Pers.) Fr.

SYNONYM: *Rozites caperatus* (Pers.) P. Karst.

COMMON NAME: The Gypsy

FAMILY: Cortinariaceae

CAP: Up to 4 in. wide; straw yellow to ochre orange, fading in age; with a hoary whitish "frosting" on the cap center; globose or oval-shaped when young, becoming convex with a broad umbo, eventually nearly flat; surface often wrinkled, moist to dry, not viscid, with small fibrillose scales; margin turned under at first

FLESH: Whitish with hyaline areas, grayish at times; thick; firm; rather fragile; odor and taste not distinctive

GILLS: Dull whitish, becoming rusty brown; attached to the stem; close to crowded; covered at first by a whitish, membranous partial veil

STEM: Up to 4½ in. long; dingy white; equal or slightly swollen below; with a persistent ring on the upper stem; solid; surface dry, bald below the ring, floccose above

SPORE PRINT: Rusty brown

ECOLOGY: Mycorrhizal with conifers, birch, and other broadleaf trees, and with bushes in the blueberry family; scattered to gregarious; summer and fall

EDIBILITY: Edible and very good, but note the combination of a persistent ring and frosted cap; there are similar but poisonous *Cortinarius* species that lack these characters

COMMENTS: The Gypsy is locally abundant in a variety of habitats but is usually most common under conifers and birch. Compare with *Cortinarius corrugatus* (p. 185), which has a wrinkled cap and lacks a membranous ring.

Cortinarius caperatus

SCIENTIFIC NAME: *Cortinarius traganus* (Fr.) Fr.

SYNONYM: None

COMMON NAME: Pungent Cort

FAMILY: Cortinariaceae

CAP: Up to 4½ in. broad; silver, pale lilac; convex to broadly convex and eventually flat; surface dry, fibrillose, or finely cracked at times

FLESH: Yellow to yellowish orange; firm; thick; odor pungent, pleasant, fruit-like, becoming unpleasant in age; taste mild or slightly bitter

GILLS: Tan to rusty cinnamon; attached; subdistant; fairly broad; covered at first with an abundant, white or violaceous cortinate partial veil

STEM: Up to 4¾ in. long; lilac or whitish; base enlarged; solid; surface dry, fibrillose; cortina leaving a thin, fibrillose, spore-covered ring zone on the upper stem

SPORE PRINT: Rusty brown

ECOLOGY: Mycorrhizal; scattered to gregarious in humus or moss under conifers; summer and fall; occasional

EDIBILITY: Not edible

COMMENTS: *Cortinarius camphoratus* (not illustrated) is similar but has a very unpleasant odor described as like an old goat or a rotten potato. *Cortinarius pyriodorus* (not illustrated), with a pear-like odor, is possibly a synonym. There are many other species of *Cortinarius* with violaceous colors. *Cortinarius traganus* is distinctive with its yellowish-orange flesh, silvery cap, and fruit-like odor.

Cortinarius traganus

SCIENTIFIC NAME: *Cortinarius squamulosus* Peck

SYNONYM: None

COMMON NAME: None

FAMILY: **Cortinariaceae**

CAP: Up to 4 in. broad; brown and purplish tinged at first, becoming chocolate brown, nearly blackish on the disc; roundish, becoming convex to nearly flat, rarely broadly umbonate; surface dry and densely fuzzy at first, soon broken up into rather large, dense, fibrillose scales that are darker than or the same color as the cuticle

FLESH: Pinkish white, violaceous to grayish white, becoming brownish, mottled, watery; abruptly thick over the disc, narrow toward the margin; odor mildly spicy, becoming stronger in age; taste not distinctive

GILLS: Purplish at first, soon cinnamon to chocolate brown; attached to the stem at first, soon pulling away and leaving a notch; close; rather broad; at first with a membranous partial veil; when present, the ephemeral cortina is embedded in the membranous veil

STEM: Up to 8 in. long; purplish at first, soon becoming chocolate brown; with a large, turnip-shaped bulb; fibrillose or with flattened to curved scales; firm; dry; with a membranous ring near the top of the stem, this ring can fall off at times

SPORE PRINT: Rusty brown

ECOLOGY: Mycorrhizal; gregarious in humus and moss in broadleaf and mixed woods; summer and fall; uncommon

EDIBILITY: Not edible

COMMENTS: This is a dark, rather unappealing mushroom. It is one of the few *Cortinarius* species with a membranous ring. The similar *Cortinarius torvus* (p. 193) has a violaceous cap, distant gills, and lacks the scales and the bulbous stem.

Cortinarius squamulosus

SCIENTIFIC NAME: *Cortinarius torvus* (Fr.) Fr.

SYNONYM: None

COMMON NAME: Stocking Webcap

FAMILY: Cortinariaceae

Cap: Up to 3½ in. wide; purplish brown to copper brown at first, becoming brown to buff in age, with a silvery bloom at times; convex to broadly convex, nearly flat at maturity; surface moist, not viscid, finely silky to nearly bald; margin turned under well into maturity

FLESH: Mottled violaceous and white, yellowish around larvae tunnels, thick over the disc; odor sweet, pungent; taste not distinctive, or slightly bitter

GILLS: Dark purplish becoming purplish brown, and brown in age, edges whitish and even; attached to the stem; distant; broad; at first covered with a membranous veil

STEM: Up to 3½ in. long; violet at first, soon whitish, at times brownish; solid; surface dry; base enlarged; sheathed from the base with a whitish or grayish-violet veil material that ends on the upper stem to form a fragile, folded-over ring

SPORE PRINT: Rusty brown

ECOLOGY: Mycorrhizal; gregarious on soil or litter in broadleaf and mixed woods, often with beech or oak; summer and fall; common

EDIBILITY: Not edible

COMMENTS: The purplish colors when young, distant gills, and the sheathing veil forming a ring are distinctive features. Compare with *Cortinarius squamulosus* (p. 192), which is scaly, has closer gills, and lacks the purplish colors.

Cortinarius torvus

SCIENTIFIC NAME: *Volvariella bombycina* (Schaeff.) Singer

SYNONYM: None

COMMON NAME: Silky Tree Volvariella

FAMILY: Pluteaceae

CAP: Up to 8 in. wide; white, yellowish at the center in age; oval, becoming bell-shaped, convex, and finally nearly flat; surface covered by a dense coating of white, silky hairs, dry, lacking warts

FLESH: White; soft; thin; odor not distinctive; taste pleasant

GILLS: White at first, becoming pink to brownish pink in age; free from the stem; crowded; broad; edges even or finely scalloped; no partial veil

STEM: Up to 8 in. long; white; equal or tapering upward; surface bald, smooth, dry; encased at the base with a rather deep, membranous, brown, or brown and white volva

SPORE PRINT: Salmon pink

ECOLOGY: Solitary to gregarious on dead and living wood of broadleaf trees, especially maples; summer and fall; uncommon

EDIBILITY: Edible

COMMENTS: This is a striking and distinctive mushroom. Its furry cap, salmon spores, and prominent, brown, bag volva are a unique combination. When emerging from the volva, the cap may be moist or even a bit slimy. It soon becomes dry.

Volvariella bombycina

SCIENTIFIC NAME: *Pluteus tomentosulus* Peck

SYNONYM: None

COMMON NAME: None

FAMILY: Pluteaceae

CAP: Up to 2¾ in. wide; white or tinged slightly pink near the margin; conical to convex, becoming broadly convex at maturity; umbonate; surface tomentose, dry; margin faintly striate in age

FLESH: White, unchanging when cut; thin; odor and taste not distinctive

GILLS: White becoming brownish pink; free from the stem; crowded; broad; edges even; no partial veil

STEM: Up to 4 in. long; white with white basal mycelium; equal or tapering slightly upward; solid; surface fibrillose to granular, appressed tomentose, often longitudinally grooved

SPORE PRINT: Brownish pink

ECOLOGY: Saprobic on the dead wood of conifers and broadleaf trees; summer and fall; occasional

EDIBILITY: Unknown

COMMENTS: This is a seldom-reported species that may be more common than records indicate. *Pluteus pellitus* (not illustrated) is larger and lacks the tomentose cap.

Pluteus tomentosulus

SCIENTIFIC NAME: *Pluteus cervinus* (Schaeff.) P. Kumm.

SYNONYM: *Pluteus atricapillus* (Batsch) Fayod

COMMON NAME: Deer Mushroom

FAMILY: Pluteaceae

CAP: Up to 4¾ in. wide; dark to pale brown, often darkest on the center; convex to broadly convex, becoming flat in age, often with a flattened umbo; bald or obscurely fibrillose; dry, becoming tacky when wet

FLESH: White, unchanging when damaged; thick; rather soft; odor like radish; taste mild or slightly of radish

GILLS: White, becoming pinkish and then deep salmon in age; free from the stem; close to crowded; broad; edges even; no partial veil

STEM: Up to 4 in. long; whitish; equal or tapering upward; solid; surface bald or with grayish or brown fibers, dry; with white mycelium at the base

SPORE PRINT: Brownish pink or salmon

ECOLOGY: Saprobic; solitary, scattered, or gregarious on the dead wood of broadleaf trees and reportedly conifer wood as well; spring, summer, and fall; common

EDIBILITY: Edible but not very popular

COMMENTS: This is another species complex. Several medium to large, brown *Pluteus* species have been called this from time to time. The species described here is abundant and in a general sense fits the author's concept of *Pluteus cervinus*.

Pluteus cervinus

SCIENTIFIC NAME: *Pluteus petasatus* (Fr.) Gillet

SYNONYM: None

COMMON NAME: None

FAMILY: Pluteaceae

CAP: Up to 5 in. wide; whitish to pale brown, darker over the center; convex to broadly convex becoming flat; surface tacky when wet, soon dry, bald becoming scaly or with dark fibers over the center, and occasionally outward; margin not striate

FLESH: White, unchanging when cut; thick; firm; odor and taste not distinctive, or faintly radish-like

GILLS: White to cream, becoming pinkish brown in age; free from the stem; broad; edges even; no partial veil

STEM: Up to 4½ in. long; whitish, bottom brownish; equal or enlarged downward; surface dry, bald, down to a fibrillose base

SPORE PRINT: Brownish pink

ECOLOGY: Scattered to gregarious or clustered on the dead wood of broadleaf trees, often in wood mulch and sawdust, at times appearing terrestrial when growing from buried wood; late spring, summer, and fall; occasional

EDIBILITY: Edible

COMMENTS: This species intergrades with the Deer Mushroom, *Pluteus cervinus* (p. 196). The whitish cap and the dark fibers are key macroscopic features. Microscopic work is needed to clinch the identification. The *Pluteus cervinus* group is a complex that may contain several as yet unnamed species.

Pluteus petasatus

SCIENTIFIC NAME: *Rhodocollybia maculata* var. *scorzonerea* (Fr.) Lennox

SYNONYM: *Rhodocollybia maculata* (Alb. and Schwein.) Singer

COMMON NAMES: Spotted Rhodocollybia, Spotted Toughshank

FAMILY: Marasmiaceae

CAP: Up to 4 in. wide; pinkish buff at first, then whitish, with watery, brown areas and spots, becoming brownish orange on part or most of the cap and with darker-brown spots; convex, broadly convex, becoming flat; surface dry to moist, not striate

FLESH: White in the cap, yellowish in the stem, unchanging when bruised; odor slightly fragrant; taste bitter

GILLS: Yellowish, pale cream, or pinkish buff, developing rusty stains; narrowly attached to the stem, or notched; crowded; edges finely scalloped; no partial veil

STEM: Up to 4½ in. wide; white to yellowish, with rusty stains; equal; becoming hollow; at times with a base that is slightly rooting; surface dry, often with white mycelium at the base

SPORE PRINT: Pinkish buff to yellowish

ECOLOGY: Saprobic; scattered to gregarious in humus or on rotten wood in conifer and mixed woods; summer and fall; uncommon

EDIBILITY: Not edible

COMMENTS: This species is more common in northern areas of the Appalachians. *Rhodocollybia maculata* var. *maculata* (not illustrated) has white gills and generally paler colors. Otherwise it is very similar. It is the commoner of the two varieties.

Rhodocollybia maculata

SCIENTIFIC NAME: *Entoloma strictius* var. *isabellinum* Peck

SYNONYM: *Nolanea strictior* (Peck) Pomerl.

COMMON NAME: Twisted Stalk Entoloma

FAMILY: Entolomataceae

CAP: Up to 2½ in. wide; silvery, butterscotch brown, or tan; convex to bell-shaped or flat with a prominent central umbo; surface bald or finely silky, hygrophanous, often streaked, dry to moist

GILLS: Buff, becoming salmon pink; close; barely attached to the stem; fairly broad; edges even; no partial veil

FLESH: White to brownish when wet; thin; odor variously described as sweet, mealy, disagreeable, and not distinctive; taste not distinctive

STEM: Up to 4 in. long; grayish; straight and twisted; slightly enlarged downward; surface dry, finely silky; base with white mycelium

SPORE PRINT: Salmon pink

ECOLOGY: Saprobic in broadleaf and mixed woods; scattered to gregarious in humus and on dead wood; summer and fall; common

EDIBILITY: Poisonous

COMMENTS: *Entoloma strictius* var. *strictius* (not illustrated) has a much darker, olive-brown cap. Most authors consider the species illustrated here as simply *Entoloma strictius*.

Entoloma strictius

SCIENTIFIC NAME: *Entoloma abortivum* (Berk. and M. A. Curtis) Donk

SYNONYM: *Clitopilus abortivus* (Berk. and M. A. Curtis) Sacc.

COMMON NAMES: Aborted Entoloma, Hunters Heart

FAMILY: Entolomataceae

CAP: Up to 5 in. broad; pale gray to grayish brown; convex to broadly convex becoming flat; surface dry, smooth to fibrillose, not striate

FLESH: White, unchanging when exposed, soft, thick, fragile; odor mild; taste mealy or metallic

GILLS: Pale gray to pink, to dull salmon in age; decurrent; close; edges even; no partial veil

STEM: Up to 3½ in. long; grayish white; equal or enlarged slightly near the base; bald or appressed fibrillose; with white mycelium at the base

SPORE PRINT: Salmon reddish

ECOLOGY: Parasitic on various species of *Armillaria* mushrooms, resulting in aborted cauliflower-like growths, usually in the vicinity of the normal *Entoloma*, at times with normal *Armillaria* fruitings; these aborted honey mushrooms may appear when the gilled *Entoloma* is not fruiting; scattered to gregarious; on dead wood or on the ground; late summer and fall; common

EDIBILITY: Both the abortions and the gilled mushrooms are edible; there are other salmon-spored mushrooms that are poisonous, so eating the gilled *Entoloma abortivum* is recommended only when found in close proximity to the abortions; note that its gills are decurrent

COMMENTS: It was once thought that the *Armillaria* species was parasitizing the *Entoloma*. The author has seen *Armillaria mellea* (p. 112), *Desarmillaria tabescens* (p. 114), and *Armillaria gallica* (p. 113) as victims of this species. The cauliflower-like abortions are white and in age become brownish with a pinkish or watery-whitish interior. Beware of decaying abortions. They should be somewhat spongy but not soft and foul smelling.

Entoloma abortivum

SCIENTIFIC NAME: *Phyllotopsis nidulans* (Pers.) Singer

SYNONYM: None

COMMON NAME: Mock Oyster

FAMILY: Tricholomataceae

CAP: Up to 3 in. wide; orange to yellowish orange; convex to flat, fan-shaped; surface dry, with a dense coating of white fuzz on part or most of the cap; margin turned under at first

FLESH: Pale orange; soft; odor usually pungent and foul, like sulfur or spoiled cabbage, occasionally not distinctive; taste disagreeable

GILLS: Bright to pale orange; close, fairly narrow; edges even; no partial veil

STEM: Absent or poorly developed

SPORE PRINT: Pale pink to pinkish brown

ECOLOGY: Saprobic; solitary or in overlapping clusters on dead wood of conifers and broadleaf trees; usually in cool weather, spring, summer, fall, and early winter; fairly common

EDIBILITY: Not edible

COMMENTS: The odor when present is a key identification feature. It is memorable. When absent it could be confused with *Tapinella panuoides* (p. 206), which has a brown spore print and lacks hairs on its cap.

Phyllotopsis nidulans

SCIENTIFIC NAME: *Pholiota highlandensis* (Peck) Quadr. and Lunghini

SYNONYM: *Pholiota carbonaria* (Fr.) Singer

COMMON NAME: Burnsite Pholiota

FAMILY: Strophariaceae

CAP: Up to 2¼ in. wide; yellowish brown to reddish brown; convex to broadly convex, becoming flat; surface viscid in wet weather, dry or tacky in dry weather, bald; margin incurved at first

FLESH: Yellow or colored like the cap; thin; odor not distinctive; taste not distinctive, or slightly disagreeable

GILLS: Pale yellowish becoming pale cinnamon; attached; close; broad; edges even; covered at first by a yellowish, cortina-like partial veil

STEM: Up to 2 in. long; whitish to yellowish; fibrillose scaly below, pruinose above; generally equal; cylindrical; solid or stuffed, becoming hollow in age; with or without an apical ring zone

SPORE PRINT: Dark Brown

ECOLOGY: Saprobic on burnt wood; scattered to gregarious, often clustered on charred wood in fire pits, old lumberyards, and after forest fires; spring, summer, and fall; occasional

EDIBILITY: Unknown

COMMENTS: This is a very variable mushroom, and there are other *Pholiota* species that occur in burned areas. These are awaiting DNA analysis. So for now, consider this a species complex.

Pholiota highlandensis

SCIENTIFIC NAME: *Pholiota squarrosoides* (Peck) Sacc.

SYNONYMS: None

COMMON NAME: Scaly Pholiota

FAMILY: Strophariaceae

CAP: Up to 4½ in. wide; cuticle color whitish to yellowish, buttons totally covered with tawny scales; as the cap expands, the cuticle is partially exposed but still mostly covered with scales; convex, becoming broadly convex; surface viscid to tacky on the cuticle under the scales

FLESH: White; firm; thick; odor variously described as garlicky, of cooked chicken, and of cornflakes; taste not distinctive

GILLS: White, becoming rusty brown from the spores; attached or barely reaching the stem; close to crowded; edges even; covered at first by a cortina-like partial veil

STEM: Up to 5 in. long; colored like the cap, silky and whitish at the apex above the rusty-colored ring zone when it is present; staining brown at the base at times; stuffed or solid; equal; often curved; surface dry with colored, curved scales similar to those on the cap

SPORE PRINT: Cinnamon brown

ECOLOGY: Usually saprobic but occasionally parasitic on the wood of broadleaf trees, especially maple, beech, and birch; mostly clustered; late summer and fall; common

EDIBILITY: Not recommended, edible for some but digestive upsets have occurred

COMMENTS: *Pholiota squarrosa* (not illustrated) is very similar but has a dry cap cuticle, a shaggier aspect, and a greenish tint to the gills. It is less common in the Appalachians. Both species form eye-catching clusters.

Pholiota squarrosoides

203

SCIENTIFIC NAME: *Pholiota aurivella* (Batsch) P. Kumm.

SYNONYM: None

COMMON NAME: Golden Pholiota

FAMILY: Strophariaceae

CAP: Up to 5 in. wide; orange at first, then yellow to tawny brown, at times whitish; convex to broadly convex to nearly flat, at times with a broad umbo; surface covered with reddish-brown, irregular to triangular-shaped scales that may be washed off in wet weather, glutinous at first, viscid in age

FLESH: Yellow or whitish; firm; rather thick; odor and taste not distinctive

GILLS: Whitish or pale yellow, becoming rusty brown in age; attached to sub-decurrent; close; rather narrow; edges even; covered at first by a cortina-like partial veil

STEM: Up to 3 in. long; yellow or yellowish brown; with fibrillose, whitish to brown recurved scales; central or eccentric; equal or tapering upward; surface floccose above the ring zone, fibrillose below, dry, at times sticky near the base

SPORE PRINT: Brown

ECOLOGY: Parasitic and saprobic on the wood of living and dead broadleaf and conifer trees; most common in the fall, but also occurs in summer and late spring; common

EDIBILITY: Not recommended; some people can't tolerate it and suffer digestive problems

COMMENTS: *Pholiota limonella* (not illustrated) and perhaps some other species require a microscope and possibly DNA analysis to distinguish them from this species. Consider it a species complex.

Pholiota aurivella

SCIENTIFIC NAME: *Pholiota angustipes* (Peck) Sacc.

SYNONYMS: None

COMMON NAME: None

FAMILY: **Strophariaceae**

CAP: Up to 3 in. wide; brownish, tan, yellowish, or paler at times, convex to flat, at times with a low broad umbo; surface with appressed, brown scales, dry, slightly viscid when wet

FLESH: Yellowish or whitish; thin; odor not distinctive; taste slightly bitter

GILLS: Whitish, yellowish, becoming tawny to cinnamon buff; attached to the stem, pulling away and leaving traces on the upper stem; close; narrowed outward; edges even, with a fibrillose cortina

STEM: Up to 3 in. long; whitish to yellowish, at times reddish toward the base; equal or base chiseled; surface dry, with yellowish or tan scales; with an evanescent, apical ring zone that may disappear in age

SPORE PRINT: Rusty brown

ECOLOGY: Saprobic; usually clustered on the ground but probably growing from buried wood of broadleaf and conifer trees, occasionally on stumps; summer and fall; uncommon

EDIBILITY: Unknown

COMMENTS: This is the only scaly, terrestrial-appearing *Pholiota* likely to be encountered in the Appalachians. It is most often seen in lawns near trees and on stumps in parks and cemeteries. *Pholiota terrestris* (not illustrated) also appears terrestrial. It is common in Western states and is rare in the Appalachians.

Pholiota angustipes

SCIENTIFIC NAME: *Tapinella atrotomentosa* (Batsch) Šutara

SYNONYM: *Paxillus atrotomentosus* (Batsch) Fr.

COMMON NAME: Velvet Foot

FAMILY: Tapinellaceae

CAP: Up to 6 in. wide; yellowish brown, olive brown to orangish buff; convex becoming flat, at times with a depressed center; surface dry, velvety to felt-like, with matted hairs, cracking at times; margin incurved at first, often becoming scalloped in age

FLESH: Whitish to yellowish, not staining when damaged; thick; tough; odor and taste not distinctive

GILLS: Whitish, tan, yellowish brown to dull brown, not changing color when damaged; subdecurrent to decurrent; close; forked, veined, or both near the stem; edges even; no partial veil

STEM: Up to 4 in. long; dark brown to blackish brown owing to a thick covering of hairs, the apex can be whitish at times; equal or tapering slightly in either direction; eccentric to nearly lateral at times

SPORE PRINT: Dull yellowish brown to brownish yellow

ECOLOGY: Saprobic; solitary, gregarious, or in small clusters on decaying conifer wood, sometimes on partially buried wood; summer and fall; occasional to fairly common

EDIBILITY: Poisonous

COMMENTS: This species was formerly placed in the genus *Paxillus,* which is a genus of mycorrhizal mushrooms. Despite its rather drab colors, it is a very attractive mushroom.

Tapinella atrotomentosa

SCIENTIFIC NAME: *Tapinella panuoides* (Fr.) E .-J. Gilbert

SYNONYM: *Paxillus panuoides* (Fr.) Fr.

COMMON NAME: None

FAMILY: Tapinellaceae

CAP: Up to 4 in. wide; yellow, yellowish orange, buff or yellowish brown, at times with olive tints; fan- or shell-shaped; surface coated at first with fuzzy hairs, becoming bald in age; margin incurved at first and at maturity lobed or wavy

FLESH: Whitish to pale cream; odor not distinctive, or slightly pleasant; taste not distinctive, or slightly bitter

GILLS: Dull orange to yellow; crimped or wrinkled; moderately thick; often forked or with cross veins; edges even; no partial veil

STEM: Absent or nearly so

SPORE PRINT: Pale brown to yellowish brown

ECOLOGY: Saprobic on the wood of conifers; solitary or usually gregarious or in small clusters; summer and fall; occasional

EDIBILITY: Poisonous

COMMENTS: *Phyllotopsis nidulans* (p. 201) is very similar but has pinkish spores and often has an unpleasant odor. *Pseudomerulius curtisii* (p. 300) is another look-alike. It has gills that are so wrinkled that they are almost honeycombed or pore-like.

Tapinella panuoides

SCIENTIFIC NAME: *Galerina marginata* (Batsch) Kühner
SYNONYM: *Galerina autumnalis* (Peck) A. H. Smith and Singer
COMMON NAMES: Deadly Galerina, Autumn Galerina
FAMILY: Hymenogastraceae

CAP: Up to 2½ in. wide; brown to tawny brown, becoming yellowish on drying out; convex becoming flat, sometimes with a broad umbo; bald, moist; viscid in wet conditions; margin faintly translucent striate

FLESH: Brownish buff; thin; odor not distinctive, or slightly mealy; taste not recorded

GILLS: Yellowish brown, becoming cinnamon brown; attached to subdecurrent, at times pulling away from the stem in age; close; broad; edges even; covered at first by a white, membranous partial veil

STEM: Up to 3 in. long; whitish, buff, or brown like the cap, darkening from the base upward, eventually dark brown all over; fibrillose; becoming hollow; dry; with a white ring that becomes brown from the spores and that may be appressed against the stem and disappear entirely

SPORE PRINT: Rusty brown

ECOLOGY: Saprobic; gregarious or clustered on dead wood of broadleaf and conifer trees, often moss-covered logs; common in cool weather spring, fall, and rarely in summer

EDIBILITY: Deadly poisonous

COMMENTS: To prevent confusion with species of *Armillaria* that have white spores, it is important to note that this mushroom has brown spores. This will separate it from edible white-spored *Armillaria* species. When conditions are optimal, fruitings of both species may appear on the same log at the same time. There are many confusing brown mushrooms growing on wood. This species gets attention because it contains amatoxins, which can cause death owing to liver failure. It is a classic example of why one should not eat a single mushroom to learn the effect.

Galerina marginata

SCIENTIFIC NAME: *Gymnopilus luteus* (Peck) Hesler

SYNONYM: *Pholiota lutea* Peck

COMMON NAME: Yellow Gymnopilus

FAMILY: Cortinariaceae

CAP: Up to 4 in. wide; pale buff, yellow, bright yellow, yellowish orange, at times darker at the center; convex at first, with a turned-under margin, becoming nearly flat; surface dry, silky to appressed fibrillose

FLESH: Pale yellow; thick; odor pleasant, sweet, resembling almond extract or anise; taste bitter

GILLS: Pale yellow, becoming brown from the spores; attached but soon pulling away, becoming notched, sometimes leaving remnants on the upper stem; close; edges even; at first covered by a membranous to cortinate partial veil

STEM: Up to 3½ in. long; colored like the cap or slightly paler; equal or enlarged toward the base; dry; fibrillose; solid; usually curved, with an apical, spore-stained fibrous ring

SPORE PRINT: Rusty orange to rusty brown

ECOLOGY: Saprobic on the dead wood of broadleaf trees, reportedly on conifer wood as well; usually gregarious or small clusters but may be solitary; summer and fall; common

EDIBILITY: Not edible; bitter and hallucinogenic

COMMENTS: Reportedly containing psilocybin, a controlled substance, so it is considered an illegal drug in the United States. The similar Big Laughing Gym, or *Gymnopilus junonius* (not illustrated), is brownish orange. Both are known to alter perception and in some cases to cause nausea.

Gymnopilus luteus

SCIENTIFIC NAME: *Crepidotus crocophyllus* (Berk.) Sacc.

SYNONYM: None

COMMON NAME: Yellow-Gilled Crep

FAMILY: Crepidotaceae

CAP: Up to 1½ in. broad; ground color whitish, buff, yellowish, covered with brown scales; semicircular, to kidney-shaped, convex becoming broadly convex to occasionally flat

FLESH: Whitish; soft; thin; not gelatinous; odor not distinctive; taste mild or slightly bitter

GILLS: Variable in color; yellow, orange, buff, yellowish orange, whitish at times, becoming brownish; radiating from the point of attachment; close to subdistant; broad; rather thick; attached laterally to the substrate; edges even; no partial veil

STEM: Absent

SPORE PRINT: Brown

ECOLOGY: Saprobic; gregarious or scattered on dead wood of broadleaf and occasionally conifer trees; spring, summer, and fall; common

EDIBILITY: Unknown, small and unsubstantial

COMMENTS: *Crepidotus mollis* (not illustrated) is a similar common species with white gills. Genus *Crepidotus* is made up of mostly small, fragile, white, stemless, wood-decaying mushrooms. None are considered good edibles.

Crepidotus crocophyllus

SCIENTIFIC NAME: *Agrocybe firma* (Peck) **Singer**

SYNONYM: *Naucoria firma* Peck

COMMON NAME: None

FAMILY: Bolbitiaceae

CAP: Up to 3 in. wide; blackish brown, hygrophanous, fading to tawny brown, center may be paler at first, margin may be buff; convex to flat; sometimes broadly umbonate; surface dry, tacky when wet, may have a frosted appearance when young, water will form beads on the young cap cuticle

FLESH: Whitish to pale yellow, becoming brownish in older specimens; firm; odor not distinctive, or mealy; taste mild becoming bitter and unpleasant

GILLS: Dirty buff to light brown, at times grayish brown to yellowish brown; close; adnate, at times leaving a decurrent tooth on the stem; edges even; no partial veil

STEM: Up to 4 in. long; whitish above, becoming brownish below; equal or slightly enlarged below; pruinose, apex striate; firm; base with white rhizomorphs

SPORE PRINT: Dark brown

ECOLOGY: Saprobic on the decaying wood of broadleaf trees, scattered to gregarious, sometimes in clusters; late summer and fall; infrequent in the spring; occasional in summer and fall

EDIBILITY: Unknown

COMMENTS: Unlike many species in this genus, *Agrocybe firma* does not have a partial veil or ring.

Agrocybe firma

SCIENTIFIC NAME: *Psathyrella candolleana* (Fr.) Maire

SYNONYM: *Hypholoma candolleanum* (Fr.) Quél.

COMMON NAME: Common Psathyrella

FAMILY: Psathyrellaceae

CAP: Up to 4 in. wide; honey-colored, becoming cream to white; with silky, white fibers when young; conic to convex when young, becoming nearly flat in age; surface hygrophanous, flocculose; margin faintly striate, with whitish partial-veil remnants, splitting at times in age

FLESH: Pale yellow to white or slightly brownish; thin; fragile; odor and taste not distinctive

GILLS: White becoming brownish gray and finally dark purplish brown; attached to the stem; close to crowded; edges even; with a thin, whitish, fragile partial veil when young

STEM: Up to 4½ in. long; white; equal; thin and fragile; hollow; surface dry, fibrillose to nearly bald; partial veil at times may leave an obscure, apical ring zone

SPORE PRINT: Purplish brown

ECOLOGY: Saprobic; often appearing terrestrial but growing on wood or the buried wood of dead broadleaf trees; scattered to gregarious in woodlands, parks, and lawns; late spring, summer, and fall; common

EDIBILITY: Edible but without much substance

COMMENTS: This is a species group of very similar species requiring microscopic examination to identify.

Psathyrella candolleana

SCIENTIFIC NAME: *Psathyrella delineata* (Peck) A. H. Smith

SYNONYMS: None

COMMON NAME: None

FAMILY: Psathyrellaceae

CAP: Up to 4 in. wide; rich reddish brown to dark brown, fading to dull orangish brown to tan; convex to broadly convex, becoming flat; surface very wrinkled and radially grooved, often with whitish fibers at first; margin with remnants of the partial veil

FLESH: Whitish, or watery brown; odor and taste not distinctive

GILLS: Grayish brown at first, becoming dark brown; attached to the stem; close; edges even, with a whitish edge; covered at first with a thin, fibrillose, whitish partial veil

STEM: Up to 4 in. long; white, pale brownish toward the base; equal or enlarged slightly at the base; hollow; surface silky above, fibrillose below, dry; no ring but may have small patches of the partial veil

SPORE PRINT: Dark purplish brown to black

ECOLOGY: Saprobic on the dead wood of broadleaf trees; usually gregarious but also solitary or in small clusters; late spring, summer, and fall; common

EDIBILITY: Reported as edible; the author has not tried it

COMMENTS: This is a common mushroom on rotten wood. It is common in late spring and early fall in the northern Appalachians. *Psathyrella rugocephala* (not illustrated) has larger spores and is usually smaller but otherwise is nearly identical. It is also reported to be edible.

Psathyrella delineata

SCIENTIFIC NAME: *Psathyrella echiniceps* (G. F. Atkinson) A. H. Smtih

SYNONYM: *Hypholoma echiniceps* G. F. Atkinson

COMMON NAME: None

FAMILY: Psathyrellaceae

CAP: Up to 4 in. wide; buff to tawny; obtuse to convex and finally nearly flat; surface dry, covered with dark-brown to blackish fibers or scales, uneven to wrinkled; margin with partial-veil remnants

FLESH: Pale to dark buff, thick, brittle; odor and taste not distinctive, or slightly unpleasant

GILLS: Pale brown becoming dark reddish brown to purplish brown, edges whitish and minutely fringed; attached to the stem; close; broad, especially at the stem; covered at first by a whitish partial veil

STEM: Up to 4¾ in. long; white to pale yellow; equal or enlarged downward; hollow, surface coated below with dark-brown or blackish fibers, apex white and pruinose; at times with a ring zone; base with white, cottony mycelium

SPORE PRINT: Purplish brown

ECOLOGY: Saprobic on the dead wood of broadleaf trees; scattered or in small groups or clusters; late summer and fall; uncommon

EDIBILITY: Unknown

COMMENTS: It is likely that this species will end up in the genus *Lacrymaria*. A similar lawn species is *Lacrymaria lacrymabunda* (p. 173). It lacks the dark fibers on the stem.

Psathyrella echiniceps

SCIENTIFIC NAME: *Hypholoma lateritium* (Schaeff.) P. Kumm.

SYNONYMS: *Hypholoma sublateritium* (Fr.) Quél., *Naematoloma sublateritium* (Fr.) P. Karst.

COMMON NAME: Brick Cap

FAMILY: Strophariaceae

CAP: Up to 3½ in. wide; brick red becoming pinkish buff or yellowish toward the margin; convex to broadly convex, becoming flat in age; bald; moist, slightly viscid in wet weather; margin turned under at first; margin with scattered partial-veil patches or fibers

FLESH: White to pale buff; thick; firm; odor not distinctive; taste mild to slightly bitter

GILLS: Whitish to gray, then dark gray and finally purple brown; attached to the stem; close; at first covered with a thin, hairy partial veil

STEM: Up to 4 in. long; whitish above, reddish brown below, sometimes staining yellowish at the base; equal; dry; hollow with age; with a faint ring zone that becomes more noticeable when covered by the dark spores; area above the ring zone is silky and nearly bald, below it the stem is fibrillose to slightly hairy

SPORE PRINT: Purplish brown

ECOLOGY: Saprobic; clustered on the dead stumps and logs of broadleaf trees; common.

EDIBILITY: Mild-tasting collections are edible; Dr. Thomas Volk reports that adding an acidic ingredient like tomato sauce brings out the flavor of this species

COMMENTS: Most years this is a readily available, late-season edible species in broadleaf woodlands. Compare with *Hypholoma capnoides* (p. 216), which is not brick red and occurs on conifer wood.

Hypholoma lateritium (at right, shown under ultraviolet light)

SCIENTIFIC NAME: *Hypholoma capnoides* (Fr.) P. Kumm.

SYNONYM: *Naematoloma capnoides* (Fr.) P. Karst.

COMMON NAME: Conifer Tuft

FAMILY: Strophariaceae

CAP: Up to 2¾ in. wide; reddish orange at first; becoming yellowish orange to cinnamon, with a pale, yellowish-white margin; convex becoming flat; surface bald or with scattered buff fibrils, moist, not viscid, not striate; margin turned under at first, at times with patches of the partial veil

FLESH: Whitish to pale buff or yellowish; thick; odor and taste not distinctive

GILLS: White to gray, eventually purplish or purplish brown; attached; close; covered at first with an ephemeral white to buff partial veil

STEM: Up to 4 in. long; yellowish above a faint ring zone, colored like the cap below; generally equal; surface floccose to finely scaly; hairy at the base

SPORE PRINT: Purplish brown

ECOLOGY: Saprobic; growing gregariously or in clusters on the wood of conifers, especially pines and hemlock; fall and early winter; common

EDIBILITY: Edible, mediocre quality

COMMENTS: Compare with the Brick Cap, or *Hypholoma lateritium* (p. 215), which is more reddish and grows on the wood of broadleaf trees. The poisonous *Hypholoma fasciculare* (not illustrated) is more yellowish, with greenish-tinged gills.

Hypholoma capnoides

SCIENTIFIC NAME: *Stropharia rugosoannulata* Farl. ex Murrill

SYNONYM: None

COMMON NAME: Wine Cap

FAMILY: Strophariaceae

CAP: Up to 6 in. wide; colored like burgundy wine or reddish brown to reddish purple, fading to buff in age, one variety has yellowish-buff coloration; convex or bell-shaped, becoming broadly convex; surface tacky in wet conditions, dry, bald, smooth; may become cracked in age

FLESH: White, unchanging when damaged; thick; firm; odor and taste not distinctive

GILLS: Grayish, becoming purplish brown; attached to the stem; close to crowded; edges even, finely eroded, may be slightly fringed; covered at first by a thick, white- to cream-colored partial veil

STEM: Up to 6 in. tall; white, discoloring to yellowish or brownish in age; equal or slightly enlarged below; solid; surface dry, fibrous, smooth at times; with a distinctive apical ring that is grooved on top, the edge and underside has claw or hook-like appendages

SPORE PRINT: Purple brown

ECOLOGY: Saprobic; scattered to gregarious on wood mulch, wood chips, sawdust, and straw in gardens, saw mills, and compost piles; late spring through fall, most common in June and September

EDIBILITY: Edible, but care should be taken to avoid eating any from areas treated with insecticides or herbicides

COMMENTS: This species occasionally gets larger than the measurements above. Its key features are its habitat and the grooved, upper ring above with the claw-like appendages below. This mushroom is easily cultivated and is considered by some to be a choice edible.

Stropharia rugosoannulata

SCIENTIFIC NAME: *Stropharia hardii* G. F. Atkinson

SYNONYM: None

COMMON NAME: Hard's Stropharia

FAMILY: Strophariaceae

CAP: Up to 4 in. wide; yellow, pale yellow to brownish yellow with darker fibers or scales; convex becoming flat; surface tacky at first, becoming dry

FLESH: Whitish; thick; odor not distinctive or slightly mealy; taste not distinctive

GILLS: Whitish when young, then grayish brown with whitish edges, becoming purplish brown in age; attached to the stem or notched; close; edges even; covered at first by a membranous partial veil

STEM: Up to 4½ in. long; white, at times with yellow tinges; equal or bulbous at the base; surface dry, nearly smooth or scaly; base with white rhizomorphs; with a membranous ring on the upper stem, which often falls off

SPORE PRINT: Purplish brown

ECOLOGY: Saprobic; solitary or scattered in soil and woody humus in low, moist, broadleaf forests; summer and fall; occasional to locally common

EDIBILITY: Unknown

COMMENTS: This species can often be found along streams and in low areas with stinging nettles and jewel weed. It often has a hole or holes in the gills as an entry area to the flesh, which is partially hollowed out by insects, eventually leaving the gills to droop.

Stropharia hardii

SCIENTIFIC NAME: *Coprinopsis atramentaria* (Bull.)
  Redhead, Vilgalys and Moncalvo

SYNONYM: *Coprinus atramentarius* (Bull.) Fr.

COMMON NAME: Alcohol Ink Cap

FAMILY: Psathyrellaceae

CAP: Up to 3 in. wide; gray to grayish brown; oval becoming conic to convex;
  margin upturned in age; surface smooth, often scaly on the disc

FLESH: White, buff to pale gray; thin; soft; odor and taste not distinctive

GILLS: White to gray becoming black and inky; crowded; nearly free; edges
  even; broad; no true partial veil

STEM: Up to 4 in. long; white; equal; fibrous; hollow; covered with small, flattened, white hairs; a ring zone may be present on the lower stem

SPORE PRINT: Black

ECOLOGY: Gregarious or in dense clusters on decaying wood of broadleaf
  trees, often appearing terrestrial when growing from buried roots; spring,
  summer, and fall; common in urban areas

EDIBILITY: Edible, but should not be consumed with or after drinking
  alcohol

COMMENTS: The unpleasant symptoms of this species when consumed
  with alcohol include nausea, a flushed and hot feeling, vomiting, rapid
  breathing, headache, and gastrointestinal disturbances. Some have even
  had a reaction when having a drink a day or two after consuming the Alcohol Ink Cap. Compare with *Coprinopsis variegata* (p. 220), which has a
  scaly cap. *Coprinopsis acuminata* (p. 174) has a more conical cap and is usually slightly smaller.

Coprinopsis atramentaria

SCIENTIFIC NAME: *Coprinopsis variegata* (Peck) Redhead, Vilgalys, and Moncalvo

SYNONYMS: *Coprinus variegatus* Peck, *Coprinus quadrifidus* Peck

COMMON NAME: Scaly Inky Cap

FAMILY: Psathyrellaceae

CAP: Up to 3 in. wide; whitish or hyaline; with whitish to tan scales that are remnants of the universal veil; oval, becoming conic or convex in age; floccose

FLESH: White to tan; soft; thin; odor slightly unpleasant or not distinctive; taste not distinctive

GILLS: Whitish becoming gray then black; very crowded; soon dissolving into a black liquid; without a true partial veil

STEM: Up to 4¾ in. long; white; equal; fibrillose or slightly scaly; hollow; the base has brown mycelial stands; sometimes with a sheath or ring near the base

SPORE PRINT: Black

ECOLOGY: Gregarious on decaying wood of broadleaf trees, sometimes appearing terrestrial when growing from buried roots; spring, summer, and fall; common

EDIBILITY: Not poisonous but not recommended since some individuals have experienced gastrointestinal distress after consuming this mushroom

COMMENTS: When young, clusters of this mushroom are quite pretty. But like other inky caps, mature specimens are "inky" and rather unattractive.

Coprinopsis variegata

SCIENTIFIC NAME: *Coprinus comatus* (O. F. Müll.) Pers.

SYNONYM: None

COMMON NAMES: Shaggy Mane, Lawyer's Wig

FAMILY: Agaricaceae

CAP: Up to 2 in. wide and 6 in. long; white with a brownish center, surface dry and covered with white to reddish-brown scales, which are often curved; oval to cylindrical; never expanding, liquefying from the margin upward

FLESH: White, becoming black in age; odor and taste not distinctive

GILLS: White becoming pinkish and finally black; attached at first, becoming free from the stem; crowded; edges even or pruinose; with a membranous partial veil present when young

STEM: Up to 12 in. long; white; enlarged downward or equal; fragile, hollow but with a thin, string-like tissue throughout; surface bald to fibrillose, with a ring near the middle or the bottom of the stem

SPORE PRINT: Black

ECOLOGY: Saprobic; scattered, gregarious, or in clusters on lawns from buried wood, hard-packed soil, and in wood-mulched flower beds; late summer and fall, occasional in spring; common

EDIBILITY: Edible and the caps are good; cooking on the day of collection is recommended since this species deteriorates into an inky mess rather quickly; stems are usually discarded or cooked separately because they have a tougher consistency

COMMENTS: This mushroom is seldom found in the woods. If it is, it usually will be along a trail or road. Even though quite fragile, it has been known to break through blacktop road surfaces.

Coprinus comatus

SCIENTIFIC NAME: *Gomphidius glutinosus* (Schaeff.) Fr.

SYNONYM: None

COMMON NAME: Slimy Spike

FAMILY: Gomphidiaceae

CAP: Up to 4 in. wide; grayish purple to reddish brown; convex, broadly convex, to nearly flat in age; surface glutinous, smooth; margin with remnants of the partial veil at times

FLESH: Whitish, at times tinted pink, yellow in the stem base; thick; odor not distinctive; taste acidic

GILLS: Pale grayish white to smoky gray in age; prominently decurrent; thick and rather waxy; close; broad; edges even; covered at first by a hyaline, slime-encased, whitish cortina

STEM: Up to 4 in. long; white with a yellow base; with an apical, hyaline but black-stained ring zone; tapered toward the base; surface fibrillose to tomentose and at times slimy below

SPORE PRINT: Smoky gray to blackish

ECOLOGY: Mycorrhizal; solitary, scattered or in small groups in humus and moss in conifer and mixed woods; to be expected in higher altitudes; summer and fall; uncommon

EDIBILITY: Edible

COMMENTS: Species in the genus *Chroogomphus* (not illustrated) have a similar aspect and spore color. Their caps are not glutinous. *Gomphidius glutinosus* is much more common in northern areas and in high-altitude and boggy conifer woods, often with spruce and fir.

Gomphidius glutinosus

SCIENTIFIC NAME: *Agaricus arvensis* Schaeff.

SYNONYM: *Psalliota arvensis* (Schaeff.) Gillet

COMMON NAME: Horse Mushroom

FAMILY: Agaricaceae

CAP: Up to 8 in. wide; white or pale yellowish when young, becoming yellow in age or when rubbed; convex at first, becoming flat; surface dry, often with flat scales over the center; the margin may have traces of the partial veil

FLESH: White and thick; may bruise slowly yellowish; odor sweet, similar to anise or almonds; taste mild

GILLS: White or grayish, sometimes tinged pink becoming brownish and finally dark brown; close; free; edges even; covered at first by a membranous partial veil, which may show a cog-wheeled pattern of V's, persists until the cap expands

STEM: Up to 6 in. long; white or becoming yellowish on handling; solid; equal or larger at the base; with a large ring near the top of the stem; surface smooth or at times becoming scaly below the ring

SPORE PRINT: Dark brown

ECOLOGY: Saprobic in grass or on soil; scattered, solitary, or gregarious, often in treeless areas; it commonly fruits near spruce trees, but the reason for this association is unknown; late spring, summer, and fall; occasional to locally abundant

EDIBILITY: The Horse Mushroom and its complex of related species are edible and have excellent flavor and texture; avoid similar species with an unpleasant odor; do not eat when collected in areas where pesticides or herbicides are used; the dark-brown spore color is important here to eliminate any confusion with a deadly *Amanita*

COMMENTS: This is a large and impressive mushroom. The edible woodland species *Agaricus silvicola* (not illustrated) is very similar but is usually less robust. The large size, anise odor, and lack of bright-pink gills will separate this species from the edible common Field Mushroom, *Agaricus campestris* (p. 224). The deadly Destroying Angel, *Amanita bisporigera* (p. 9), has white gills, a white spore print, and a saccate volva.

Agaricus arvensis

223

SCIENTIFIC NAME: *Coprinellus domesticus* (Bolton) Vilgalys, Hopple, and Jacq. Johnson

SYNONYM: None

COMMON NAME: Rug Inky Cap

FAMILY: Psathyrellaceae

CAP: Up to 2¾ in. wide; honey yellow and whitish toward the margin; oval then conic or convex; surface with whitish or tan scales or granules that are remnants of a universal veil and are easily washed off; granules may be missing entirely; striate, moist

FLESH: Whitish; thin; fragile; odor and taste not distinctive

GILLS: Whitish then brownish black, eventually partially liquefying; free or barely attached to the stem; close

STEM: Up to 3¾ in. long; white; equal or slightly enlarged below; hollow; sometimes with a volva-like collar at the base; usually emanating from a dense carpet of orange fibers, this carpet is often visible when no fruiting bodies are present

SPORE PRINT: Black or blackish brown

ECOLOGY: Gregarious on decaying wood of broadleaf trees, this species can sometimes be found on carpets or on wood in bathrooms and damp basements; summer and fall; occasional

EDIBILITY: Unknown

COMMENTS: *Coprinellus radians* (not illustrated) is very similar, and microscopic examination is needed to separate them. Formerly this species was placed in the genus *Coprinus*.

Coprinellus domesticus

SCIENTIFIC NAME: *Coprinellus micaceus* (Bull.) Vilgalys, Hopple, and Jacq. Johnson

SYNONYM: *Coprinus micaceus* (Bull.) Fr.

COMMON NAME: Mica Cap

FAMILY: Psathyrellaceae

CAP: Up to 1¼ in. wide; tawny brown, amber, reddish brown, fading in age; oval to bell-shaped becoming broadly convex; dry; at first with glistening, mica-like particles; margin striate and in decomposition flaring upward

FLESH: Watery whitish to pale brownish; thin; odor and taste not distinctive

GILLS: Whitish to grayish brown, becoming black and partially dissolving; crowded; barely attached to the stem; no partial veil

STEM: Up to 3 in. long; whitish; equal; hollow; fragile; surface bald, fibrous, or silky

SPORE PRINT: Black

ECOLOGY: Saprobic on the wood of broadleaf trees, often appearing terrestrial when growing from buried roots; usually on dead wood but also on diseased living trees; clustered; abundant; spring through late fall; very common

EDIBILITY: Edible with good flavor but without much substance

COMMENTS: Consider this a species complex since a microscope is needed to identify closely related species. It is abundant in urban areas as well as in woodlands. It is one of the species commonly called "inky caps" owing to the partial dissolving of the gills into a black liquid.

Coprinellus micaceus

SCIENTIFIC NAME: *Bolbitius titubans* (Bull.) Fr.

SYNONYM: *Bolbitius vitellinus* (Pers.) Fr.

COMMON NAME: Yellow Bolbitius

FAMILY: Bolbitiaceae

CAP: Up to 3 in. wide; yellow, becoming white in age; oval to conic when young, becoming flat in age; at times with a persistently yellowish umbo; fragile; surface viscid at times, becoming pocked or veined when drying, bald, striate in age

FLESH: Yellowish; thin; odor and taste mild

GILLS: Whitish or pale yellowish, becoming brownish; free or barely reaching the stem; close to subdistant; no partial veil

STEM: Up to 4 in. long; shiny white or tinted yellow; equal; finely hairy at the apex; no ring

SPORE PRINT: Rusty cinnamon

ECOLOGY: Saprobic; scattered to gregarious on manure piles, fertilized lawns, and gardens; spring, summer, and fall; common

EDIBILITY: Not edible

COMMENTS: This common farmland mushroom appears in the morning and shrivels by late afternoon. The entire mushroom may collapse in wet weather.

Bolbitius titubans

SCIENTIFIC NAME: *Bolbitius callistus* (Peck) Watling

SYNONYM: *Pluteolus callistus* (Peck) Peck

COMMON NAME: None

FAMILY: Bolbitiaceae

CAP: Up to 2 in. wide; colors variable and changeable, deep reddish brown, reddish orange, in age the margin is pale orangish buff and the center is reddish orange; conic becoming convex and finally flat; surface viscid to glutinous, striate

FLESH: Yellowish; very thin; odor not distinctive; taste unknown

GILLS: Yellowish, becoming rusty brown; barely reaching the stem; close; narrow; thin; edges even; no partial veil

STEM: Up to 3 in. long; yellow to yellowish becoming rusty and then dull brown; surface coated at first with a white dusting; equal; hollow

SPORE PRINT: Rusty brown

ECOLOGY: Saprobic on humus and woody debris in broadleaf and swampy broadleaf and mixed woods; summer and fall; rare

EDIBILITY: Unknown

COMMENTS: This seldom-collected mushroom is likely one of a group of similar as-yet-to-be-determined species. In Europe it is reported to have a blue cap, but North American collections and the original description do not describe a blue-capped species. The author has seen a collection from Pennsylvania that had a blue, furfuraceous coating on the stem. The species described here, while rare, is one that does occur occasionally in the Appalachians.

Bolbitius callistus

SCIENTIFIC NAME: *Simocybe centunculus* (Fr.) P. Karst.

SYNONYM: *Naucoria centunculus* (Fr.) P. Kumm.

COMMON NAME: American Simocybe

FAMILY: Crepidotaceae

CAP: Up to 1 in. wide; brown, olive brown, darker in the center; convex, becoming flat in age; surface bald, velvety or silky, striate at times

FLESH: Brown; thin; odor and taste not distinctive

GILLS: Whitish, grayish brown, or yellowish brown; attached to the stem; close to subdistant; edges frayed or finely sawtoothed; no partial veil

STEM: Up to 1½ in. long; dingy whitish to brownish olive; equal or slightly tapering upward; pruinose, becoming nearly bald in age; base with white mycelium

SPORE PRINT: Olive brown

ECOLOGY: Saprobic; solitary, scattered, or gregarious on decaying wood of broadleaf trees; summer and fall; occasional

EDIBILITY: Unknown

COMMENTS: The habitat on wood and the distinctly striate cap and brown spores are key features for this mushroom.

Simocybe centunculus

SCIENTIFIC NAME: *Conocybe apala* (Fr.) Arnolds

SYNONYM: *Conocybe lactea* (J. E. Lange) Métrod

COMMON NAME: White Dunce Cap

FAMILY: Bolbitiaceae

CAP: Up to 1½ in. wide; white or pale buff in age; conical with the margin uplifted at maturity; fragile surface dry, striate

FLESH: Whitish or watery; insubstantial; fragile; odor and taste not distinctive

STEM: Up to 4 in. long; whitish or watery; equal or enlarged slightly below, sometimes with a small basal bulb; hollow; surface dry, bald, or pruinose

GILLS: Whitish, becoming tawny to brownish; close; nearly free; narrow; no partial veil

SPORE PRINT: Reddish brown

ECOLOGY: Saprobic; scattered usually in lawns but also in humus-rich areas; spring, summer, and fall; common

EDIBILITY: Unknown

COMMENTS: An ephemeral species best observed in the morning as it often wilts by midafternoon. It is very common in hot humid weather. Fruitings of above average size have been observed in the Southern Appalachians.

Conocybe apala

SCIENTIFIC NAME: *Panaeolina foenisecii* (Pers.) Maire

SYNONYM: *Panaeolus foenisecii* (Pers.) J. Schröt.

COMMON NAMES: Haymaker, Lawn Mower's Mushroom

FAMILY: Bolbitiaceae

CAP: Up to 1 in. wide; reddish brown to grayish brown, becoming lighter on drying, often producing zones of light and dark colors; ovoid, conic to bell-shaped, becoming convex to nearly flat; surface dry to moist, not viscid; margin smooth or at times striate in age

FLESH: Watery tan to light brown; thin, fragile; odor and taste not distinctive

GILLS: Purplish brown to chocolate brown; attached to the stem or pulling away from it; edges even; no partial veil

STEM: Up to 3 in. long; dull whitish to pinkish brown, at times with a whitish bloom; usually equal but may be enlarged downward; hollow; fragile; surface bald or with minute hairs at the apex

SPORE PRINT: Dark brown to purplish brown

ECOLOGY: Saprobic on grass in lawns and parks; late spring and summer; very abundant

EDIBILITY: Not poisonous but not recommended

COMMENTS: There are many similar little brown mushrooms with black or rusty brown spores. None of these fragile, thin-fleshed mushrooms are good edibles and some of them are poisonous. Because of its abundance, it is one of the mushrooms most commonly consumed by toddlers and dogs.

Panaeolina foenisecii

SCIENTIFIC NAME: *Macrocystidia cucumis* (Pers.) Joss.

SYNONYM: None

COMMON NAME: Cucumber Cap

FAMILY: Marasmiaceae

CAP: Up to 2 in. wide; reddish brown, dark reddish brown with a yellowish-buff margin, fading in age to grayish buff with a brownish center; bell-shaped or convex to broadly convex, becoming nearly flat; surface moist, hygrophanous, smooth, pruinose, or silky at times

FLESH: Brownish; thin; odor pungent, like cucumbers or fish; taste unpleasant, fishy, or mealy

GILLS: Whitish becoming pink or pinkish yellow, discoloring to dark brown where damaged; notched or narrowly attached to the stem; close to subdistant; rather broad; edges even; no partial veil

STEM: Up to 2 in. long; colored like the cap, at times paler above, in age dark brown throughout; equal; tough, fibrous, compressed at times; brittle; surface dry, pruinose

SPORE PRINT: Pinkish brown to pale pink

ECOLOGY: Saprobic; terrestrial on wood-rich soil, or on well-decayed wood; gregarious in broadleaf forests or in wood chips; summer and fall; occasional

EDIBILITY: Not edible

COMMENTS: This species is common in the Pacific Northwest. It is becoming more common in the East, possibly facilitated by being imported in wood mulch.

Macrocystidia cucumis

SCIENTIFIC NAME: *Entoloma quadratum* (Berk. and M. A. Curtis) E. Horak

SYNONYMS: *Entoloma salmoneum* (Peck) Sacc., *Inocephalus quadratus* (Berk and M. A. Curtis) T. J. Baroni

COMMON NAME: Salmon Entoloma

FAMILY: Entolomataceae

CAP: Up to 2 in. wide; bright salmon orange fading to dirty orange, at times with olivaceous stains; bell-shaped to sharply conical, expanding at maturity but maintaining a sharp, pointed umbo; surface moist, sticky when wet

FLESH: Orange; thin; fragile; odor and taste not distinctive

GILLS: Salmon orange; subdistant; fairly broad; narrowly attached to the stem; no partial veil

STEM: Up to 4 in. long; salmon orange; equal; sometimes twisted; hollow; with whitish or pale-orange mycelium at the base; equal; surface striate, translucent striate

SPORE PRINT: Salmon pink

ECOLOGY: Saprobic; single to scattered in moss or litter, most commonly under conifers but also under broadleaf trees; summer and fall; common

EDIBILITY: Poisonous

COMMENTS: Except for the color, this pretty species is very much like the yellow *Entoloma murrayi* (p. 237). Some mycologists place this mushroom in the genus *Inocephalus*. Some mycologists consider the olivaceous-stained variety to be a different species.

Entoloma quadratum

SCIENTIFIC NAME: *Entoloma murrayi* (Berk. and M. A. Curtis) Sacc.

SYNONYMS: *Nolanea murrayi* (Berk. and M. A. Curtis) Dennis, *Inocephalus murrayi* (Berk. and M. A. Curtis) Rutter and Watling

COMMON NAME: Yellow Unicorn Entoloma

FAMILY: Entolomatacea

CAP: Up to 1¼ in. broad; yellow, whitish yellow to orangish yellow; bell-shaped to sharply conical, expanding at maturity but maintaining a sharp, pointed umbo; surface moist, bald, translucent striate

FLESH: Pale yellow; thin; fragile; odor and taste not distinctive

GILLS: Pale yellow; subdistant; narrowly attached to the stem; no partial veil

STEM: Up to 4 in. long; white or yellowish; equal; striate; sometimes twisted; hollow; with white mycelium at the base

SPORE PRINT: Salmon pink

ECOLOGY: Saprobic; single to scattered in litter or moss, most commonly in wet, broadleaf forests but also under conifers; summer and fall; common

EDIBILITY: Not edible

COMMENTS: This is an attractive little mushroom. *Entoloma quadratum* (p. 236) is a look-alike, but it is orange. Species of *Hygrocybe* and *Humidicutis* may have similar colors, but they lack the acute conical shape and have whitish spores. Some mycologists place this species in the genus *Inocephalus*.

Entoloma murrayi

SCIENTIFIC NAME: *Entoloma conicum* (Sacc.) Hesler
SYNONYM: *Nolanea conica* Sacc.
COMMON NAME: Conic Entoloma
FAMILY: Entolomataceae

CAP: Up to ¾ in. wide; dull watery cinnamon to pinkish, fading to grayish cinnamon; conic becoming broadly conic to convex, umbonate; surface silky shiny when dry, translucent striate when wet, hygrophanous

FLESH: Watery brownish; thin; odor and taste not distinctive

GILLS: White at first, becoming pinkish; barely attached or free from the stem; close to subdistant; fairly broad; narrow at the margin; no partial veil

STEM: Up to 2¼ in. long; dark brown, purplish brown to nearly black; bald; straight; hollow; somewhat elastic; base with white mycelium

SPORE PRINT: Salmon pink

ECOLOGY: Saprobic; scattered or gregarious in litter or soil in broadleaf and mixed woods; summer and fall; common

EDIBILITY: Not edible, probably poisonous

COMMENTS: The shiny, pinkish-brown, hygrophanous cap helps set this species apart from *Entoloma alboumbonatum* (not illustrated), which has a whitish cap.

Entoloma conicum

SCIENTIFIC NAME: *Inocybe tahquamenonensis* D. E. Stuntz

SYNONYM: None

COMMON NAME: None

FAMILY: Inocybaceae

CAP: Up to 1¼ in. wide; black, blackish brown, dark purplish brown; or reddish brown; convex becoming broadly convex to flat; at times with a low, broad umbo; surface dry, covered with dark-purplish-brown, reddish-brown or blackish-brown scales

FLESH: Reddish purple; odor not distinctive, or mildly of radish; taste not distinctive

GILLS: Reddish purple, becoming reddish brown, and finally chocolate brown; attached to the stem; subdistant; rather thick; moderately broad; edges even, becoming ragged at times: no partial veil

STEM: Up to 3 in. long; colored like the cap; equal; solid; dry; covered with flat or curved scales

SPORE PRINT: Brown

ECOLOGY: Mycorrhizal; scattered to gregarious in soil and litter in moist broadleaf and mixed woods; summer and fall; common

EDIBILITY: Not edible, probably poisonous

COMMENTS: This is a dark-colored mushroom, probably overlooked by many collectors. It is easily identified and rather attractive despite its dark colors. It is named for Tahquamenon Falls State Park in Northern Michigan, where it was first discovered.

Inocybe tahquamenonensis

SCIENTIFIC NAME: *Inocybe lilacina* (Peck) Kauffman

SYNONYMS: *Inocybe geophylla* var. *lilacina* (Peck) Gillet, *Inocybe geophylla* (Bull.) P. Kumm.

COMMON NAME: Lilac Fiber Cap

FAMILY: **Cortinariaceae**

CAP: Up to 1½ in. wide; lilac to reddish violet overall becoming mottled with white; conic to bell-shaped to nearly flat with a broad umbo; surface dry, silky or nearly smooth; margin incurved at first, often splitting in age

FLESH: White or tinted lilac; thick over the center, thin outward; odor unpleasant, yeasty, of rancid meal or sweat-soaked clothing; taste slightly disagreeable or acrid

GILLS: Whitish to pale lilac when young, becoming grayish brown; attached to the stem or notched; close; fairly broad; edges even; cortina present but soon disappearing

STEM: Up to 2½ in. long; lilac when young, pinkish brown in age, apex white and powdery; equal; solid; surface dry, floccose; partial veil may leave a ring zone

SPORE PRINT: Brown

ECOLOGY: Mycorrhizal; scattered to gregarious in broadleaf, conifer, and mixed woods; late summer and fall; uncommon

EDIBILITY: Poisonous

COMMENTS: Similarly colored species in the genus *Cortinarius* will have a rusty-brown spore print. Some mycologists consider this species to be a variety of *Inocybe geophylla* (not illustrated), a very similar species with whitish coloration. It also is likely that there might be a cluster of undescribed species with violet colors.

Inocybe lilacina

SCIENTIFIC NAME: *Inocybe rimosa* (Bull.) P. Kumm.

SYNONYM: *Inocybe fastigiata* (Schaeff.) Quél.

COMMON NAME: Corn Silk Inocybe

FAMILY: Inocybaceae

CAP: Up to 3½ in. wide; yellowish to reddish tan, splitting in a spoke-like pattern and revealing white flesh; conical to bell-shaped becoming convex to nearly flat, usually with an umbo; surface dry, slippery when wet, silky or finely fibrillose

FLESH: White; odor mealy to rancid, yeasty, resembling sweat-soaked clothing, at times of corn silk; taste not distinctive

GILLS: Whitish, becoming gray and eventually brownish; attached to the stem; close; narrow; edges even; partial veil lacking

STEM: Up to 3½ in. long; whitish to pale yellowish; equal; surface dry, smooth, silky fibrillose, longitudinally striate

SPORE PRINT: Brown

ECOLOGY: Mycorrhizal; scattered to gregarious in humus, lawns, and moss under conifers and broadleaf trees; summer and early fall; common

EDIBILITY: Poisonous

COMMENTS: It is likely several species are lumped under the names *Inocybe fastigiata* and *Inocybe rimosa*. *Inocybe* is a genus that requires a microscope to name all but the most distinctive species.

Inocybe rimosa

SCIENTIFIC NAME: *Inocybe unicolor* Peck

SYNONYM: None

COMMON NAME: None

FAMILY: Inocybaceae

CAP: Up to 2 in. wide; yellowish buff, ochraceous buff to tawny; convex becoming flat; surface densely wooly, fibrous to scaly, the scales usually darker and larger over the disc, dry; margin turned under at first

FLESH: Whitish; thick on the distinct, becoming narrow toward the margin; odor and taste not distinctive

GILLS: Dull yellow ochre, becoming cinnamon brown, edges whitish; attached, pulling away in age; close; broad; at first with a thin, ochre, cortinate partial veil

STEM: Up to 1½ in. long; whitish with ochre to yellowish-tawny or orangish fibers or scales; dry; equal; remnants of the partial veil usually not prominent

SPORE PRINT: Brown

ECOLOGY: Mycorrhizal; usually gregarious or scattered in grass, moss, and soil, in lawns, roadsides, and occasionally in woodlands, usually under oaks; summer and fall; common

EDIBILITY: Not edible, probably poisonous

COMMENTS: *Inocybe caesariata* is a similar European mushroom, and this name has sometimes been used for this American species. *Inocybe* is a large genus of small, brown-spored mushrooms with fibrous caps. Most species require a microscope to make a positive identification.

Inocybe unicolor

SCIENTIFIC NAME: *Psathyrella epimyces* (Peck) A. H. Sm.

SYNONYM: None

COMMON NAME: None

FAMILY: Psathyrellaceae

CAP: Up to 2 in. wide; whitish, becoming dingy white or grayish in age; globe-shaped becoming broadly convex to nearly flat; surface dry, not hygrophanous, silky fibrillose or with small scales; margin with remnants of the partial veil at first

FLESH: Whitish; thick; odor and taste not distinctive

GILLS: Pale pinkish buff, becoming blackish brown from the spores; attached to the stem or barely reaching it; moderately broad; close; edges even with a whitish edge; covered at first by an ephemeral partial veil

STEM: Up to 2 in. long; colored like the cap; equal or tapering upward; floccose or mealy; solid or stuffed, becoming hollow; dry; rarely with a ring

SPORE PRINT: Blackish

ECOLOGY: Parasitic on the Shaggy Mane, *Coprinus comatus* (p. 221); host caps are deformed as to being barely recognizable; normal fruitings are usually in the vicinity; host becomes vase-shaped, and the *Psathyrella* fruits from inside the vase; fall; rare, but where it occurs, it is to be expected every year

EDIBILITY: Unknown

COMMENTS: In a genus of mostly saprobic mushrooms, this is the only known species that is parasitic on another fungus. It is also unusual that the host mushroom is a saprobe. Most mushrooms that are parasitized by fleshy fungi are mycorrhizal species.

Psathyrella epimyces

SCIENTIFIC NAME: *Volvariella surrecta* (Knapp) Singer

SYNONYM: *Volvaria surrecta* (Knapp) Ramsb.

COMMON NAME: Piggyback Rosegill

FAMILY: Pluteaceae

CAP: Up to 3 in. wide; whitish, at time with a yellowish-brown center; nearly round at first, soon convex to broadly convex, becoming almost flat; surface dry, fibrillose to finely scaly, at times silky and nearly smooth

FLESH: Whitish; relatively thin; odor and taste not distinctive

GILLS: White becoming pinkish; free from the stem; crowded; broad; edges even or at times somewhat eroded; no partial veil

STEM: Up to 3 in. long; white; surface dry, appressed fibrillose or velvety; emerging from a rather prominent, white, sack-like volva

SPORE PRINT: Pinkish salmon

ECOLOGY: Parasitic on species of *Clitocybe,* especially *Clitocybe nebularis* (not illustrated), also reported on species of *Tricholoma* and *Melanoleuca*; late summer and fall; rare

EDIBILITY: Unknown

COMMENTS: This mushroom is seldom encountered but easily identified when it is located. No other mushroom is known that has a sack-like volva and is parasitic on other mushrooms. It has been reported on both mycorrhizal and saprobic species.

Volvariella surrecta

BOLETES

Boletes are fleshy fungi that usually have a stereotypically umbrella-shaped cap. The underside of the cap has pores, which are the ends of tubes in which the spores are produced. Most occur on the ground, and most form mycorrhiza with various tree species. Unlike many of the polypores that are most commonly found on wood, boletes do not have a woody texture. At one time all were placed in the genus *Boletus*, but now there are many genera. Some important features to note include taste, presence or absence of a partial veil, scabers, reticulations or glandular dots on the stem, and color changes of the flesh and pores when bruised.

There are many good edibles among the boletes, and no species in the Appalachians are known to be deadly poisonous. Nonlethal poisonings have been reported with some species that have a blue oxidation reaction when the flesh or pores are bruised. Most species with red tube mouths should be avoided as well. These will also usually stain blue when bruised. Some species of *Suillus* have slimy caps that are best peeled before cooking. There are many boletes that, although not poisonous, have an extremely bitter taste. A few have a peppery taste. Many find that preserving edible boletes by slicing and then drying on a food dehydrator intensifies their flavor. Once crisp, they can be stored for years in a plastic bag or other sealed container. They can be reconstituted in water or milk and used as if fresh.

Boletus edulis and closely related species are among the most popular edible species in the world. A few of the many common names include Porcini, Cep, Steinpilz, and King Bolete. Productive collecting areas are often kept secret.

Boletes species

Hemileccinum species

Boletes longicurvipes

Keys to Boletes

Blue-staining boletes

A. Flesh and pores immediately staining dark or bright blue

1. Cap yellow: *Neoboletus pseudosulphureus* (p. 279)
2. Cap whitish: *Gyroporus cyanescens* (p. 277)
3. Cap brown: *Cyanoboletus pulverulentus* (p. 278)
4. Cap blackish brown to chocolate brown; often on wood: *Boletellus chrysenteroides* (p. 267)
5. Cap brownish orange to reddish brown; pores reddish: *Boletus subvelutipes* (p. 251)

Boletus subvelutipes

B. Flesh or pores staining bluish, sometimes slowly

1. Cap red; medium to large; flesh staining slowly blue, fading to yellow: *Baorangia bicolor* (p. 268)
2. Cap red; small to medium; yellow pores staining bluish green: *Hortiboletus rubellus* (p. 269)
3. Cap red; shiny; stem with raised reticulations: *Exsudoporus frostii* (p. 266)
4. Cap buffy gray; mature pores bruise strongly blue or greenish: *Boletus pallidus* (p. 257)
5. Cap dingy white to gray; flesh staining blue, stem often reticulate: *Caloboletus inedulis* (p. 271)
6. Cap reddish; fertile surface gill-like: *Phylloporus leucomycelinus* (p. 301)

Baorangia bicolor

Not staining blue when bruised and not reticulate

1. Cap brown with pale spots: *Xanthoconium affine* var. *maculosus* (p. 273)
2. Cap tan; wrinkled or corrugated: *Xerocomus hortonii* (may bruise slowly and faintly blue) (p. 272)
3. Cap reddish brown to yellowish brown; bright-yellow pores: *Aureoboletus innixus* (p. 270)
4. Cap orange brown to chestnut brown; pores not bright yellow: *Gyroporus castaneus* (p. 275)
5. Cap purplish red to burgundy: *Gyroporus purpurinus* (p. 276)
6. Cap blackish brown; fuzzy, with cottony pointed or flattened scales: *Strobilomyces strobilaceus* (p. 281)
7. Cap tawny olive to tan; growing on *Scleroderma citrinum*: *Pseudoboletus parasiticus* (p. 284)

8. Cap brown to tan, taste peppery: *Chalciporus piperatus* (p. 280)

Xerocomus hortonii

Not staining blue when bruised, with reddish-brown to vinaceous spores

1. Cap black to blackish gray: *Tylopilus alboater* (p. 261)
2. Cap grayish purple; stem purple; spores vinaceous: *Tylopilus plumbeoviolaceus* (p. 259)

3. Cap purplish pink to grayish violet; stem violet to brown: *Tylopilus violatinctus* (p. 260)
4. Cap brown or tan; stem with dark reticulations; under conifers: *Tylopilus felleus* (p. 258)
5. Cap orange to orange red: *Tylopilus ballouii* (p. 262)

Austroboletus gracilis

With reticulate stems

1. Cap red; shiny; raised reticulations: *Exsudoporus frostii* (p. 266)

2. Cap tan to dark brown; found under broadleaf trees; white reticulations: *Boletus variipes* (p. 255)

3. Cap reddish brown, to yellowish tan; found under conifers; white reticulations: *Boletus edulis* (p. 252)

4. Cap brown or tan; found under conifers; prominent brown reticulations: *Tylopilus felleus* (p. 258)

5. Cap yellowish, gray, or brownish; prominent yellow reticulations: *Retiboletus ornatipes* (p. 264)

6. Cap gray to brown or whitish; prominent gray or white reticulations: *Retiboletus griseus* (p. 263)

7. Cap gray to whitish; reticulations reddish, sometimes faint: *Boletus inedulis* (p. 271)

8. Cap violet to liver brown when young; white reticulations; under oaks: *Boletus separans* (p. 254)

9. Cap reddish brown; reticulations brownish; under conifers: *Boletus subcaerulescens* (p. 253)

10. Cap orange to yellow; long stemmed; prominent, ragged reticulations: *Heimioporus betula* (p. 265)

11. Cap pale gray to brown; long stemmed, prominent reticulations: *Boletellus russellii* (p. 283)

12. Cap wrinkled to corrugated; tan; only occasionally with reticulations: *Xerocomus hortonii* (p. 272)

Tylopilus felleus

With scabers on the stem

1. Cap black or dark gray; under birch and conifers in mixed woods: *Leccinum snellii* (p. 288)

2. Cap dark brown to blackish brown; under oaks: *Leccinellum crocipodium* (p. 285)

3. Cap orange, yellow, or tan; under oaks: *Leccinum rugosiceps* (p. 286)

4. Cap orange under Norway spruce: *Leccinum piceinum* (p. 287)

Leccinum snellii

Viscid capped and in the genus *Suillus*

1. Cap yellow; under white pine: *Suillus americanus* (p. 290)

2. Cap yellow; orange or brown under larch: *Suillus clintonianus* (p. 295)

3. Cap yellow to ochre; under broadleaf trees or pines; odor indistinct: *Suillus subaureus* (p. 298)

4. Cap yellow to ochre; under conifers; odor sweet, similar to almond extract: *Suillus punctipes* (p. 297)

5. Cap white; under white pine; stem with numerous pinkish-tan smears or dots: *Suillus placidus* (p. 292)

6. Cap tan or brown; ring on the stem; under pines; taste of cap slime acidic: *Suillus acidus* (p. 296)

7. Cap dark brown; under pines; no ring on the stem: *Suillus brevipes* (p. 293)

8. Cap dark brown; membranous ring on the stem: *Suillus luteus* (p. 294)

9. Cap cinnamon to vinaceous brown; no stem ring; stem with glandular dots: *Suillus granulatus* (p. 291)

Suillus salmonicolor

Dry capped and having radially arranged pores

1. Cap brown, under ash: *Boletinellus merulioides* (p. 282)

2. Cap brown, under oaks: *Bothia castanella* (p. 299)

3. Cap red under white pine: *Suillus spraguei* (p. 289)

4. Cap brown, on conifer wood, lacking a stem: *Pseudomerulius curtisii* (p. 300)

5. Cap brown to tan, taste peppery: *Chalciporus piperatus* (p. 280)

Suillus spraguei

SCIENTIFIC NAME: *Boletus subvelutipes* Peck

SYNONYMS: None

COMMON NAME: Red-Pored Bolete

FAMILY: Boletaceae

CAP: Up to 5 in. wide; variable in color, brownish orange; yellowish brown to reddish brown, often dull brown in age or in rainy weather; convex to broadly convex, becoming nearly flat in age; surface dry, velvety when young, at times cracking in age, immediately staining blackish blue when bruised

FLESH: Yellow becoming white, instantly staining blackish blue when exposed; odor not distinctive; taste slightly acidic or not distinctive

PORES: Various shades of red and orange, often with a yellow marginal rim, becoming duller in age; small; circular; no partial veil

STEM: Up to 4 in. long; yellow at the apex, yellow and red downward, surface red pruinose in a random or vertically lined arrangement, at times forming a false reticulation, not truly reticulate or barely so at the extreme apex, instantly staining dark blackish blue when bruised; equal or enlarged downward; solid

SPORE PRINT: Olive brown

ECOLOGY: Mycorrhizal; solitary, scattered to gregarious in humus, moss, and grass in broadleaf and mixed woods, often under oaks and hemlock; summer and fall; very common

EDIBILITY: Poisonous; gastrointestinal problems have been reported, though others have eaten it without problems; there are many red-pored boletes, so which ones have caused digestive issues and which ones have not is unclear

COMMENTS: Red-pored boletes are notoriously poorly differentiated and difficult to identify. Much work needs to be done on this group's taxonomy and distribution. *Boletus subvelutipes* as considered here is one of the first boletes to appear. Some important features are the reddish or yellowish hairs usually present at the stem base and the red, pruinose dusting over a yellowish ground color on the stem.

Boletus subvelutipes

SCIENTIFIC NAME: *Boletus edulis* Bull.

SYNONYM: *Boletus chippewaensis* A. H. Smith and Thiers

COMMON NAMES: King Bolete, Porcini, Cep

FAMILY: Boletaceae

CAP: Up to 8 in. wide; reddish orange, reddish brown to yellowish tan; convex, broadly convex to nearly flat in age; surface slightly viscid when moist, slightly tacky when dry; smooth to slightly wrinkled or pitted

FLESH: White, unchanging when exposed; thick; odor and taste not distinctive

PORES: White, becoming yellow with olive tints in age; unchanging when bruised, or staining yellowish brown at times; small, becoming larger in mature caps; circular; no partial veil

STEM: Up to 4½ in. long; white to pale brownish; surface with white reticulations on the upper stem, at times extending downward, dry; enlarged club-shaped to downward, at times nearly equal

SPORE PRINT: Olive brown

ECOLOGY: Mycorrhizal with conifers, especially with Norway spruce, pines, and hemlock; solitary, scattered, or gregarious in humus, moss, and grass in conifer and mixed woodlands and parks

EDIBILITY: Edible and choice; the poisonous *Boletus huronensis* (not illustrated) is rare in the Appalachians, its flesh blues slightly when bruised, and its stem is barely reticulate or not at all

COMMENTS: This is a very famous edible mushroom. It is to be approached as a complex of closely related species. As considered here it is a species found under conifers, with a tacky cap, pores that go from white to yellowish, and a whitish stem with white reticulations. How many species are going under this general description and name is yet to be determined. Our common species may actually be *Boletus chippewaensis*. All of the varieties are good edibles. The variability and popularity of this complex is evidenced by the fact that there have been nineteen varieties and twenty forms described! *Boletus subcaerulescens* (p. 253), once considered a variety, has pores that stain blue-green when bruised. Compare with the Bitter Bolete, or *Tylopilus felleus* (p. 258), which has brown reticulations and a pinkish-brown spore print. *Boletus variipes* (p. 255) and *Boletus separans* (p. 254) are similar edible species that associate with broadleaf trees.

Boletus edulis

SCIENTIFIC NAME: *Boletus subcaerulescens* (E. A. Dick and Snell) Both, Bessette, and A. R. Bessette

SYNONYM: *Boletus edulis* f. *subcaerulescens* (E. A. Dick and Snell) Vassilkov

COMMON NAME: None

FAMILY: Boletaceae

CAP: Up to 6 in. wide; cocoa-colored to reddish brown, mottled with yellow at times, with pale-cinnamon coloration in age; margin often whitish or pale yellow, incurved at first, with a narrow band or sterile tissue, nearly round, becoming convex and finally flat; surface dry with flattened fibers, or nearly bald, often wrinkled or pitted

FLESH: White, dull vinaceous near the cuticle and near the tubes, unchanging when exposed or bruising blue by the tubes; thick at the cap center; odor not distinctive, or lemony; taste nutty

PORES: Whitish to cream at first, becoming yellow then greenish yellow and finally dingy olive with brownish areas; staining bluish green and then brownish where bruised; circular to angular; small; no partial veil

STEM: Up to 5 in. long; rusty brown to brownish vinaceous, paler at the apex, white at the base, with white to brownish reticulation over most of the stem; reticulation becoming torn at times; fuzzy around the reticulations; surface dry; solid; base with white mycelium, at times with a root-like extension

SPORE PRINT: Olive gray

ECOLOGY: Mycorrhizal with Scots pine, Norway spruce, and possibly other conifers; solitary, scattered, or gregarious in humus and moss in conifer and mixed woods; late spring, summer, and fall; occasional to locally abundant

EDIBILITY: Edible and choice

COMMENTS: This species was formerly considered a variety of *Boletus edulis* (p. 252). The brown stem with brownish reticulations and blue-green color change of the bruised pores will help distinguish this species.

Boletus subcaerulescens

253

SCIENTIFIC NAME: *Boletus separans* Peck

SYNONYM: *Xanthoconium separans* (Peck) Halling and Both

COMMON NAME: Lilac Bolete

FAMILY: Boletaceae

CAP: Up to 6 in. wide; variable in color, ranging from dark purple to pale reddish buff, whitish or yellowish, typically liver brown or violaceous brown; surface often wrinkled or pitted, velvety, or bald at times, slightly sticky when young, becoming dry

FLESH: White, unchanging when exposed; fairly thick; odor and taste not distinctive

PORES: Whitish, becoming yellowish and finally bright brownish yellow; not staining when bruised, or staining slightly brighter yellow or brown; depressed around the stem; small; stuffed when young

STEM: Up to 5 in. long; whitish or colored like the cap, only paler; apex and base typically white, with white reticulation, prominent or faint, usually over at least half of the stem; equal or enlarged downward; solid; surface bald, dry, at times wrinkled

SPORE PRINT: Yellowish brown to pale reddish brown

ECOLOGY: Mycorrhizal; solitary, scattered to gregarious in parks, broadleaf and mixed woods, often in grass, humus, and moss; under oaks; summer and early fall; common

EDIBILITY: Edible and good

COMMENTS: After heavy rains this species can be nearly white on all parts. Usually lilac tints will be visible on the cap or stem. In many guides this species will be called *Xanthoconium separans*. Compare with *Boletus variipes* (p. 255), *Boletus edulis* (p. 252), and *Boletus nobilis* (not illustrated). The lilac tints are not present in these species.

Boletus separans

SCIENTIFIC NAME: *Boletus variipes* Peck

SYNONYM: None

COMMON NAME: None

FAMILY: Boletaceae

CAP: Up to 6 in. wide; creamy tan, grayish brown, yellowish brown, or brown (dark brown in *Boletus variipes* var. *fagicola*); convex, becoming broadly convex, nearly flat at times in age; surface dry, somewhat velvety, cracking in dry weather; margin even

FLESH: White, unchanging when exposed; thick; odor and taste not distinctive

PORES: White, becoming yellowish to yellowish olive in age; not staining when bruised; circular; small; stuffed at first; no partial veil

STEM: Up to 5 in. long; whitish to various shades of brown or tan; surface dry with usually prominent white or occasionally brown reticulation; equal or enlarged downward, at times swollen in the middle; solid

SPORE PRINT: Olive brown

ECOLOGY: Mycorrhizal; solitary, scattered to gregarious in humus, moss, and grass under oaks and other broadleaf trees, also reported under hemlock; summer and early fall; common

EDIBILITY: Edible and good but frequently infested with fly larvae

COMMENTS: This is one of the first boletes to appear in the summer. *Boletus atkinsonii* (not illustrated) and *Boletus nobilis* (not illustrated) are similar. Both have much less prominent reticulations, have a paler stem, and are less common. They are also edible. Compare with *Boletus edulis* (p. 252), which has a tacky cap and associates with conifers, especially spruce. Both varieties of *Boletus variipes* are illustrated here.

Boletus variipes

Boletes variipes var. *fagicola*

SCIENTIFIC NAME: *Boletus auripes* Peck

SYNONYM: *Aureoboletus aureissimus*

COMMON NAME: **Butter Foot Bolete**

FAMILY: **Boletaceae**

CAP: Up to 4½ in. wide; chestnut brown to yellow brown, fading in age; nearly round to convex, becoming broadly convex to nearly flat in age; surface velvety at first, then smooth and dry

FLESH: Yellow, not changing on exposure, or rarely slightly bluish; at times becoming deeper yellow; firm; thick; odor and taste not distinctive

PORES: Yellow, becoming olive to brownish yellow at maturity, unchanging when bruised; very small; round to angular; no partial veil

STEM: Up to 3 in. long; bright yellow, at times tinged brown, often discoloring brownish in age; club-shaped or enlarged below when young, often becoming nearly equal in age; surface usually with yellowish reticulations at the apex, dry, fibrillose, striate to somewhat roughened

SPORE PRINT: Yellow brown to olive brown

ECOLOGY: Mycorrhizal; solitary, scattered to gregarious in humus, moss, and grass in broadleaf woods and parks, often under oaks; summer and early fall; occasional to locally abundant

EDIBILITY: Edible

COMMENTS: This is a handsome mushroom with its plush, brown cap contrasting with its bright-yellow stem. It has no close look-alike in the Appalachians.

Boletus auripes

SCIENTIFIC NAME: *Boletus pallidus* Frost

SYNONYM: None

COMMON NAME: Pale Bolete

FAMILY: Boletaceae

CAP: Up to 5 in. wide; whitish to buffy gray, pinkish buff when young, dingy brown in age, tinted rose at times; convex to broadly convex and finally nearly flat, at times with a central depression; surface dry, bald, or finely velvety

FLESH: Whitish or pale yellow; unchanged or staining slightly blue when bruised; odor not distinctive; taste slightly bitter or not distinctive

PORES: whitish to yellowish when young, becoming yellow to greenish yellow in age; staining greenish blue then gray when bruised, there may be no staining when very young; reaching the stem or depressed around it; small; circular becoming angular; no partial veil

STEM: Up to 5 in. long; whitish when young, developing brownish streaks near the base, at times yellow at the apex and with reddish streaks downward; equal or enlarged downward; solid; surface dry, smooth, apex at times slightly reticulate

SPORE PRINT: Olive brown

ECOLOGY: Mycorrhizal; solitary, scattered, or gregarious in humus, moss, or grass in broadleaf woods and parks, often under oaks; summer and fall; common

EDIBILITY: Edible

COMMENTS: This mushroom fruits commonly most summers, often in parks and cemeteries under red oak.

Boletus pallidus

SCIENTIFIC NAME: *Tylopilus felleus* (Bull.) P. Karst.

SYNONYM: *Boletus felleus* Bull.

COMMON NAME: Bitter Bolete

FAMILY: Boletaceae

CAP: Up to 11 in. wide: various shades of tan and brown; nearly round at first, becoming convex to broadly convex and finally nearly flat; surface bald, dry, somewhat viscid when wet

PORES: White, becoming dingy pink or reddish tan, often staining brown when bruised; nearly circular; no partial veil

FLESH: White, staining slightly pink where exposed; soft; thick; odor not distinctive; taste very bitter

STEM: Up to 8 in. long; pale buff or brown except for a whitish apex; enlarged downward, bulbous at times; surface dry, distinctly reticulate, with brown reticulations

SPORE PRINT: Pinkish brown to reddish brown

ECOLOGY: Mycorrhizal with conifers; solitary to gregarious; terrestrial on humus and moss; often on rotten conifer stumps in conifer and mixed forests; summer and fall; common

EDIBILITY: Not edible owing to the bitter taste

COMMENTS: The bitter taste, brown reticulations, and pinkish pores will separate this species from *Boletus edulis* (p. 252), which has a mild taste, white reticulations, and white to yellowish pores. There are several brown-capped species of *Tylopilus* often found in lawns under oaks. Many of these have a mild taste and are edible, but none are considered to be very flavorful.

Tylopilus felleus

SCIENTIFIC NAME: *Tylopilus plumbeoviolaceus* (Snell and E. A. Dick) Snell and E. A. Dick

SYNONYM: *Boletus plumbeoviolaceus* Snell and E. A. Dick

COMMON NAME: Violet-Gray Bolete

FAMILY: Boletaceae

CAP: Up to 5½ in. wide; violet to purple or grayish purple when young, becoming brown tinted and finally tan or dull cinnamon; surface dry, with a bloom at first, becoming bald and shiny

FLESH: White, unchanging when exposed; firm; odor not distinctive; taste very bitter

PORES: White at first, becoming pinkish to dull reddish tan, staining brown when bruised; small; circular to angular; depressed around the stem at maturity; no partial veil

STEM: Up to 5½ in. tall; violaceous, reddish violet, grayish violet, becoming brownish, base whitish; equal or enlarged downward; surface dry, occasionally reticulated near the apex

SPORE PRINT: Vinaceous

ECOLOGY: Mycorrhizal; solitary to gregarious or in small clusters in humus or grass under oaks, hemlock; in broad leaf or mixed woodlands; summer and early fall; occasional to common

EDIBILITY: Not edible, bitter

COMMENTS: This is a beautiful bolete when young. Its stem retains its violet color into maturity, and the contrast with the mature cap will distinguish this species from the more uniformly colored *Tylopilus violatinctus* (p. 260).

Tylopilus plumbeoviolaceus

SCIENTIFIC NAME: *Tylopilus violatinctus* T. J. Baroni and Both

SYNONYM: None

COMMON NAME: Pale Violet Bitter Bolete

FAMILY: Boletaceae

CAP: Up to 5 in. wide; violet to purplish at first, soon purplish pink or grayish violet, and finally drab brownish, bruising rusty violet to dark violet; roundish, becoming convex to broadly convex and finally nearly flat; surface dry, velvety when young, becoming nearly bald and shiny in age

FLESH: White, unchanging when cut or slowly turning grayish; fairly thick; odor not distinctive; taste very bitter

PORES: White, eventually becoming dull pinkish brown, unchanging when bruised or slowly staining brownish olive; small; nearly round; no partial veil

STEM: Up to 5½ in. long; at first violaceous, becoming brownish in age, base and apex usually whitish; equal or enlarged below; usually not reticulate but the apex can be reticulate at times and rarely reticulations can extend halfway down the stem

SPORE PRINT: Reddish brown

ECOLOGY: Mycorrhizal; solitary, scattered to gregarious in humus in mixed woods, often with hemlock, red oak, and beech; summer and early fall; occasional

EDIBILITY: Unknown

COMMENTS: Compare with *Tylopilus plumbeoviolaceus* (p. 259), which has a dark-purple stalk. *Tylopilus rubrobrunneus* (not illustrated) is also similar, but its stem develops olivaceous stains. All of these purplish species lose most of their violet colors in age, making them difficult to identify at that stage.

Tylopilus violatinctus

SCIENTIFIC NAME: *Tylopilus alboater* (Schwein.) Murrill

SYNONYM: None

COMMON NAME: Black Velvet Bolete

FAMILY: Boletaceae

CAP: Up to 6 in. wide; black to blackish gray, paler in age; convex to broadly convex, in age becoming flat; surface dry, velvety, with a thin, whitish or violaceous bloom, cracking in age

FLESH: White to pale grayish, pink to reddish when exposed, eventually becoming blackish; firm; thick; odor and taste not distinctive

PORES: Whitish to pale gray, becoming dull pinkish at maturity, staining reddish, the stains slowly turning black; small; angular to irregular; no partial veil

STEM: Up to 4½ in. long; pale gray to dark gray, palest at the apex; staining reddish to blackish when bruised; equal or enlarged downward; solid; surface dry, with a faint, whitish bloom at times, usually not reticulate

SPORE PRINT: Pink to pinkish red

ECOLOGY: Mycorrhizal with oaks; solitary, scattered to gregarious in humus or moss in broadleaf woods; summer and fall; occasional to locally abundant

EDIBILITY: Edible and good

COMMENTS: The young caps have a smooth cuticle reminiscent of mole skin. *Tylopilus griseocarneus* (not illustrated) is similar, but its stem is prominently reticulate. The hemlock associate *Tylopilus atratus* (not illustrated) is smaller and lacks reddish staining.

Tylopilus alboater

SCIENTIFIC NAME: *Tylopilus balloui* (Peck) Singer

SYNONYMS: *Rubinoboletus balloui* (Peck) Heinem. and Rammeloo, *Gyroporus ballouii* (Peck) E. Horak

COMMON NAME: Burnt-Orange Bolete

FAMILY: Boletaceae

CAP: Up to 5 in. wide; bright orange to orangish red, fading to dull orange, cinnamon, or tan in age; surface dry, fairly smooth, bald, velvety, or cracked into small patches; margin incurved at first

FLESH: White, staining pinkish tan to lilac brown when damaged; soft; mild odor unpleasantly similar to chlorine; taste mild to slightly bitter

PORES: White, becoming tan, pinkish, or brownish to smoky brown in age, staining brown when bruised; somewhat angular; no partial veil

STEM: Up to 4½ in. long; white, yellow, or orange, staining brownish when damaged; equal or tapering in either direction; solid; surface dry, smooth or scurfy, not usually reticulate

SPORE PRINT: Pale brown, tan, or reddish brown

ECOLOGY: Mycorrhizal with oaks and beech, and possibly with pines and other broadleaf and conifer trees; solitary, scattered, gregarious or clustered; summer and fall; occasional

EDIBILITY: Reported as edible but slightly bitter

COMMENTS: This species is more common from Virginia southward. Its orange color when young makes this a rather distinctive species.

Tylopilus balloui

SCIENTIFIC NAME: *Retiboletus griseus* (Frost) Manfr. Binder and Bresinsky

SYNONYM: *Boletus griseus* Frost

COMMON NAME: Gray Bolete

FAMILY: Boletaceae

CAP: Up to 5 in. wide; pale to dark gray at first, sometimes brownish or whitish in age; convex to broadly convex, becoming nearly flat in age; surface dry, appressed fibrillose, dull at times, becoming finely scaly at maturity

FLESH: Whitish, at times staining dingy red or brownish when exposed, dark yellowish brown around larval tunnels; thick; odor and taste not distinctive

PORES: White to grayish or grayish brown; unchanging or staining brownish or gray where bruised, circular, small; usually attached to the stem; no partial veil

STEM: Up to 4 in. long; whitish to grayish with a yellowish base; equal or tapering downward; solid; surface dry, prominently reticulate over most of the stem

SPORE PRINT: Olive brown

ECOLOGY: Mycorrhizal with oaks and possibly other broadleaf trees; scattered to gregarious in humus, moss, and lawns under broadleaf trees or in mixed woods; summer and early fall; common

EDIBILITY: Edible

COMMENTS: *Retiboletus ornatipes* (p. 264) has a yellow stem and often has mustard-yellowish colors on its cap.

Retiboletus griseus

SCIENTIFIC NAME: *Retiboletus ornatipes* (Peck) Manfr. Binder and Bresinsky

SYNONYM: *Boletus ornatipes* Peck

COMMON NAME: **Ornate Stalked Bolete**

FAMILY: **Boletaceae**

CAP: Up to 6 in. wide; smoke gray, brownish olive, or mustard yellow; convex, flat in age; surface smooth, felt-like, dry, finely tomentose to bald and shiny; margin with a narrow, sterile band of tissue

FLESH: Yellow to dull buff, tinted reddish under the cap cuticle, unchanging when exposed; firm; odor not distinctive; taste bitter, slightly bitter to not distinctive

PORES: Honey yellow, brownish olive to brown in age, staining brighter yellow or orange when bruised; circular, randomly arranged; no partial veil

STEM: Up to 6 in. long; bright yellow to orangish yellow; equal or tapered in either direction; surface dry with prominent, raised, elongate, yellow reticulations, usually extending all the way down the stem; staining dark yellowish orange when bruised

SPORE PRINT: Olive brown

ECOLOGY: Mycorrhizal with oaks; solitary, scattered to gregarious in moss and humus in broadleaf and mixed woodlands; summer and early fall; common

EDIBILITY: Edible but bitter; generally the more yellow pigment in the cap, the more bitter the taste

COMMENTS: *Retiboletus griseus* (p. 263) can look similar but lacks the yellow colors on the upper stem and cap.

Retiboletus ornatipes

SCIENTIFIC NAME: *Heimioporus betula* (Schwein.) E. Horak

SYNONYMS: *Austroboletus betula* (Schwein.) E. Horak, *Boletellus betula* (Schwein.) E. -J. Gilbert

COMMON NAME: Shaggy-Stalked Bolete

FAMILY: Boletaceae

CAP: Up to 3 in. wide; red, reddish orange, becoming yellow in age, margin often yellow; convex to broadly convex; surface moist, viscid when wet, shiny when dry, bald, at times becoming pitted or wrinkled in age

PORES: Yellow to greenish yellow, not staining when bruised; circular; not radially arranged; fairly small; no partial veil

FLESH: Pale yellow to tinted orange or reddish in the stem, not changing when exposed; odor not distinctive; taste not distinctive, or slightly acidic

STEM: Up to 7 in. long; yellow, or yellow with a reddish ground color; equal; solid; firm; basal base with whitish mycelium; at times with rhizomorphs; surface dry with coarse, raised reticulations to shaggy ribs

SPORE PRINT: Olive brown

ECOLOGY: Mycorrhizal; solitary to scattered in oak pine woods and at times with hemlock and beech; summer and early fall; very common in the southern Appalachians

EDIBILITY: Edible

COMMENTS: This striking, shaggy-stalked, long-legged bolete with an orange to yellow cap has no look-alike. Its long stem makes it easy to find.

Heimioporus betula

SCIENTIFIC NAME: *Exsudoporus frostii* (J. L. Russell) Vizzini, Simonini, and Gelardi

SYNONYMS: *Boletus frostii* J. L. Russell, *Butyriboletus frostii* (J. L. Russell) G. Wu, Kuan Zhao, and Zhu L. Yang

COMMON NAMES: Frost's Bolete, Candy Apple Bolete

FAMILY: Boletaceae

CAP: Up to 5 in. broad; candy-apple red, with yellowish areas in age; nearly round, convex, broadly convex to nearly flat; surface bald, shiny, moist, viscid when wet; margin incurved when young, with a yellow rim at maturity

PORES: Dark red to pale red, often with golden droplets when young; quickly staining blackish blue when damaged; depressed around the stem; round; small; no partial veil

FLESH: Pale yellow to yellow, staining blue when exposed; firm; odor not distinctive; taste slightly sour

STEM: Up to 4 in. long; red or occasionally with yellowish areas showing where the red reticulations are damaged or at the base, slowly staining blue when bruised; coarsely reticulate; solid; equal or enlarging downward

SPORE PRINT: Olive brown

ECOLOGY: Mycorrhizal with oaks and possibly other broadleaf trees; solitary to scattered or gregarious in humus, grass, and moss in broadleaf and mixed woods and parks; summer and early fall; occasional to locally common

EDIBILITY: Edible; most red-pored boletes should be avoided, but this one is so distinctive as to be recommended; it has a lemony or sour taste, which lends itself to seafood sauces and other dishes where a bit of tartness is desired

COMMENTS: This is no doubt one of the most beautiful boletes. When young, it is one of the most distinctive. The raised-stem reticulation and shiny red cap are a distinctive combination. Some say it is too pretty to eat.

Exsudoporus frostii

SCIENTIFIC NAME: *Boletellus chrysenteroides* (Snell) Snell

SYNONYM: *Boletus chrysenteroides* Snell

COMMON NAME: None

FAMILY: Boletaceae

CAP: Up to 3 in. broad; dark blackish brown at first, then reddish brown, chocolate brown, or yellowish brown; convex to broadly convex; surface dry, velvety at first, becoming fibrillose, often cracking in age, tan to whitish in the cracks; margin even

PORES: Pale yellow to bright yellow, becoming greenish yellow, staining blue when bruised; round to angular; no partial veil

FLESH: Pale yellow to whitish, reddish around larval tunnels, staining blue when exposed; odor and taste not distinctive

STEM: Up to 1½ in. long; reddish brown to blackish brown, paler upward, at times yellow at the apex, staining blue when bruised, the stains eventually becoming reddish; equal or enlarged downward; surface dry, with fibers, scales, or scabers

SPORE PRINT: Olive brown

ECOLOGY: Mycorrhizal; solitary or in small groups on well-decayed wood or in lignin-rich humus in broadleaf and mixed woods; summer and fall; occasional

EDIBILITY: Edible

COMMENTS: The dark-brown cap, frequent habitat on wood, and the blue staining will set this species apart from similar-looking boletes.

Boletellus chrysenteroides

SCIENTIFIC NAME: *Baorangia bicolor* (Kuntze) G. Wu, Halling, and Zhu L. Yang

SYNONYM: *Boletus bicolor* Peck

COMMON NAME: Red and Yellow Bolete

FAMILY: Boletaceae

CAP: Up to 5 in. wide; dark red to purple red or rose pink, becoming yellowish in age; convex to broadly convex, to nearly flat; surface dry, velvety, bald to finely wooly, often becoming cracked in age

FLESH: Yellow, slowly staining blue when exposed, then becoming yellow again; odor not distinctive, or reportedly of bouillon or curry; taste not distinctive

PORES: Bright yellow at first, becoming olive yellow in age, staining greenish blue when bruised; tubes are very short; angular; small; no partial veil

STEM: Up to 4 in. long; yellow at the apex, reddish below; not staining, or slowly staining grayish blue when bruised; equal to club-shaped; surface dry, bald, not reticulate

SPORE PRINT: Olive brown

ECOLOGY: Mycorrhizal with oaks; scattered to gregarious in broadleaf and mixed woods; summer and early fall; common

EDIBILITY: Edible with caution; similar species have caused diarrhea and other digestive upsets

COMMENTS: Key features are the very shallow tubes and the weak and slow blue staining or absence of staining of the flesh. The poisonous *Boletus sensibilis* (not illustrated) stains blue quickly when damaged and has a sweet, curry odor. This is another bolete species complex requiring further study and DNA analysis.

Baorangia bicolor

SCIENTIFIC NAME: *Hortiboletus rubellus* (Krombh.) Simonini

SYNONYMS: *Xerocomellus rubellus* (Krombh.) Šutara, *Boletus rubellus* Krombh, *Boletus fraternus* Peck

COMMON NAME: Ruby Bolete

FAMILY: Boletaceae

CAP: Up to 3 in. wide; dark red, fading to brick red in age, at times fading to pinkish red; convex to nearly flat; surface bald, dry, and velvety, at times cracking in age

FLESH: Bright yellow to pale yellow in the cap, with reddish to orange spots at the stem base; slowly staining blue on exposure; fairly thick; odor and taste not distinctive

PORES: Yellow, staining bluish green when bruised; angular at maturity, thick walled; usually depressed around the stem; no partial veil

STEM: Up to 3 in. long; yellow at the apex, pinkish to red below; equal or tapered downward; base with whitish mycelium; surface usually with red points and dots; staining brownish where handled

SPORE PRINT: Olive brown

ECOLOGY: Mycorrhizal with broadleaf trees, often associated with oak and beech; solitary, scattered to gregarious on soil, moss, or humus in broadleaf and mixed woods, often along trails or on wood edges

EDIBILITY: Unknown

COMMENTS: *Hortiboletus campestris* (not illustrated) is very similar. There are other look-alikes, including *Boletus subfraternus* (not illustrated) and *Boletus harrisonii* (not illustrated). All require a microscope for positive identification.

Hortiboletus rubellus

SCIENTIFIC NAME: *Aureoboletus innixus* (Frost) Halling, A. R. Bessette and A. E. Bessette

SYNONYMS: *Boletus innixus* Frost, *Pulveroboletus innixus* (Frost) Singer, *Boletus caespitosus* Peck

COMMON NAME: Clustered Brown Bolete

FAMILY: Boletaceae

CAP: Up to 3 in. wide; reddish brown, yellowish brown to dull cinnamon; convex to broadly convex; surface dry or slightly tacky when moist; at times cracking in age

FLESH: White to yellow; with ruddy staining in the cap and brownish in the stem, vinaceous right under the cuticle; odor variously reported as pungent, resembling witch hazel, like the flesh of *Scleroderma citrinum*, or not distinctive; taste not distinctive

Pores: Bright yellow at first, becoming dull yellow in age, not staining when bruised; randomly arranged; circular or angular; no partial veil

STEM: Up to 3 in. long; yellowish, streaked vertically with brown; basal mycelium yellowish; club-shaped, often distinctly swollen lower mid stem, tapered down below the swelling; rather stout; surface smooth or fibrillose, dry above, viscid at the base, more so when rubbed

SPORE PRINT: Olive brown

ECOLOGY: Mycorrhizal; solitary, scattered to gregarious, often in small clusters in humus, lawns, or moss, in broadleaf woods, often with oaks; summer and early fall; common

EDIBILITY: Edible

COMMENTS: *Aureoboletus auriporus* (not illustrated) has similar colors. Its cap and stem are viscid, and its stem base has ample, white mycelium. *Aureoboletus innixus* is a very common species.

Aureoboletus innixus

SCIENTIFIC NAME: *Caloboletus inedulis* (Murrill) Vizzini

SYNONYM: *Boletus inedulis* (Murrill) Murrill

COMMON NAME: None

FAMILY: Boletaceae

CAP: Up to 5 in. wide; gray, dingy white, pinkish gray, darkening to grayish brown in age; convex to broadly convex, becoming nearly flat in age; surface dry, velvety when young, becoming bald, cracking in age

FLESH: White to yellowish; staining pale blue when exposed; thick; odor not distinctive; taste bitter

PORES: Pale yellow becoming olive yellow, staining blue when bruised; small; round; not radially arranged; depressed around the stem; no partial veil

STEM: Up to 4 in. long; whitish or yellow near the apex, pinkish to reddish below, staining blackish at the base when handled; solid; surface dry, often with reddish reticulations at the apex

SPORE PRINT: Olive brown

ECOLOGY: Mycorrhizal with oaks, poplars, and hemlock; scattered to gregarious in humus, moss, and grass in broadleaf, mixed woods, and parks; summer and early fall; uncommon

EDIBILITY: Not edible, bitter

COMMENTS: *Caloboletus calopus* (not illustrated) is similar but is larger and has an olive-brown to grayish-brown cap that becomes dark yellowish brown in age.

Caloboletus inedulis

SCIENTIFIC NAME: *Xerocomus hortonii* (A. H. Sm. and Thiers) Manfr. Binder and Besl

SYNONYM: *Boletus hortonii* A. H. Sm. and Thiers

COMMON NAME: Horton's Bolete

FAMILY: Boletaceae

CAP: Up to 4 in. wide; tan, ochre brown, yellowish brown, or reddish brown; convex to broadly convex; surface, bald, deeply pitted to corrugated, dry to slightly viscid when moist

FLESH: Whitish to pale yellow; at times bruising slightly bluish; odor and taste not distinctive

PORES: Yellow at first, becoming olive yellow in age, at times staining weakly and slowly blue when bruised, occasionally with reddish stains; circular to angular; no partial veil

STEM: Up to 4 in. long; whitish to yellow, at times with reddish stains when handled; equal or enlarged downward; solid; surface dry, pruinose, flocculose or with minute, pale scabers, apex reticulate at times

SPORE PRINT: Olive brown

ECOLOGY: Mycorrhizal; scattered to gregarious in broadleaf woods especially under hickory; summer and fall; occasional to locally abundant

EDIBILITY: Edible

COMMENTS: *Leccinum rugosiceps* (p. 286) has a similarly colored and often wrinkled cap. Its stem has brown scabers, and its flesh turns dull reddish when cut. *Hemileccinum subglabripes* (not illustrated) has similar colors and scabers, but its cap is not corrugated.

Xerocomus hortonii

SCIENTIFIC NAME: *Xanthoconium affine* var. *maculosus* (Peck) Singer

SYNONYM: None

COMMON NAME: Spotted Bolete

FAMILY: Boletaceae

CAP: Up to 4 in. wide; dark brown, yellowish brown, reddish brown to orangish brown with cream to yellowish spots; convex, broadly convex to nearly flat; surface dry, somewhat velvety, at times finely wrinkled

FLESH: White, unchanging when exposed, yellowish around larval tunnels; odor and taste not distinctive

PORES: White at first, becoming yellow to yellowish brown in age, staining brown where bruised; circular to angular; no partial veil

STEM: Up to 4 in. long; streaked with brown in age, ground color whitish; base usually white; bruising pinkish tan or brown; generally equal or tapering in either direction; solid; surface dry, bald, rarely reticulate

SPORE PRINT: Bright yellowish brown

ECOLOGY: Mycorrhizal with beech and oaks; scattered to gregarious in broadleaf and mixed woods; summer and early fall; fairly common

EDIBILITY: Edible

COMMENTS: *Xanthoconium affine* var. *affine* (not illustrated) is very similar. It lacks the spotted cap and is usually a paler brown color. *Xanthoconium purpureum* (p. 274) usually has a cap with some purple or reddish coloration.

Xanthoconium affine var. *maculosus*

273

SCIENTIFIC NAME: *Xanthoconium purpureum* Snell and E. A. Dick

SYNONYM: None

COMMON NAME: None

FAMILY: Boletaceae

CAP: Up to 4½ in. wide; variable in color, maroon, brownish, purplish red, purple, brownish red, at times with yellowish areas; convex to broadly convex, becoming nearly flat; surface minutely velvety when young, dry to moist, not viscid

FLESH: White, unchanging when exposed; fairly thick; odor and taste not distinctive

PORES: White to cream, becoming brownish yellow to nearly yellowish brown in age, staining brownish when bruised; circular to angular; no partial veil

STEM: Up to 4½ in. long; streaked the color of the cap with a pale ground color, base white; equal or enlarged downward; surface dry, smooth, occasionally reticulate

SPORE PRINT: Bright yellowish brown

ECOLOGY: Mycorrhizal; solitary, scattered to gregarious in humus and grass, under oaks in broadleaf woods or parks; summer and early fall; common

EDIBILITY: Edible

COMMENTS: *Xanthoconium affine* var. *affine* (not illustrated) is very similar. It has a brownish cap that lacks the maroon or purple coloration. The cap of *Xanthoconium purpureum* has a quick green color flash when exposed to a drop of household ammonia. *Xanthoconium affine* reacts differently, having a rusty-tan reaction to ammonia. These two species are closely related, and it is possible that they may turn out to be varieties rather than different species.

Xanthoconium purpureum

SCIENTIFIC NAME: *Gyroporus castaneus* (Bull.) Quél.

SYNONYM: None

COMMON NAMES: Chestnut Bolete, Carrot Stem Bolete

FAMILY: Gyroporaceae

CAP: Up to 3 in. wide; orangish brown, chestnut brown, yellowish brown, or rarely dull dark brown; convex, broadly convex to nearly flat in age, center slightly depressed at times; surface velvety to nearly bald, dry; margin splitting at times

FLESH: White, not staining on exposure; brittle; thick; odor and taste not distinctive

PORES: White to buff, or yellowish, not staining when bruised, with brown stains in age; generally circular, small; no partial veil

STEM: Up to 3 in. long; colored like the cap or paler, especially at the apex; equal or irregular, swollen in the middle or below, at times constricted at the base or apex; surface dry, slightly fuzzy, or bald; stuffed with pith, becoming hollow; brittle

SPORE PRINT: Pale yellow

ECOLOGY: Mycorrhizal with oaks, beech, and pines; solitary to scattered in broadleaf and mixed woods, often in sandy soil along trails or on road banks; summer and early fall; common

EDIBILITY: Edible

COMMENTS: There are two varieties of this species. One is smaller and has an orangish-brown cap. The other one has a dull, darker-brown cap and is generally larger. One of these may get a new species name.

Gyroporus castaneus

SCIENTIFIC NAME: *Gyroporus purpurinus* Singer ex Davoodian and Halling

SYNONYM: None

COMMON NAME: None

FAMILY: Gyroporaceae

CAP: Up to 3 in. wide; purplish red to burgundy; convex to broadly convex and eventually nearly flat; surface dry, somewhat velvety or bald, at times wrinkled, or finely cracked in age

FLESH: White, unchanging when exposed; odor and taste not distinctive

PORES: Whitish to buff, becoming yellowish at maturity, not staining when bruised, or staining slowly brownish; depressed around the stem; circular to angular; small; no partial veil

STEM: Up to 2½ in. long; colored like the cap; generally equal or enlarged downward, not staining when bruised; surface dry, somewhat velvety, not reticulate; hollow; basal mycelium white

SPORE PRINT: Bright yellow

ECOLOGY: Mycorrhizal; scattered to gregarious in soil and humus in broad-leaf and mixed woods, often with oaks and pines, prefers sandy soil; summer and early fall; uncommon

EDIBILITY: Edible

COMMENTS: *Gyroporus castaneus* (p. 275) is brownish orange and is much more common.

Gyroporus purpurinus

SCIENTIFIC NAME: *Gyroporus cyanescens* var. *violaceotinctus*
Watling

SYNONYM: None

COMMON NAME: Bluing Bolete

FAMILY: Gyroporaceae

CAP: Up to 4 in. wide; pale buff, cream, to pale tan; convex to broadly convex, becoming nearly flat in age; surface coarsely roughened or floccose-scaly, dry, bruising blue where damaged

FLESH: Whitish to pale yellow, immediately staining dark blue when exposed; brittle; odor and taste not distinctive

PORES: White, yellowish, or pale tan, bruising dark blue when damaged; usually depressed around the stem; circular; small; no partial veil

STEM: Up to 4 in. long; colored like the cap, staining blue where touched; equal, irregular, or swollen downward; textured like the cap, becoming nearly bald in age; hollow or with a soft pith

SPORE PRINT: Pale yellow

ECOLOGY: Mycorrhizal with birch, spruce, and fir; solitary, scattered to gregarious in humus or moss, frequently in disturbed sandy soil, often along road banks and trails; summer and fall; occasional

EDIBILITY: Edible

COMMENTS: This is a rather drab mushroom that has a stunning oxidation reaction. All parts of this mushroom bruise deep blue when touched. *Gyroporus cyanescens* var. *cyanescens* (not illustrated) is very similar, but its context stains greenish blue and then blue when exposed. There is an uncommon non-bluing variety that has been observed in West Virginia and North Carolina.

Gyroporus cyanescens
var. *violaceotinctus*

277

SCIENTIFIC NAME: *Cyanoboletus pulverulentus* (Opat.) Gelardi, Vizzini, and Simonini

SYNONYM: *Boletus pulverulentus* Opat.

COMMON NAME: None

FAMILY: Boletaceae

CAP: Up to 3 in. wide; olive brown, yellowish brown, or dark reddish brown, instantly bruising blackish blue where touched; velvety, soon smooth and shiny; convex to broadly convex and finally nearly flat

FLESH: Yellow, staining immediately deep blue when exposed, reddish brown at the base; fairly thick; odor and taste not distinctive

PORES: Yellow, becoming golden to brownish yellow in age; instantly bruising blue when bruised, and then eventually turning dull brown; reaching the stem; angular; no partial veil

STEM: Up to 3 in. long; apex bright yellow, becoming golden yellow and then reddish orange to brownish below, staining dark blue to black where bruised; nearly equal or chiseled at the base; solid; surface powdery to granular, at times with raised vertical lines, rarely slightly reticulate

SPORE PRINT: Olive brown

ECOLOGY: Mycorrhizal; solitary to scattered in humus and moss in broadleaf and conifer woods; summer and early fall; occasional

EDIBILITY: Reported as edible; the author has not tried it

COMMENTS: The intense, dark-blue oxidation reaction on all parts is a remarkable feature of this mushroom.

Cyanoboletus pulverulentus

SCIENTIFIC NAME: *Neoboletus pseudosulphureus* (Kallenb.) Klofac

SYNONYM: *Boletus pseudosulphureus* Kallenb.

COMMON NAME: None

FAMILY: Boletaceae

CAP: Up to 5 in. wide; bright yellow, becoming duller yellow to tawny in age; typically with rusty spots, quickly staining blue when bruised; nearly round at first, then convex, becoming broadly convex to nearly flat; surface dry, velvety when young, nearly bald in age

FLESH: Bright yellow to greenish yellow, instantly staining blue when exposed; thick; odor not distinctive; taste acidic, astringent, or not distinctive

PORES: Bright yellow, becoming olive and finally tan, staining blue quickly when bruised, then the stains slowly turning brown; depressed around the stem; small; round to angular; no partial veil

STEM: Up to 5 in. long; yellow, at times with reddish tints near the base, staining blue and then grayish brown when bruised; enlarged downward; solid, thick; surface dry, not reticulate

SPORE PRINT: Olive brown

ECOLOGY: Mycorrhizal; solitary, scattered to gregarious in humus, grass, and moss under oaks and pines in broadleaf and conifer woods; summer and early fall; uncommon

EDIBILITY: Unknown

COMMENTS: All parts of this distinctive mushroom stain blue when bruised. As with so many species, there are questions about whether this mushroom is the same as its European namesake.

Neoboletus pseudosulphureus

279

SCIENTIFIC NAME: *Chalciporus piperatus* (Bull.) Bataille
SYNONYM: None

COMMON NAME: Peppery Bolete

FAMILY: Boletaceae

CAP: Up to 2 in. wide; yellowish brown, reddish brown to tan; convex to nearly flat; surface dry or slightly sticky when wet, bald, or finely fibrillose, shiny

FLESH: Yellow to pinkish buff, darkening to cinnamon brown in age; unchanging when cut; flesh in the stem yellowish; fairly thick; odor not distinctive or slightly unpleasant; taste acrid

PORES: Cinnamon brown to reddish brown or copper colored, becoming darker in age, becoming darker brown when bruised; subdecurrent; somewhat radially arranged; angular; no partial veil

STEM: Up to 2 in. long; colored like the cap or slightly paler; base yellow, often with yellow mycelium; usually equal; surface dry, bald to fibrillose

SPORE PRINT: Brown

ECOLOGY: Mycorrhizal with conifers and aspens; scattered to gregarious in lawns, humus, and moss; summer and fall; common

EDIBILITY: Not edible

COMMENTS: *Chalciporus piperatoides* (not illustrated) is nearly identical, but its pores stain blue when bruised. These two species are rather unusual since very few boletes have a peppery or acrid taste.

Chalciporus piperatus

SCIENTIFIC NAME: *Strobilomyces strobilaceus* (Scop.) Berk.

SYNONYM: *Strobilomyces floccopus* (Vahl.) P. Karst.

COMMON NAME: Old Man of the Woods

FAMILY: Boletaceae

CAP: Up to 5 in. wide; grayish ground color; with blackish-brown to grayish-black scales that can be pointed or, more commonly, flattened; convex, broadly convex to nearly flat; surface cottony, dry; margin with flaps of the partial veil

FLESH: Whitish, quickly staining orange to brownish orange when exposed, eventually turning black; odor and taste not distinctive

PORES: White, becoming gray, and eventually black; staining reddish and then black when bruised; angular; rather large; random to somewhat radially arranged; covered at first by a cottony, whitish to gray partial veil

STEM: Up to 5½ in. long; colored like the cap; generally equal but can taper in either direction; solid; usually longer than the width of the cap; surface shaggy, with an apical ring or ring zone, sometimes reticulate above the ring zone

SPORE PRINT: Blackish brown to black

ECOLOGY: Mycorrhizal; solitary to scattered, often under oaks in humus, grass, and moss in broadleaf and mixed woods and parklands; common

EDIBILITY: Edible

COMMENTS: Many mycologists have tried to sort out the various *Strobilomyces* species by the pointedness or flatness of the scales and by the ornamentation of the spores. It turns out that we have several species that differ from those of Europe. So we have a complex waiting for clarification. All of these very similar species may be called the Old Man of the Woods. The genus *Strobilomyces* is easy to identify in the field. Species identification requires microscopic examination of the spores. All are edible but not very popular.

Strobilomyces strobilaceus

SCIENTIFIC NAME: *Boletinellus merulioides* (Schwein.) **Murrill**

SYNONYM: *Gyrodon merulioides* (Schwein.) Singer

COMMON NAMES: Ash Tree Bolete, Ash Bolete

FAMILY: Boletinellaceae

CAP: Up to 5 in. wide; various shades of brown, yellowish brown, olive brown, or reddish brown, bruising dull yellowish brown; often kidney-shaped, depressed in the center to nearly funnel-shaped in age; margin incurved at first, wavy in age; surface dry to slightly viscid when wet, bald, soft, and leathery

FLESH: Yellow, unchanging or staining slightly bluish green when exposed; thick at the cap center, thin outward; odor musty or not distinctive; taste not distinctive

PORES: Cream, pale yellow, golden yellow to greenish yellow, when bruised staining olive to pale greenish blue or brownish; subdecurrent to decurrent; large, irregular, elongated, with numerous cross veins; radially arranged; nearly gill-like at times; no partial veil

STEM: Up to 2 in. long; yellowish above, brownish below, at times bruising dark brown or near the base bluish; off-center; lacking glandular dots, scabers, or reticulations

SPORE PRINT: Olive brown

ECOLOGY: Symbiotic with the leaf-curl ash aphid; the mushroom receives nutrition from the aphid's excretions; the sclerotia of the mushroom provides a protected home for the young aphids, a remarkable arrangement; scattered to gregarious under ash trees; summer and early fall; common

EDIBILITY: Edible but generally considered of mediocre quality

COMMENTS: With the decline of ash trees from the assault by the Emerald Ash Borer, this very common mushroom could become rare.

Boletinellus merulioides

SCIENTIFIC NAME: *Boletellus russellii* (Frost) E.-J. Gilbert
SYNONYM: *Frostiella russellii* (Frost) Murrill
COMMON NAME: Russell's Bolete
FAMILY: Boletaceae

CAP: Up to 5 in. tall; pale gray, reddish brown, yellowish brown, often cracking in age, revealing a yellow ground color; nearly round, becoming convex; surface velvety when young, dry; margin incurved at first

FLESH: Pale yellow to greenish yellow, brownish around larval tunnels, not staining when exposed; odor and taste not distinctive

PORES: Yellow to greenish yellow, at times staining brighter yellow where bruised; angular; fairly large; no partial veil

STEM: Up to 8 in. tall; reddish brown, brown, or tan; generally equal; often curved or doglegged; solid; surface coarsely lacerate reticulate, the ridges becoming torn and giving the stem a shaggy appearance, dry, at times sticky at the base

SPORE PRINT: Olive brown

ECOLOGY: Mycorrhizal with oaks and other broadleaf trees, occasionally with hemlock and pine; solitary to scattered in humus, soil, or moss; summer and fall; uncommon

EDIBILITY: Edible

COMMENTS: In stature this species resembles the more common *Heimioporus betula* (p. 265). The orangish-red, moist to sticky cap of *Heimioporus betula* will distinguish it. *Aureoboletus projectellus* (not illustrated) is also similar. Its stem is reticulate but not as shaggy, and its cap margin projects over the edge of the pore surface. Some mycologists now place this species in the genus *Frostiella*.

Boletellus russellii

SCIENTIFIC NAME: *Pseudoboletus parasiticus* (Bull.) Šutara

SYNONYM: *Boletus parasiticus* Bull.

COMMON NAME: Parasitic Bolete

FAMILY: Boletaceae

CAP: Up to 3 in. wide; olive, tawny olive, becoming yellowish brown in age; nearly round, then convex to broadly convex, nearly flat in age; surface dry, bald, shiny when young, cracking at times; margin incurved at first

FLESH: White to yellowish, unchanging when exposed; odor and taste not distinctive

PORES: Yellow at first; to olive yellow in age, often with brown stains, unchanging when bruised, or rarely slightly greenish blue when damaged; subdecurrent at times; fairly large; angular; no partial veil

FLESH: White to yellowish, unchanging when exposed; odor and taste not distinctive

STEM: Up to 2½ in. long; olive to brown; nearly equal; usually curved; solid; with white mycelium at the connection with the host *Scleroderma*; surface dry; covered with fibers that darken in age

SPORE PRINT: Olive brown

ECOLOGY: Parasitic on the Pigskin Poison Puffball, or *Scleroderma citrinum* (p. 413); one to five fruitings attached to the base of the *Scleroderma*; summer and fall; occasional

EDIBILITY: Edible

COMMENTS: There are several boletes that look like this one, but its habitat is unique. No other bolete is found attached to *Scleroderma citrinum* (p. 413). The only other known parasitic member of this genus is an Asian species, *Pseudoboletus astraeicola*, which is parasitic on earth stars in the genus *Astraeus*.

Pseudoboletus parasiticus

SCIENTIFIC NAME: *Leccinellum crocipodium* (Letell.) Della Maggiora and Trassin.

SYNONYM: *Leccinellum nigrescens* (Singer) Bresinsky and Manfr. Binder

COMMON NAME: None

FAMILY: Boletaceae

CAP: Up to 5 in. wide; dark brown to blackish brown, becoming pale yellowish brown in age; convex to broadly convex; margin incurved at first and remaining so to near maturity; surface dry or moist, not viscid, wrinkled, pitted, becoming cracked in age and revealing a pale color underneath

FLESH: Pale yellow, slowly staining pinkish gray to dull red when exposed, finally blackish; odor not distinctive; taste slightly acidic or not distinctive

PORES: Pale lemon yellow to dingy yellow, staining brownish when bruised; depressed around the stem; circular to angular; small; no partial veil

STEM: Up to 3 in. long; pale yellow to buff with brown scabers that darken in age, at times dull reddish near the base; equal or tapering in either direction, at times swollen in the middle or near the base; solid; surface dry, at times the scabers form a pattern resembling a reticulum at the stipe apex

SPORE PRINT: Honey yellow

ECOLOGY: Mycorrhizal with oaks; scattered to gregarious, often in lawns under oaks; summer and early fall; uncommon to occasional

EDIBILITY: Edible

COMMENTS: Compare with *Leccinellum rugosiceps* (p. 286), which also often occurs in lawns under oaks. It lacks the dark-gray to black coloration, and it stains reddish. It appears that the European species with this name is different, so a new name in the future is likely.

Leccinellus crocipodium

285

SCIENTIFIC NAME: *Leccinum rugosiceps* (Peck) Singer

SYNONYM: *Boletus rugosiceps* Peck

COMMON NAME: Wrinkled Leccinum

FAMILY: Boletaceae

CAP: Up to 6 in. wide; orange, yellow, tan, brownish in age; nearly round at first, becoming convex to broadly convex; surface dry, wrinkled and pitted, becoming less wrinkled at maturity, cracked in age, revealing pale or whitish flesh beneath the cuticle; margin with sterile flaps of tissue

FLESH: White, slowly staining burgundy or reddish when exposed; most noticeable at the junction of the cap and stem; firm; odor and taste not distinctive

PORES: Whitish, light yellowish to olive brown, rarely reddish brown, occasionally staining brown when bruised; circular; small; no partial veil

STEM: Up to 4 in. long; yellow base color, covered by orangish-brown scabers that darken in age; equal or tapered in either direction; solid

SPORE PRINT: Olive brown

ECOLOGY: Mycorrhizal with oaks, especially pin oak; scattered to gregarious or in small clusters in park lawns and broadleaf woodlands; summer to early fall; common

EDIBILITY: Edible

COMMENTS: This mushroom is a frequent associate of pin oak and typically occurs in park lawns. Compare with *Xerocomus hortonii* (p. 272), which has a persistently rugose cap and lacks orangish-brown scabers. *Hemileccinum subglabripes* (not illustrated) has similar colors and yellowish scabers that sometimes become orange in age; its cap is not corrugated.

Leccinum rugosiceps

SCIENTIFIC NAME: *Leccinum piceinum* Pilát and Dermek
SYNONYM: None
COMMON NAME: Spruce Scaber Stalk
FAMILY: Boletaceae

CAP: Up to 5 in. wide; convex to broadly convex; orange to rusty cinnamon; surface dry; margin with overhanging flaps of tissue

FLESH: White, staining directly to purplish gray and then to purplish black when exposed; odor and taste not distinctive

PORES: Whitish, becoming yellowish to olive brown in age; unchanging or brownish when bruised; small; no partial veil

STEM: Up to 6 in. long; whitish; equal or enlarged downward; surface with a covering of brownish to blackish scabers, dry

SPORE PRINT: Yellowish brown to olive brown

ECOLOGY: Mycorrhizal; solitary, scattered to gregarious in humus under Norway spruce; late spring, summer and fall; common

EDIBILITY: Not recommended; poisonings have been reported from this or very similar species

COMMENTS: Orange to reddish capped *Leccinum* species have presented some of the most problematic taxonomic issues of any bolete group. Names of conifer-associated species include *Leccinum vulpinum* (not illustrated) and *Leccinum aurantiacum* (not illustrated). These names, as well as *Leccinum piceinum*, are of European species but have been used—probably incorrectly—for some North American mushrooms. The situation is made more complicated because it is likely some European species have been introduced in North America on the roots of imported trees. Until they are sorted out by DNA analysis, the most prudent name for all orange-capped scaber-stemmed boletes is *Leccinum* species.

Leccinum piceinum

SCIENTIFIC NAME: *Leccinum snellii* A. H. Sm., Thiers, and Watling

SYNONYM: None

COMMON NAME: Snell's Leccinum

FAMILY: Boletaceae

CAP: Up to 3½ wide; black, dark brown, often with paler areas where the cuticle has been damaged by slugs and insects; convex, broadly convex to nearly flat in age; surface dry, fibrillose

FLESH: White, when exposed staining reddish in the cap and stem apex, staining bluish-green in the lower stem, rather thin; odor and taste not distinctive

PORES: Whitish, becoming gray to grayish brown, unchanging when bruised or staining slightly tan; small; circular; no partial veil

STEM: Up to 4½ in tall; whitish but covered with black or gray scabers, at times with bluish-green stains near the base; equal or tapering upward; solid; surface dry, not reticulate

SPORE PRINT: Brown

ECOLOGY: Mycorrhizal with yellow birch and possibly other birches and conifers; solitary to scattered in humus or soil in mixed woodlands; summer and fall; common

EDIBILITY: Edible

COMMENTS: This is one of relatively few *Leccinum* species that can be identified using macroscopic features. The reddish staining in the cap flesh combined with bluish-green staining in the stem are good features. It appears now that our North American species may be the same as the European *Leccinum variicolor*, in which case this older name has priority and may be the accepted name if these two names do belong to the same species. This genus is characterized by having scabers on the stem, which in many species darken as the mushroom ages. Reddish-orange- to orange-capped species are also common, but much work is needed to sort out their taxonomy. Names of *Leccinum* species in most field guides should be considered tentative until many more studies are completed.

Leccinum snellii

SCIENTIFIC NAME: *Suillus spraguei* (Berk. and M. A. Curtis) Kuntze

SYNONYM: *Suillus pictus* (Peck) Kuntze

COMMON NAME: Painted Bolete

FAMILY: Suillaceae

CAP: Up to 4½ in. wide; covered with conspicuous, thick, red to pinkish-red scales or hairy patches, fading to yellowish in age; convex to broadly convex, nearly flat in age; dry; margin usually with remnant flaps of the partial veil

FLESH: Yellow, not staining blue when exposed, may slowly stain slightly reddish; firm when young; odor and taste not distinctive

PORES: Yellow, becoming brownish in age or where damaged by slugs and insects; radially arranged; fairly large; angular; subdecurrent at times; covered at first by a white to grayish partial veil that usually tears irregularly, leaving remnants on the margin and at times a ring on the upper stem

STEM: Up to 5 in. tall; covered with reddish scales or hairy patches over a yellowish or whitish ground color; surface fibrous, dry; with or without an apical, whitish or grayish ring

SPORE PRINT: Olive brown

ECOLOGY: Mycorrhizal; scattered to gregarious in humus and moss under eastern white pine, usually with native trees; summer and early fall; common

EDIBILITY: Edible

COMMENTS: This bolete is most often found under native white pine. It is seldom found in pine plantations. *Suillus pictus* is commonly used as the name for this species. Unlike most *Suillus* species, it is not viscid and has a fuzzy cap.

Suillus spraguei

289

SCIENTIFIC NAME: *Suillus americanus* (Peck) Snell
SYNONYM: *Suillus sibiricus* (Singer) Singer
COMMON NAMES: Chicken-fat Suillus, American Suillus
FAMILY: Suillaceae

CAP: Up to 3½ in. wide; bright yellow to ochre yellow, with reddish to brownish patches or streaks; rounded with an incurved margin at first, becoming convex to flat, occasionally with an umbo; margin usually with yellowish to whitish partial-veil fragments; surface viscid to glutinous

FLESH: Yellow, staining purplish brown when exposed; thin; odor and taste not distinctive

PORES: Yellow at first, becoming dull ochraceous; staining reddish brown when bruised; fairly large, angular or somewhat elongated; somewhat radially arranged; reaching the stem or depressed around it, at times subdecurrent; covered when young by a fuzzy, white partial veil

STEM: Up to 4 in. long; colored like the cap, with resinous dots and smears; often bruising reddish brown; equal, becoming hollow; slender; often slightly curved; surface dry, typically without a ring

SPORE PRINT: Cinnamon brown

ECOLOGY: Mycorrhizal with eastern white pine; usually gregarious, often in lawns, on moss or needle litter, most common under planted white pines; summer and fall; common

EDIBILITY: Edible but of little value

COMMENTS: *Suillus americanus* is very common under planted white pines, even small trees. It is less common under mature pines in native forests.

Suillus americanus

SCIENTIFIC NAME: *Suillus granulatus* (L.) Roussel
SYNONYM: None
COMMON NAMES: Butterball, Granulated Bolete
FAMILY: Suillaceae

CAP: Up to 4 in. wide; cinnamon to vinaceous brown, orangish brown, or tan, becoming brownish buff in age, mottled; convex to broadly convex, nearly flat in age; surface often streaked or checkered, viscid to glutinous when wet, often with streaks of dried gluten

FLESH: Whitish, becoming yellowish when exposed and bruised, with a watery, greenish line above the tubes; odor and taste not distinctive

PORES: Whitish to pinkish buff when young, soon honey yellow to dark mustard yellow, brownish in age or at times when bruised; small; irregular

STEM: Up to 3 in. long; whitish to pale yellowish in age, especially near the apex; with pinkish-tan to brown glandular dots, especially at the apex; equal; dry; solid

SPORE PRINT: Cinnamon brown to reddish brown

ECOLOGY: Mycorrhizal with eastern white pine and possibly hemlock and other pines; scattered to gregarious in humus, grass and moss; summer and fall; very common

EDIBILITY: Edible; peeling is recommended

COMMENTS: This is one of the most common members of this genus, and it is also one of the first to appear. It is often more common in parks and cemeteries than it is in woodlands.

Suillus granulatus

SCIENTIFIC NAME: *Suillus placidus* (Bonord.) Singer

SYNONYM: None

COMMON NAME: White Suillus

FAMILY: Suillaceae

CAP: Up to 3½ in. wide; white, becoming yellowish in age; convex to broadly convex and finally flat; surface viscid, bald

FLESH: Whitish to pale yellow, slowly staining pale vinaceous, especially in the stem base when exposed; odor and taste not distinctive

PORES: Whitish to yellowish, becoming dull yellow in age, unchanging when bruised; at times with pinkish droplets when young and moist; angular; attached to the stem or subdecurrent; no partial veil

STEM: Up to 3½ in. long; white or yellowish, with conspicuous pinkish-tan smears and glandular dots that become darker in age; sticky when moist; equal or tapered in either direction; solid, often becoming hollow; basal mycelium white

SPORE PRINT: Cinnamon brown

ECOLOGY: Mycorrhizal with eastern white pine, scattered to gregarious in humus or moss in pine or mixed woods; summer and fall; occasional

EDIBILITY: Edible

COMMENTS: Look for this species in stands of mature trees with white pine. It is more common in northern areas of the Appalachians.

Suillus placidus

SCIENTIFIC NAME: *Suillus brevipes* (Peck) Kuntze

SYNONYM: None

COMMON NAME: Short-Legged Suillus

FAMILY: Suillaceae

CAP: Up to 4 in. wide; dark reddish brown, yellowish brown to tan, often lighter in age; convex to broadly convex in age; surface bald, viscid to glutinous; margin incurved at first

FLESH: White, becoming yellowish, unchanging when exposed; thick; soft; odor and taste not distinctive

PORES: Whitish to pale yellow, becoming dingy olivaceous yellow in age; small; no partial veil

STEM: Up to 2 in. long; white to pale yellow; equal or tapered in either direction; solid; surface dry, glandular dots absent or inconspicuous in age

SPORE PRINT: Cinnamon brown

ECOLOGY: Mycorrhizal with pines; scattered to gregarious in soil, humus, or moss; late summer and fall; occasional to locally common

EDIBILITY: Edible; peeling is recommended

COMMENTS: This species looks much like the Slippery Jack, *Suillus luteus* (p. 294), but without a ring on the stem. It also resembles *Suillus granulatus* (p. 291), which has a much more obviously glandular dotted stem.

Suillus brevipes

SCIENTIFIC NAME: *Suillus luteus* (L.) Roussel

SYNONYM: None

COMMON NAME: Slippery Jack

FAMILY: Suillaceae

CAP: Up to 5 in. wide; dark reddish brown to cinnamon brown, yellowish brown, or ochre; nearly round, becoming convex to broadly convex, eventually flat; surface bald, viscid when moist, shiny when dry; margin with partial veil flaps at times

FLESH: White to pale yellow, unchanging when exposed; thick; odor and taste not distinctive

PORES: White to pale yellow at first, becoming dark yellow or olive yellow in age, unchanging when bruised; angular; covered at first by a white partial veil that is often rimmed with purple at the stem

STEM: Up to 3 in. long; white, apex often yellowish, in age developing purplish or brownish stains; equal or enlarged downward; solid; with a skirt-like, white ring with a purple underside on the upper stem; with glandular dots above the ring

SPORE PRINT: Cinnamon brown

ECOLOGY: Mycorrhizal; scattered to gregarious in humus under Scots pine and Austrian pine, also reported under white pine and spruce; fall; common

EDIBILITY: Edible; peeling the cuticle and, in older specimens, removing the tube layer is recommended; not peeling the cap and not removing the tubes has resulted in digestive upsets

COMMENTS: This is a common bolete that is often abundant late in the season. It is thought to be a European species that has been imported on the roots of Scots pine.

Suillus luteus

SCIENTIFIC NAME: *Suillus clintonianus* (Peck) Kuntze

SYNONYM: *Suillus proximus* A.H. Sm. and Thiers

MISAPPLIED NAME: *Suillus grevillei* (Klotzsch) Singer

COMMON NAME: Larch Bolete

FAMILY: **Suillaceae**

CAP: Up to 4 in. wide; color variable; orange, yellow, reddish brown, chestnut brown; convex to broadly convex becoming nearly flat; surface bald, smooth, slimy when wet, sticky when dry; margin at time with remnants of the partial veil

FLESH: Pale yellow to yellowish orange, at times bruising pinkish brown; odor and taste not distinctive

PORES: Honey yellow to mustard yellow, staining brown where bruised, becoming olive tinged in age; fairly small; angular; reaching the stem or subdecurrent; covered at first by a yellow, brownish, or whitish partial veil, which is cottony inside and slimy outside

STEM: Up to 4 in. long; below the ring orangish brown, reddish brown, or streaked brown over a yellowish ground color, at times yellowish; yellow or reddish yellow above the ring; equal or enlarged downward; surface scurfy without glandular dots

SPORE PRINT: Light brown to olive brown

ECOLOGY: Mycorrhizal with tamarack (native larch) in Pennsylvania and New York and with planted European larch throughout the central Appalachians; occurs in humus, lawns, moss, and in bogs; summer and fall; common wherever larch trees are present

EDIBILITY: Edible; peeling is recommended

COMMENTS: This species seems to thrive equally in cold northern bogs and dry park lawns. It has been called *Suillus grevillei* in many field guides. Recent DNA studies have revealed that our species differs from the very similar European *Suillus grevillei.*

Suillus clintonianus

295

SCIENTIFIC NAME: *Suillus acidus* (Peck) Singer

SYNONYMS: *Suillus intermedius* (A. H. Sm. and Thiers) A. H. Sm. and Thiers, *Suillus subalutaceus* (A. H. Sm. and Thiers) A. H. Sm. and Thiers

COMMON NAME: Sour Cap Suillus

FAMILY: Suillaceae

CAP: Up to 6 in wide; brown, tan, or yellowish, when dry with brown streaks or appressed fibers over a pale ground color; surface smooth, viscid to glutinous, shiny when dry, covered with acidic-tasting gluten; margin incurved at first, and in age with gluten-covered partial-veil remnants

FLESH: Whitish to pale yellow or orangish yellow in the cap, not changing when exposed; darker orange to salmon orange in the stem; odor not distinctive, taste acidic or not distinctive, the sour taste comes mostly from the gluten

PORES: Pale yellow to dull yellow in age, unchanging or slowly staining pale brown when bruised; with drops of liquid when fresh; angular; not distinctly radially arranged; covered at first by a glutinous partial veil

STEM: Up to 4 in. long; whitish, pale yellow to ochre yellow; at maturity with reddish to brownish glandular dots and smears that eventually blacken; solid; enlarged downward or equal; with a two-edged, gluten-covered ring on the upper stem

SPORE PRINT: Cinnamon brown

ECOLOGY: Mycorrhizal with red pine and eastern white pine; scattered to gregarious in humus or moss in conifer or mixed woods; summer and fall; common

EDIBILITY: Edible

COMMENTS: The acidic taste of the cap cuticle gives this species its name. The very dark glandular dots and smears in age are typical of *Suillus acidus*. Previously it was separated from *Suillus subalutaceus*, based mainly on the cap color and how acidic the cap cuticle tasted. It is now considered to be one variable species.

Suillus acidus

SCIENTIFIC NAME: *Suillus punctipes* (Peck) Singer

SYNONYM: None

COMMON NAME: Spicy Suillus

FAMILY: Suillaceae

CAP: Up to 2½ in. wide; yellow to ochraceous, or tawny, eventually dull ochre orange; convex, broadly convex, to nearly flat; surface with tufts of tiny gray or brownish fibrils, in age becoming smooth

FLESH: Whitish or pale yellow, unchanging when exposed; thick over the center, thin at the margin; odor of bitter almonds or almond extract; taste not distinctive

PORES: Brown to grayish brown, pale brown to yellowish brown or olive; not staining when bruised; exuding brown droplets when fresh; small; circular to angular; no partial veil

STEM: Up to 3 in. long; colored much like the cap, but less yellowish; equal or enlarged downward; often curved; solid; surface densely covered with brown to dark-brown glandular dots and smears, not reticulate, base stained reddish at times

SPORE PRINT: Olive brown to brown

ECOLOGY: Mycorrhizal with white pine and other conifers; scattered to gregarious in humus or moss in conifer and mixed woods; late summer and fall; common

EDIBILITY: Edible but not popular

COMMENTS: *Suillus tomentosus* (not illustrated) is very similar, but the pore surface stains blue when bruised and it lacks the almond extract odor. The sweet scent of *Suillus punctipes* will help clinch its identification since no other common bolete has this aroma.

Suillus punctipes

297

SCIENTIFIC NAME: *Suillus subaureus* (Peck) Snell
SYNONYM: None
COMMON NAME: None
FAMILY: Suillaceae

CAP: Up to 5 in. wide; yellow; convex to broadly convex, becoming nearly flat; surface viscid when moist; bald or at times with appressed, reddish-brown fibrils; margin with a transient cottony roll of tissue

FLESH: Yellow, unchanging or slightly reddening when exposed; odor not distinctive; taste slightly acidic

PORES: Yellow to yellowish orange or apricot, unchanging when bruised; radially arranged; angular; no partial veil

STEM: Up to 3 in. long; yellow, staining brownish when handled; equal or enlarged downward; solid; surface with yellowish glandular dots, not reticulate

SPORE PRINT: Olive brown

ECOLOGY: Mycorrhizal with white pine, oaks, and aspens; solitary to scattered in humus and moss in broadleaf and mixed woods; summer and fall; occasional

EDIBILITY: Edible

COMMENTS: This species is unusual for a *Suillus* in that it often can be found where no conifers are present. The reddish-brown cap fibrils are often obscure or absent.

Suillus subaureus

SCIENTIFIC NAME: *Bothia castanella* (Peck) Halling, T. J. Baroni, and Manfr. Binder

SYNONYM: *Suillus castanellus* (Peck) A. H. Sm. and Thiers

COMMON NAME: Both's Bolete

FAMILY: Boletaceae

CAP: Up to 3 in. wide; medium brown, burgundy brown, paler at times; convex to broadly convex, becoming nearly flat in age; surface dry to slightly viscid when wet, floccose becoming bald; margin usually even, at times somewhat wavy

FLESH: Whitish in the cap, whitish to pale yellow in the stem; unchanging when exposed; odor and taste not distinctive

PORES: Tan or buff to pinkish brown, darkening in age to yellowish brown, bruising slowly brown to reddish brown; subdecurrent; radially arranged; angular to elongate; fairly large; no partial veil

STEM: Up to 3 in. long; colored like the cap or paler, especially near the apex, brownish buff at times; generally equal or tapering in either direction; surface dry, nearly bald, or reticulate at the apex; solid

SPORE PRINT: Dull yellow to yellowish brown

ECOLOGY: Mycorrhizal with oaks and possibly other broadleaf trees; solitary, scattered, gregarious, or in loose clusters in broadleaf and mixed woods; summer and early fall; occasional

EDIBILITY: Unknown

COMMENTS: This rather odd bolete has been placed in several genera over the years. It has been determined to be worthy of its own genus. It was named in honor of the late Ernst Both, the preeminent bolete expert from the area around Buffalo, New York.

Bothia castanella

SCIENTIFIC NAME: *Pseudomerulius curtisii* (Berk.) Redhead and Ginns

SYNONYM: *Meiorganum curtisii* (Berk.) Singer, J. García, and L. D. Gómez

COMMON NAME: None

FAMILY: Tapinellaceae

CAP: Up to 2½ in. wide; olive yellow to brownish yellow or reddish brown, especially when wet; convex to nearly flat; semicircular to fan-shaped; surface dry, bald or, at times, slightly fuzzy; margin wavy and undulating

FLESH: Pale yellow; odor not distinctive; taste slightly bitter or not distinctive

PORES: Yellowish orange, orange, or brownish orange; corrugated and wavy; gill-like; forked; with cross veins; no partial veil

STEM: Absent or rudimentary

SPORE PRINT: Yellowish olive

ECOLOGY: Saprobic; solitary or in overlapping clusters on decaying conifer wood, at times from buried wood; summer and fall; occasional

EDIBILITY: Unknown

COMMENTS: Compare with *Tapinella panuoides* (p. 207), which has gills that are less irregular and less corrugated.

Pseudomerulius curtisii

SCIENTIFIC NAME: *Phylloporus leucomycelinus* Singer

SYNONYM: None

COMMON NAME: Gilled Bolete

FAMILY: Boletaceae

CAP: Up to 4 in. wide; bright red, dark red, reddish brown, or olive brown; convex, broadly convex to nearly flat in age; surface bald to velvety, dry, often cracked in age; margin incurved at first

FLESH: Yellow or buff, at times tinged reddish under the cuticle; firm; thick at the cap center; odor and taste not distinctive

GILLS: Bright yellow to golden yellow; subdecurrent to decurrent; subdistant; at times forking, with cross veins; sometimes somewhat poroid near the stem; no partial veil

STEM: Up to 3 in. long; yellow with reddish areas, equal or tapering downward; solid; firm; surface scurfy with reddish-brown dots, at times ribbed near the apex; base with white mycelium

SPORE PRINT: Yellow to yellowish ochraceous

ECOLOGY: Mycorrhizal with oak and beech; solitary, scattered to gregarious in humus, moss, or grass; summer and early fall; fairly common

EDIBILITY: Edible

COMMENTS: Gilled bolete sounds contradictory, but except for the gills, the look and feel of this mushroom is like a bolete. Microscopically it is a bolete. *Phylloporus rhodoxanthus* (not illustrated) is very similar, but it has yellow mycelium at the stipe base.

Phylloporus leucomycelinus

POLYPORES

Polypores are a very diverse group of pored fungi that are saprobic, or parasitic, and are important recyclers of wood. Unlike the boletes, which also have pores, most polypores are tough, leathery, or woody. Some have stems. Others form shelf-like growths on the sides of trees, stumps, and logs. Polypores can appear terrestrial when growing from buried wood or roots. A few species are perennials, adding a new growth ring each year like trees.

There are some fleshy species that are good edibles when young. These include *Grifola frondosa*, *Laetiporus sulphureus*, *Polyporus umbellatus*, and *Fistulina hepatica*. The larger of these—generally those with caps or clusters over 6 inches wide—are keyed out below as "large, fleshy polypores." Other large polypores are tough, fibrous, or woody. These are keyed out as "large, woody polypores."

Despite the fact that they are not polypores, two *Stereum* species are included in this section because their upper surface resembles a polypore. However, unlike true polypores, their fertile surface is smooth or wrinkled and does not have pores. They are keyed out with similar-looking polypores as "thin-fleshed, tough, with or without pores, on dead wood."

"Terrestrial-appearing polypores" usually occur on buried wood and may appear to be growing on the ground. Species keyed out as "large-pored, maze or gill-like polypores" have a spore-bearing surface that has large, elongated pores. Some of these have pores that are maze to gill-like. Those polypore species keyed out as "medium-sized, tough to woody polypores" generally have small pores and are less than six inches wide.

Grifola frondosa

Ganoderma applanatum

Daedaleopsis confragosa

Daedalea quercina

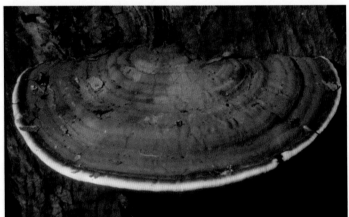

Keys to Polypores

Large, fleshy polypores

1. Orange and yellow fruit body; on broadleaf tree wood: *Laetiporus sulphureus* (p. 308)

2. Orange and yellow fruit body; on conifer wood: *Laetiporus huroniensis* (p. 309)

3. Whitish, gray, or brownish; staining black where bruised: *Meripilus sumstinei* (p. 312)

4. Tan to brownish; massive; not staining black when bruised: *Bondarzewia berkeleyi* (p. 313)

5. Tan, gray, or brownish; dense clusters of roundish caps on the ground: *Polyporus umbellatus* (p. 311)

6. Gray to brown; dense clusters of irregular caps on roots (usually oaks): *Grifola frondosa* (p. 310)

7. Brownish orange, dark brown to black; on broadleaf tree wood: *Ischnoderma resinosum* (p. 345)

8. Yellowish brown or brownish orange; on conifer roots and stumps: *Phaeolus schweinitzii* (p. 314)

Large, woody polypores

1. Shelving; cap surface cracked, brown; pores brown on locust wood: *Phellinus robiniae* (p. 332)

2. Shelving; cap not deeply cracked; gray or brownish; pores white: *Ganoderma applanatum* (p. 331)

3. Shelving; cap with bands of reddish brown, margin whitish: *Fomitopsis pinicola* (p. 334)

4. Shelving; cap gray to brownish; hoof-shaped; often on birch or beech: *Fomes fomentarius* (p. 333)

5. Fan-shaped; with a stem; shiny reddish brown; on hemlock: *Ganoderma tsugae* (p. 342)

6. Irregular, hard, black mass usually on birch trees: *Inonotus obliquus* (p. 329)

Large-pored, maze or gill-like polypores

1. Cap large; fleshy; scaly; stem base black at maturity: *Cerioporus squamosus* (p. 315)

2. Cap medium to large; fleshy; stem base not black: *Polyporus craterellus* (p. 316)

3. Cap small; roundish; margin fringed with small hairs: *Lentinus arcularius* (p. 317)

4. Cap small; kidney- to fan-shaped; fibrillose to scaly: *Neofavolus alveolaris* (p. 317)

5. Cap zoned; fruiting body flexible; fertile surface gill-like: *Trametes betulina* (p. 323)

6. Cap reddish brown to yellowish red; fertile surface gill-like: *Gloeophyllum sepiarium* (p. 318)

7. Cap tan, brown, or grayish; thick; hard; fertile surface maze-like: *Daedalea quercina* (p. 322)

8. Cap gray to brown; zoned; fertile surface with elongated pores: *Daedaleopsis confragosa* (p. 321)

9. Cap whitish; fertile surface with elongated pores: *Trametes gibbosa* (p. 324)

Terrestrial-appearing polypores

1. Not in large clusters; pores blue to bluish gray: *Neoalbatrellus caeruleoporus* (p. 352)

2. Not in large clusters; pores white to pale gray; cap gray: *Boletopsis griseus* (p. 350)

3. Not in large clusters; pores white: *Laeticutis cristata* (p. 351)

4. Not in large clusters; pores brown; cap shiny brown: *Coltricia cinnamomeus* (p. 349)

5. Large clusters of overlapping, irregular caps, near or on roots: *Grifola frondosa* (p. 310)

6. Large clusters of generally round caps: *Polyporus umbellatus* (p. 311)

7. Irregular, fan-shaped caps, or pore-covered, finger-like projections: *Abortiporus biennis* (p. 353)

Albatrellus ovinus

Thin-fleshed, tough, with or without pores, on dead wood

1. No pores; small; cap yellowish orange to cinnamon brown: *Stereum complicatum* (p. 327)

2. No pores; cap with multicolored zones: *Stereum ostrea* (p. 326)

3. With pores, which become spine-like in age; cap and pores violet at first: *Trichaptum biforme* (p. 328)

4. With pores; cap with multicolored zones: *Trametes versicolor* (p. 325)

5. With pores and a stem; cap yellowish buff to tan; stem base black: *Cerioporus leptocephalus* (p. 346)

6. With pores and a stem; cap tan to dark red brown; stem base black: *Picipes badius* (p. 347)

Medium-sized, tough to woody polypores

1. Cap bright orange to cinnabar red: *Pycnoporus cinnabarinus* (p. 340)
2. Cap dark orange to brownish: *Pycnoporellus fulgens* (p. 319)
3. Cap orange to yellowish orange; thick: *Hapalopilus croceus* (can be large at times) (p. 339)
4. Cap whitish; moss covered; on the base of broadleaf trees, especially maple: *Oxyporus populinus* (p. 337)
5. Cap whitish; fruiting on conifers; with a volva: *Cryptoporus volvatus* (p. 336)
6. Cap pink to reddish brown at first: *Rhodofomes cajanderi* (p. 343)
7. With pores; cap pinkish brown to cinnamon brown; spongy when young: *Hapalopilus nidulans* (p. 338)
8. Cap whitish to cream or ochre when young; staining green when bruised: *Niveoporofomes spraguei* (p. 344)
9. Cap gray to brownish; hoof-shaped; often on birch or beech: *Fomes fomentarius* (p. 333)

Heterobasidion annosum

Polyporus radicatus

SCIENTIFIC NAME: *Laetiporus sulphureus* (Bull.) Murrill

SYNONYM: None

COMMON NAMES: Sulphur Shelf, Chicken Mushroom

FAMILY: Fomitopsidaceae

CAP: Up to 12 in. wide; some combination of bright yellow and bright orange, fading in age to orangish yellow or whitish; when fresh the margin is usually yellow; semicircular to fan-shaped; upper surface velvety, wrinkled, uneven, more or less zonate; margin blunt and wavy

FLESH: Yellow or yellowish white; soft and firm at first, becoming fibrous and whitish in age; odor and taste not distinctive

PORES: Sulphur yellow, very small

STEM: Absent

SPORE PRINT: White

ECOLOGY: Saprobic; usually in dense, overlapping clusters, or at times scattered to rarely single on the living and dead wood of broadleaf trees, especially oaks and wild cherry, occasionally on conifers; late spring, summer, and fall; common

EDIBILITY: Edible and popular; stomach upsets have been reported, some regarding alcohol consumption and others involving eating caps gathered from conifer wood; the late bolete expert Ernst Both reported gastrointestinal problems when he ate fruitings growing on honey locust; when young and fresh, the entire mushroom is edible; as it ages only the tender margins should be consumed, as it becomes too fibrous for safe consumption

COMMENTS: *Laetiporus cincinnatus* (not illustrated) is very similar but has a pale pore surface and usually grows in large rosettes on top of oak stumps. It is an excellent edible.

Laetiporus sulphureus

SCIENTIFIC NAME: *Laetiporus huroniensis* Burds. and Banik

SYNONYM: None

COMMON NAME: None

FAMILY: Fomitopsidaceae

CAP: Up to 12 in. wide; orange, with pale-yellow and whitish areas at times; fading in age to orange yellow or whitish; semicircular to fan-shaped; upper surface velvety, somewhat wrinkled

FLESH: Yellow or yellowish white; soft and firm at first, becoming fibrous and whitish in age; odor and taste not distinctive

PORES: Pale yellow to yellow; very small

STEM: Absent

SPORE PRINT: White

ECOLOGY: Saprobic and possibly parasitic on conifer wood, especially hemlock; usually in shelving clusters on conifer stumps and logs in mature forests; late spring and summer; uncommon

EDIBILITY: Not recommended; edible for some and reportedly quite good, but the conifer habitat (see *Laetiporus sulphureus*) and lack of more reports weigh against calling it a safe edible

COMMENTS: This mushroom can be very easily confused with *Laetiporus sulphureus* (p. 308) if the host tree is not identified.

Laetiporous huroniensis

SCIENTIFIC NAME: *Grifola frondosa* (Dicks.) Gray

SYNONYM: *Polyporus frondosus* (Dicks.) Fr.

COMMON NAMES: Hen of the Woods, Sheephead, Maitake

FAMILY: Meripilaceae

FRUIT BODY: Up to 2 ft. across; a dense cluster of overlapping caps, attached to branches arising from a short, thick, common stem; gray to brownish gray, becoming dark brown in age; individual caps are fan-shaped to irregular; surface area bald to fibrous, vaguely zoned or radially streaked; margins thin and wavy

FLESH: White; unchanging when exposed; firm, becoming fibrous in age; odor nutty or not distinctive; taste not distinctive

PORES: White to cream; small; angular

STEM: Whitish, solid, thick, tough; repeatedly branched; off-center at times

SPORE PRINT: White

ECOLOGY: Parasitic and saprobic, usually on oaks but also on other broadleaf trees, including beech, wild cherry, and yellow birch; fruitings are usually at or near the base of the tree or stump; late summer and fall; common

EDIBILITY: Edible and very popular; can reach enormous proportions, but fruit bodies that are basketball-sized or smaller are best for culinary use

COMMENTS: Three similar species are typically found earlier in the summer: *Meripilus sumstinei* (p. 312) is similar but stains black where bruised. *Bondarzewia berkeleyi* (p. 313) has much wider, fan-shaped caps. *Polyporus umbellatus* (p. 311) has clusters of roundish caps. All of these are edible when young.

Grifola frondosa

SCIENTIFIC NAME: *Polyporus umbellatus* (Pers.) Fr.

SYNONYMS: *Grifola umbellata* (Pers.) Pilát., *Cladomeris umbellata* (Pers.) Quél.

COMMON NAME: Umbrella Polypore

FAMILY: Polyporaceae

FRUIT BODY: Up to 16 in. wide; consists of a roundish or oblong cluster of roundish caps, each up to 1¼ in. wide, grayish brown, yellowish brown, or whitish; generally circular in outline; center depressed, margin uplifted

FLESH: White, unchanging when cut; fairly soft, becoming more fibrous in age; odor and taste not distinctive

PORES: White to cream; decurrent; small

STEM: Up to 3 in. long; whitish above, brownish toward the base; irregular, generally central; branching and fusing into the base of the cluster; base with an underground sclerotium

SPORE PRINT: White

ECOLOGY: Saprobic and parasitic on the roots of beech and other broadleaf trees, appearing terrestrial; late spring, summer, and early fall; uncommon to rare, fruits repeatedly in the same area

EDIBILITY: Edible and generally considered to be quite good

COMMENTS: *Grifola frondosa* (p. 310), the Hen of the Woods, is similar and much more common. Its fronds do not end in round caps, and it is a late summer and fall mushroom usually found at the base of oak trees and stumps.

Polyporus umbrellatus

SCIENTIFIC NAME: *Meripilus sumstinei* (Murrill) M. J. Larsen and Lombard

MISAPPLIED NAME: *Meripilus giganteus* (Pers.) P. Karst.

COMMON NAME: Black Staining Polypore

FAMILY: Meripilaceae

FRUIT BODY: Up to 14 in. wide; composed of multiple, fan-shaped individual caps up to 7 in. wide, sharing a thick basal connection; whitish, yellow, or grayish yellow, grayish brown in age, staining black from rain or from handling

FLESH: White; firm; fibrous, rather tough; odor mild when young, unpleasant in age, like burning rubber; taste not distinctive

PORES: Colored like the caps, staining black where rubbed; pores small and angular

STEM: Up to 4 in. long; whitish to reddish brown; tough, thick, often off-center

SPORE PRINT: White

ECOLOGY: Parasitic and saprobic on the roots of broadleaf trees, especially oaks; summer; common

EDIBILITY: Edible when young

COMMENTS: Compare with the Hen of the Woods, or *Grifola frondosa* (p. 310), which fruits later in the season and lacks the black staining. Berkeley's Polypore, or *Bondarzewia berkeleyi* (p. 313), is similar. It does not stain black. All three are edible when young and fresh. *Meripilus giganteus* was a name applied to this mushroom until it was determined that this name belongs to a different fungus found in Europe.

Meripilus sumstinei

SCIENTIFIC NAME: *Bondarzewia berkeleyi* (Fr.) Bondartsev and Singer

SYNONYM: None

COMMON NAME: Berkeley's Polypore

FAMILY: Bondarzewiaceae

CAP: Up to 14 in. wide; tan, yellowish brown to grayish brown, obscurely or markedly zoned at times; fan-shaped caps, usually in a layered, rosette-like cluster that can be up to 3 feet across; surface densely matted, fibrillose to nearly bald, dry, wrinkled, may be pitted; margin wavy

FLESH: Whitish; very thick; firm; odor of anise when young, later not distinctive; taste mild, becoming bitter in age

PORES: White to creamy, becoming slightly brownish where bruised and exuding white latex when cut; decurrent; angular, often torn, irregular; developing first near the stem

STEM: Up to 4 in. long above ground; rooting and arising from an underground sclerotium; yellowish brown to dull white; dry; tough

SPORE PRINT: White

ECOLOGY: Parasitic and saprobic on broadleaf trees, especially oaks; solitary to gregarious at the base of trees and stumps; late spring, summer, and early fall; common

EDIBILITY: Edible when young, becoming tough and bitter in age

COMMENTS: This is the largest fungus fruit body that is found in the Appalachians. It is to be expected in mature oak woods. Compare with *Meripilus sumstinei* (p. 312), which bruises black, and *Grifola frondosa* (p. 310), which has much smaller caps. All three are edible when young.

Bondarzewia berkeleyi

SCIENTIFIC NAME: *Phaeolus schweinitzii* (Fr.) Pat.

SYNONYM: *Polyporus schweinitzii* Fr.

COMMON NAME: Dyers Polypore

FAMILY: Polyporaceae

CAP: Up to 15 in. wide; colors variable, surface yellow or orange at first, becoming olive brown to reddish brown from the center outward; margin typically yellowish; zoned at times; in age shades of brown dominate; fruiting can be one large, roundish or semicircular cap, or more often caps are fused into overlapping layers; surface dry, densely covered with matted hairs that may disappear in age, leaving a bald and at times shiny surface

FLESH: Yellowish brown; fibrous; tough; spongy; watery; odor slightly fragrant or not distinctive; taste unknown

PORES: Yellow, greenish yellow, or brownish, bruising brown; decurrent; irregular; round, angular, or elongate and curved

STEM: Up to 2 in. long, up to 2 in. thick, at times indistinct; pale to dark brown; surface dry, velvety

SPORE PRINT: Whitish to cream

ECOLOGY: Parasitic and saprobic on the roots or stumps of conifers, often on white pine; summer and fall; fairly common, especially in older conifer forests

EDIBILITY: Not edible

COMMENTS: As the common name indicates, this mushroom is often used to dye wool yarn.

Phaeolus schweinitzii

SCIENTIFIC NAME: *Cerioporus squamosus* (Huds.) Quél.

SYNONYM: *Polyporus squamosus* (Huds.) Fr.

COMMON NAMES: Dryad's Saddle, Pheasant Back Mushroom

FAMILY: Polyporaceae

CAP: Up to 18 in. wide; pale tan to creamy yellow or whitish, overlaid with often radially-arranged, reddish-brown, dark-brown, to nearly black, appressed scales; in age often black in the center or above where the stem attaches; kidney- to fan-shaped, or nearly circular when young

FLESH: White, unchanging when cut; thick at the cap center, thin outward; soft at first, soon becoming corky and tough; odor of cucumbers or watermelon rind; taste mealy

PORES: Whitish to creamy, in age becoming yellowish with black spots; large, decurrent, rather angular, arranged radially, exuding clear moisture droplets in wet weather

STEM: Up to 3½ in. long; white, in age becoming black from a covering of black scales starting at the base; lateral to eccentric; thick; solid; tough, with a tenacious connection to the wood

SPORE PRINT: White

ECOLOGY: Saprobic or occasionally parasitic on a variety of broadleaf trees; American elm is a favorite host in the northern Appalachians; solitary or usually gregarious or in clusters; most common in spring, also found in summer and fall; abundant

EDIBILITY: Edible when young, but very fibrous, tough, and rather bland

COMMENTS: This species is frequently encountered by morel hunters. *Polyporus craterellus* (p. 316) is similar. It is much less scaly, has pores that are randomly arranged, and lacks black coloration.

Cerioporus squamosus

315

SCIENTIFIC NAME: *Polyporus craterellus* Berk. and M. A. Curtis

SYNONYM: *Polyporus fagicola* Murrill

COMMON NAME: None

FAMILY: Polyporaceae

CAP: Up to 4 in. wide; ochre, buff, or tan; with flat, reddish-brown scales or tufts of hairs; flat, depressed in the center to funnel-shaped; surface smooth to slightly wrinkled under the scales; margin fringed

FLESH: White; tough; odor and taste not distinctive, or mealy

PORES: Whitish to cream or yellowish; decurrent; large and angular

STEM: Up to 2 in. long; colored like the cap; equal or tapering toward the base; central or eccentric; surface fuzzy, becoming less so in age

SPORE PRINT: White

ECOLOGY: Saprobic on the dead wood of broadleaf trees, most often on fallen limbs; late spring, summer, and fall; occasional

EDIBILITY: Reported as edible

COMMENTS: Confusing this species with *Cerioporus squamosus* (p. 315) is possible. Note that *Polyporus craterellus* is much less scaly, is smaller in size, and lacks black anywhere on the fruit body.

Polyporus craterellus

SCIENTIFIC NAME: *Neofavolus alveolaris* (DC.) Sotome and T. Hatt.

SYNONYMS: *Polyporus alveolaris* (DC.) Bondartsev and Singer, *Favolus alveolarius* (Bosc) Quél., *Polyporus mori* (Pollini) Fr.

COMMON NAME: Hexagonal Pored Polypore

FAMILY: Polyporaceae

CAP: Up to 2½ in. wide; orangish yellow to reddish orange, fading in age to buff or cream; fan-shaped to kidney-shaped, occasionally circular; convex, depressed near the point of attachment; surface radially fibrillose to scaly; margin turned under at first, at times fringed with hairs in age

FLESH: White to cream; thin; tough; odor and taste not distinctive, or slightly bitter

PORES: Whitish to yellowish white; decurrent; roughly diamond-shaped, or hexagonal; large; radially arranged

STEM: Up to 1 in. long; whitish; eccentric to nearly lateral, occasionally central; solid

SPORE PRINT: White

ECOLOGY: Saprobic on small dead limbs and sticks of broadleaf trees, usually with the bark still intact; spring and summer; common

EDIBILITY: Edible but very tough

COMMENTS: This is the smallest of the three common large-pored polypores of spring. *Cerioporus squamosus* (p. 315) is much larger and has dark scales. *Lentinus arcularius* (p. 320) lacks the orange to reddish-orange colors.

Neofavolus alveolaris

SCIENTIFIC NAME: *Gloeophyllum sepiarium* (Wulfen)
P. Karst.

SYNONYM: None

COMMON NAME: Yellow-Red Gilled Polypore

FAMILY: Gloeophyllaceae

FRUIT BODY: Up to 4 in. wide; reddish brown to yellowish red; semicircular to kidney-shaped; nearly flat; surface covered with short, dense hairs, becoming matted and felt-like and nearly bald in age

FLESH: Dark yellowish brown to dark rusty brown; tough; fibrous; odor not distinctive; taste slightly bitter

FERTILE SURFACE: Orange, golden brown, brownish; irregular, gill-like with cross-walls, may be poroid near the stem, maze-like at times; gill edges often saw-toothed

STEM: None

SPORE PRINT: White

ECOLOGY: Saprobic; solitary to gregarious, usually on conifer wood, often causing decay on the wood of bridges, decks, and other structures; throughout the year; common

EDIBILITY: Not edible

COMMENTS: *Trametes betulina* (p. 323) has paler colors and white flesh. *Gloeophyllum trabeum* (not illustrated) is less hairy and usually occurs on broadleaf tree wood; like *Gloeophyllum sepiarium*, it is often found on structural wood.

Gloeophyllus sepiarium

SCIENTIFIC NAME: *Pycnoporellus fulgens* (Fr.) Donk

SYNONYM: *Polyporus fibrillosus* P. Karst.

COMMON NAME: None

FAMILY: Polyporaceae

CAP: Up to 4 in. wide; fan-shaped to semicircular; pale to dark orange or yellowish brown; surface radially fibrillose to fuzzy, becoming nearly bald in age, often zonate; margin often whitish

FLESH: Orange to rusty red; thin; tough, corky; odor and taste not distinctive

PORES: Cream to pale orange, dark orange, or brownish orange; circular to angular, becoming stretched, and spine-like; small; no partial veil

STEM: Absent

SPORE PRINT: Whitish

ECOLOGY: Saprobic usually on the dead wood of conifers and occasionally on broadleaf tree wood; solitary to scattered, at times in overlapping clusters; summer and fall; occasional

EDIBILITY: Not edible

COMMENTS: *Pycnoporus cinnabarinus* (p. 340) has a bright-orange pore surface and smaller pores. It does not have a white margin.

Pycnoporellus fulgens

SCIENTIFIC NAME: *Lentinus arcularius* (Batsch) Zmitr.

SYNONYM: *Polyporus arcularius* (Batsch) Fr.

COMMON NAME: **Spring Polypore**

FAMILY: **Polyporaceae**

CAP: Up to 3 in. wide; tan or buff ground color, covered with yellowish-brown to dark-brown scales; circular; convex to flat, with a central depression; dry; margin fringed with hairs

FLESH: White or cream colored; thin; tough, leathery; odor and taste not distinctive

PORES: White, yellowish cream, becoming tan in age, unchanging when bruised; decurrent; angular or polygonal; large; radially arranged

STEM: Up to 2½ in. long; brown to yellowish brown; equal or with a swollen base; central or slightly off-center; scaly to hairy

SPORE PRINT: White to creamy white

ECOLOGY: Saprobic on the dead wood of broadleaf trees, especially oaks; occasionally appearing terrestrial; solitary, gregarious, or in small clusters; spring and early summer; fairly common

EDIBILITY: Not edible, tough

COMMENTS: Another spring polypore, *Neofavolus alveolaris* (p. 317), is smaller and has brownish-orange scales over a yellowish ground color. *Cerioporus squamosus* (p. 315) is much larger and has dark scales. *Lentinus brumalis* (p. 348) has much smaller pores and a dark-brown cap. It fruits in the fall but can still be found in the spring. The genus *Polyporus* has been and is being split up.

Lentinus arcularius

SCIENTIFIC NAME: *Daedaleopsis confragosa* (Bolton) J. Schröt.

SYNONYM: *Daedalea confragosa* (Bolton) Pers.

COMMON NAME: Thin-Maze Flat Polypore

FAMILY: Polyporaceae

FRUIT BODY: Up to 6 in. wide; grayish to olivaceous brown or reddish brown; semicircular to kidney-shaped; broadly convex to flat; tough, fibrous; surface zoned, radially wrinkled, uneven, shallowly grooved, finely velvety when young

FLESH: White to pinkish brown; tough, fibrous; odor not distinctive; taste slightly bitter

FERTILE SURFACE: Whitish, grayish to pale brown, often staining pinkish to reddish when bruised; fibrous, tough, elongated pore walls toward the margin, more pore-like near the point of attachment; often labyrinthine

STEM: Absent

SPORE PRINT: White

ECOLOGY: Saprobic; solitary to gregarious on oaks and other broadleaf tree logs and stumps; throughout the year; common

EDIBILITY: Not edible

COMMENTS: Compare with *Daedalea quercina* (p. 322), which is larger and has a thick maze-like undersurface. *Trametes gibbosa* (p. 324) has a similar pore surface. It is whitish and not zoned.

Daedaleopsis confragosa

SCIENTIFIC NAME: *Daedalea quercina* (L.) Pers.

SYNONYM: None

COMMON NAME: Oak Mazegill

FAMILY: Fomitopsidaceae

FRUIT BODY: Up to 8 in. wide; brownish yellow, ash gray, tan, or brown; broadly convex to flat; semicircular to kidney-shaped; leathery to woody, velvety when young, becoming bald and cracked or furrowed in age; often zoned, especially near the margin

FLESH: Whitish to pale brown; fibrous, very tough; thick; odor not distinctive; taste unknown

FERTILE SURFACE: Whitish, buff, to pale yellowish brown or grayish brown; maze-like to gill-like, thick-walled, fairly well separated; fibrous, tough

STEM: None

SPORE PRINT: White

ECOLOGY: Saprobic on oaks and occasionally on other broadleaf tree wood; solitary or gregarious, often with fused caps; throughout the year; common

EDIBILITY: Not edible

COMMENTS: The name *Daedalea* is derived from Daidalos, builder of the labyrinth of the Minotaur in Crete. Compare with *Daedaleopsis confragosa* (p. 321), which is smaller and thinner and has a maze-like fertile surface with walls much closer together and often more poroid.

Daedalea quercina

SCIENTIFIC NAME: *Stereum complicatum* (Fr.) Fr.

SYNONYM: *Stereum hirsutum* var. *complicatum* (Fr.) Rick.

COMMON NAME: Crowded Parchment

FAMILY: Stereaceae

CAP: Up to ¾ in. wide; yellowish orange, bright cinnamon buff, cinnamon brown, margin buff, or yellow; fan-shaped to semicircular; densely velvety with appressed hairs

FLESH: Thin; very flexible; tough; odor not distinctive; taste unknown

FERTILE SURFACE: Cream, buff, orange, whitish, or cinnamon buff; smooth; no pores

STEM: Absent

SPORE PRINT: White

ECOLOGY: Saprobic on the dead wood of broadleaf trees, especially oaks; encompassing twigs and limbs or in masses or rows on stumps and logs, the caps often are overlapped and fused together; throughout the year; very common

EDIBILITY: Not edible

COMMENTS: This is one of the most common species in oak woods.

Stereum complicatum

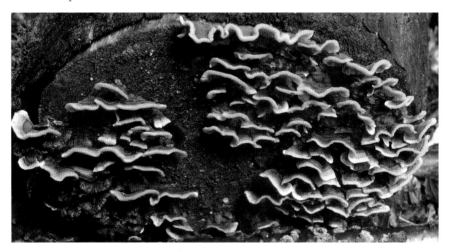

SCIENTIFIC NAME: *Trichaptum biforme* (Fr.) Ryvarden

SYNONYM: *Trichaptum pargamenum* (Fr.) G. Cunn.

COMMON NAME: Violet-Tooth Polypore

FAMILY: Polyporaceae

CAP: Whitish, buff, or tan, with a violet margin, fading in age; surface zonate, velvety to smooth, hairy at times; often with a covering of algae

FLESH: White to ochraceous; thin; tough; odor not distinctive; taste unknown

FERTILE SURFACE: Deep violet fading to buff, or brownish; margin usually retaining some violet coloration; with pores at first, the pores soon becoming ragged and spine-like, appearing like a toothed mushroom

STEM: Absent

SPORE PRINT: White

ECOLOGY: Saprobic; growing in overlapping clusters on the dead wood of broadleaf trees; throughout the year; abundant

EDIBILITY: Not edible

COMMENTS: This is one of the most common wood-rotting mushrooms in the broadleaf forests. *Trichaptum abietinum* (not illustrated) is nearly identical and is considered a distinct species. It occurs on conifer wood.

Trichaptum biforme

SCIENTIFIC NAME: *Inonotus obliquus* (Ach. ex Pers.) Pilát

SYNONYM: *Fuscoporia obliqua* (Ach. ex Pers.) Aoshima

COMMON NAME: Chaga

FAMILY: Polyporaceae

CANKER: Up to 16 in. wide; an amorphous, black, cracked, and very hard mass; appearing burnt

STEM: Absent

ECOLOGY: Parasitic on black and yellow birches and reportedly on other broadleaf trees; usually solitary, often emerging from a wound on the tree; throughout the year; occasional

EDIBILITY: Not edible, used to make a tea

COMMENTS: The actual spore-producing fruiting is a short-lived and seldom-observed crust fungus with small pores. It is a yellowish-brown, reddish-brown to grayish-brown crust found on birch and other broadleaf tree logs. It is soon devoured by insects. The canker has received quite a bit of attention as a medicinal species. While the chemistry is promising and the anecdotal reports numerous, more study is needed to determine the role this fungus might play in the immune system and cancer treatment.

Inonotus obliquus

SCIENTIFIC NAME: *Climacodon septentrionalis* (Fr.) P. Karst.

SYNONYM: *Steccherinum septentrionale* (Fr.) Banker

COMMON NAME: Northern Tooth

FAMILY: Meruliaceae

FRUIT BODY: Whitish, becoming buff to yellowish brown in age; layered; shelving; semicircular to fan-shaped caps, which are up to 12 in. wide and up to 2 in. thick; the entire fruiting is up to 15 in. high; convex to flat; upper surface dry, roughened, usually very hairy

FLESH: Whitish, zoned; fibrous, very tough, elastic; odor mild at first then resembling ham and eventually unpleasant; taste mild at first becoming bitter

SPINES: Dull white to pinkish brown; crowded; pointed; pliant

STEM: Absent

SPORE PRINT: White

ECOLOGY: Parasitic in large clusters on broadleaf trees, especially sugar maple and beech; summer and fall; fairly common

EDIBILITY: Not edible

COMMENTS: Clusters of this species are often seen high up on the trunks of infected trees. They are annual but rather long-lived and can be observed for a month or more.

Climacodon septentrionalis
Photo by William Roody

SCIENTIFIC NAME: *Ganoderma applanatum* (Pers.) Pat.

SYNONYM: *Ganoderma megaloma* (Lév.) Bres.

COMMON NAME: Artist's Conk

FAMILY: Ganodermataceae

FRUIT BODY: Up to 30 in. wide; gray, brown, or grayish brown to nearly black in age, margin whitish; fan-shaped, semicircular, or irregular, shelf-like; surface thick, hard, furrowed, often cracked, may be covered with brown spores; perennial

FLESH: Brown; hard, woody; odor not distinctive; taste unknown

PORES: White, staining brown where bruised; very small; circular

STEM: Usually absent; when present, short and attached laterally

SPORE PRINT: Brown or reddish brown

ECOLOGY: Saprobic and parasitic on broadleaf and conifer wood; solitary, scattered, or in overlapping clusters; throughout the year; common

EDIBILITY: Not edible

COMMENTS: A hand lens is needed to see the pores. This fungus is used by artists who etch pictures on the underside. Compare with *Fomes fomentarius* (p. 333), which is hoof-shaped and smaller. *Ganoderma megaloma* may turn out to be the proper name for our American Artist's Conk. *Ganoderma applanatum* is reported to be a European species.

Ganoderma applanatum

SCIENTIFIC NAME: *Phellinus robiniae* (Murrill) A. Ames
SYNONYM: *Phellinus rimosus* (Berk.) Pilát
COMMON NAME: Cracked-Cap Polypore
FAMILY: Hymenochaetaceae

CAP: Up to 16 in. wide and 8 in. deep; brown to dark brown, marginal fresh growth rich brownish red; semicircular, kidney-shaped, or irregular bracket-shaped; surface velvety at first, becoming cracked and furrowed, often partially covered with algae or moss

FLESH: Various shades of brown; woody, very hard; odor fragrant when fresh; taste unknown

PORES: Brown; very small

STEM: Absent

SPORE PRINT: Brown

ECOLOGY: Saprobic and parasitic on the heartwood of locust trees, especially black locust; solitary or several on a tree or stump; perennial, lasting several years; common

EDIBILITY: Not edible

COMMENTS: Both of the above names are being used for what appears to be the same species. Both could be reduced to one species and placed in the genus *Fulvifomes*. *Phellinus everhartii* (not illustrated) is similar. It occurs on oaks.

Phellinus robiniae

SCIENTIFIC NAME: *Fomes fomentarius* (L.) Fr.

SYNONYMS: *Fomes excavatus* (Berk.) Sacc.

COMMON NAME: Tinder Polypore, Punk

FAMILY: Polyporaceae

FRUIT BODY: Up to 8 in. wide; gray, brown, or blackish gray, margin often with a whitish and brownish zone; hoof-shaped; layered at times; surface concentrically furrowed, zoned, hard and crust-like, woody, finely cracked

FLESH: Light brown to yellowish brown; fibrous, tough to woody; odor not distinctive; taste unknown

PORES: Light brown; circular; small

STEM: None

SPORE PRINT: White

ECOLOGY: Parasitic and saprobic on the wood of broadleaf trees, especially beech and birch; perennial; common

EDIBILITY: Not edible

COMMENTS: The common names refer to the fact that this conk when dried is extremely flammable and an excellent fire starter. It was used in the ignition of revolutionary war rifles. It was also found on the person of the five-thousand-year-old ice man found frozen in the Italian Alps. It is used today by campers and survivalists. Compare with *Ganoderma applanatum* (p. 331), which is flatter, not hoof-shaped, and usually larger.

Fomes fomentarius

SCIENTIFIC NAME: *Fomitopsis pinicola* (Sw.) P. Karst.

SYNONYMS: *Fomes pinicola* (Sw.) Fr., *Fomes excavatus* (Berk.) Sacc.

COMMON NAMES: Red-Belt Conk, Red-Belted Polypore

FAMILY: Fomitopsidaceae

FRUIT BODY: Up to 18 in. wide; surface usually blackish-brown near the point of attachment, with reddish-brown zones outward, with a narrow band of creamy white at the margin; semicircular to fan-shaped, becoming nearly flat; broadly attached to the substrate; surface bald and shiny at first, becoming dull in age

FLESH: Creamy white; leathery to woody; odor unpleasant or like citrine, taste sour or bitter

PORES: Creamy white, becoming brownish in age, not changing when bruised; small; at times exuding drops of clear liquid when young

STEM: Absent

SPORE PRINT: Light yellow

ECOLOGY: Saprobic and parasitic primarily on conifers but occasionally on broadleaf trees; solitary or gregarious on stumps, on logs, and on wounds of living trees; throughout the year; common

EDIBILITY: Not edible

COMMENTS: The Red-Belt Conk is a common sight wherever large conifers are found. It is most commonly a saprobe but will take advantage of a wound scar or a tree weakened by other factors.

Fomitopsis pinicola

SCIENTIFIC NAME: *Fomitopsis betulina* (Bull.) B. K. Cui, M. L. Han, and Y. C. Dai

SYNONYM: *Piptoporus betulinus* (Bull.) P. Karst.

COMMON NAMES: Birch Polypore, Ice Man Polypore

FAMILY: Polyporaceae

CAP: Up to 10 in. wide; white to pale brown or gray; shell- to kidney-shaped; surface smooth and bald, becoming a mosaic of brown and white, finely spotted, cracking in age; margin turned under

FLESH: White, firm, becoming tough and corky; thick; odor pleasant; taste bitter, becoming more so with age

PORES: White to cream, becoming yellowish brown; small, circular to angular, becoming ragged in age

STEM: Up to 2 in. long; white to reddish brown; often rudimentary or absent

SPORE PRINT: White

ECOLOGY: Saprobic and weakly parasitic on various species of birch trees; solitary to scattered on birch trees and logs; summer and fall, fruit bodies visible year round; common

EDIBILITY: Edible when young but fibrous and rather bitter

COMMENTS: Pieces of this mushroom were being carried by Ötzi, the name given to a five-thousand-year-old man whose frozen body was found in the Italian Alps. Oils in this fungus are effective against intestinal parasites, which were found in his intestine. It has also been shown to have styptic effects and possibly other antibiotic properties as well. It can be found powdered in immune-system-enhancing capsules in contemporary health food stores.

Fomitopsis betulina

SCIENTIFIC NAME: *Cryptoporus volvatus* (Peck) Shear
SYNONYM: None
COMMON NAMES: Globe Polypore, Veiled Polypore
FAMILY: Polyporaceae

FRUIT BODY: Up to 2 in. wide; dull white to cream colored, yellowish brown to tan in age; round to hoof shaped; outer surface leathery, tough, bald, dry, at times with a lacquered look; resembles a puffball; the fertile pore surface and flesh is totally incased in a universal veil; the interior consists of a fleshy layer with a pore surface underneath

FLESH: White; solid, tough with a corky interior; odor resinous; taste bitter Pores: s that are encased in the fruitingemoving the universal veil will reveal the small, white, or brownish pores which are often covered with pale spores.

STEM: Absent

SPORE PRINT: Cream to pinkish

ECOLOGY: Saprobic and mildly parasitic; solitary to gregarious usually on standing conifers, especially pines; spring, summer, and fall; occasional, locally common

EDIBILITY: Not edible

COMMENTS: This is the only polypore with a universal veil. It appears just before the tree dies from other causes or soon afterward. Insects of various kinds are known to burrow into the pore surface and flesh. They serve as one vector for dispersing the spores.

Cryptoporus volvatus

SCIENTIFIC NAME: *Oxyporus populinus* (Schumach.) Donk

SYNONYM: None

COMMON NAME: Mossy Maple Polypore

FAMILY: Schizoporaceae

CAP: Up to 8 in. across; whitish to grayish white or creamy white, margin tan at times; fan- to kidney-shaped; surface covered with dense, matted fibers, becoming bald in age, often covered with moss; margin sharp, uneven

FLESH: White to ochre; watery; firm; odor not distinctive; taste unknown

PORES: White to cream; circular to angular; very small

STEM: Absent

SPORE PRINT: White

ECOLOGY: Parasitic on broadleaf trees, usually maples, where it is solitary or gregarious, usually on wounds near the base of the tree; throughout the year; common

EDIBILITY: Not edible

COMMENTS: The habitat and moss covering make identifying this polypore fairly easy. The species epithet "populinus," which refers to *Populus* tree genus, is a misnomer since it usually fruits on maple and not poplar trees.

Oxyporus populinus

SCIENTIFIC NAME: *Hapalopilus nidulans* (Fr.) P. Karst.

SYNONYM: *Hapalopilus rutilans* (Pers.) Murrill

COMMON NAME: Tender Nesting Polypore

FAMILY: Polyporaceae

CAP: Up to 4½ in. wide; dull orange, pinkish brown to cinnamon brown; irregularly bracket-shaped to kidney- or fan-shaped; surface dry, with matted hairs to nearly bald, occasionally furrowed

FLESH: Colored like the cap; soft and spongy when young, becoming tough and hard in age; odor and taste not distinctive

PORES: Brownish orange to cinnamon brown; not staining, or staining slightly darker brown when bruised; angular; small; no partial veil

STEM: Absent

Spore Print: White

ECOLOGY: Saprobic on the dead wood of broadleaf trees, including oaks, beech, and birches; solitary, in small groups, or in overlapping clusters; summer and fall; occasional

EDIBILITY: Poisonous; it affects the kidneys and central nervous system

COMMENTS: A drop of KOH (potassium hydroxide) on all parts of this mushroom will produce a color reaction to lilac or purple. It is a treasured find for those who make dyes from mushrooms.

Hapalopilus nudulans

SCIENTIFIC NAME: *Hapalopilus croceus* (Pers.) Donk

SYNONYM: None

COMMON NAME: None

FAMILY: Hapalopilaceae

CAP: Up to 10 in. wide; orange to yellowish orange; semicircular to fan-shaped, convex; rather thick; soft and watery when young, becoming corky when dry; surface uneven, finely velvety when young

FLESH: Bright orange when fresh, becoming darker orange and eventually brownish in age; firm to spongy, eventually becoming hard; odor not distinctive; taste slightly bitter or not distinctive

PORES: Bright reddish orange to yellowish orange with whitish areas at times, brownish in age when dry; small; angular

STEM: Absent

SPORE PRINT: White

ECOLOGY: Saprobic and parasitic on the wood of broadleaf trees, especially oaks; usually solitary but occasionally in groups; summer and early fall; uncommon to occasional, rare in some areas

EDIBILITY: Not edible

COMMENTS: In several European countries this species is considered rare and a species of concern. While not common, it can be found occasionally in Appalachian woods with mature oaks.

Hapalopilus croceus

SCIENTIFIC NAME: *Pycnoporus cinnabarinus* (Jacq.) P. Karst.

SYNONYM: *Trametes cinnabarina* (Jacq.) Fr.

COMMON NAME: Cinnabar Polypore

FAMILY: Polyporaceae

CAP: Up to 4 in. wide; brilliant cinnabar red to bright orange, becoming pale orange and finally whitish in age; usually semicircular and laterally attached, but may be circular and have a central point of attachment when growing on top of a log; surface suede-like to nearly smooth to uneven or wrinkled or pockmarked in age

FLESH: Orangish red; leathery, fibrous, tough, becoming hard when dry; odor and taste not distinctive

PORES: Cinnabar red to orange, holding their color longer than the cap; rather small; round to angular

STEM: Absent

SPORE PRINT: White

ECOLOGY: Saprobic on the dead wood of broadleaf trees, often on wild cherry and oaks, reportedly on conifers as well; its typical habitat is in open, well-aerated areas on logs; gregarious or in shelving rows, caps are often fused together; throughout the year; common

EDIBILITY: Not edible

COMMENTS: *Pycnoporus sanguineus* (not illustrated) has thinner caps and a generally more southerly range.

Pycmoporus cinnabarinus

SCIENTIFIC NAME: *Fistulina hepatica* (Schaeff.) With.

SYNONYM: None

COMMON NAMES: Beefsteak Polypore, Ox Tongue

FAMILY: Fistulinaceae

FRUITBODY: Up to 10 in. wide; bright red, pinkish red, reddish orange at first, becoming dark red to brownish red with age; semicircular to fan-shaped; broadly convex to flat; surface finely granular, sticky to slimy when wet, at times with red droplets

FLESH: Mottled whitish, reddish, and pinkish, slowly darkening after exposure; thick; watery; exuding a red liquid when squeezed; odor not distinctive; taste sour-acidic

PORES: Whitish, becoming yellowish to pinkish tan; circular; the tubes are separate from each other when viewed with a hand lens; closely packed

SPORE PRINT: Pinkish brown to pinkish salmon; reportedly white in California

ECOLOGY: Saprobic and weakly parasitic on oaks and other broadleaf trees; solitary or in small overlapping clusters usually near the base of trees and stumps; summer and fall; occasional

EDIBILITY: Edible; can be marinated and eaten raw; the acidic taste is a challenge when cooking this mushroom

COMMENTS: The texture and color of this fungus resemble raw beef. The pores when separated reveal tubes that are not attached to each other. This differs from most pored fungi.

Fistulina hepatica

SCIENTIFIC NAME: *Ganoderma tsugae* Murrill

SYNONYM: **None**

COMMON NAME: **Hemlock Varnish Shelf**

FAMILY: **Ganodermataceae**

FRUIT BODY: Up to 12 in. wide, occasionally larger; reddish brown when mature; the margin is yellow or whitish while actively growing, becoming progressively darker and more brownish toward the stem; shiny and appearing varnished except for the white areas; fan-to kidney-shaped

FLESH: Whitish, fairly soft and corky at first, becoming tough and fibrous; odor and taste not distinctive

PORES: Creamy white, becoming brown when bruised or in age; very small

STEM: Up to 6 in. long, occasionally absent; brownish red to blackish brown; shiny and appearing varnished; lateral, eccentric to central at times

SPORE PRINT: Brown

ECOLOGY: Parasitic and saprobic on hemlock and other conifers, rarely on broadleaf trees; solitary, gregarious, or in shelving clusters; late spring through fall; common

EDIBILITY: Not edible, but it is powdered and made into a tea

COMMENTS: Several similar species occur on broadleaf trees. These include *Ganoderma lucidum*, *Ganoderma curtisii*, and *Ganoderma sessile*. None of these species are illustrated here. *Ganoderma lucidum* is available in Asian markets and health food stores under the names Lingzhi and Reishi. It has been used for centuries as a folk medicine in Asia.

Ganoderma tsugae

SCIENTIFIC NAME: *Rhodofomes cajanderi* (P. Karst.) B. K. Cui, M. L. Han, and Y. C. Dai

SYNONYMS: *Fomitopsis subrosea* (Weir) Bondartsev and Singer, *Fomitopsis cajanderi* (P. Karst.) Kotl. and Pouzar

COMMON NAMES: Rosy Polypore, Rosy Conk

FAMILY: Fomitopsidaceae

FRUIT BODY: Up to 5 in. wide; pink, reddish brown; grayish brown, margin typically whitish; semicircular or fan-shaped, irregular; broadly convex to flat; finely hairy at first, nearly bald in age; wrinkled at times

FLESH: Rosy pink, becoming pinkish brown; pliant, corky, becoming woody in age; odor not distinctive; taste unknown

PORES: Pink, rosy pink, to pinkish brown; small; circular to angular

STEM: Absent

SPORE PRINT: Whitish

ECOLOGY: Saprobic and parasitic; solitary or in shelving groups on conifer wood and occasionally on the wood of broadleaf trees, at times laterally fused with other caps; throughout the year; occasional to fairly common

EDIBILITY: Not edible

COMMENTS: *Fomitopsis rosea* (not illustrated) is similar when young. It has a hoof-shaped cap that becomes brownish black and crusty in age.

Fomitopsis cajanderi

SCIENTIFIC NAME: *Niveoporofomes spraguei* (Berk. and M. A. Curtis) B. K. Cui, M. L. Han, and Y. C. Dai

SYNONYMS: *Tyromyces spraguei* (Berk. and M. A. Curtis) Murrill, *Fomitopsis spraguei* (Berk. and M. A. Curtis) Gilb. and Ryvarden

COMMON NAME: None

FAMILY: Fomitopsidaceae

FRUIT BODY: Up to 3½ in. wide; whitish to cream with areas of orange or ochre, especially toward the margin, becoming gray or washed-out white in age, when young the margin stains green when handled or in contact with wax paper; irregular roundish when young, becoming shelf-like; surface roughened and hairy toward the cap margin

FLESH: Zoned hyaline and white, staining green when young; firm becoming fibrous and hard; odor pungent; taste bitter

PORES: Cream to pale brown; round to slightly angular; small; edges thick, becoming thin and torn in age

STEM: Absent

SPORE PRINT: White

ECOLOGY: Parasitic and saprobic on the wood of broadleaf trees, especially oaks; typically near the base of a tree or stump; solitary or gregarious; summer and fall; common

EDIBILITY: Not edible

COMMENTS: When young, the ochre cap margin, which stains green, and the presence of liquid droplets are keys to identification and a treat for photographers.

Niveoporofomes spraguei

SCIENTIFIC NAME: *Ischnoderma resinosum* (Schrad.) P. Karst.

SYNONYM: None

COMMON NAME: Resinous Polypore

FAMILY: Hapalopilaceae

CAP: Up to 10 in. wide; brownish orange to dark brown, often blackish near the point of attachment; semicircular to fan-shaped; surface furrowed, zoned at times; exuding gold to brownish droplets when young, especially on the underside and on the growing margin, which is whitish, thick, and rounded

FLESH: Whitish to pale yellow, becoming brownish in age; soft when young, becoming fibrous; odor not distinctive; taste slightly bitter or not distinctive

PORES: White, bruising brownish, becoming brown in age; small; at times with gold to brownish liquid droplets, especially when young

STEM: Absent

SPORE PRINT: Whitish

ECOLOGY: Usually saprobic but parasitic at times on the wood of broadleaf trees; solitary or in overlapping clusters; late summer and fall; common

EDIBILITY: Edible when young and soft; reports on its quality vary greatly; not a popular edible

COMMENTS: This is a common mushroom in beech maple forests.

Ischnoderma resinosum

SCIENTIFIC NAME: *Cerioporus leptocephalus* (Jacq.) Zmitr.

SYNONYMS: *Polyporus elegans* Fr., *Polyporus varius* (Pers.) Fr., *Polyporus leptocephalus* (Jacq.) Fr.

COMMON NAME: Elegant Polypore

FAMILY: Polyporaceae

CAP: Up to 3 in. wide; yellowish, buff to pale tan; convex, broadly convex to flat, at times depressed and funnel-shaped, circular to fan-shaped; surface dry, bald, not zoned; margin striate at times in age, even or undulating

FLESH: whitish, buff, or yellowish, unchanging when exposed; corky to woody; odor and taste not distinctive

PORES: White to buff or grayish, becoming darker in age, at times bruising slightly brownish; decurrent; small; no partial veil

STEM: Up to 2 in. long; white to tan or brownish above, becoming black and velvety from the base upward; central, off-center to lateral; equal or tapering downward; tough; surface dry and bald

SPORE PRINT: White

ECOLOGY: Solitary to scattered on dead wood of broadleaf trees, usually on decorticated limbs and sticks; summer and fall; common

EDIBILITY: Not edible

COMMENTS: Some mycologist consider *Polyporus varius* to be a separate species, based primarily on its size, striations, and cap color. Recent studies indicate that *Polyporus elegans* and *Polyporus varius* are the same. Both *Polyporus leptocephalus* and *Polyporus varius* were first described in 1821. There is a question as to which name was published first.

Cerioporus leptocephalus

SCIENTIFIC NAME: *Picipes badius* (Pers.) Zmitr. and Kovalenko

SYNONYMS: *Polyporus badius* (Pers.) Schwein., *Royoporus badius* (Pers.) A. B. De.

COMMON NAME: Black-Footed Polypore, Bay-Colored Polypore

FAMILY: Polyporaceae

CAP: Up to 8 in. wide; rich reddish brown, grayish brown, yellowish brown, to tan, center dark reddish brown to black; broadly convex with a central depression, nearly flat in age; roundish to kidney-shaped; surface dry, bald; margin incurved at first, sometimes becoming uplifted at maturity

FLESH: White, unchanging when cut; very tough; thin; odor and taste not distinctive

PORES: White to cream, becoming dingy in age; very small; decurrent; very shallow

STEM: Up to 2 in. long; apex colored like the pores, brown to black below; equal or tapering downward; relatively short, off-center, lateral, or central; surface bald, smooth, dry

SPORE PRINT: White

ECOLOGY: Saprobic; scattered to gregarious on the dead wood of broadleaf trees, reported occasionally on conifer wood; late spring through early winter; common

EDIBILITY: Not edible

Comments: Mature caps are a deep reddish brown and are the most likely to be encountered. Young caps can be a very pale grayish brown or tan, but the central depression will usually have reddish-brown to black coloration.

Picipes badius

SCIENTIFIC NAME: *Lentinus brumalis* (Pers.) Zmitr.

SYNONYM: *Polyporus brumalis* (Batsch) Fr.

COMMON NAME: Winter Polypore

FAMILY: Polyporaceae

CAP: Up to 3 in. wide; circular; convex to flat with a central depression; dark yellowish brown, dark brown, or nearly black; surface dry, smooth, or with fine dark hairs; margin fringed with hairs at times

FLESH: White or cream colored; thin; tough, leathery; odor and taste not distinctive

PORES: White, yellowish cream, becoming yellowish tan in age, unchanging when bruised; decurrent; oblong or somewhat angular; small

STEM: Up to 2½ in. long; colored like the cap or paler; equal or with a swollen base; central or slightly off-center; surface smooth, scurfy to finely hairy

SPORE PRINT: White to creamy white

ECOLOGY: Saprobic on the dead wood of broadleaf trees, especially birch, in cool weather; solitary or in small groups; late fall, winter, and spring; fairly common

EDIBILITY: Not edible, tough

COMMENTS: *Lentinus arcularius* (p. 320) has larger pores and a tan, scaly cap. It usually fruits in the spring. The genus *Polyporus* has been and is being split up. Both of these species have been placed in that genus in older texts.

Lentinus brumalis

SCIENTIFIC NAME: *Coltricia cinnamomea* (Jacq.) Murrill

SYNONYM: None

COMMON NAME: Shiny Cinnamon Polypore

FAMILY: Hymenochaetaceae

CAP: Up to 2 in. wide; reddish cinnamon, at times in age with a dark-brown center and brownish yellow outward, with a very thin, white margin, zoned with various shades of brown; flat to depressed or umbilicate; circular; surface appressed fibrillose, silky-shiny

FLESH: Rusty brown to orange; fibrous-tough, leathery, becoming rigid in age; odor not distinctive, taste unknown

PORES: Reddish brown to yellowish brown or cinnamon brown, large; angular; usually not descending onto the stem

STEM: Up to 1½ in. long; dark reddish brown to dark brown; equal or tapering downward, at times with a basal bulb; central; velvety; tough

SPORE PRINT: Yellowish brown

ECOLOGY: Mycorrhizal; solitary, in small groups or fused together; often on bare soil or moss on road banks and trails; under broadleaf trees and in mixed woods; summer and fall; common

EDIBILITY: Not edible

COMMENTS: *Coltricia perennis* (not illustrated) is larger and has a cap that is not silky-shiny.

Coltricia cinnamomea

SCIENTIFIC NAME: *Boletopsis grisea* (Peck) Bondartsev and Singer

SYNONYM: None

MISAPPLIED NAMES: *Boletopsis subsquamosa* (L.) Kotl. and Pouzar, *Boletopsis leucomelaena* (Pers.) Fayod

COMMON NAMES: Gray False Bolete, Kurotake

FAMILY: Bankeraceae

CAP: Up to 5 in. wide; whitish, gray, brownish to black; nearly circular; convex, broadly convex to nearly flat; surface dry, smooth at first, often becoming cracked and scaly; margin incurved at first, at maturity becoming wavy, often furrowed and splitting in age

FLESH: White to gray; firm and rather tough; thick; odor not distinctive, becoming fragrant when dry; taste slightly bitter

PORES: White to pale gray, becoming brownish in age; attached to subdecurrent; small; no partial veil

STEM: Up to 3 in. tall; white to grayish; generally equal; central to eccentric; solid; fibrillose-scaly

SPORE PRINT: Whitish to pale yellowish tan

ECOLOGY: Mycorrhizal with conifers; solitary, scattered to gregarious in humus under pine and hemlock in mixed woods; late summer and fall; occasional to locally common

EDIBILITY: Edible but rather tough and bitter at times

COMMENTS: Older field guides often use the names *Boletopsis subsquamosa* (not illustrated) for this species. It is a twin-like spruce associate. *Boletopsis leucomelaena* is a name that has been used for both species. Except for the tough flesh, these polypores could be mistaken for a bolete.

Boletopsis grisea

SCIENTIFIC NAME: *Laeticutis cristata* (Schaeff.) Audet
SYNONYM: *Albatrellus cristatus* (Schaeff.) Kotl. and Pouzar
COMMON NAME: Crested Polypore
FAMILY: Albatrellaceae

CAP: Up to 8 in. wide; yellowish brown, reddish brown to yellowish green; convex to flat; roughly circular or irregular; margin lobed; surface dry, glabrous, often cracking, forming scaly areas

FLESH: White, staining yellowish green where exposed and around larval tunnels; tough; odor not distinctive; taste bitter or not distinctive

PORES: White, often with greenish or yellowish stains; decurrent; small; angular

STEM: Up to 2 in. long; white to greenish or colored like the cap; thick; solid; central or eccentric; branching at times; surface smooth, dry

SPORE PRINT: White

ECOLOGY: Probably mycorrhizal with oaks and other broadleaf trees; scattered to gregarious in humus and lawns in broadleaf and mixed woods and parks; summer and early fall; fairly common

EDIBILITY: Not edible

COMMENTS: Commonly called *Albatrellus cristatus* in many older field guides.

Laeticutis cristata

SCIENTIFIC NAME: *Neoalbatrellus caeruleoporus* (Peck) Audet
SYNONYM: *Albatrellus caeruleoporus* (Peck) Pouzar
COMMON NAME: Blue Albatrellus
FAMILY: **Albatrellaceae**

CAP: Up to 4 in. wide; blue to grayish blue, fading to grayish brown to tan; generally circular in outline; convex to flat, depressed in the center; surface smooth to slightly felt-like

FLESH: Whitish to pale buff, unchanging when exposed; fairly soft; odor and taste not distinctive

PORES: Colored like the cap or paler, not fading as rapidly as the cap; decurrent; small; angular

STEM: Up to 3 in. long; colored like the cap, fading in age, becoming gray or brownish; generally equal; central to eccentric; surface smooth to slightly rough upward

SPORE PRINT: White

ECOLOGY: Mycorrhizal with hemlock and possibly other conifers; solitary, gregarious, or in small clusters on the ground, in moss or humus, in conifer and mixed woods; late summer and fall; uncommon

EDIBILITY: Edible

COMMENTS: It is always a treat to find this blue mushroom in prime condition. The author's collections always have been under hemlock in mixed woods.

Neoalbatrellus caeruleoporus

SCIENTIFIC NAME: *Abortiporus biennis* (Bull.) Singer

SYNONYM: *Sporotrichopsis terrestris* (Schulzer) Stalpers

COMMON NAME: Aborted Polypore

FAMILY: Meruliaceae

FRUITING BODY: Up to 8 in. wide in the "normal" form but usually smaller; white, tan, brown, or reddish brown; extremely variable in form, at times forming a layered rosette of fan-shaped caps with pores on the underside, at other times forming a pore-covered amorphous mass, sometimes with pore-covered finger-like projections

FLESH: Whitish to pinkish to pale tan; fibrous, tough; odor unpleasant; taste not distinctive

PORES: White to buff, bruising pinkish to reddish brown; fairly large, angular or irregular, at times becoming torn and ragged, and appearing like a maze of spine-like pores; sometimes exuding red droplets

STEM: When present, whitish to buff and velvety to fuzzy, rooted; tapering downward, often rudimentary or absent

SPORE PRINT: White

ECOLOGY: Usually saprobic and found solitary to gregarious or in a clustered mass or rosette from buried roots around broadleaf tree stump in woodlands, or in lawns; parasitic at times; summer and fall; occasional

EDIBILITY: Not edible

COMMENTS: This mushroom and its variability have been a challenge to taxonomists for many years. At last count it had been placed in twenty-three different genera!

Abortiporus biennis

Chanterelles and Allies

CHANTERELLES ARE MUSHROOMS in the genus *Cantharellus* and *Craterellus*. These are terrestrial, mycorrhizal mushrooms. They do not have sharp-edged gills. Instead their underside is smooth, wrinkled, or covered with thick, blunt-edged gills. Many are orange or yellow, and some have gray to blackish colors. Several have fruity odors, and most are considered good to choice edibles. Their often fruity fragrance is a factor in their use in cookies and ice cream or as an alcohol flavoring.

Key to Chanterelles and Allies

1. Cap bright red to pinkish red: *Cantharellus cinnabarinus* (p. 362)
2. Cap orange but appearing purplish from a covering of purple fibers: *Cantharellus lewisii* (p. 363)
3. Cap yellowish brown to ochre: *Cantharellus appalachiensis* (p. 360)
4. Cap orange to orangish yellow; very small; fertile surface gill-like: *Cantharellus minor* (p. 361)
5. Cap orange to orangish yellow; medium sized; fertile surface gill-like: *Cantharellus cibarius* species complex (p. 358)
6. Cap yellowish orange to pinkish orange; medium sized; fertile surface smooth or broadly wrinkled: *Cantharellus lateritius* (p. 357)
7. Cap gray, dark brown, or blackish; fertile surface smooth or broadly wrinkled: *Craterellus fallax* (p. 364)
8. Cap yellowish with orange to reddish-orange scales, funnel-shaped; fertile surface whitish: *Turbinellus floccosus* (p. 366)
9. Yellowish upper surface; club- to top-shaped; outer surface yellowish to orange: *Clavariadelphus truncatus* (p. 365)

Craterellus tubaeformis

Craterellus cinereus

SCIENTIFIC NAME: *Cantharellus lateritius* (Berk.) Singer

SYNONYM: *Craterellus cantharellus* (Schw.) Fr.

COMMON NAME: Smooth Chanterelle

FAMILY: Cantharellaceae

CAP: Up to 5 in. wide; pale yellow, yellowish orange to pinkish orange; broadly convex with a depressed center to funnel-shaped; surface usually smooth but very convoluted at times, dry, bald; margin thin and incurved at first, becoming uplifted in age, often wavy

FLESH: White, at times tinted yellowish orange; thick becoming thin toward the margin; odor fragrant, fruity, similar to apricots; taste not distinctive

FERTILE SURFACE: Pale yellow, or tinted pink or orange; nearly smooth or with broad wrinkles

STEM: Up to 3½ in. long; creamy white or colored like the fertile surface, bruising slowly yellowish brown to dull orange; surface smooth, dry; tapering downward; white mycelium at the base

SPORE PRINT: Orangish buff to pinkish yellow

ECOLOGY: Mycorrhizal with oaks; scattered or gregarious, at times in small clusters under broadleaf trees in humus and in grassy areas; summer and early fall; very common

EDIBILITY: Edible and very popular; its fruitiness lends itself to sweet dishes such as sorbet and cookies; it is also used as a flavoring for vodka

COMMENTS: In areas with large oak trees, this chanterelle can be collected in large quantities. The fruitings last for several days, but gathering them at their peak is best since they frequently become infested with insect larvae. Like other species of *Cantharellus*, there may be more than one look-alike species using this name. When the fertile surface is wrinkled, it can resemble members of the *Cantharellus cibarius* species complex (p. 358).

Cantharellus lateritius

SCIENTIFIC NAME: *Cantharellus cibarius* species complex

SYNONYM: None

COMMON NAME: Chanterelle

FAMILY: Cantharellaceae

CAP: Up to 5 in. wide; pale yellow, yellowish orange to orange; broadly convex with a depressed center to funnel-shaped; surface usually smooth but very convoluted at times, dry, bald; margin thin and incurved at first, becoming uplifted in age, often wavy

FLESH: White; thick; firm; odor fruity, resembling apricots; taste pleasant or not distinctive

FERTILE SURFACE: yellow, white, orange, or pinkish, often colored like the cap or slightly paler; with blunt-edged, gill-like ridges; no partial veil

STEM: Up to 3 in. long; creamy white or colored like the fertile surface; usually tapering downward; surface smooth, dry

SPORE PRINT: Variously recorded as white, pink, salmon, yellow and so on

ECOLOGY: Mycorrhizal; scattered to gregarious in humus and moss under broadleaf and conifer trees, hemlock and spruce are two frequent associates; summer; common

EDIBILITY: All similar chanterelles are edible and considered quite good

COMMENTS: The poisonous Jack O'Lantern, *Omphalotus illudens* (p. 126), has similar coloration. It grows on wood that may be buried, is generally larger, and most often fruits in clusters. It has sharp-edged gills. In eastern North America, what has been considered one species using the European species name *Cantharellus cibarius* is now known to be a complex of six or more species (and still counting). The true *Cantharellus cibarius* is not known to occur in North America.

Cantharellus cibarius complex

SCIENTIFIC NAME: *Hygrophoropsis aurantiaca* (Wulfen) Maire

SYNONYM: None

COMMON NAME: False Chanterelle

FAMILY: Hygrophoropsidaceae

CAP: Up to 3 in. wide; color variable, some combination of orange, yellow, whitish, brownish, and brownish orange, usually convex to broadly convex, finally flat, often with a depressed center; surface dry, velvety or bald, center occasionally becoming minutely scaly in age; margin turned under for most of the life of the cap

GILLS: Pale yellowish orange to deep bright orange, rarely whitish; close or crowded; decurrent; very narrow; abundantly forked, edges even and often rather thick; no partial veil

FLESH: Buff or tinted orange; thin; odor and taste not distinctive

STEM: Up to 4 in. long; usually colored like the cap but may be paler or darker; equal or slightly enlarged at the base; often curved, off center at times to nearly lateral; tough; surface dry, velvety, or minutely hairy; base with white mycelium

SPORE PRINT: White

ECOLOGY: Saprobic; scattered to gregarious on woody debris or duff under conifers and occasionally broadleaf trees; summer and fall

EDIBILITY: Not recommended; considered edible by some, but others have experienced gastrointestinal problems

COMMENTS: This mushroom's variability suggests that this is a species complex waiting for DNA analysis. As described here, the numerous forking of the gills is a key feature. *Cantharellus* species are somewhat similar but have thick gill-like folds, are much firmer, and have a fruity odor.

Hygrophoropsis aurantiaca

SCIENTIFIC NAME: *Cantharellus appalachiensis* R. H. Petersen

SYNONYM: None

COMMON NAME: Appalachian Chanterelle

FAMILY: Cantharellaceae

CAP: Up to 2 in. wide; yellowish brown to ochre, at times with a greenish tinge; convex at first, becoming flat with a central depression, funnel-shaped at times; surface bald, wrinkled at times, moist at first, becoming dry; margin turned under at first, becoming wavy and uplifted in age

FLESH: Whitish to yellowish brown, unchanging when exposed; thin; odor fragrant, fruity; taste not distinctive

FERTILE SURFACE: Cream, yellowish, or tan; gill like; blunt-edged; forked with numerous cross veins; no partial veil

STEM: Up to 2 in. long; colored like the cap or paler, whitish at the base; equal or tapering downward; surface bald, smooth; hollow in age

SPORE PRINT: Cream to pale salmon

ECOLOGY: Mycorrhizal with oaks and possibly other broadleaf trees; scattered, gregarious, or in small clusters in humus and moss in broadleaf and mixed woods; summer; fairly common

EDIBILITY: Edible

COMMENTS: This species was described from the southern Appalachians. It can be found throughout the entire region.

Cantharellus appalachiensis

SCIENTIFIC NAME: *Cantharellus minor* Peck

SYNONYM: None

COMMON NAMES: Small Chanterelle, Mini Chanterelle

FAMILY: Cantharellaceae

CAP: Up to 1 in. wide; orange to yellowish orange; broadly convex to nearly flat with a central depression; surface bald, dry to slightly moist

FLESH: Orange to pale yellow; thin; odor not distinctive or slightly fragrant, taste not distinctive

FERTILE SURFACE: Yellow to orange; gill-like; decurrent; rather blunt edges; no partial veil

STEM: Up to 2½ in. long; colored like the cap or paler; equal or tapering slightly in either direction; becoming hollow; often curved; surface bald, dry, furrowed at times

SPORE PRINT: Pale yellowish orange

ECOLOGY: Mycorrhizal; scattered to gregarious in humus, soil, and moss in broadleaf and mixed woods, often associated with oaks; summer and early fall; common

EDIBILITY: Edible but too small to be of much value

COMMENTS: This is a perfect mini chanterelle. *Humidicutus marginata* (p. 84) and *Gloioxanthomyces nitidus* (p. 72) have similar colors but are larger and have a fertile surface with sharp-edged gills.

Cantharellus minor

SCIENTIFIC NAME: *Cantharellus cinnabarinus* (Schwein.) Schwein.

SYNONYM: None

COMMON NAMES: Cinnabar Chanterelle, Vermillion Chanterelle

FAMILY: Cantharellaceae

CAP: Up to 2 in. wide; bright red to pinkish red; broadly convex to flat with a central depression, funnel-shaped at times; surface dry, bald, finely roughened

FLESH: Whitish, tinged orange near the cap surface; very thin; odor sweet or not distinctive; taste mild or slightly peppery

FERTILE SURFACE: Colored like the cap or paler; with blunt, distant, gill-like ridges; decurrent; forked; veined; narrow; no partial veil

STEM: Up to 2 in. long; colored like the cap or slightly paler; often whitish toward the bottom; equal or tapering downward; surface dry, basal mycelium white to yellowish

SPORE PRINT: Pinkish cream

ECOLOGY: Mycorrhizal with various broadleaf trees, especially oaks and beech; often in sandy soil; summer and early fall; common

EDIBILITY: Edible but small, so large quantities are needed to make a side dish

COMMENTS: The bright red to pinkish red over most of the mushroom makes this a distinctive and beautiful species. The very similar *Cantharellus texensis* is an edible, southern species not known from the Appalachians.

Cantharellus cinnabarinus

SCIENTIFIC NAME: *Cantharellus lewisii* Buyck and V. Hofst.

SYNONYM: None

COMMON NAME: Amethyst Chanterelle

FAMILY: Cantharellaceae

CAP: Up to 4 in. wide; orangish yellow to orange, with purplish-lilac appressed fibrils; with yellowish areas bleeding through the purple, center dark brownish purple to nearly black at times; margin turned under at first and remaining so to maturity

FLESH: Pale whitish, quickly yellowing when exposed, finally rusty; tough; odor fruity, similar to apricots; taste pleasant

FERTILE SURFACE: Cream to yellowish or pale grayish yellow, edges blunt, and at times paler than the sides; intervenose; no partial veil

STEM: White to yellowish, staining yellow to rusty where handled; longer than the width of the cap

SPORE PRINT: Whitish to pale cream

ECOLOGY: Mycorrhizal with broadleaf trees, often in floodplain forests; summer; rare in the Appalachians, to be expected in the southernmost areas of the region

EDIBILITY: Edible

COMMENTS: This mushroom is common in East Texas and Louisiana. The photograph here was taken in the Blue Ridge Mountains of South Carolina.

Cantharellus lewisii

SCIENTIFIC NAME: *Craterellus fallax* A. H. Sm.

SYNONYM: **None**

COMMON NAME: **Black Trumpet**

FAMILY: **Cantharellaceae**

FRUITBODY: Up to 3½ in. tall; gray, sooty brown to blackish; tubular becoming deep funnel-shaped; sterile surface dry, roughened to minutely scaly; margin incurved at first, then flaring, wavy and often recurved in age

FLESH: Grayish brown; thin; brittle; odor fragrant or fruity; taste not distinctive

FERTILE SURFACE: Smoky gray to blackish, becoming salmon buff from the spores; smooth, or with broad wrinkles, dry; no partial veil

STEM: Blackish; contiguous with the fertile surface; short; hollow; with white basal mycelium

SPORE PRINT: Pale pinkish orange to salmon buff

ECOLOGY: Mycorrhizal; scattered, gregarious to clustered, in moss, humus, or on soil, in mixed woods and broadleaf forests, especially under oaks; summer and fall; common

EDIBILITY: Edible and very good

COMMENTS: *Cantharellus cinereus* (p. 356) has similar colors, but its underside has prominent ridges and veins. It is edible but rather bitter. *Craterellus cornucopioides* is a European species with pale spores. A similar, as-yet-unnamed species on the West Coast of North America also has a pale spore print.

Craterellus fallax

SCIENTIFIC NAME: *Clavariadelphus truncatus* Donk

SYNONYM: None

COMMON NAME: Club Coral

FAMILY: Gomphaceae

FRUIT BODY: Up to 6 in. tall; exterior (fertile surface) pale yellow to pinkish buff or ochraceous orange; club- to top-shaped, broadest at the flattened apex; surface smooth or wrinkled vertically, channeled at times, base with white hairs; upper surface yellow or colored like the exterior, sterile and often hollow; stem contiguous with the fertile surface and not well-differentiated

FLESH: White; thin; firm at first, becoming spongy; hollow; odor pleasant; taste sweet

SPORE PRINT: Pale brownish yellow

ECOLOGY: Mycorrhizal with conifers; usually gregarious, occasionally solitary in conifer or mixed woods; in humus or moss; summer and fall; occasional to uncommon

EDIBILITY: Edible

COMMENTS: This species occurs most often under native conifers. The author has not found it in conifer plantations.

Clavariadelphus truncatus

SCIENTIFIC NAME: *Turbinellus floccosus* (Schwein.) Earle ex Giachini and Castellano

SYNONYM: *Gomphus floccosus* (Schwein.) Singer

COMMON NAME: Wooly Chanterelle

FAMILY: Gomphaceae

Cap: Up to 5 in. wide; yellow ground color, with numerous orange to reddish-orange scales that become brownish orange in age

FRUIT BODY: Up to 6 in. long; vase-shaped to funnel-shaped

FLESH: White; solid; thick; fibrous; odor and taste not distinctive

FERTILE SURFACE: Creamy white to yellowish, may bruise purplish; wrinkled or with decurrent, elongated, blunt ridges; veined; at times almost poroid

STEM: Up to 3 in. long; creamy white at first, becoming brownish, often short and barely discernable from the fruiting surface; solid becoming hollow

SPORE PRINT: Ochre yellow

ECOLOGY: Mycorrhizal with conifers, especially hemlock in Appalachia; solitary, gregarious to scattered in humus, moss, or soil; summer and fall; locally abundant

EDIBILITY: Not recommended; eaten by some but many cannot tolerate it and suffer gastrointestinal issues

COMMENTS: Once thought to be related to chanterelles, it is now known to be not at all closely related to *Cantharellus* and *Craterellus*. It is thought to be more closely related to coral mushrooms in the genus *Ramaria*.

Turbinellus floccosus

Club-Like and Coral-Like Fungi

T HIS ARTIFICIAL GROUPING includes a diverse assemblage of species that either resemble coral to some extent or are spatula or club-like. Fourteen genera are included here. Many species, especially those in the genus *Ramaria*, require chemical tests and a microscope to identify with certainty. The species covered here can be identified using macroscopic features. The different fungi are keyed out based on branching, habitat, color, and texture.

Key to Club-Like and Coral-Like Fungi

1. Fruiting body branched; whitish; tough; on soil or humus: *Tremellodendron schweinitzii* (p. 369)

2. Fruiting body branched; buff to pinkish tan; fragile; on wood: *Ramaria stricta* (p. 371)

3. Fruiting body branched; whitish to yellowish buff; branch tips crowned with three to six points; on wood: *Artomyces pyxidatus* (p. 370)

4. Fruiting body branched; whitish to pinkish; fragile; on soil or humus: *Ramariopsis kunzei* (p. 373)

5. Fruiting body branched; orange to pinkish orange to ochre; on soil or humus: *Ramaria formosa* (p. 372)

6. Fruiting body branched; whitish to pinkish gray, branches appearing feathery; on soil or humus: *Clavulina coralloides* (p. 374)

7. Fruiting body branched; gray and thick above, brown and hairy below; on soil or humus: *Clavulina ornatipes* (p. 375)

8. Fruiting body branched; yellowish-appearing in rosettes: *Thelephora vialis* (p. 380)

9. Fruiting body unbranched; buff to pinkish gray; clustered on soil, moss, or humus: *Clavaria fumosa* (p. 376)

10. Fruiting body unbranched; yellow; clustered on soil, moss, or humus: *Clavulinopsis fusiformis* (p. 377)

11. Fruiting body unbranched or branched; yellow, club-shaped or irregular; scattered on moss or humus: *Neolecta irregularis* (p. 383)

12. Fruiting body unbranched; yellow to cream above, brown below; cap fan- to spatula-shaped: *Spathulariopsis velutipes* (p. 384)

13. Fruiting body unbranched; yellowish upper surface; club- to top-shaped; on soil or humus: *Clavariadelphus truncatus* (p. 365)

14. Fruiting body branched but tightly clustered; cream, whitish to yellow; forming a clump, on roots: *Sparassis spathulata* (p. 382)

15. Fruiting body resembles a cluster of wet, curly noodles; white, cream, or yellowish; on roots: *Sparassis americana* (p. 381)

16. Fruiting body usually unbranched; whitish, becoming black; woody; club-like; on wood: *Xylaria polymorpha* (p. 388)

17. Fruiting body usually unbranched; gray or black; thin strands; on magnolia cones: *Xylaria magnoliae* (p. 387)

18. Fruiting body usually unbranched; reddish orange; club-shaped; on buried moth and butterfly larvae and pupae: *Cordyceps militaris* (p. 386)

19. Fruiting body unbranched; reddish brown becoming black; club-shaped; on buried false truffles in the genus Elaphomyces: *Tolypocladium ophioglossoides* (p. 385)

20. Fruiting body unbranched and small, fruiting on submerged sticks: *Vibrissea truncorum* (p. 379)

21. Fruiting body unbranched and small, fruiting on very wet humus and moss: *Mitrula elegans* (p. 378)

Clavaria fragilis

Ramaria species

SCIENTIFIC NAME: *Tremellodendron schweinitzii* (Peck) G. F. Atk.

SYNONYMS: *Tremellodendron pallidum* Burt, *Sebacina pallida* Oberw., Garnica, and K. Riess

COMMON NAME: False Coral Mushroom

FAMILY: Sebacinaceae

FRUITING BODY: Up to 6 in. wide; white, dingy white, cream, or yellowish, at times greenish from an algae covering; coral-like with a central base and compact clusters of fused, erect branches with blunt tips; at first appearing as a whitish mass, the coral-like branches grow slowly over several weeks; surface bald, tough, appearing rather waxy

FLESH: Colored like the surface; very tough, flexible, cartilaginous; odor not distinctive; taste bitter or rancid

STEM: A dingy, white, central base

SPORE PRINT: White

ECOLOGY: Mycorrhizal with oaks and possibly other broadleaf trees; solitary but usually scattered to gregarious on soil, moss, and humus in broadleaf woods and lawns; summer and fall; common

EDIBILITY: Not edible, tough

COMMENTS: Unlike coral mushrooms in the genera *Ramaria* and *Clavaria*, this mushroom is tough and not brittle or fragile. It is not closely related to these coral mushrooms. Even though it does not look much like most jelly fungi, it is related to that group. Its fruiting body is very long lasting when compared to most terrestrial mushrooms, at times lasting more than a month. *Tremellodendron pallidum* is a name commonly used for this mushroom in older texts. Eventually it is likely to be placed in the genus *Sebacina*.

Tremellodendron schweinitzii

SCIENTIFIC NAME: *Artomyces pyxidatus* (Pers.) Jülich

SYNONYM: *Clavicorona pyxidata* (Pers.) Doty

COMMON NAME: Crown Coral

FAMILY: Auriscalpiaceae

FRUIT BODY: Up to 5 in. tall, whitish, buff to pale yellowish, darkening to pale tan; coral-like with repeatedly forked candelabra-like branches, which terminate in a shallow depression, crowned with 3 to 6 points

FLESH: Whitish; tough, pliant; odor not distinctive; taste slightly peppery

STEM: Colored like the branches or brownish; short

SPORE PRINT: White

ECOLOGY: Saprobic on broadleaf tree wood, usually on logs, often on the wood of maple, aspen, and tulip trees; late spring, summer, and fall; common

EDIBILITY: Edible

COMMENTS: This is one of three common coral mushrooms that grow on logs. The other two, *Ramaria stricta* (p. 371) and *Ramaria concolor* (not illustrated), lack the crowned tips and have an anise odor.

Artomyces pyxidatus

SCIENTIFIC NAME: *Ramaria stricta* (Pers.) Quél.

SYNONYM: None

COMMON NAME: Straight Branched Coral

FAMILY: Ramariaceae

FRUIT BODY: Up to 4½ in. tall and 4 in. wide; coral-like; branches buff, yellowish buff to pinkish tan, bruising brown, when young the branch tips are yellowish to greenish; slender, repeatedly forked branches, the entire cluster often appearing very straight and erect

FLESH: Whitish, bruising brown; tough, rather elastic; odor sweet, like anise; taste metallic or bitterish

STEM: Absent or rudimentary; better described as a base; colored like the fruit body; with white rhizomorphs

SPORE PRINT: Ochre yellow

ECOLOGY: Saprobic and possibly mycorrhizal since most other species in this genus form mycorrhiza; clustered, solitary to gregarious on decaying broadleaf and conifer wood, often on buried wood; summer and fall; common

EDIBILITY: Not edible

COMMENTS: *Ramaria concolor* (not illustrated) is very similar but lacks the yellowish to greenish branch tips and often has an acrid taste. *Artomyces pyxidatus* (p. 370) is another wood-rotting coral mushroom. It has crown-like tips at the end of the branches.

Ramaria stricta

SCIENTIFIC NAME: *Ramaria formosa* (Pers.) Quél.

SYNONYM: *Clavaria formosa* Pers.

COMMON NAME: Yellow-Tipped Coral

FAMILY: Ramariaceae

FRUIT BODY: Up to 6 in. wide and 6 in. tall; coral-like; branches orangish salmon to coral pink or pinkish orange with blunt, yellowish tips, fading in age to yellowish or ochre, brownish where damaged; usually arising from a massive base that has a smooth to wrinkled surface

FLESH: Colored like the branches; fibrous above, spongy below; rather soft; brittle when dry; odor not distinctive; taste reportedly astringent, bitter, or not distinctive

STEM: Indistinct, better described as a base; massive or nearly absent; with white hairs

SPORE PRINT: Yellow to brownish yellow

ECOLOGY: Mycorrhizal; solitary, scattered to gregarious, at times in arcs or rows; on soil, in moss or humus under conifer and broadleaf trees; summer and fall; locally common

EDIBILITY: Poisonous; has been known to cause diarrhea and gastrointestinal disturbances

COMMENTS: When fresh this is one of the more attractive coral fungi. In age it fades and resembles several other coral mushrooms.

Ramaria formosa

SCIENTIFIC NAME: *Ramariopsis kunzei* (Fr.) Corner

SYNONYM: *Clavulinopsis kunzei* (Fr.) Jülich

COMMON NAME: White Coral

FAMILY: Clavariaceae

FRUIT BODY: Up to 3¼ in. tall and 3 in. wide; white, often tinged pink or pinkish orange; branched, coral-like, repeatedly forking branches arising from a central point; brittle; surface moist; tips bluntly pointed

FLESH: White, unchanging when cut; brittle, fragile; odor and taste not distinctive

STEM: Rudimentary, very short

SPORE PRINT: White

ECOLOGY: Considered saprobic, but possible connections with ericaceous plants and mosses are being investigated; solitary, scattered, or gregarious on soil, humus, and moss in broadleaf and conifer woods; summer and early fall; common

EDIBILITY: Not recommended; some similar coral fungi are poisonous

COMMENTS: The similar *Ramariopsis lentofragilis* (not illustrated) has a pale tan spore print, is more robust, and lacks the pinkish tinges.

Ramariopsis kunzei

SCIENTIFIC NAME: *Clavulina coralloides* (L.) J. Schröt.

SYNONYMS: *Clavulina cristata* (Holmsk.) J. Schröt., *Clavaria cristata* (Holmsk.) Pers.

COMMON NAME: Crested Coral

FAMILY: Clavulinaceae

FRUIT BODY: Up to 3 in. wide and high; whitish, at times pinkish gray in age; coral-like, with several branches emerging from a solid, pubescent base; the branch tips are fine and often flattened, with a feathery appearance; surface smooth or finely wrinkled

FLESH: Whitish; solid; pliant; odor and taste not distinctive

STEM: Not well defined; whitish; pubescent

SPORE PRINT: White

ECOLOGY: Mycorrhizal; scattered to gregarious, typically in humus and under conifers but also in broadleaf woods; summer and fall; common

EDIBILITY: Edible

COMMENTS: *Clavulina cinerea* (not illustrated) is very similar but is pale gray to ash gray overall. *Clavulina coralloides* is frequently parasitized by *Helminthosphaeria clavariarum* (not illustrated), a Pyrenomycete. Affected fruiting bodies will become gray to black from the base upward. A view through a hand lens will reveal blackish dots (perithecia).

Clavulina coralloides

SCIENTIFIC NAME: *Clavulina ornatipes* (Peck) Corner

SYNONYM: *Clavaria ornatipes* Peck

COMMON NAME: Fuzzy-Foot Coral

FAMILY: Clavulinaceae

FRUIT BODY: Up to 3 in. tall; consisting of a sterile stem base and a branched fertile area

FERTILE SURFACE: Gray to pinkish gray, becoming brownish in age; consisting of two to twelve rather thick branches; somewhat wrinkled; branch tips uneven

FLESH: Brown to grayish; flexible; odor and taste not distinctive

STEM: Dark reddish brown; densely hairy; overlapped unevenly at the top by the fertile surface

SPORE PRINT: White

ECOLOGY: Saprobic; solitary or gregarious in moss or humus in broadleaf and mixed woods; summer and early fall; uncommon to rare

EDIBILITY: Unknown

COMMENTS: The colors combined with the fuzzy stem set this species apart from all other coral mushrooms. *Clavulina cinerea* (not illustrated) is similar in color but lacks a hairy stem.

Clavulina ornatipes

SCIENTIFIC NAME: *Clavaria fumosa* Pers.

SYNONYM: *Clavaria rubicundula* Leathers

COMMON NAMES: Smoky Clavaria, Smoky Worm Coral

FAMILY: Clavariaceae

FRUIT BODY: Up to 5 in. tall; vinaceous buff to pale pinkish gray; composed of clustered cylindrical clubs with pointed or rounded tips; at times flattened or grooved; surface smooth and bald; hollow in age

FLESH: White or colored like the outside surface; very fragile, insubstantial; odor and taste not distinctive, or similar to iodine

STEM: Not well differentiated

SPORE PRINT: White

ECOLOGY: Saprobic in moss, soil, and grass, in broadleaf and mixed woods and in parklands; summer; occasional to locally common

EDIBILITY: Unknown

COMMENTS: Some mycologists prefer the name *Clavaria rubicundula* for this fungus. It is not clear whether they are actually synonyms.

Clavaria fumosa

SCIENTIFIC NAME: *Clavulinopsis fusiformis* (Sowerby) Corner

SYNONYM: *Ramariopsis fusiformis* (Sowerby) R. H. Petersen

COMMON NAME: Spindle-Shaped Yellow Coral

FAMILY: Clavariaceae

FRUIT BODY: Up to 5½ in. tall; pale to bright yellow; cylindrical to flattened thin clubs, narrowing at the apex, with roundish to somewhat pointed tops; the club tips are often reddish to brown in age; unbranched; clustered

FLESH: Yellowish; thin; brittle; odor not distinctive; taste bitter

STEM: Not well differentiated

SPORE PRINT: White to pale yellow

ECOLOGY: Saprobic, possibly mycorrhizal; usually growing in dense clusters with fused bases, occasionally scattered; on soil or humus, or in moss and grass, under conifers and broadleaf trees; summer and early fall; common

EDIBILITY: Reported as edible; the bitter taste is a deterrent

COMMENTS: *Clavulinopsis aurantiocinnabarina* (not illustrated) is closely related. It is orange and has a mild taste.

Clavulinopsis fusiformis

SCIENTIFIC NAME: *Mitrula elegans* Berk.

SYNONYMS: Misapplied name; *Mitrula paludosa* Fr.

COMMON NAME: Swamp Beacon.

FAMILY: Sclerotiniaceae

FRUITBODY: Up to 2 in. tall; consists of a club-like shape made up of a pale stem and yellow or orange head

FLESH: Pale yellow in the head, hyaline in the stem

FERTILE SURFACE: Translucent yellow to orange, becoming dull orange in age; clearly defined from the whitish stem; slightly gelatinous; smooth; elliptic to spindle-shaped, pear-shaped or irregularly rounded, lobed at times

STEM: Translucent, hyaline, pale grayish, or pinkish; equal or tapering upward; smooth or slightly textured

ECOLOGY: Saprobic; scattered to gregarious in very wet humus and moss, near water or partially submerged; late spring and summer; fairly common

EDIBILITY: Unknown

COMMENTS: *Mitrula lunulatospora* (not illustrated) is similar and occurs in the same habitats. Its fertile surface is pinkish to buff.

Mitrula elegans

SCIENTIFIC NAME: *Vibrissea truncorum* (Alb. & Schwein.) Fr.

SYNONYM: None

COMMON NAME: Water Club

FAMILY: Vibrisseaceae

CAP: Up to ¼ in. wide

FERTILE SURFACE: Pale yellow to yellow or orange or reddish orange; hemispheric to convex; bald; smooth; margin turned under

STEM: Up to ¾ in. long; whitish to pale gray, translucent, equal; curved at times; slightly roughened

ECOLOGY: Saprobic on partially or totally submerged sticks and limbs in cold streams; spring and early summer; occasional to locally common

EDIBILITY: Unknown, insignificant

COMMENTS: Aquatic macrofungi are unusual. *Vibrissea truncorum* is usually found in streams. Habitat helps distinguish *Vibrissea foliorum,* which occurs in vernal woodland pools on nutshells, leaves, and humus.

Vibrissea truncorum

SCIENTIFIC NAME: *Thelephora vialis* Schwein.

SYNONYM: None

COMMON NAME: Vase Thelephore

FAMILY: Thelephoraceae

CAP: Up to 4 in. long; color yellowish with whitish margins or the reverse, especially in age; variable in shape, spoon- to fan-shaped or fused, appearing in rosettes, arising from a central base; margin fringed at times

FLESH: Whitish to grayish; thick; leathery; odor slightly unpleasant, becoming foul when drying; taste not distinctive

FERTILE SURFACE: Yellowish becoming brownish or grayish violet to gray, margins paler; slightly wrinkled; at times with nipple-like projections

STEM: Up to 2 in long; whitish to gray, somewhat hairy; rather thick; solid

SPORE PRINT: Olive buff to brownish

ECOLOGY: Mycorrhizal, often associated with oaks; solitary to scattered on humus and soil in broadleaf and mixed woods; summer and early fall; fairly common

EDIBILITY: Not edible

COMMENTS: It has been reported as a good edible in Asia, but as leathery as it is, it is questionable that this is the same fungus that we have in eastern North America.

Thelephora vialis

SCIENTIFIC NAME: *Sparassis americana* R. H. Petersen

SYNONYM: None

COMMON NAME: Conifer Cauliflower Mushroom

FAMILY: Sparassidaceae

FRUIT BODY: Up to 12 in. wide; white, cream, or yellowish, a clustered mass of flattened, crimped, leafy lobes, emanating from a solid base above the stem; with a curly, lettuce-like appearance, only more ruffled

FLESH: White; fibrous; thin; odor not distinctive, or slightly fragrant; taste not distinctive

STEM: Up to 5 in. long; dark brown to black, thick; tapering toward the base; rooting

SPORE PRINT: White

ECOLOGY: Parasitic and saprobic on the wood of conifers, usually growing from buried roots; summer and fall; uncommon to occasional, more common in southern Appalachian areas

EDIBILITY: Edible and quite good; cleaning can be a chore but worth it; thorough cooking is recommended

COMMENTS: In older books this species was called *Sparassis crispa*, a European species. *Sparassis radicata* is a much larger species of the Pacific Northwest. *Sparassis spathulata* (p. 382) has thicker lobes and is usually found around oak trees and stumps.

Sparassi americana

SCIENTIFIC NAME: *Sparassis spathulata* (Schwein.) Fr.

SYNONYM: None

COMMON NAME: Eastern Cauliflower Mushroom

FAMILY: Sparassidaceae

FRUIT BODY: Up to 12 in. wide; creamy white, yellowish, the edges are often white in young fruitings; forms a cluster of long, wavy, flat, smooth, bald branches; the branches taper down to a solid, stem-like base; not deeply rooting but at times with a cord-like root

FLESH: White; thin; flexible; fibrous; becoming tough with age; odor pleasant when young, becoming pungent and fetid in age, like old cabbage; taste not distinctive

STEM: Absent

SPORE PRINT: White

ECOLOGY: Saprobic and parasitic; solitary or gregarious; usually growing from buried roots of living and dead oaks, reported on conifer roots as well; summer and early fall; locally common

EDIBILITY: Edible and quite good

COMMENTS: This species looks a bit like a ball or oblong cluster of old-fashioned ribbon candy. Several species of polypores look similar. They have pores on the undersides of their branches, unlike *Sparassis spathulata* which has a smooth fertile surface, lacking pores. *Sparassis americana* (p. 381) has thinner, more ruffled fronds and occurs on conifer roots. It is a good edible as well.

Sparassis spathulata

SCIENTIFIC NAME: *Neolecta irregularis* (Peck) Korf and
  J. K. Rogers

SYNONYM: *Spragueola irregularis* (Peck) Nannf.

COMMON NAME: Irregular Earth Tongue

FAMILY: Neolactaceae

FRUIT BODY: Up to 3 in. long; bright yellow, base yellow or whitish; generally club-shaped but bent, contorted, and lobed; longitudinally furrowed; compressed; branching at times

FLESH: Yellowish; thin; odor not distinctive; taste unknown

STEM: Whitish or yellow, rudimentary, sometimes absent

SPORE PRINT: Does not print well; spores are cream to yellowish

ECOLOGY: Probably saprobic or weakly parasitic; solitary, scattered to gregarious, or in clusters in moss and humus under conifers, most commonly at high elevations; late summer and fall; occasional to locally common

EDIBILITY: Unknown

COMMENTS: *Clavulinopsis fusiformis* (p. 377) looks similar but is unbranched and nearly always grows in clusters, usually with broadleaf trees. *Neolecta vitellina* (not illustrated) is also a look-alike, but it too is unbranched and not as contorted.

Neolecta irregularis

SCIENTIFIC NAME: *Spathulariopsis velutipes* (Cooke and Farl.) Maas Geest.

SYNONYM: *Spathularia velutipes* Cooke and Farl.

COMMON NAME: Velvety Fairy Fan

FAMILY: **Cudoniaceae**

FRUIT BODY: Up to 2½ in. long, and up to 1½ in. wide; yellowish to cream colored; spatula- to fan-shaped, with a flattened head; with a distinct stem

FLESH: Whitish; insubstantial; odor not distinctive; taste unknown

FERTILE SURFACE: Creamy to pale yellowish; fan- or spoon-shaped; flattened to compressed; fitting like a bonnet over the top of the stem

STEM: Reddish brown to brown or tan; equal or tapering downward; hollow, rather flexible; surface velvety; base with orange mycelium

SPORE PRINT: Yellowish brown

ECOLOGY: Saprobic on woody debris and humus in broadleaf, conifer, and mixed woods; scattered to usually gregarious in moss, soil, or well-decayed wood; summer and fall; locally common

EDIBILITY: Not edible

COMMENTS: *Spathularia flavida* (not illustrated) and *Spathularia rufa* (not illustrated) are similar. Neither has the reddish-brown stem typical of *Spathulariopsis velutipes*.

Spathulariopsis velutipes

SCIENTIFIC NAME: *Tolypocladium ophioglossoides* (J. F. Gmel.) Quandt, Kepler, and Spatafora

SYNONYMS: *Elaphocordyceps ophioglossoides* (J. F. Gmel.) G.H. Sung, J. M. Sung, and Spatafora, *Cordyceps ophioglossoides* (J. F. Gmel.) Fr.

COMMON NAME: Goldenthread Cordyceps

FAMILY: Ophiocordycipitaceae

FRUIT BODY: Up to 4¼ in. long; club-shaped, the upper portion roughened or pimply; apex larger than the base

FLESH: Whitish; thick; firm; odor not distinctive; taste unknown

FERTILE SURFACE: Up to 1¼ in. tall; yellowish brown to reddish brown, becoming black in age; rough feeling owing to a finely bumpy surface; cylindrical to oval

STEM: Up to 3 in. long; dark olive green, yellowish, or black; smooth; equal; base with yellow rhizomorphs

SPORE PRINT: Does not print well

ECOLOGY: Parasitic on *Elaphomyces* species; scattered or gregarious, following the fruiting pattern of *Elaphomyces*, often in low, boggy woods under hemlock and black birch; summer and fall; fairly common but often overlooked

EDIBILITY: Unknown

COMMENTS: Careful digging is often required to find the intact connection of the yellow threads of this fungus and the false truffle, a species of *Elaphomyces*. Species of *Geoglossum* and *Trichoglossum* (not illustrated) are similar. They are lubricous and lack the bumpy surface. They do not parasitize false truffles.

Tolypocladium ophioglossoides

SCIENTIFIC NAME: *Cordyceps militaris* (L.) Fr.

SYNONYM: None

COMMON NAME: Caterpillar Fungus

FAMILY: Cordycipitaceae

FRUIT BODY: Up to 2 in. long; narrowly club-shaped; consisting of a pale stem and orange head

FLESH: Pale watery orangish yellow; brittle; odor and taste not distinctive

FERTILE SURFACE: Pale but appearing orangish red and feeling roughened owing to a thick covering of orange pimples; cylindrical to spindle-shaped, or compressed

STEM: Whitish to yellowish with orange near the fertile head; cylindrical; often curved

SPORE PRINT: Does not print well

ECOLOGY: Parasitic on the buried pupae and occasionally the larvae of moths and butterflies; solitary or in small groups in humus, soil, or well-decayed wood; summer and fall; fairly common

EDIBILITY: Not edible

COMMENTS: Careful excavation will reveal the insect victim at the bottom of the stem. Several species of larvae and pupae are parasitized. Larger pupae often produce larger clubs. At times, multiple clubs may arise from one pupa. There are many insect-killing fungi. This is the one most commonly collected.

Cordyceps militaris

SCIENTIFIC NAME: *Xylaria magnoliae* J. D. Rogers

SYNONYM: None

COMMON NAME: Magnolia Cone Xylaria

FAMILY: Xylariaceae

FRUIT BODY: Up to 3 in. long; multiple upright, curved, thin strands, typically not branching

FLESH: Gray; very thin; tough; odor and taste not distinctive

FERTILE SURFACE: Covered with white asexual spores when young, becoming gray and finally black when the sexual spores mature

STEM: Absent or very rudimentary

SPORE PRINT: Black

ECOLOGY: Saprobic, found only on magnolia cones; gregarious to clustered; summer and fall; fairly common

EDIBILITY: Not edible

COMMENTS: The magnolia-cone habitat makes this fungus very easy to identify. It is sometimes found with a small, whitish, gilled mushroom, *Strobilurus conigenoides* (not illustrated), which also is a magnolia-cone decomposer.

Xylaria magnoliae

SCIENTIFIC NAME: *Xylaria polymorpha* (Pers.) Grev.

SYNONYM: None

COMMON NAME: Dead Man's Fingers

FAMILY: Xylariaceae

FRUIT BODY: Up to 4 in. long; gray or whitish, becoming black from the spores; generally club-shaped, but at times irregular and branching; woody

FLESH: White; tough, rather corky; odor not distinctive; taste unknown

FERTILE SURFACE: Whitish to gray becoming black; crust-like and powdery at first; with tiny warts in age

STEM: Dark gray to black; very short; hard; cylindrical; often barely discernable from the fertile section

SPORE PRINT: Black

ECOLOGY: Saprobic on the dead wood of broadleaf trees; often densely clustered around stumps, sometimes appearing to be terrestrial; all seasons; common

EDIBILITY: Not edible

COMMENTS: *Xylaria longipes* (not illustrated) has a more prominent stem, is more slender, and tends to fruit scattered rather than densely clustered. *Xylaria hypoxylon* (not illustrated) is less robust and has flattened tips that are whitish and often branched. There are other species of *Xylaria*. Microscopic examination is needed to identify most species in this genus.

Xylaria polymorpha

Spine Fungi

I N   A N   O B V I O U S example of convergent evolution, several groups of only distantly related fungi have developed spine- or whisker-like structures on which the spores are produced. These are sometimes referred to as "teeth." Fleshy species of *Hericium* are good and distinctive edibles. Species of *Hydnum* are also edible. Other genera, such as *Hydnellum*, *Climacodon*, and *Bankera*, are rather tough and not edible. Many species are used to dye wool yarn. Important features in the key are presence or absence of a stem, habitat, and tough or tender flesh.

Key to Spine Fungi

1. Stem present; fruiting body tough; with blue colors: *Hydnellum caeruleum* (p. 394)

2. Stem present; fruiting body tough; brown; stem spongy: *Hydnellum spongiosipes* (p. 392)

3. Stem present; fruiting body tough; with orange colors: *Hydnellum aurantiacum* (p. 393)

4. Stem present; fruiting body fleshy; buff, whitish, with orange or tan tints: *Hydnum repandum* (p. 395)

5. Stem present; cap covered with erect, brown to black scales: *Sarcodon imbricatus* (p. 391)

6. Stem present or absent; fruiting body gelatinous; translucent: *Pseudohydnum gelatinosum* (p. 399)

7. Stem absent; on wood; white; spines form an unbranched, beard-like mass: *Hericium erinaceus* (p. 397)

8. Stem absent; on wood; white; branched, long spines on the branch tips: *Hericium americanum* (p. 398)

9. Stem absent; on wood; white; branched; short spines along the branches: *Hericium coralloides* (p. 396)

10. Stem absent; on living trees; whitish; in large, shelving clusters: *Climacodon septentrionale* (p. 330)

Hydnum umbilicatum

Hydnellum species

SCIENTIFIC NAME: *Sarcodon imbricatus* (L.) P. Karst.

SYNONYM: *Hydnum imbricatum* L.

COMMON NAME: Scaly Tooth

FAMILY: Bankeraceae

CAP: Up to 8 in. wide; surface tan to pale brown, becoming dark brown in age, covered with coarse, dark-brown to blackish scales that are pointed, somewhat concentrically arranged, and erect at first, becoming flatter especially toward the margin; convex with a central depression that often deepens at maturity; margin incurved at first, then flattening out and often becoming torn at maturity

FLESH: White to pale brown; soft to firm; odor not distinctive; taste mild to slightly bitter

SPINES: Pale grayish brown, becoming darker reddish brown to brown in age; decurrent

STEM: Up to 4 in. tall; whitish, tan, becoming gray brown to brown; tapering upward; becoming hollow; surface dry, smooth, or with partially (or rarely completely) formed spines

SPORE PRINT: Brown

ECOLOGY: Mycorrhizal; solitary, scattered to gregarious on soil, humus, or moss, usually under conifers but also under broadleaf trees; summer and early fall; locally common

EDIBILITY: Edible but generally not highly rated, bitter at times

COMMENTS: There are other scaly *Sarcodon* species, including *Sarcodon scabrosus* (not illustrated), which has paler and flatter scales and a greenish to black base of the stem. Several of the species are very bitter.

Sarcodon imbricatus
Photo by Alan Bessette

SCIENTIFIC NAME: *Hydnellum spongiosipes* (Peck) Pouzar
SYNONYM: None
COMMON NAME: Velvet Tooth
FAMILY: Bankeraceae

CAP: Up to 4 in. wide; cinnamon brown to reddish brown, at times with a grayish-brown bloom, bruising dark brown; convex becoming broadly convex to nearly flat; surface dry, fuzzy, uneven, not zoned; margin uneven owing to fusing, at times with a ring of secondary growth

FLESH: Two-layered; upper layer is pale to dark brown, thick, spongy; lower layer cinnamon brown to purplish brown, thin, corky; odor and taste mealy or not distinctive

SPINES: Pale to dark brown, or violet brown, becoming darker when bruised; decurrent

STEM: Up to 4 in. long; dark brown; enlarged downward; spongy; surface velvety

SPORE PRINT: Brown

ECOLOGY: Mycorrhizal with oaks; scattered to gregarious in humus, moss, and soil in broadleaf woods; summer and fall; common

EDIBILITY: Not edible

COMMENTS: This is a common species, especially under white oak. The spongy base of the stem is a good identification feature.

Hydnellum spongiosipes

SCIENTIFIC NAME: *Hydnellum aurantiacum* (Batsch) P. Karst.

SYNONYM: None

COMMON NAME: Orange Rough-Cap Tooth

FAMILY: Bankeraceae

CAP: Up to 7 in. wide; orange buff to whitish, becoming salmon orange and finally rusty brown with a tan, rusty-orange to whitish margin; convex to broadly convex to nearly flat, with a slightly uplifted margin; surface bald or finely hairy, dry, uneven with lumps and cavities

FLESH: Buff in the cap, orange in the stem; fibrous and tough; two-layered, with upper layer spongy and lower layer tough; odor disagreeable; taste mild or unpleasant

SPINES: Whitish or orange at first, becoming gray and finally brown with grayish tips; subdecurrent

STEM: Up to 3 in. long; orangish brown, felted to fuzzy, dry; solid; base with orange mycelium

SPORE PRINT: Brown

ECOLOGY: Mycorrhizal with conifers; usually gregarious in moss or humus, but may be scattered or solitary; summer and fall; occasional to locally abundant

EDIBILITY: Not edible

COMMENTS: *Hydnellum chrysinum* (not illustrated) is nearly identical. A microscope is needed to distinguish them.

Hydnellum aurantiacum

SCIENTIFIC NAME: *Hydnellum caeruleum* (Hornem.) P. Karst.

SYNONYM: None

COMMON NAME: Bluish Tooth

FAMILY: Bankeraceae

CAP: Up to 4½ wide; blue or whitish, becoming bluish and finally brown, especially in the center; convex or top-shaped to nearly flat; often appearing in fused rows; surface dry, velvety, pitted, and irregular

FLESH: Zoned blue and white or with brownish-orange tints; tough but pliant; odor variously described as mealy, unpleasantly anise-like, of cooked meat, and not distinctive; taste mild, mealy, or slightly acidic

SPINES: Light bluish gray, becoming brown in age with pale tips; decurrent

STEM: Up to 2½ in. long; orange to orangish brown; equal or enlarged downward; surface smooth, often covered with debris

SPORE PRINT: Brown

ECOLOGY: Mycorrhizal; solitary, scattered, or gregarious in humus under conifers, often with fused caps; late summer and fall; uncommon

EDIBILITY: Not edible

COMMENTS: The variability of reports of odors and tastes could be explained by the possibility that this may be another example of a species complex. In pristine condition, this is a gorgeous mushroom.

Hydnellum caeruleum

SCIENTIFIC NAME: *Hydnum repandum* L.

SYNONYM: *Dentinum repandum* (L.) Gray

COMMON NAMES: Sweet Tooth, Hedgehog

FAMILY: Hydnaceae

CAP: Up to 6 in. wide; buff, whitish, tan, pale orange, pinkish orange, reddish orange, to brownish orange, bruising dark orange; convex to nearly flat, at times depressed in the center; surface dry, felted, often becoming pitted or cracked; margin incurved at first, wavy at maturity

FLESH: White, staining yellowish ochre when damaged; thick; firm; brittle; odor not distinctive, or variously described as nut-like, sweet, and pleasant; taste not distinctive, or slightly peppery

SPINES: Creamy white to orange, darkening when bruised; reaching the stem, infrequently decurrent

STEM: Up to 4 in. long, white or colored like the cap, bruising ochre; central or occasionally off-center; equal; solid

SPORE PRINT: White

ECOLOGY: Mycorrhizal with conifers and broadleaf trees; single, scattered, or gregarious in humus and moss; summer and fall; common

EDIBILITY: Edible and good

COMMENTS: The edible *Hydnum umbilicatum* (p. 390) is similar but has an umbilicate cap center and is generally smaller. It prefers conifer and mixed woods. *Hydum repandum* var. *albidum* (not illustrated) is an edible, pure-white variety that stains orange where bruised.

Hydnum repandum

SCIENTIFIC NAME: *Hericium coralloides* (**Scop.**) **Pers.**

SYNONYM: *Hericium ramosum* (Bull.) Letell.

COMMON NAMES: Coral Tooth Mushroom, Comb Tooth

FAMILY: **Hericiaceae**

FRUIT BODY: Up to 10 in. wide, and up to 8 in. high; white to pale pink, becoming tan in age; an irregular-shaped cluster of spreading branches with short spines arranged in rows along the branches, arising from a common base; with a general "feathery" or coral-like appearance

FLESH: White, unchanging when exposed; soft; rather thin; odor and taste not distinctive

SPINES: White; short

STEM: Whitish; rudimentary; attached laterally

SPORE PRINT: White

ECOLOGY: Saprobic on the dead wood of broadleaf trees; solitary to gregarious; summer and fall; common

EDIBILITY: Edible; becoming bitter in age

COMMENTS: There are two similar species that are good edibles. *Hericium americanum* (p. 398) has longer spines that occur in tufts at the ends of its branches. *Hericium erinaceus* (p. 397) is unbranched and has thick flesh.

Hericium coralloides

SCIENTIFIC NAME: *Hericium erinaceus* (Bull.) Pers.

SYNONYM: None

COMMON NAMES: Lion's Mane, Pom Pom Mushroom

FAMILY: Hericiaceae

FRUIT BODY: Up to 10 in. wide and 10 in. tall; white, becoming yellowish in age; an oval or roundish, branchless mass of beard-like spines; solid; attached laterally to the wood

FLESH: White, unchanging when exposed; thick; rather elastic; odor and taste not distinctive, becoming sour in age

SPINES: White; short in relation to the fleshy base

STEM: White; stout; tough; more of a base than a stem

SPORE PRINT: White

ECOLOGY: Saprobic and parasitic on the wood of living broadleaf trees and logs and stumps of dead trees, especially oaks and beech; usually solitary; summer and fall, occasional in spring; fairly common

EDIBILITY: Edible and good; becoming yellowish and unpalatable in age

COMMENTS: This mushroom has been successfully cultivated and is available fresh in upscale supermarkets and dried in Asian markets. *Hericium americanum* (p. 398) is similar, but its fruit body is branched, unlike *Hericium erinaceus*, which forms one unbranching mass. It is a good edible as well.

Hericium erinaceus

SCIENTIFIC NAME: *Hericium americanum* Ginns

SYNONYM: None

COMMON NAMES: Goat's Beard, Bear's Head, Lion's Mane

FAMILY: Hericiaceae

FRUIT BODY: Up to 12 in. wide, and up to 20 in. high; usually white, becoming yellowish in age, at times pinkish when young; a multibranched mass with moderately long spines arising in tufts from the branch tips

FLESH: White, unchanging when cut; fibrous; odor and taste not distinctive

SPINES: White and relatively long

STEM: White; rudimentary to absent, often forming a rather thick base rather than an elongated stem

SPORE PRINT: White

ECOLOGY: Saprobic and parasitic on the wood of broadleaf trees, especially beech, rarely on conifer wood; solitary or in small groups; late summer and fall; common

EDIBILITY: Edible and good; becoming bitter and unpalatable in age when the fruit body becomes yellowish

COMMENTS: This species is the only *Hericium* in Appalachia that is branched and has long spines. Compare with the unbranched *Hericium erinaceus* (p. 397) and *Hericium coralloides* (p. 396), which has short spines and a coral-like appearance. All three are good edibles.

Hericium americanum

SCIENTIFIC NAME: *Pseudohydnum gelatinosum* (Scop.)
P. Karst.

SYNONYM: None

COMMON NAME: Jelly Tooth

FAMILY: Incertae sedis

CAP: Up to 3 in. wide; whitish to grayish brown, spoon- to shallow-shell-shaped; downy or covered with whitish fuzz, at times smooth and nearly bald

FLESH: Translucent hyaline; gelatinous; not slimy unless water-soaked; odor and taste not distinctive

FERTILE SURFACE: Colored like the cap; covered with whitish, soft, pendulous spines

STEM: Up to 2 in. tall; translucent hyaline; usually off-center, appearing as an extension of the cap surface; at times nearly absent

SPORE PRINT: White

ECOLOGY: Saprobic on well-decayed, often moss-covered, conifer wood, especially hemlock; gregarious to scattered, or in overlapping fused clusters; late summer and fall; common

EDIBILITY: Edible but bland; can be candied

COMMENTS: This is a unique fungus whose relationships with other fungi have yet to be determined. It has been placed in the Exidiaceae and the Tremellaceae families. Whatever the case, a jelly fungus with spores produced on spines is unique.

Pseudohydnum gelatinosum

PUFFBALLS AND RELATED FUNGI

G ASTEROMYCETES ARE A diverse group of fungi whose spores are produced within a protective covering. Most are round or oval-shaped at first. Some, like the stinkhorns, develop a stem that ruptures the protective covering, leaving a sack-like structure at the stem base. Most form a spore mass internally, and the outer surface either deteriorates, ruptures, or forms a slit-like ostiole. It is an artificial group that includes mycorrhizal genera such as *Scleroderma*, *Pisolithus*, *Calostoma*, and *Astreus*. "Earth balls," "gelatinous stalked puffballs," "dye maker's puffball" and the "barometer earth star" are common names for some of these mycorrhizal species. Saprobic genera include the *Geastrum* earthstars, the common puffballs in *Calvatia* and *Lycoperdon*, and the bird's nest fungi in *Cyathus* and *Crucibulum*. Also, the stinkhorns in the genera *Phallus* and *Mutinus* are common saprobes. There are also several mycorrhizal genera whose fruit bodies develop underground, including the genera *Elaphomyces*, *Rhizopogon*, *Tuber*, and *Gautiera*.

CLOCKWISE FROM ABOVE:

Mutinus elegans

Geastrum saccatum

Gautiera magnicellaris

Key to Puffballs and Related Fungi

1. Stem present; strong, unpleasant odor; white fruiting surface under the greenish slime: *Phallus ravenelii* (p. 418)

2. Stem present; strong, unpleasant odor; red fruiting surface under the greenish slime: *Phallus rubicundus* (p. 417)

3. Stem present; mild odor; yellow spore case; with collar-like fragments: *Calostoma lutescens* (p. 411)

4. Stem present; mild odor; gray to greenish-yellow spore case: *Calostoma ravenelii* (p. 412)

5. Stem absent; spore case with star-like rays: *Astraeus hygrometricus* (p. 416)

6. Stem absent; very small nests of small, whitish peridioles: *Crucibulum laeve* (p. 410)

7. Stem absent; very small nests of small, gray to black peridioles: *Cyathus stercoreus* (p. 409)

8. Stem absent; soccer ball sized or larger, white: *Calvatia gigantea* (p. 405)

9. Stem absent; softball sized, spores olive brown: *Calvatia craniiformis* (p. 403)

10. Stem absent; softball sized, spores purple brown: *Calvatia cyathiformis* (p. 404)

11. Stem absent; small, on lawns: *Lycoperdon marginatum* (p. 407)

12. Stem absent; small, on wood: *Lycoperdon pyriforme* (p. 408)

13. Stem absent; with a sterile base, small to medium, cuticle with spines; on humus: *Lycoperdon perlatum* (p. 406)

14. Stem absent; small to medium; with a scaly and hard outer skin: *Scleroderma citrinum* (p. 413)

15. Stem absent; interior with white peridioles embedded in sticky, black goo: *Pisolithus arhizus* (p. 414)

16. Stem absent; fruiting underground: *Elaphomyces americanus* (p. 415)

SCIENTIFIC NAME: *Calvatia craniiformis* (Schwein.) Fr.

SYNONYM: None

COMMON NAMES: Brain Puffball, Skull Puffball

FAMILY: Agaricaceae

FRUIT BODY: Up to 6 in. wide; surface white to tan, smooth at first, soon becoming cracked into numerous scale-like patches that flake off in age; often wrinkled; skull-shaped, roundish, or like an inverted pear

FLESH: White and firm, becoming bright yellowish green and soft and finally olive brown and powdery as the spores mature; odor pleasant; taste not distinctive

STERILE BASE: White at first, dark brown in age; chambered; with white rhizomorphs at the bottom

ECOLOGY: Saprobic; scattered to gregarious, rarely clustered, in grasslands, brushy areas, and broadleaf forests; summer and fall; fairly common

EDIBILITY: Edible when pure white inside, becoming bitter as the spores mature

COMMENTS: See comments under *Calvatia cyathiformis* (p. 404).

Calvatia craniiformis

403

SCIENTIFIC NAME: *Calvatia cyathiformis* (Bosc) Morgan

SYNONYM: None

COMMON NAME: Purple-Spored Puffball

FAMILY: Agaricaceae

FRUIT BODY: Up to 7 in. wide, usually the size of a large grapefruit; roundish to pear-shaped; exterior white to pinkish tan, eventually tan or brownish; smooth at first, becoming cracked, breaking into thin, irregular plates that eventually flake off

FLESH: White and firm, becoming yellowish and soft, finally purplish brown and powdery as the spores mature; odor pleasant; taste not distinctive

STERILE BASE: white to yellowish; chambered; often with folds or wrinkles; makes up about one-third of the fruit body; in extreme age it forms a cup-like structure and is the last remaining part of the fruit body

ECOLOGY: Saprobic; scattered to gregarious, at times in arcs or circles; in grassy areas; summer and fall; common

EDIBILITY: Edible when the interior is pure white, becoming bitter as the spores mature

COMMENTS: *Calvatia craniiformis* (p. 403) is similar but has a yellow-brown interior when mature. *Calvatia gigantea* (p. 405) is larger and white. All three are edible when their interiors are pure white. Any puffball smaller than an orange should be cut in half vertically to be sure that there are no immature mushroom structures inside. These would be present in the egg stage of poisonous *Amanita* species.

Calvatia cyathiformis

SCIENTIFIC NAME: *Calvatia gigantea* (Batsch) Lloyd

SYNONYM: *Langermannia gigantea* (Batsch) Rostk.

COMMON NAME: Giant Puffball

FAMILY: Agaricaceae

FRUIT BODY: Up to 20 in. wide; white to creamy white; generally round, sometimes somewhat flattened, at times with a vertical crease; surface dry, felt-like, smooth or pockmarked

FLESH: White at first; firm; changing color as the spores mature to yellowish green and finally greenish brown; odor not distinctive when young, becoming fetid in age; taste pleasant when young

STEM: Absent; attached to the ground by a thick, basal rhizomorph

ECOLOGY: Saprobic; in lawns, brushy areas, and woodlands, often near canals and drainage ditches; summer and fall; occasional

EDIBILITY: Edible when white inside

COMMENTS: Specimens over fifty-five pounds have been found. It is more commonly about the size of a soccer ball or slightly larger.

Calvatia gigantea

SCIENTIFIC NAME: *Lycoperdon perlatum* Pers.

SYNONYM: *Lycoperdon gemmatum* Batsch.

COMMON NAME: Gem-Studded Puffball

FAMILY: Lycoperdaceae

FRUIT BODY: Up to 3 in. tall; pear-shaped; dull whitish to light tan, becoming brown in age; with white or brown spines, and with granules and smaller spines throughout, becoming much less common on the surface of the sterile base; at times the spines break off, leaving small, round pits; developing a large, centrally located pore-like opening at maturity

FLESH: White and fleshy at first, becoming olive brown from the maturing spores; powdery in age; odor and taste not distinctive when immature, odor unpleasant when mature

STERILE BASE: White, brown in age; chambered, making up about a third to half of the fruit body

SPORES: Yellowish to olive brown

ECOLOGY: Saprobic; solitary, scattered, or usually gregarious or clustered in humus under broadleaf and conifer trees; summer and fall; common

EDIBILITY: Edible while still white inside; becomes bitter as the spores mature

COMMENTS: Cutting the fruit body vertically should reveal a homogenous white center. If partially developed cap, gills, and stem are observed, it is not a puffball but the button stage of a possibly deadly poisonous *Amanita*. Toxic species of *Scleroderma* have a hard outer skin and flesh, and they lack spines.

Lycoperdon perlatum

SCIENTIFIC NAME: *Lycoperdon marginatum* Vittad.

SYNONYM: None

COMMON NAME: Peeling Puffball

FAMILY: Lycoperdaceae

FRUIT BODY: Up to 2 in. wide; white; round when young, becoming somewhat pear-shaped or flattened at maturity; surface covered with white, low, sharp spines, with angular patches under the spines; the surface flakes off in irregular patches at maturity

FLESH: Firm and white at first, becoming olive brown to grayish brown; becoming powdery; odor and taste not distinctive

STERILE BASE: White to olive brown, small; chambered

SPORES: Olive brown to grayish brown

ECOLOGY: Saprobic; scattered to gregarious; most often in lawns or on poor soil, at times in conifer, broadleaf, and mixed woodlands; summer and fall; common

EDIBILITY: Edible when white throughout, but too small to be of much culinary value

COMMENTS: This common lawn species is easily identified when the skin starts to peel off.

Lycoperdon marginatum

SCIENTIFIC NAME: *Lycoperdon pyriforme* Schaeff.

SYNONYM: *Morganella pyriformis* (Schaeff.) Kreisel and D. Krüger.

COMMON NAME: Pear-Shaped Puffball

FAMILY: Lycoperdaceae

FRUIT BODY: Up to 2 in. tall; whitish, becoming yellowish brown, tan to red-dish brown; pear-shaped to nearly round; surface with granules or warts, often becoming bald, sometimes cracking in age

FLESH: White and firm at first; becoming greenish yellow to olive brown as the spores mature; odor unpleasant at maturity; taste mild when young

STERILE BASE: Whitish; with numerous white rhizomorphs

SPORES: Greenish yellow, becoming olive brown; powdery at maturity

ECOLOGY: Saprobic on broadleaf and conifer wood; gregarious to densely clustered, at times fruiting luxuriantly on wood-mulched trails; late summer and fall; common

EDIBILITY: Edible before the spores mature and the flesh turns yellowish or brown; the flavor is bland, and they are best incorporated into dishes with more flavorful species

COMMENTS: This puffball is readily available most years. It is one of the few that grow on wood. It is likely this species will be placed in the genus *Morganella* at some time in the future. *Lycoperdon perlatum* (p. 406) is somewhat similar but has spines and is usually terrestrial.

Lycoperdon pyriforme

SCIENTIFIC NAME: *Cyathus stercoreus* (Schwein.) De Toni

SYNONYM: None

COMMON NAME: Dung-Loving Bird's Nest

FAMILY: Nidulariaceae

FRUIT BODY: Up to ½ in. wide and tall; outer surface pale at first, becoming brownish; shaggy-hairy at first, becoming less so in age; inner surface bald and shiny, dark brown to black; goblet-shaped; covered at first with a whitish covering; peridioles dark gray to black

ECOLOGY: Saprobic; gregarious to clustered on manured soil, humus, wood chips, and other similar substrates; summer and fall; common

EDIBILITY: Not edible

COMMENTS: This is a common species in fertilized gardens. Compare with *Cyathus striatus* (not illustrated), which has vertical lines inside the cup, and with *Cyathus olla* (not illustrated), which lacks the shaggy hairs on the outside of the cup. *Crucibulum laeve* (p. 410) has pale, colored peridioles.

Cyathus stercoreus

SCIENTIFIC NAME: *Crucibulum laeve* (Huds.) Kambly

SYNONYM: *Crucibulum vulgare* Tul. and C. Tul.

COMMON NAME: Common Bird's Nest

FAMILY: Nidulariaceae

FRUIT BODY: Less than ½ in. wide and tall; exterior yellowish orange becoming pale yellow; cup-like; hairy to velvety; interior whitish; smooth; containing usually 3 to 10 white to tan "eggs" (peridioles), which contain the spores; covered at first by a whitish membrane that is coated with yellowish-orange fibers; the cup is generally round and wider at the top

ECOLOGY: Saprobic on woody debris, wood chips, twigs, blackberry stems, and other organic debris; scattered to densely gregarious; summer and fall; common

EDIBILITY: Not edible

COMMENTS: Large quantities of this species can be observed in honeycomb-like masses in gardens on wood mulch and wood chips. It has also been reported fruiting on cardboard, cloth, old furniture, and leather. It is our only common bird's nest fungus with pale, colored peridioles.

Crucibulum laeve

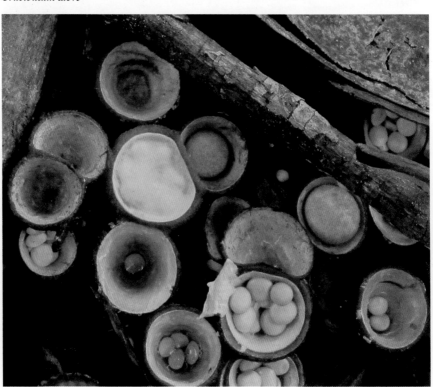

SCIENTIFIC NAME: *Calostoma lutescens* (Schwein.) Burnap
SYNONYM: None
COMMON NAME: Collared Calostoma
FAMILY: Calostomataceae

SPORE CASE: Up to 1 in. wide; the outer layer pale to lemon yellow, peeling away and leaving collar-like fragments around the spore case; inner surface yellow, globular, not gelatinous; with a slit-like ostiole in the center that is surrounded by bright red ridges; odor not distinctive; taste unknown

FLESH: Whitish to buff spore mass, becoming powdery at maturity; odor not distinctive; taste unknown

STEM: Up to 3½ in. tall; usually pale yellow, at times whitish or tinged reddish, brownish in age, often covered with debris; nearly equal; consisting of longitudinal, interwoven strands; spongy, becoming leathery and eventually hard

SPORES: Whitish to buff, becoming powdery at maturity

ECOLOGY: Mycorrhizal with oaks and probably other broadleaf trees; solitary, scattered to gregarious in broadleaf and mixed woods on soil, moss, or humus, often in sandy soil, on road banks, and along trails; summer, fall, and winter; generally occasional, but common in the southern Appalachians

EDIBILITY: Not edible

COMMENTS: *Calostoma cinnabarina* (not illustrated) is reddish orange and gelatinous. *Calostoma ravenelii* (p. 412) has a grayish spore case and lacks the collar-like fragments.

Calostoma lutescens

SCIENTIFIC NAME: *Calostoma ravenelii* (Berk.) Massee

SYNONYM: *Calostoma microsporum* G. F. Atk.

COMMON NAME: Ravenel's Calostoma

FAMILY: Calostomataceae

SPORE CASE: up to ¾ in. wide; grayish to greenish yellow, with a slit-like ostiole in the center that is surrounded by bright red ridges; globular; covered at first by a scurfy, grayish to yellowish coating that breaks apart and forms wart-like patches; not gelatinous; odor not distinctive; taste unknown

FLESH: Whitish spore mass, becoming creamy white and powdery at maturity; odor not distinctive; taste unknown

STEM: Up to 2 in. tall; pale yellow, becoming brownish; usually covered with debris

SPORES: Whitish, becoming creamy white at maturity

ECOLOGY: Mycorrhizal; solitary, scattered to gregarious on the ground in mixed woods, often along trails on road banks; summer, fall, and winter; occasional to locally abundant

EDIBILITY: Not edible

COMMENTS: *Calostoma lutescens* (p. 411) has a yellow, fragmented necklace surrounding the spore case. *Calostoma cinnabarina* (not illustrated) is reddish orange, gelatinous, and larger.

Calostoma ravenelii

SCIENTIFIC NAME: *Scleroderma citrinum* Pers.

SYNONYM: None

COMMON NAMES: Pigskin Poison Puffball, Common Earth Ball

FAMILY: Sclerodermataceae

FRUIT BODY: Up to 4 in. wide; round to oval; exterior surface is tan, pale brown, yellowish, or golden brown; attached to the substrate by a mass of mycelial strands; scaly and hard; eventually the exterior develops an opening from which the spores become dispersed, leaving the exterior cuticle looking like a bowl with an irregular rim

FLESH: White at first, hard, and firm, soon darkening to grayish purple and finally black at maturity; may stain pink when rubbed; in age the interior is a mass of spores; odor waxy when young, becoming slightly unpleasant in age; taste not distinctive

STEM: Absent

SPORE PRINT: None, the spores are black

ECOLOGY: Mycorrhizal with broadleaf and conifer trees; solitary, scattered to gregarious or sometimes in small clusters on soil, moss, humus, and occasionally on well-decayed wood; summer and fall; common

EDIBILITY: Poisonous; edible puffballs are never scaly and hard

COMMENTS: This species is occasionally found parasitized by *Pseudoboletus parasiticus* (p. 284). As far as is known, this is the only species parasitized by this bolete. The pigskin in the common name refers to the pebbly skin of an American football.

Scleroderma citrinum

SCIENTIFIC NAME: *Pisolithus arhizus* (Scop.) Rauschert
SYNONYM: *Pisolithus tinctorius* (Pers.) Coker and Couch
COMMON NAME: Dye Makers' False Puffball
FAMILY: Sclerodermataceae

FRUIT BODY: Up to 4 in. wide and 5 in. tall, usually smaller; tan, brown, or yellowish, soon streaked with black; variable in shape, round, pear- to club-shaped; outer surface thin and fragile, smooth, soon cracking or deteriorating, revealing the spore-bearing interior

FLESH: A mass of white to yellowish peridioles embedded in sticky, black, gelatinous goo; the peridioles mature into a brown, powdery spore mass; odor not distinctive at first, becoming fragrant and foul at maturity; taste unknown

STEM: Colored like the upper surface; usually rudimentary to nearly absent, rarely elongated; at times with yellowish rhizomorphs

SPORES: Brown

ECOLOGY: Mycorrhizal with conifers and broadleaf trees, often pines and oaks; solitary, scattered to gregarious in soil, often in very disturbed areas; at times partially buried; summer and fall; occasional to common

EDIBILITY: Not edible

COMMENTS: This fungus is no great beauty, and because of its sticky, black matrix, it can be unpleasant to handle. It forms mycorrhiza with a variety of trees and can thrive in poor soils. When united with seedlings, *Pisolithus* species significantly increase the growth rate of the trees. It does well in disturbed soils such as that of reclaimed strip mines. The common name refers to its use in dyeing wool various shades of brown and black. There are other, similar species that require a microscope to positively identify.

Pisolithus arhizus

SCIENTIFIC NAME: *Elaphomyces americanus* Castellano sp. Nov.

MISAPPLIED NAME: *Elaphomyces muricatus* Fr.

COMMON NAME: American Elaphomyces

FAMILY: Elaphomycetaceae

FRUIT BODY: Up to ¾ in. wide; yellowish brown; roughly globose; outer surface thick; with warts

FLESH: Marbled with white to whitish veins that become brown at maturity; odor not distinctive; taste unknown

STEM: Absent

SPORES: Dark brown; powdery

ECOLOGY: Mycorrhizal with conifers; scattered to gregarious; buried in sandy soil in mixed woods, often with hemlock and white pine; summer and fall; common

EDIBILITY: Not edible

COMMENTS: This species is frequently parasitized by *Tolypocladium ophioglossoides* (p. 385). It is commonly consumed by red and gray squirrels. These rodents are an agent in its spore dispersal. There are many species in this genus, and there are several other genera that fruit underground. Some in the genus *Tuber* are considered choice edibles.

Elaphomyces americanus
Photo by Todd Elliott

SCIENTIFIC NAME: *Astraeus hygrometricus* (Pers.) Morgan

SYNONYM: None

COMMON NAME: Barometer Earth Star

FAMILY: Diplocystaceae

FRUIT BODY: Up to 3½ in. wide; consisting of a puffball-like spore case that is surrounded by pointed flaps or rays of leathery tissue, which may be folded up over the spore case or expanded outward; the variably colored rays can be gray, reddish gray, reddish brown to black, or checkered with tan, brown, or gray patches; rarely smooth; inner spore case white and solid at first, becoming gray, whitish to brown; round; thin; papery; roughened or fuzzy; with a central irregular perforation

FLESH: Whitish to buff or brownish spore sack; odor and taste not distinctive

STEM: Absent

SPORES: Yellowish brown

ECOLOGY: Mycorrhizal; solitary, scattered to gregarious in sandy or loose soil, usually with pines or oaks; partially buried at first; summer, fall, and early winter; occasional to locally abundant

EDIBILITY: Not edible

COMMENTS: This species gets its common name because the fungus responds to humid or wet weather by opening its star-like rays. In dry conditions the rays elevate and cover the spore sack. There are many earth stars in the unrelated genus *Geastrum*. They are saprobic, lack the checkered rays, and are not closely related to *Astraeus hygrometricus*. Recent studies indicate the proper name for our American *Hygrometricus* species should be either *Astraeus morganii* or *Astraeus smithii*.

Astraeus hygrometricus

SCIENTIFIC NAME: *Phallus rubicundus* (Bosc) Fr.

SYNONYM: None

COMMON NAME: None

FAMILY: Phallaceae

FRUIT BODY: Up to 6 in. tall, occasionally larger; lance-like; reddish pink or reddish orange, becoming yellow to whitish toward the bottom, occasionally whitish or yellow throughout; often curved or drooping; hollow; at times with a reddish partial veil hanging below the fertile surface; base emerging from a whitish to pale-brown sack, the remains of the egg-like universal veil; surface often has elongated pits

FLESH: Reddish orange; fragile odor probably not distinctive but difficult to determine owing to the strong odor of the slime; taste unknown

FERTILE SURFACE: Up to 1¾ in. high; olive brown; when slime covered, draped over the top of the fruitbody; lower edge not fused to the stem; base color red, which is revealed when insects and rain remove the foul-smelling slime

SPORE PRINT: None; spores are yellowish and contained in the olive-brown slime

ECOLOGY: Saprobic on woody debris such as wood chips and sawdust; usually gregarious or scattered in wood mulch piles and gardens; late spring, summer, and early fall; generally uncommon but locally abundant

EDIBILITY: Not edible, at least in the mature stage

COMMENTS: Compare with *Mutinus elegans* (p. 401), whose fertile surface is fused to the stem. *Phallus rubicundus* has become common in certain areas in the last twenty years. It probably has been helped to spread by commercially sold wood mulch. Described from South Carolina, it was thought to be a subtropical species. It has now been found as far north as New York and Wisconsin. As with other stinkhorns, the slime contains the spores, which are dispersed by flies, carrion beetles, and other insects.

Phallus rubicundus

SCIENTIFIC NAME: *Phallus ravenelii* Berk. and M. A. Curtis

SYNONYM: None

COMMON NAME: Ravenel's Stinkhorn

FAMILY: Phallaceae

FRUIT BODY: Up to 6 in. tall; phallus-shaped; stem portion white to cream or pinkish; equal; thick; spongy, hollow; surface finely honeycombed, extending under the head; at first emerging from a rubbery, whitish, or pinkish egg-like universal veil, in age the veil remains as a sack-like volva at the base of the stem; often with white rhizomorphs

FLESH: Whitish; odor difficult to determine owing to the strong odor of the slime; taste mild in the egg stage

FERTILE SURFACE: Whitish but covered with an olive-green to olive-brown fetid slime; extending over the stem apex; surface moist, granular, not pitted; apex with a white-rimmed circular hole

SPORE PRINT: None; the spores are in the slime

ECOLOGY: Saprobic; scattered to gregarious on woody debris, often in wood chips and wood mulch; summer and fall; fairly common

EDIBILITY: Not edible when mature; the egg stage is edible but generally not considered worth eating

COMMENTS: *Phallus impudicus* (not illustrated) is similar but has a pitted head. *Phallus duplicatus* (not illustrated) differs in having a net-like veil draped over the stem. All of these species are often detected by their odor before they are found. Spores are contained in the greenish slime. Insects are attracted to the stench and provide their main means of spore dispersal.

Phallus ravenelii

MUSHROOMS WITH CUP-SHAPED OR FLAT FRUITING BODIES

T HE FUNGI AS presented here range from fragile cups to rubbery, urn-like fruitings. Three nearly flat crust fungi are included in this section. Most species are saprobic, occurring on dead wood. Color is used as a primary identifying feature, along with the presence or absence of hairs. These features, along with size and fleshiness, will enable the reader to identify the species covered here. See also the key to jelly and rubbery fungi for similar species and species that are included in both keys.

Aleuria aurantia

Peziza species

Key to Mushrooms with Cup-Shaped or Flat Fruiting Bodies

1. Cup red; not hairy; late winter to spring; medium size: *Sarcoscypha austriaca* (p. 430)

2. Cup red; not hairy; late spring to fall; small: *Sarcoscypha occidentalis* (p. 429)

3. Cup red with tufts of hair; small: *Microstoma floccosum* (p. 428)

4. Cup reddish orange; small; soon flat; with prominent marginal hairs: *Scutellina scutellata* (p. 427)

5. Cup green; small; host wood with green stains: *Chlorociboria aeruginascens* (p. 422)

6. Cup yellowish green, olive brown to orangish brown; small; on dead wood: *Chlorencoelia versiformis* (p. 421)

7. Cup reddish brown to brown or black; rubbery; medium size; on logs and stumps: *Bulgaria inquinans* (p. 440)

8. Cup reddish brown to dark brown; clustered elongated cups: *Wynnea americana* (p. 431)

9. Cup yellowish tan inside to reddish brown outward; rubbery; medium size; on small limbs on the ground: *Galiella rufa* (p. 438)

10. Cup hyaline to pinkish buff; rubbery; small to medium size; on dead broadleaf tree wood: *Neobulgaria pura* (p. 441)

11. Cup black, small, with accompanying matchstick-like asexual stage: *Holwaya mucida* (p. 425)

12. Cup creamy to pale yellow with a fringed margin: *Tarzetta cupularis* (p. 423)

13. Crust gray to black; forming small, tightly grouped, raised, irregular plates: *Xylobolus frustulatus* (p. 432)

14. Crust grayish white, becoming black; lacking raised plates: *Kretzschmaria deusta* (p. 433)

15. Crust yellow; on wood or usually parasitic on the jelly fungus *Exidia glandulosa*: *Trichoderma sulphureum* (p. 443)

SCIENTIFIC NAME: *Chlorencoelia versiformis* (Pers.) J. R. Dixon

SYNONYM: *Chlorosplenium versiforme* (Pers.) P. Karst.

COMMON NAME: None

FAMILY: Hemiphacidiaceae

FRUIT BODY: Up to 1 in. wide; broadly cup-shaped to flat; inner fertile surface yellowish green, olive green, with olive-brown or orangish-brown tints; outer surface reddish brown, velvety

FLESH: Pale buff; very thin; odor and taste not distinctive

STEM: Dull reddish brown; very short; tapering downward

ECOLOGY: Saprobic; scattered to gregarious on well-decayed wood in wet forests; summer and fall; uncommon

EDIBILITY: Unknown

COMMENTS: *Chlorencoelia torta* (not illustrated) is nearly identical and differentiated by microscopic features.

Chlorencoelia versiformis

SCIENTIFIC NAME: *Chlorociboria aeruginascens* (Nyl.) Kanouse ex C.S. Ramamurthi, Korf, and L. R. Batra

SYNONYM: *Chlorosplenium aeruginascens* (Nyl.) P. Karst.

COMMON NAME: Blue Green Wood Stain

FAMILY: Helotiaceae

FRUIT BODY: Up to ½ in. wide; cup-shaped to nearly flat; outer surface bluish green; finely roughened; fertile surface bluish green, at times yellowish; smooth

FLESH: Bluish green; thin; odor not distinctive; taste unknown

STEM: Up to ¼ in. long; bluish green; slender; usually off-center; tapering downward

ECOLOGY: Saprobic on decorticated wood of broadleaf and conifer wood; staining the wood green; summer and fall; common

EDIBILITY: Not edible

COMMENTS: The stained wood is found more often than the green cups. *Chlorociboria aeruginosa* (not illustrated) is very similar. It usually has a central stem. Examination of the spores is needed to positively separate these two.

Chlorociboria aeruginascens

SCIENTIFIC NAME: *Tarzetta cupularis* (L.) Svrček

SYNONYM: *Geopyxis cupularis* (L.) Sacc.

COMMON NAME: Toothed Cup, Elf Cup

FAMILY: **Pyronemataceae**

FRUIT BODY: Up to ¾ in. wide and tall; creamy to grayish yellow or brownish yellow; orb- to globe-shaped at first, becoming cup-shaped with a serrated margin; surface granular

FLESH: Pale; thin; odor not distinctive; taste unknown

FERTILE SURFACE: Creamy to grayish tan or yellowish; smooth; covered at first with a hairy veil; the remains of those hairs linger on the edge of the margin, which then appears scalloped or serrated

STEM: Short and indistinct; colored like the outside of the cup

SPORE PRINT: None

ECOLOGY: Mycorrhizal; on soil or among mosses, often in disturbed areas such as roadsides and trails; solitary or in small groups, in broadleaf and mixed woods; summer and fall; fairly common

EDIBILITY: Unknown and too small to be of consequence

COMMENTS: This small fungus is easily overlooked. There are several other similar, little brown cup fungi requiring a microscope to identify. The presence of a veil in very young cups is a good identification feature, as is the serrated edge on mature specimens.

Tarzetta cupularis

SCIENTIFIC NAME: *Helvella macropus* (Pers.) P. Karst.

SYNONYM: None

COMMON NAME: Scurfy Elfin Cup

FAMILY: Helvellaceae

FRUIT BODY: Up to 1½ in. wide, upper surface dark brown to grayish brown; pubescent, granular to fuzzy, especially toward the margin; outer surface shallow, cup-shaped to nearly flat, supported by a stem that is longer than the cup is wide; margin incurved at first

FLESH: White; thin; brittle; odor and taste not distinctive

FERTILE SURFACE: Light gray to grayish brown, at times with olive tints; smooth to wrinkled; bald; moist

STEM: Up to 2¼ in. long; gray to grayish brown with a whitish base; equal or enlarged downward; solid; contiguous with the cup

SPORES: Hyaline

ECOLOGY: Probably mycorrhizal; solitary to gregarious on the ground or in moss under oaks and conifers in mixed woods; occasional

EDIBILITY: Not edible

COMMENTS: *Helvella cupuliformis* (not illustrated) is very similar. It usually has a shorter stem, but examination of the spores is needed to distinguish these two. It is likely that there is a group of similar species here awaiting further study to sort them out.

Helvella macropus

SCIENTIFIC NAME: *Holwaya mucida* (Schulzer) Korf and Abawi

SYNONYM: *Crinula caliciiformis* Juel.

COMMON NAME: Match Stick Fungus

FAMILY: Bulgariaceae

FRUIT BODY: Two forms occur, often appearing at the same time; sexual spores are produced in the cup form and asexual spores are produced in the match stick form

SEXUAL STAGE: Up to ½ in. wide; black; cup- to saucer-shaped, the cup appears inverted at times; with a short to prominent black stem; inner surface dull black; surface smooth, shiny, viscid when wet; outer surface dull, smooth to scurfy

FLESH: Very thin; odor and taste unknown

ASEXUAL STAGE: Up to ¾ in. tall; match stick-like, a head supported by a stem; head is gray, whitish, at times with black areas; surface smooth, shiny, or dull

FLESH: Thin; odor and taste unknown

SPORES: Hyaline

ECOLOGY: Saprobic; scattered or in groups on the dead wood of broadleaf trees, often emerging from cracks in the bark or from moss; basswood is a common host; fall and early winter; occasional

EDIBILITY: Not edible

COMMENTS: The asexual match stick stage is the most noticeable. Careful observation of the wood will usually reveal the black cups as well. Until recently the asexual stage was given its own name, *Crinula caliciiformis*.

Holwaya mucida

SCIENTIFIC NAME: *Phlebia incarnata* (Schwein.) Nakasone and Burds.

SYNONYMS: *Merulius incarnatus* Schwein., *Byssomerulius incarnatus* (Schwein.) Gilb.

COMMON NAME: **Coral-Pink Merulius**

FAMILY: **Phanerochaetaceae**

CAP: Up to 2 in. wide; bright coral pink to reddish, fading in age to salmon buff, margin often white, surface occasionally with a fuzzy, white coating; semicircular to fan-shaped; margin usually scalloped

FLESH: Whitish to buff; waxy, gelatinous, spongy, or somewhat leathery; odor not distinctive; taste unknown

FERTILE SURFACE: Typically white to cream, at times yellowish or pinkish; often appearing pored; densely covered with kinked ridges with numerous cross veins and branches

STEM: None

SPORE PRINT: White

ECOLOGY: Saprobic and possibly parasitic; in overlapping clusters on the wood of broadleaf trees, usually in association with *Stereum ostrea* (p. 326) and possibly parasitic on that species; summer and fall; occasional

EDIBILITY: Unknown

COMMENTS: The relationship with *Stereum ostrea* (p. 326) has not been established as of this writing. Compare with *Merulius tremellosus* (not illustrated), which is yellowish to orange and lacks coral-pink coloration.

Byssomerulius incarnata

SCIENTIFIC NAME: *Scutellinia scutellata* (L.) Lambotte

SYNONYM: None.

COMMON NAME: Eyelash Cup

FAMILY: Pyrenomataceae

FRUIT BODY: Up to ¾ in. wide; cup-shaped to flat; inner fertile surface reddish orange to red; outer surface orange or brownish orange, somewhat hairy; edge of the cup with brown to black, stiff hairs best observed with a hand lens

FLESH: Pale reddish orange; thin, brittle, unsubstantial; odor and taste not distinctive

STEM: Absent

SPORE PRINT: None

ECOLOGY: Saprobic; scattered to gregarious on well-decayed wood or wet soil near decaying wood; spring through fall; common

EDIBILITY: Not edible

COMMENTS: This is our most common *Scutellinia*. A microscope is needed to positively identify it because there are other similar species. The common name refers to the eyelash-like hairs on the cup margin. Compare with *Microstoma floccosum* (p. 428), which has an elongated, hairy cup. It is much less common than the Eyelash Cup.

Scutellinia scutellata

SCIENTIFIC NAME: *Microstoma floccosum* (Schwein.) Raitv.

SYNONYM: *Anthopeziza floccosa* (Schwein.) Kanouse

COMMON NAME: Shaggy Scarlet Cup

FAMILY: Sarcoscyphaceae

FRUIT BODY: Up to 1¾ in. tall; bright red with conspicuous white hairs on the outside and, especially, at the upper margin; cup- to goblet-shaped with a distinct stem

FLESH: Pinkish buff; thin; odor and taste not distinctive

FERTILE SURFACE: Bright red; smooth; not hairy

STEM: White; slender; hairy

SPORE PRINT: None

ECOLOGY: Saprobic; gregarious to clustered on broadleaf sticks and limbs; late spring and summer; occasional

EDIBILITY: Not edible, insignificant

COMMENTS: This is a small species, but the combination of its bright-red coloration and white hairs make it quite attractive. Compare with *Scutellina scutellata* (p. 427), which lacks a stem and has hairs only on the cup rim.

Microstoma floccosum

SCIENTIFIC NAME: *Sarcoscypha occidentalis* (Schwein.) Sacc.

SYNONYM: None

COMMON NAME: Stalked Scarlet Cup

FAMILY: Sarcoscyphaceae

FRUIT BODY: Up to ½ in. wide; inner surface scarlet red, outer surface pinkish red to whitish; goblet- or cup-shaped, becoming nearly flat; bald on both surfaces

FLESH: Very thin; odor and taste not distinctive

STEM: Up to 1 in. long, usually shorter; pinkish red or whitish; surface smooth, bald

ECOLOGY: Saprobic on broadleaf twigs and sticks, often along streams and runoffs; scattered or in small clusters; late spring and summer; fairly common

EDIBILITY: Not edible; too small to be of much value

COMMENTS: *Microstoma floccosum* (p. 428) is similar in size and color but has a hairy exterior. *Scutellinia scutellata* (p. 427) has hairs on the cap margin. Other species of *Sarcoscypha* are larger, lack a stem, and fruit earlier in the season.

Sarcoscypha occidentalis

SCIENTIFIC NAME: *Sarcoscypha austriaca* (Beck ex Sacc.) Boud.

MISAPPLIED NAME: *Sarcoscypha coccinea* (Gray) Boud.

COMMON NAME: Scarlet Cup

FAMILY: Sarcoscyphaceae

FRUIT BODY: Up to 2 in. wide; inner surface scarlet red, outer surface whitish, pinkish to orangish; often oval to irregularly shaped when young; becoming cup-shaped, and then somewhat flattened in age; margin often lobed and irregular; outer surface granulose to scurfy or downy; inner surface bald, smooth to somewhat wrinkled

FLESH: Pinkish to cream, thin, becoming brittle in age; odor and taste not distinctive

STEM: Absent or rudimentary

ECOLOGY: Saprobic on dead broadleaf limbs and sticks, often partially buried; solitary, but more often in small groups or clusters; usually in spring but at times in winter or late fall; occasional to fairly common

EDIBILITY: Not recommended; reportedly edible when well-cooked

COMMENTS: This bright-red species is often found by morel hunters. It can sometimes be found in woods that are partially covered in snow. *Sarcoscypha dudleyi* (not illustrated) is nearly identical. A microscope is needed to distinguish it from *Sarcoscypha austriaca*. *Sarcoscypha occidentalis* (p. 429) is smaller, has a stem, and fruits in late spring and summer.

Sarcoscypha austriaca

SCIENTIFIC NAME: *Wynnea americana* Thaxt.

SYNONYM: None

COMMON NAMES: Moose Antlers, Rabbit Ears

FAMILY: Sarcoscyphaceae

FRUIT BODY: Up to 5 in. long; blackish brown to dark reddish brown; composed of clustered, elongated cups that are fused at the bases; outer surface coated with small granular dots, wrinkled at times in age

FLESH: Brown; firm; somewhat tough; odor and taste not distinctive

Fertile Inner Surface: pinkish purple to reddish brown, becoming dark brown in age; smooth, bald

STEM: Rudimentary; attached to an underground mass of fungal tissue called a "sclerotium"

SPORE PRINT: Pale brown

ECOLOGY: Saprobic; clustered in humus and soil in broadleaf and mixed woods; summer and fall; uncommon; most likely to be found in a very shaded, cove-forest-type habitat

EDIBILITY: Unknown

COMMENTS: The late amateur mycologist Emily Johnson collected the sclerotium from this rather distinctive fungus and planted it in her local park. The next year it was producing fruit bodies. The sclerotium helps the fungus survive unfavorable conditions, apparently including being transplanted!

Wynnea americana

SCIENTIFIC NAME: *Xylobolus frustulatus* (Pers.) P. Karst.

SYNONYM: None

COMMON NAME: Ceramic Parchment

FAMILY: Stereaceae

CAP: Up to ¾ in. wide; sides gray to blackish; resembling small, crust-like plates or barely raised knobs; hard and woody

FLESH: Brownish; woody; odor and taste not distinctive

FERTILE SURFACE: Pinkish buff, gray, to whitish, finely powdered

STEM: Absent

SPORE PRINT: Whitish to pale pinkish or tinged orange

ECOLOGY: Gregarious, often in tight, puzzle-like pieces in groups on oak logs and stumps, rarely on the wood of other broadleaf trees; at times the plates are fused, forming larger units; throughout the year; abundant

EDIBILITY: Not edible

COMMENTS: This small, woody fungus is very common and very easy to find because it usually fruits in dense colonies and is common and visible throughout the year.

Xylobolus frustulatus

SCIENTIFIC NAME: *Kretzschmaria deusta* (Hoffm.) P. M. D. Martin

SYNONYM: *Ustulina deusta* (Hoffm.) Lind

COMMON NAME: Carbon Cushion

FAMILY: Xylariaceae

FRUIT BODY: Grayish white; rather soft crust forming sheets up to 20 in. wide; becoming black, bumpy, brittle, resembling burnt wood; irregular with multiple lobes

FLESH: Gray; very thin; odor not distinctive, taste unknown

STEM: None

SPORE PRINT: Dark brown to black

ECOLOGY: Parasitic and saprobic on the wood of broadleaf trees, especially beech; late spring, summer, and fall; common

EDIBILITY: Not edible

COMMENTS: This unassuming fungus has drab colors and is often over-looked. It is abundant and is a threat to standing trees, causing a butt rot.

Kretzschmaria deusta

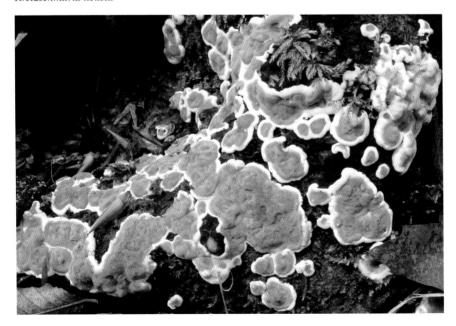

JELLY AND RUBBERY FUNGI

SPECIES IN THIS group are gelatinous or rubbery in texture. With the exception of *Leotia lubrica* (p. 439), all of these fungi are found on wood. Many jelly fungi shrivel to an inconspicuous crust in dry conditions and become much more noticeable and jelly-like when wet. Some are saprobes, whereas others parasitize polypores and other wood-rotting fungi.

Key to Jelly and Rubbery Fungi

1. Black; irregular strips or clumps of fused, gelatinous caps: *Exidia glandulosa* (p. 442)

2. Black to brown; globose becoming cup shaped; rubbery: *Bulgaria inquinans* (p. 440)

3. Inner surface tan, outer surface olivaceous to brown; goblet- to cup-shaped: *Galiella rufa* (p. 438)

4. Hyaline to pinkish buff; cup- to cushion- or top-shaped; rubbery: *Neobulgaria pura* (p. 441)

5. Pale yellow to olivaceous; on soil or humus; stem contiguous with irregular cap: *Leotia lubrica* (p. 439)

6. Orange; spoon- or tongue-shaped to funnel-like, with a split side: *Guepinia helvelloides* (p. 437)

7. Yellowish orange to orange; shoehorn- to fan-shaped; underside ribbed; often on structural wood: *Dacryopinax spathularia* (p. 444)

8. Coral pink to reddish with white areas; with ridges and cross veins: *Phlebia incarnata* (p. 426)

Phaeotremella foliacea

Dacrymyces chrysospermus

SCIENTIFIC NAME: *Auricularia angiospermarum* Y. C. Dai, F. Wu, and D. W. Li

MISAPPLIED NAME: *Auricularia auricula* (Hook) Underw.

COMMON NAMES: Tree Ear, Wood Ear, Jelly Ear

FAMILY: Auriculariaceae

FRUIT BODY: Up to 6 in. wide; various shades of brown; irregular cup-shaped to nearly convex or ear-shaped; rubbery, gelatinous when moist, becoming hard and tough when dry; margin lobed and wavy; outer surface (usually upper side) reddish brown to yellowish brown, minutely hairy to appearing frosted, often wrinkled; inner fertile surface colored like the outer surface, smooth, lubricous, may be wrinkled or veined

FLESH: Tan to reddish brown; gelatinous when wet, cartilaginous when dry; odor and taste not distinctive

STEM: Rudimentary or absent

SPORES: White

ECOLOGY: Saprobic on dead limbs, stumps, and logs of broadleaf trees; throughout the year; fairly common

EDIBILITY: Edible; similar species are often used in Asian cooking, where they provide texture rather than flavor

COMMENTS: Many field guides have used the name *Auricularia auricula* for this species. This appears to be a European species, not known from the Appalachians. A microscope is needed to sort out other similar species, such as *Auricularia fuscosuccinea* (not illustrated). *Auricularia angiospermarum* is probably the most common species of all *Auricularia* in the Appalachians. All are edible but are known more for texture than flavor.

Auricularia angiospermarum

SCIENTIFIC NAME: *Guepinia helvelloides* (DC.) Fr.

SYNONYM: *Phlogiotis helvelloides* (DC.) G. W. Martin

COMMON NAME: Apricot Jelly Fungus

FAMILY: Exidiaceae

FRUIT BODY: Up to 5 in. tall, usually smaller; pinkish orange, reddish orange, or yellowish orange; spoon-shaped to tongue-shaped, or funnel-shaped with a split side; gelatinous; surface smooth, at times with a white hoariness; base with white mycelium

FLESH: Pinkish; thin; gelatinous; flexible; odor and taste not distinctive

SPORE PRINT: White

ECOLOGY: Saprobic; solitary or gregarious on soil or on decaying wood in conifer and mixed woods; late summer and fall; uncommon to rare

EDIBILITY: Edible but bland

COMMENTS: This species is more common in western North America and in northern areas of eastern North America. It is seldom reported in Appalachia and probably should be considered rare.

Guepinia helvelloides

SCIENTIFIC NAME: *Galiella rufa* (Schwein.) Nannf. and Korf

SYNONYM: *Bulgaria rufa* Schwein.

COMMON NAME: Hairy Rubber Cup

FAMILY: Sarcosomataceae

FRUIT BODY: Up to 1½ in. wide; inner surface tan, yellowish tan, orange to reddish brown; smooth; concave; outer surface blackish brown, reddish brown or olivaceous when young; wrinkled; densely hairy; margin with a jagged fringe; goblet- to cup-shaped

FLESH: Translucent; rubbery; gelatinous; thick; odor and taste not distinctive

STEM: Absent or less than half an inch long; dark brown, base densely hairy

SPORES: Hyaline

ECOLOGY: Saprobic on small, fallen limbs of broadleaf trees, the wood may be partially buried; usually gregarious, at times in small clusters; early summer to mid-summer; common

EDIBILITY: Not edible

Comments: This fungus has a rubbery feel that, combined with its coloration, makes it easy to identify. *Bulgaria inquinans* (p. 440) is somewhat similar. It has a black inner surface and fruits on logs and stumps.

Galiella rufa

SCIENTIFIC NAME: *Leotia lubrica* (Scop.) Pers.

SYNONYM: *Leotia viscosa* Fr.

COMMON NAME: Jelly Babies

FAMILY: Leotiaceae

CAP: Up to 1¼ in. wide; pale dull yellow to yellowish buff or olivaceous; irregularly rounded; convoluted or convex; rubbery; gelatinous; surface smooth or furrowed, moist to slightly viscid; margin distinctly incurved

FLESH: Colored like the surface; gelatinous; odor and taste not distinctive

STEM: Up to 2 in. long; colored like the cap or paler; rubbery; gelatinous; hollow at times; surface slippery in wet weather, smooth, or with tiny pale flakes

SPORE PRINT: Does not print well

ECOLOGY: Saprobic and possibly mycorrhizal at times; scattered to densely gregarious in humus and moss under broadleaf and conifer trees, often in mixed woods; summer and fall; common

EDIBILITY: Unknown

COMMENTS: *Leotia viscosa* is now considered a synonym. It is rather striking, with a dark-green to black cap and a yellowish-orange stem. It is less common than the yellowish-buff variety.

Leotia lubrica

SCIENTIFIC NAME: *Bulgaria inquinans* (Pers.) Fr.

SYNONYM: None

COMMON NAME: Black Jelly Drops

FAMILY: Bulgariaceae

FRUIT BODY: Up to 1½ in. wide and tall; outer surface reddish brown to brown, finally black, scurfy; inner surface black, shiny, smooth, bald; nearly globose or turbinate at first, expanding to cup-shaped, finally convex to flat

FLESH: Dark brown to black; tough, rubbery, gelatinous; odor not distinctive; taste unknown

STEM: Absent or rudimentary

SPORES: Dark brown to black

ECOLOGY: Saprobic on oak logs and other broadleaf wood; usually gregarious or clustered; summer and fall; occasional

EDIBILITY: Unknown

COMMENTS: *Galiella rufa* (p. 438) is similar in aspect and texture but is not black. It is usually found on small limbs, which are often partially buried. *Bulgaria inquinans* is usually found on logs and stumps.

Bulgaria inquinans

SCIENTIFIC NAME: *Neobulgaria pura* (Pers.) Petr.

SYNONYM: *Bulgaria pura* (Pers.) Fr.

COMMON NAME: Beech Jelly Disc

FAMILY: Leotiaceae

Fruit Body: Up to 1 in. tall and wide; hyaline, pinkish to reddish buff throughout; shaped irregularly, resembling shallow cups or cushions, at times top-shaped, distorted when in clusters; rubbery to watery gelatinous; outer surface slightly uneven, inside surface smooth

Flesh: Colored like the outside of the cups; thin; odor and taste not distinctive

Stem: Absent

Ecology: Saprobic on decaying broadleaf wood, especially beech; generally gregarious or clustered; late summer and fall; uncommon

Edibility: Unknown

Comments: This fungus may be more common than records indicate. It may just be overlooked or underreported.

Neobulgaria pura

SCIENTIFIC NAME: *Exidia glandulosa* (Bull.) Fr.

SYNONYM: None

COMMON NAME: Black Jelly Roll

FAMILY: Auriculariaceae

FRUIT BODY: Black fused caps up to 16 in. wide; dark brown to black; gelatinous; shiny; reviving when wet

FLESH: Dark brown to black; gelatinous; odor and taste not distinctive

FERTILE SURFACE: Usually with small pimples, smooth at times

STEM: Absent

ECOLOGY: Saprobic on the fallen, dead wood of oaks and other broadleaf trees; throughout the year, most abundant in spring and fall; common

EDIBILITY: Edible

COMMENTS: In dry conditions, *Exidia glandulosa* shrivels to a flat, dry crust. In wet weather it expands, looking much like black jelly. It is occasionally parasitized by a yellow crust, *Trichoderma sulphureum* (p. 443). *Exidia nigricans* (not illustrated) is very similar, and a microscope is needed to confidently separate them.

Exidia glandulosa

SCIENTIFIC NAME: *Trichoderma sulphureum* (Schwein.) Jaklitsch and Voglmayr

SYNONYM: *Hypocrea sulphurea* (Schwein.) Sacc.

COMMON NAME: None

FAMILY: Hypocreaceae

FRUIT BODY: Up to 12 in. wide; a bright to pale yellow or grayish yellow, irregularly shaped crust, covering part or all of the *Exidia glandulosa* fruit body or forming an indeterminate patch on wood, margin frequently white

FLESH: Yellow; thin; tough; odor not distinctive; taste unknown

STEM: Absent

ECOLOGY: Parasitic on the black jelly fungus, *Exidia glandulosa* (p. 442), and possibly saprobic on dead wood; spring, summer, and fall; fairly common

EDIBILITY: Not edible

COMMENTS: This is an easily identified fungus when the *Exidia glandulosa* jelly fungus is visible as its host.

Trichoderma sulphureum

SCIENTIFIC NAME: *Dacryopinax spathularia* (Schwein.) G. W. Martin

SYNONYM: *Guepinia spathularia* (Schwein.) Fr.

COMMON NAME: Fan-Shaped Jelly Fungus

FAMILY: Dacrymycetaceae

FRUIT BODY: Up to ½ inch wide, up to one inch tall; orange to yellowish orange; shoehorn- to fan-shaped; rubbery to gelatinous; underside ribbed lengthwise; surface smooth or finely wrinkled

FLESH: Yellowish orange; gelatinous; thin; odor and taste not distinctive

STEM: Indistinct

ECOLOGY: Saprobic on decaying wood; gregarious to clustered, usually on decorticated wood, often on wood of decks, sheds, and other structures; summer and fall; common

EDIBILITY: Edible but bland

COMMENTS: Clusters of this species often emerge from cracks in wood, all too often from wood in structures. It shrivels when dry and revives when wet.

Dacryopinax spathularia

MORELS AND FALSE MORELS

"MOREL" IS THE GENERALLY accepted common name for mushrooms in the genus *Morchella*. The genus contains the most sought-after edible species in Appalachia. Because of their popularity, morels have many other common names. These names include "sponge mushrooms," "merkels," "snakeheads," "molly moochers," and "land fish." In addition, the various forms and species are often referred to by their colors as "grays," "yellows," and "blacks." As is the case with many edible wild mushrooms, morels should not be eaten raw. These are spring fungi with a generally conical cap, which is honeycombed with pits and ridges, reminiscent of a sponge. In most species the hollow stem is not separable from the cap. They can range from 1 to 12 inches tall. Most fruitings are between 3 and 6 inches in height.

DNA studies have shown that many of the names being used in field guides are actually those of European species. Two groups of investigators, nearly simultaneously, published different names for many North American species. This understandably has led to much confusion as what to call our familiar Appalachian morels. Adding to the confusion is the fact that there are nearly identical-looking species that have been shown by DNA studies to be different.

False morels are irregular to saddle-shaped. Some occur at the same time as morels. Their caps are wrinkled, brain-like, and are not conical. One species, *Gyromitra esculenta* (not illustrated), is toxic and has caused fatal poisonings. It is sometimes referred to as "beefsteak" or "beefsteak morel." It often occurs in northern forests in mixed woods under conifers. It is rare in the Appalachians. No false morels are recommended as table fare.

Morchella species

445

Two *Gyromitra* species

Gyromitra esculanta

Key to Morels and False Morels

1. Upper surface a stemmed cup; dark brown to grayish brown; granular to fuzzy: *Helvella macropus* (p. 424)

2. Cap tan to dark grayish brown, saddle-shaped; on soil: *Helvella elastica* (p. 452)

3. Cap brown, wrinkled, saddle-shaped; on wood or lignin-rich soil in the fall: *Gyromitra infula* (p. 451)

4. Cap ochre to yellowish brown, wrinkled, brain-like; on soil and humus in the spring: *Gyromitra korfii* (p. 450)

5. Cap gray to yellowish buff, generally conical, honeycombed; medium to large: *Morchella americana* (p. 449)

6. Cap gray to yellowish buff, generally conical, small, elongated pits: *Morchella diminutiva* (p. 448)

7. Cap pinkish buff to tan, honeycombed, ridges becoming black: *Morchella angusticeps* (p. 447)

SCIENTIFIC NAME: *Morchella angusticeps* Peck

MISAPPLIED NAME: *Morchella elata* Fr.

COMMON NAMES: Eastern Black Morel, Snakehead

FAMILY: Morchellaceae

CAP: Up to 3½ in. tall; when young with tan to brown ridges and brownish pits or pale pinkish buff all over, when mature with black ridges and brown to yellowish-brown pits; in extreme age black all over; conic to oval, often bluntly triangular; honeycombed with generally vertically arranged pits; attached directly to the stem but with a slight overhang, creating a groove around the base of the cap

FLESH: Buff to pale brownish; thin; odor pleasant; taste not distinctive

STEM: Up to 4 in. long; whitish to pale yellow; enlarged near the base; granular; hollow; ribbed at times

ECOLOGY: Saprobic, possibly mycorrhizal at times; scattered to gregarious in broadleaf forests, most often associated with tulip poplar, ash, and wild cherry, often in well-drained or sandy soil; spring; occasional to common

EDIBILITY: Edible and choice but must be thoroughly cooked; do not eat this mushroom raw; gastrointestinal problems have also occurred when it has been consumed with alcoholic beverages

COMMENTS: This is the first morel to appear in the spring. It is referred to as the "common black morel" in eastern North America. In northern areas of Appalachia, *Morchella septentrionalis* (not illustrated) occurs on or near woody debris, often under big tooth aspen and white ash. It is usually smaller than *Morchella angusticeps*. In areas landscaped with wood mulch, another black morel occurs. This is *Morchella importuna* (not illustrated). Positive identification requires a microscope. *Morchella punctipes* (not illustrated), the Half-Free Morel, has similar colors but usually has a long stem and a cap that is skirt-like over the stem, being attached about halfway up. All of these are edible when cooked.

Morchella angusticeps

SCIENTIFIC NAME: *Morchella diminutiva* M. Kuo, Dewsbury, Moncalvo, and S. L. Stephenson

SYNONYM: None

COMMON NAME: Tulip Morel

FAMILY: Morchellaceae

CAP: Up to 2 in. tall; with yellowish-buff, vertical ridges that may darken or become all yellowish in age; pits are elongate and smoky gray to grayish brown when young, becoming tan to yellowish brown at maturity, at times with reddish stains; attached directly to the stem; hollow

FLESH: Colored like the stem; thin; odor pleasant; taste not distinctive

STEM: Up to 3 in. long, usually longer than the cap; white to cream; hollow; smooth to granular

ECOLOGY: Saprobic and possibly mycorrhizal at times; scattered to gregarious in humus or grass in broadleaf forests and parks, often under tulip trees, wild cherry, hickory, apple, and ash trees; spring; fairly common

EDIBILITY: Edible and very good when thoroughly cooked

COMMENTS: This is the smallest common morel in the Appalachian forests. Larger specimens could be confused with a small *Morchella americana* (p. 449), but it has a rather random pit shape and arrangement, whereas *Morchella diminutiva* generally has elongate pits. *Morchella sceptriformis* (not illustrated) is very similar, but it is slightly larger, has a southerly range, and is found in sandy soil, often with tulip trees.

Morchella diminutiva

SCIENTIFIC NAME: *Morchella americana* Clowez and Matherly

SYNONYM: *Morchella esculentoides* M. Kuo, Dewsbury, Moncalvo, and S. L. Stephenson

MISAPPLIED NAME: *Morchella esculenta* (L.) Pers.

COMMON NAMES: Common Morel, Sponge Mushroom, Land Fish, Yellow Morel

FAMILY: Morchellaceae

CAP: Up to 10 in. tall and up to 2½ in. wide; honeycombed with irregular, randomly arranged pits and ridges; when young the pits are dark gray and the ridges are pale whitish; soon the entire cap is a homogenous, yellowish-buff color, in age becoming yellow; generally cone-shaped; hollow; attached continuously with the stem

FLESH: Whitish; thin; brittle; odor described by many as not distinctive, but most would agree there is a characteristic fragrance that can only be described as morel-like; taste not distinctive

STEM: Up to 5 in. long; white to pale yellowish; equal or enlarged downward; surface granular, ribbed at times; hollow or at times chambered at the base

ECOLOGY: Mycorrhizal and saprobic; solitary, scattered, or gregarious, sometimes in small clusters; in humus or grass under broadleaf trees, especially dying and recently dead elms, old apple and tulip trees, and occasionally in burn sites and cinders; prefers nonacidic soil; spring; fairly common

EDIBILITY: Edible and one of the best when cooked

COMMENTS: This is the species that has been called *Morchella esculenta* for many years. DNA studies have revealed that it is not that species. The confusing taxonomy of this species has not settled yet, and the name *Morchella rigida* may someday be the accepted name. In addition there are two known species that are macroscopically identical. Regardless of the names, this species complex is the most popular edible mushroom group in Appalachia. It is a rite of spring to search for them. In some years, the name "Common Morel" is a misnomer because they can be very hard to find. Conversely, in other years, one large, dying elm can yield over a hundred morels. Late in the season and under favorable conditions, this mushroom can reach heights of 12 in. or more. Once thought to be a separate species, *Morchella crassipes* is a large, late-season form, called the "Big Foot Morel." It is the best of the best for eating.

Morchella americana

SCIENTIFIC NAME: *Gyromitra korfii* (Raitv.) Harmaja

SYNONYM: *Discina korfii* Raitv.

COMMON NAME: Bull Nose False Morel

FAMILY: Discinaceae

CAP: Up to 5 in. wide, and up to 3 in. tall; convoluted, wrinkled, brain-like; at times saddle-shaped; outside fertile surface ochre to yellowish brown, occasionally reddish brown; bald, somewhat shiny; underside whitish to pale yellowish brown

FLESH: Whitish; brittle; odor and taste not distinctive

STEM: Whitish to pale tan; massive; with vertical channels and ribs; equal or enlarged downward; chambered or hollow, fused in places with the cap; surface bald or granular

SPORE PRINT: Pale yellow

ECOLOGY: Saprobic; solitary or scattered on soil and humus in broadleaf and mixed woodlands; spring; occasional to locally abundant

EDIBILITY: Not recommended; it is reportedly edible when well-cooked, but it is poisonous raw

COMMENTS: This is one of the first fleshy fungi to appear in the spring at about the same time as the Black Morel, *Morchella angusticeps* (p. 447). *Gyromitra esculenta* (p. 446) is dark reddish brown and usually occurs with conifers. Although consumed by some after repeated boiling, it has caused fatal poisonings. *Discina brunnea* (not illustrated) is more often saddle-shaped, generally darker brown, and usually fruits a bit later in the spring.

Gyromitra korfi

SCIENTIFIC NAME: *Gyromitra infula* (Schaeff.) Quél.

SYNONYM: None

COMMON NAME: Saddle-Shaped False Morel

FAMILY: Discinaceae

FRUIT BODY: Up to 4 in. tall, and up to 4 in. wide; reddish brown, dark brown, at times yellowish brown; roughly saddle-shaped; surface broadly wrinkled or with folds, moist, somewhat shiny

FLESH: Brownish; thin; brittle; odor and taste not distinctive

STEM: Up to 2½ in. long; whitish, pinkish tan, brown; minutely fuzzy or granular; base fluted at times; hollow, or chambered

SPORE PRINT: Cream colored

ECOLOGY: Saprobic; solitary, scattered to gregarious on decaying wood or woody humus in conifer and mixed woods; late summer and fall; occasional

EDIBILITY: Poisonous

COMMENTS: This is the only Appalachian false morel that fruits in the fall. It contains monomethylhydrazine, a toxin also found in the deadly poisonous *Gyromitra esculenta* (not illustrated). Species of *Helvella* are similar and also occur in the fall. They lack the brown coloration and usually are not found on decaying wood. The closely related *Gyromita ambigua* (not illustrated) has violet hues in the cap and stem. Some mycologists consider it to be a variety of *Gyromitra infula*.

Gyromitra infula

SCIENTIFIC NAME: *Helvella elastica* Bull.

SYNONYM: None

COMMON NAME: Smooth-Stalked Helvella

FAMILY: Helvellaceae

FRUIT BODY: Up to 2 in. wide; undersurface whitish, creamy buff to pale tan; resembling a folded-over cup draped over a stem, appearing saddle-shaped; smooth; moist

FERTILE SURFACE: tan, grayish tan, or dark grayish brown; smooth to somewhat wrinkled; bald; dry or moist

FLESH: White; thin; brittle; odor and taste not distinctive

STEM: Up to 4 in. long; whitish to buff; equal or enlarged downward; smooth or slightly roughened upward

ECOLOGY: Probably mycorrhizal; solitary, scattered, or gregarious in conifer, broadleaf, and mixed woods; late summer and fall; occasional

EDIBILITY: Unknown

COMMENTS: There are other similar *Helvella* species requiring microscopy to positively identify.

Helvella elastica

annulus. A ring on the stem of some mushrooms formed by the rupturing of the partial veil.

bolete. General name for a fleshy, usually terrestrial mushroom with pores.

chanterelle. A common name for mushrooms in the genera *Cantharellus* and *Craterellus*.

cortina. A partial veil over the young gills that resembles web-like fibers.

cortinate. A descriptive term for a mushroom that has a cortina.

decurrent. A connection of the stem and gills where the gills descend down the stem.

floccose. Loose, cottony fibers.

flocculose. Very fine, cottony fibers.

friable. Easily crumbled.

fruit body. The reproductive organ of a fungus, typically called a mushroom.

furfuraceous. Covered with bran-like particles, scurfy.

gasteromycete. A fungus whose spores are produced within a closed chamber (i.e., puffballs).

gills. The radially arranged, spore-producing, flat plates on the underside of many mushrooms.

glandular dots. Sticky spots on bolete stems, usually darker than the stem surface.

glutinous. Covered with a slimy, gluten-like material.

hygrophanous. An adjective for a mushroom whose color changes as it dries out.

hyphae. Strands of mycelium.

intervenose. Having veins between the gills or on the gill faces.

macro fungi. Fungi observable with the naked eye, in contrast with micro fungi.

monograph. A book or reference devoted to a single genus or family.

mycelium. The nutrient-absorbing, root-like filaments of a fungus.

mycorrhizal. Symbiotic relationship between the roots of a plant and the mycelium of a fungus.

ochraceous. A dull, brownish yellow.

olivaceus. With olive-green tints.

ostiole. A small, pore-like opening.

partial veil. A protective membrane covering the gills on some young mushrooms.

peridioles. The tiny, egg-like, spore-containing structures in the bird's nest fungi and some other fungi.

polypores. General name for a group of fibrous or woody fungi with pores, usually on wood.

poroid. An adjective describing a fungus with tubes whose spores are released via pores.

pruinose. Appearing finely dusted with powder.

pyrenomycete. A large group of small fungi with a pebble-like coating on the fertile surface.

reticulate. Having a net-like pattern, often on the stems of boletes.

reticulations. The net-like pattern on the stem and cap of certain mushrooms.

rivulose. Marked by thin, winding, or crooked lines.

saccate. An adjective for the sheath-like remnant of a membranous universal veil.

saprobic. An adjective for a fungus that gets its nutrients from dead or decaying organic matter.

scabers. Dry, raised scales on the stems of some boletes, especially in the genus *Leccinum*.

sclerotium. A firm, irregular to roundish mass of hyphae that enable the fungus to withstand drought and other unfavorable conditions.

squamulose. Covered with small scales or squamules.

subdecurrent. A connection of the stem and gills where the gills barely descend the stem.

subdistant. A descriptive term for gill spacing that is intermediate between close and distant.

subviscid. Tacky or sticky, becoming slimy when wet.

tomentose. A covering of wooly hairs, often densely matted.

umbilicate. Having a navel-like depression.

umbonate. Having a raised nob or umbo.

universal veil. An egg-like outer covering of some immature mushrooms, especially in the genus *Amanita*.

vinaceous. Having a dull reddish-brown, burgundy, or grayish-purple color.

viscid. Slimy or sticky.

volva. The often sack-like remains of the universal veil around the stem base.

wax cap. A common name given to waxy-textured members of the family Hygrophoraceae.

MUSHROOM ORGANIZATIONS

Appalachian Mushroom Organizations

Asheville Mushroom Club
PO Box 18676
Asheville, NC 28804-0676
www.ashevillemushroomclub.com

Central Pennsylvania Wild Mushroom Club
PO Box 450
Lemont, PA 16851
www.CentralPAMushroomClub.org

Mushroom Club of Georgia
4642 Crepe Myrtle Drive
Marietta, GA 30067-4622
www.gamushroomclub.org

New River Valley Mushroom Club
PO Box 64
Christiansburg, VA 24068-0064

Ohio Mushroom Society
8915 Knotty Pine Lane
Chardon, OH 44024-8887
http//ohiomushroomsociety.wordpress.com/

South Carolina Upstate Mycological Society
130 McGinty Court
E143 Poole Agricultural Center
Clemson, SC 29634-0310
www.scumsonline.com

Western Pennsylvania Mushroom Club
70 Woodland Farms Road
Pittsburgh, PA 15238
http//wpamushroomclub.org/

North American Mushroom Organization

North American Mycological Association
6018 Illinois Lane SE, Unit B
Lacey, WA 98513
http://www.namyco.org

REFERENCES

Bessette, A. E., A. R. Bessette, and D. W. Fischer. *Mushrooms of Northeastern North America*. Syracuse: Syracuse University Press, 1997.

Bessette, A. E., A. R. Bessette, W. C. Roody, and S. A. Trudell. *Tricholomas of North America: A Mushroom Field Guide*. Austin: University of Texas Press, 2013.

Bessette, A. E., W. C. Roody, and A. R. Bessette. *North American Boletes: A Color Guide to the Fleshy Pored Mushrooms*. Syracuse: Syracuse University Press, 2000.

Bessette, A. E., W. C. Roody, W. E. Sturgeon, and A. R. Bessette. *Waxcap Mushrooms of Eastern North America*. Syracuse: Syracuse University Press, 2012.

Bessette, A. E., D. B. Harris, and A. R. Bessette. *Milk Mushrooms of North America: A Field Guide to the Genus Lactarius*. Syracuse: Syracuse University Press, 2009.

Bessette, A. E., W. C. Roody, A. R. Bessette, and D. L. Dunaway. *Mushrooms of the Southeastern United States*. Syracuse: Syracuse University Press, 2007.

Beug, M. W., A. E. Bessette, and A. R. Bessette. *Ascomycete Fungi of North America*. Austin: University of Texas Press, 2014.

Binion, D. E., H. H. Burdsall Jr., O. K. Miller Jr., W. C. Roody, S. L. Stephenson, and L. N. Vasilyeva. *Macrofungi Associated with Oaks of Eastern North America*. Morgantown: West Virginia University Press, 2008.

Kauffman, C. H. *The Gilled Mushrooms (Agaricaceae) of Michigan and the Great Lakes Region*. New York: Dover, 1971.

Lincoff, G. H. *The Audubon Society Field Guide to North American Mushrooms*. New York: Chanticleer, 1981.

Miller, O. K., Jr., and H. H. Miller. *North American Mushrooms: A Field Guide to Edible and Inedible Fungi*. Guilford: Morris Book Publishing, 2006.

Roody, W. C. *Mushrooms of West Virginia and the Central Appalachians*. Lexington: University Press of Kentucky, 2003.

Smith, A. H. *The North American Species of Psathyrella*. New York: New York Botanical Garden Press, 1972.

Smith, A. H., and L. R. Hesler. *The North American Species of Pholiota*. Monticello, NY: Lubrecht and Cramer, 1968.

Trudell, S., and J. Ammirati. *Mushrooms of the Pacific Northwest*. Portland: Timber Press, 2009.

Website References

http://www.arc.gov/appalachian_region/TheAppalachianRegion.asp

http://mushroomobserver.org/

Michael Kuo http://mushroomexpert.com/

Gary Emberger http://www.messiah.edu/oakes/fungi_on_wood/

http://www.cbs.knaw.nl/publications/mycoheritage/fungi-can/fungi-can_pdf/085
.pdf

Britt Bunyard http://www.fungimag.com/fall-2012-articles/V5I3SignificantOtherLR
.pdf

Brian P Looney, Joshua M. Birkebak, P. Brandon Matheny https://openjournals.wsu
.edu/index.php/pnwfungi/article/view/1126

Roy Halling https://www.researchgate.net/publication/226936804_A_Synopsis_of_
Marasmius_Section_Globulares_

Tricholomataceae in the United_States

http://nature.mdc.mo.gov/discover-nature/field-guide/eastern-cauliflower
-mushroom

INDEX OF SCIENTIFIC NAMES

Main entries for species are indicated by **boldface.**